Practical Teaching
A Guide to PTLLS & DTLLS

Practical Teaching
A Guide to PTLLS & DTLLS

Linda Wilson

Endorsed by

City&
Guilds

DELMAR
CENGAGE Learning

Australia • Brazil • Japan • Korea • Mexico • Singapore • Spain • United Kingdom • United States

DELMAR
CENGAGE Learning

Practical Teaching: A Guide to PTLLS & DTLLS
Linda Wilson

Publishing Director: Linden Harris

Publisher: Melody Dawes

Production Controller: Eyvett Davis

Marketing Manager: Jason Bennett

Typesetter: Macmillan Publishing Solutions

Cover design: Adam Renvoize

Text design: Design Deluxe, Bath, UK

For product information and technology assistance,
contact **emea.info@cengage.com**.

For permission to use material from this text or product,
and for permission queries,
email **emea.permissions@cengage.com**.

British Library Cataloguing-in-Publication Data
A catalogue record for this book is available from the British Library.

ISBN: 978-1-84480-745-1

Cengage Learning EMEA
Cheriton House, North Way, Andover, Hampshire, SP10 5BE, United Kingdom

Cengage Learning products are represented in Canada by Nelson Education Ltd.

For your lifelong learning solutions, visit
www.cengage.co.uk

Purchase your next print book, e-book or e-chapter at
www.cengagebrain.com

Printed in China by RR Donnelley
4 5 6 7 8 9 10 – 14 13 12

Brief contents

Part Seven Wider professional practice (WPP)

Contents

Part Three Enabling learning and assessment (ELA)

Part Four Theories and principles for planning and enabling learning (TPPEL)

Part Five Continuing personal and professional development (CPPD)

Part Seven Wider professional practice (WPP)

About this book

The book is intended for and written in a style to help those who are embarking on their teaching career, gaining a teaching qualification and working towards Qualified Teacher Learning and Skills (QTLS). It is meant to be informative and user-friendly; it balances the practical aspects of the job, with the reasons why (the theory). Many of the examples are from things I have seen or recommendations I have made to student teachers. The theory relates to current thinking and policy.

Remember, teaching can be an art or a science; what works in one situation may not work in others. So try things out, go with what feels right and be confident to accept that not every lesson will be brilliant. The important factor must always be the learner's experience.

The book is split into seven main parts, each relating to a core unit in the Diploma award: preparing to teach in the lifelong learning sector (PTLLS), planning and enabling learning (PEL), enabling learning and assessment (ELA), theories and principles for planning and enabling learning (TPPEL), continuing personal and professional development (CPPD), curriculum development for inclusive practice (CDIP) and wider professional practice (WPP). Each part of the book is divided into chapters which relate to the main learning outcomes of each unit and assessment outcomes. In addition to the main parts, there are other chapters relating to information, guidance and support to help your achievement.

Throughout your qualification you are required to show evidence of how you are meeting the minimum core of literacy, language, numeracy and information communication technologies (ICT). Some teaching-related activities, mapped to the Minimum Core are included within Chapter 10.

The text and activities contained in this publication are to support your studies, but it is intended that attendance of a relevant programme of study is the primary tool to learn your craft.

Terms of reference

Learner refers to the student, trainee, candidate, delegate, apprentice, pupil.

Teacher refers to the lecturer, tutor, trainer, instructor, coach, assessor.

Session refers to the lesson, training activity, class, lecture, tutorial, seminar.

Environment refers to the classroom, workshop, lecture theatre, workplace, shop floor.

Introduction

I came into education in 1984 as a variable hours lecturer, trying to balance a career with being a mum with two toddlers. My previous career as a caterer meant that long and unsociable hours made things like childcare and a social life difficult.

At first, I taught on a Friday afternoon. In those days, full-time staff were not around on a Friday afternoon and following my induction – 'you're in room P55 with the chefs', I learnt quickly to think on my feet and that the only information that I would receive would be that which I acquired for myself.

Anyway, I survived, and despite the endless hours of preparation (nobody told me about that!) I realised that I actually liked teaching. A few more hours appeared and by the end of that first year, I was teaching 12 hours per week. The groups weren't the easiest; I'm sure they were the ones nobody wanted, but that was how it was then.

I did my teaching qualifications over the next few years. That was also a culture shock. I'd done nothing since my own full-time education and so I found studying challenging, sometimes confusing and generally time consuming. I had never had to do anything that academic before, but fortunately the group I studied with were helpful and together we got through. I've since had to do further Master's level qualifications, which I found hard, but looking back now they really helped me to develop myself.

Changes in staff and the way FE was delivered enabled me to secure a full-time position. I still loved the job and was eager to get more responsibility and a better personal profile. Catering was one of the first subjects to go down the NVQ route. This meant that I started getting involved with employers because they needed to become workplace assessors. I'd done a Train the Trainer course when I had a 'real' job, so naturally took up this initiative. As this new curriculum strategy started running through other vocational qualifications my role changed to training employers and staff. I also got involved with initial teacher training and I just became totally absorbed in teaching.

I am now Director of Learning and Development, with responsibility for Continuing Professional Development. That means I am involved in the aspects of staffing including training, managing performance and providing opportunities for development as well as ensuring staff are compliant with regulations.

I still love the teaching, although I don't do as much now and it is mainly with staff. Teaching is difficult, frustrating, funny, bureaucratic and rewarding. I hope that this book will help new teachers to cope with the skills required of the job, find a user friendly route through their teaching qualifications and develop into fine professionals.

Linda Wilson

Acknowledgements

This book is dedicated to all of the Teacher Training students I have tutored. I know that at times I have been hard, and sometimes told you things you didn't really want to hear, but, you got there and I am privileged to have been part of that process.

To all the people I have observed as part of my job, you have given me some wonderful ideas and made me a better teacher. I've seen some things I wouldn't do, but . . .

To Steve, Liz, Kerry, Marilyn and Janine, my team at work, for their encouragement, opinions and suggestions and for trialling the exercises. To Bradley, for some brilliant ideas and advice. To Richard, a fellow author, for reassurance during the writing and publication of the manuscript.

To LLUK, with whose kind permission each unit title, all the learning outcomes and assessment criteria are reproduced from *'Guidance for awarding institutions on teacher roles and initial teaching qualifications: All mandatory units of assessment. Lifelong Learning UK, August 2007'*.

To staff at Cengage Learning, the reviewers and City and Guilds for their feedback in what has been an extremely steep learning curve.

And finally, to my partner John, for his endless proofreading and commentary – and for borrowing the office!

The publisher would like to acknowledge that all photos are sourced from www.istockphoto.com.

Walk-through tour

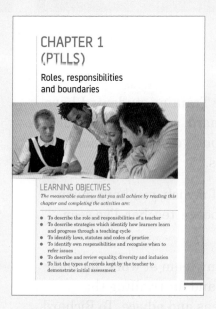

Learning objectives Featured at the beginning of each chapter, you can check at a glance what you are about to learn

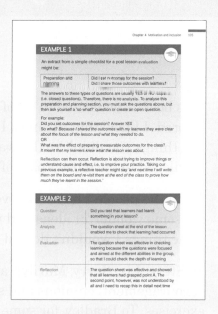

Example Practical, real-world examples illustrate key points and learning objectives in the text

Activity Put your knowledge into action with these practical activities

Note box Key information is drawn out in eye-catching boxes

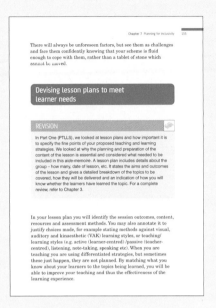

Revision Revision boxes help you recap on things learned in previous chapters

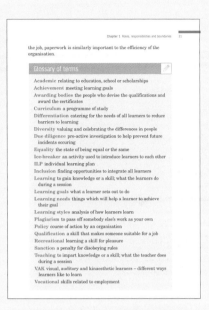

Glossary of terms Glossary of terms highlighted in the text are listed at the end of each chapter with definitions

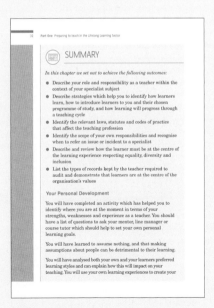

Summary Featured at the end of each chapter, summary boxes help you to consolidate what you have learned

Useful resources Further reading feature offers suggestions for print and online reading material

Part One
Preparing to teach in the Lifelong Learning Sector
(PTLLS)

This is the first unit in your Diploma in Teaching in the Lifelong Learning Sector (DTLLS) qualification

1   Roles, responsibilities and boundaries
2   Approaches to teaching and learning
3   Session planning skills
4   Motivation and inclusion
5   Assessment and record keeping

Learning Outcomes	Assessment Criteria
Understand own role, responsibilities and boundaries of role in relation to teaching	● Review own role and responsibilities, and boundaries of own role as a teacher ● Summarise key aspects of relevant current legislative requirements and codes of practice within a specific context ● Review other points of referral available to meet the potential needs of learners ● Discuss issues of equality and diversity, and ways to promote inclusion ● Justify the need for record keeping
Understand appropriate teaching and learning approaches in the specialist area	● Identify, adapt and use relevant approaches to teaching and learning in relation to the specialist area ● Evaluate a range of ways to embed elements of functional skills in the specialist area ● Evaluate the teaching and learning approaches for a specific session
Demonstrate session planning skills	● Plan a teaching and learning session which meets the needs of individual learners ● Evaluate how the planned session meets the needs of individual learners ● Analyse the effectiveness of the resources for a specific session
Understand how to deliver inclusive sessions which motivate learners	● Analyse different ways to establish ground rules with learners which underpin appropriate behaviour and respect for others ● Use a range of appropriate and effective teaching and learning approaches to engage and motivate learners ● Explain different methods of giving feedback ● Demonstrate good practice in giving feedback ● Communicate appropriately and effectively with learners ● Reflect on and evaluate the effectiveness of own teaching, making recommendations for modification as appropriate
Understand the use of different assessment methods and the need for record keeping	● Review a range of different assessment methods ● Evaluate the use of assessment methods in different contexts, including reference to initial assessment ● Justify the need for record keeping in relation to assessment

CHAPTER 1 (PTLLS)

Roles, responsibilities and boundaries

LEARNING OBJECTIVES

The measurable outcomes that you will achieve by reading this chapter and completing the activities are:

- To describe the role and responsibilities of a teacher
- To describe strategies which identify how learners learn and progress through a teaching cycle
- To identify laws, statutes and codes of practice
- To identify own responsibilities and recognise when to refer issues
- To describe and review equality, diversity and inclusion
- To list the types of records kept by the teacher to demonstrate initial assessment

Roles and responsibilities

The role and responsibility of the teacher is a complex one. We are charged with ensuring our learners gain their qualifications in a manner which is favourable to their own learning needs and those of the **awarding bodies**. We have to offer value for money. We have to consider the needs and interests of their parents and employers, as well as the learning institution. Not all learners come into learning to achieve a **qualification**; some want to gain new skills to help with their employment or simply to cope with the changing world.

The role of the Lifelong Learning Sector is quite broad. It covers further education, higher education, work-based training, training for employment, adult and community learning, the voluntary sector, the armed forces and prisons. Learners in the sector may be funded by government bodies, by their employers, by funding councils or by their own finances. Some may be supported by student loans, bursaries or scholarships. In a nutshell, lifelong learning covers everything that is not compulsory education. Learners can be aged from 14 upwards and learning can occur in any suitable environment.

The student population is ever-changing due to:

- Changes in society
- The need for equality and diversity
- Changes in funding priorities
- Expectations of learners, employers and parents
- Behaviour trends
- Technological developments

Think, for example, about the typical learners in a Further Education college.

- 14-year-old pupils trying to gain vocational qualifications as an alternative to **academic** qualifications
- 16-year-olds embarking upon training and qualifications to meet potential employment needs
- 19-year-olds developing skills or perhaps catching up on missed opportunities
- The mature student, returning to learning, maybe thinking about a change in career
- The unemployed, trying to re-enter the world of work
- The adult, gaining skills relevant to their work
- The young mum, returning to a career after a period of time and finding that the workplace has moved on
- The pensioner, trying to gain skills so that they can communicate in today's electronic era
- The social learner, learning a skill to provide pleasure and enjoyment.

The teacher will come across many of these examples, each of which describes **learning goals**, in a typical working week. The skills involved will be discussed in detail later in the book, but suffice to say if the learners are all different, so the skills required to teach them will vary. Most people come into teaching because they believe they can make a difference. The amount of energy that a teacher will expend in realising that value will astound the inexperienced teacher. A teacher needs to accept that they will face many challenges in teaching, including risks, but if something goes wrong, it should be seen as more of an opportunity than a threat. In order to succeed, you sometimes need to make mistakes; that's how we learn.

The impact of all of these influences affects the teacher, whose role is far more than just being someone who stands at the front of the class telling people things.

The role and functions of a teacher:

- Designing programmes of study
- Planning and preparing classes
- Developing interesting ways of delivering learning
- Assessing the impact of learning
- Ensuring a safe learning environment
- Marking of work and giving feedback on outcomes
- Keeping records
- Contributing to the development of the programme
- Evaluating the effectiveness of the programme
- Keeping data about retention and achievement
- Having a duty of care
- Monitoring the progress of learners
- Acting within professional codes
- Monitoring attendance and punctuality
- Contributing to the administration of the programme
- Entering learners for exams and tests
- Contributing to quality assurance requirements
- Acting as a role model
- Pastoral care

ACTIVITY 1

Let us consider the extent of that responsibility:

Look at each of the headings below and write down what you need to consider. It is probably best to focus on your particular subject. You should consider how you might tackle it, who will help you and how you will know if you have got it right.

You will find all the answers within this book, but try not to look yet. Use your existing knowledge and common sense! This will also be a good way of finding out about your own strengths and development needs at this early stage.

Roles and responsibilities	Thoughts and considerations
What will I teach?	
When will I teach it?	
How will I prepare for a lesson?	
How will I make it interesting?	
What will I do when things go wrong?	
Who else will be involved?	
How will I know when somebody has learnt something?	
Am I getting my topic across?	
What paperwork will I need to complete?	
How will I appear professional?	
Do I know enough to teach my topic?	

You probably now have lots of questions. Using this book and the guidance of your tutor, you can now embark on your own learning journey.

Getting started

Teaching is not limited to imparting your knowledge, you will also have a responsibility for helping someone to learn. One of the first rules of teaching is:

ASSUME NOTHING

Do not assume that your learners know the most effective way of learning. They will come to you with a variety of experiences, a lot of needs and maybe some misconceptions. If you assume that learners 'already know this', 'can do that' and 'expect this', you are in for a massive learning experience yourself! One of the most influential factors on someone's ability to learn is the teacher.

Creating a first impression

You only have one opportunity to do this. In the first few minutes of meeting someone, we all make a decision about them. Whether this is an accurate impression or not remains subjective; it is human nature! As learners walk in to the classroom, they survey their surroundings, look at the teacher and look at each other. This can be managed so that it has a positive effect by:

● Being on time
● Smiling

- Welcoming learners
- Looking clean and presentable
- Being prepared
- Looking calm and organised
- Being confident
- Making sure the room is prepared for the learners
- Friendly introductions.

Think about how you would feel if, when you arrived, there was no-one in the room, it was untidy, and then the teacher arrived mumbling about being busy and the photocopier not working: then the lesson started and you had no idea of the teacher's name or even the name of the person sitting next to you. Are you even in the right room? Would you feel valued? Would you have confidence in the teacher? Would you expect the course to be any good? Would you come back next week?

It seems obvious when presented like this, but because the first impression counts for so much, you should be particularly aware of it during the first session. When learners don't attend the second session, the teacher should always consider the impact they made during the first session.

How do learners learn?

When starting to teach and plan lessons, a teacher should consider the individuals in the class. We have already established that learners will arrive with a variety of learning goals. They will also have had differing experiences of teaching and learning in the past.

 **ACTIVITY 2**

Think about a good learning experience. Write down what you liked about it that made it a good experience:

Now think about a bad experience. Again, write down things that made you feel uncomfortable or unhappy with that experience:

Conclude this by listing all of the positive actions that you are going to include in your own teaching sessions. These are your values or principles: things that are so important to you that you will not accept second best.

Hopefully, one of these values will be to ensure that all of your learners receive a positive learning experience and achieve their goals. One way that this can be accomplished is by analysing how learners learn: this is one of the most fundamental tasks of the teacher. A teacher who understands what helps a learner to learn will be a better teacher because they recognise differences and are prepared to alter their teaching to suit those differences. This is called **differentiation**.

There are many theories associated with identifying how learners learn. The main ones that you may come across are:

Honey and Mumford (1982, 1992) based their analysis of how people learn on Kolb's (1984) (see Chapter 11) learning cycle. They advocate that people learn best by either doing something (activist), by thinking back on something (reflector), by investigating ideas and concepts (theorist) or by finding relevance or association (pragmatist).

EXAMPLE

Think about learning to play golf.

- A theorist will buy all the books they can find and read up on the best way to do everything, before even going to the practice range.

- An activist will buy all the gear, go down to the first tee and hit balls until they've got round to the 18th.

- A reflector will probably go down to the driving range, hit a few balls and then go to the clubhouse to analyse where and why it went wrong.

- The pragmatist will buy golf lessons, having carefully considered the commitment, and then experiment and analyse his or her way around the course.

Another is Gardner's Multiple Intelligence (1983, 1993). He states that understanding intelligence and categorising it will develop learning. The categories are:

- Linguistic – the use of language. Writers and poets are deemed to have a high linguistic intelligence.
- Logical/mathematical – patterns and reasoning. The ability to detect patterns, highly sought in science subjects.
- Musical – appreciation of musical pattern, for example learning the alphabet to song.

- Bodily/kinaesthetic – using body movements, using mental abilities to co-ordinate bodily movements.
- Spatial – using space patterns.
- Interpersonal – working with others. It requires people to understand the intentions, motivations and desires of other people. Teachers need to use this type of intelligence.
- Intrapersonal – understanding oneself; to appreciate one's feelings, fears and motivations in a bid to develop.

Last, and probably the most simple to understand is the *VAK analysis*. This is the suggestion that people learn either through visual senses (sight), auditory senses (hearing) or through kinaesthetic (doing) senses; hence VAK. The Chinese proverb reinforces that learning is about senses:

> ## I hear, I forget
> ## I see, I remember
> ## I do, I understand

Cooper (1996) analysed people's learning preferences, following the assumption that most learning occurs through the left side of the brain (noted for logic and order), yet by using the right side of the brain (noted for creativity), learning could be enhanced. The ideal, therefore, is to create a mixture of visual, auditory and kinaesthetic experiences, both to meet individual needs and to stimulate deeper learning. It follows that the teacher will exploit these differences by including teaching methods to meet all sensory needs. This is called teaching using differentiated strategies.

It is quite common for new teachers to limit their teaching style to that of their own preferred learning style. This will have an impact on the effectiveness of that teaching, in that it does not cater for those with different learning styles. Sometimes when you finish a class, you think, 'That really went well; I enjoyed that!' The reflective (and effective) teacher will think 'I wonder if everyone enjoyed that as much as I; did all my learners learn?'

Ice-breakers

During the first meeting with your learners it is important to find out what they want from the course. Usually entrants to **vocational** courses will be interviewed to assess their suitability, but in some instances, learners just enrol and the first time the teacher has an opportunity to check suitability is the first session. Whichever route, when you meet learners for the first time, you should find out about your learners, their needs, their **learning styles**, their concerns and apprehensions, and gradually introduce them to the rest of the group and their new environment. This type of activity is generally seen as an induction and will usually include an ice-breaking activity.

I	Introduce yourself
C	Create a comfortable setting
E	Encourage communication
B	Break down barriers
R	Reveal concerns
E	Encourage team spirit
A	Ascertain needs
K	Know your learners
E	Establish rules
R	Re-visit previous learning

Different ice-breakers will be used for different things, but the key to a successful **ice-breaker** is to make it fun, useful and not intimidating for learners. You should remember that learners do not usually like to draw attention to themselves at the first meeting. If you are sensitive to this, then the ice-breaker will do what it says it will do, i.e. break the ice. If you, the teacher, start the activity, maybe by introducing yourself and answering the ice-breaker questions, that will help to relax the learners and make an activity that is interesting and rewarding.

Some ideas:

1   In pairs, interview each other to find out names, an interesting
    fact about each other and maybe a favourite film or book. Then
    each person introduces their fellow learner.

    What this does. The teacher can write down the names of the
    group as a table plan, so that immediately the teacher can recall
    names: learners like to be recognised by name. The teacher can
    start to create a rapport. For example, next week you can ask how
    the children are, or if they enjoyed a particular leisure activity.
    This type of information creates a positive relationship because
    learners know that you care and are interested in them. Knowing
    about learners' favourite things reveals the type of things that
    interest them. This can tell you a little about them. For example,
    are they thoughtful, active, extrovert or introvert? If you have a
    confident group, you might also try the, 'If you were an animal,
    what kind would you be, and why?' type of question. That
    question can usually be quite enlightening as well as very funny.

2   Devise a little questionnaire, probably written to find out what
    learners already know about the subject. You can then invite
    learners to discuss what they've written and what is concerning
    them.

    What this does. In a quiet group, this type of activity will help to
    settle the learners. Be careful to include some questions that are
    quite easy in order to reassure the learner. The difficult questions
    can be off-putting, so remember to assure learners that they will be
    able to do these things soon. On a **recreational** course it will tell you
    about your learners. It introduces the course and can be revisited
    regularly so that learners can track their progress. It will help you to
    design a programme of study that meets the group's needs.

3   Split the group into smaller groups of about 4 or 5 people and ask
    them to build something. (I ask my groups to build a freestanding
    bridge using newspaper, using only a set amount of string and
    sticky tape.)

    What this does. It develops a team spirit. By getting feedback after
    the activity it initiates discussion and the teacher can identify
    the roles learners take when working within groups – leaders,

followers, doers, thinkers, artistic tendencies, etc. We use this to lead into a VAK questionnaire, because it has already established that everyone is different.

Can you see the connections between ice-breakers and the concepts of first impression and learning styles? There are balances to be made – are your first impressions still the same after the ice-breaker? Do the answers to the ice-breaker bear any resemblance to their learning style analysis? These first activities are pieces of a jigsaw that will gradually fit together to make a picture, but remember that some of the pieces you put in might have to be moved if they are not quite right!

The teaching cycle

Teaching and learning should be a structured process. Teaching (and learning) will follow a cycle and the teacher makes use of this to ensure achievement. The teaching cycle is a continuous process, which can be joined at any point, but needs to be followed through to be effective. The process follows the strategy of moving from the known to the unknown.

Figure 1A The teaching cycle

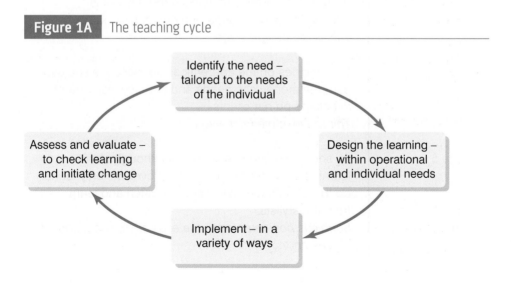

Think of our earlier examples of learners, from both the learner's and the teacher's viewpoint. Let us put them into the teaching cycle using the following case studies:

Sophie is a 16-year-old. She has had her careers interview and wants to be a hairdresser.

Stage 1	Sophie has discovered that she doesn't need high grade GCSEs, which is good because she doesn't think she'll get very many. She is artistic in her style and loves chatting to people. She has held a Saturday job in a local hairdressing salon and enjoyed it. She thinks she would like to own her own salon one day. *This is the evaluation stage.*
Stage 2	Sophie wants to go to college, but she also needs to earn some money. She finds out about the courses offered at two local colleges and a large hairdressing chain. *This is the identify need stage.*
Stage 3	She discovers that she has two main choices. She either goes to college full-time and continues with her Saturday job or she can join an apprenticeship programme where she works each day but is released to go to college one day per week. *This is the design stage.*
Stage 4	She decides on the apprenticeship, because she can earn the money she needs and practice skills learnt in college on her clients. *This is the implement stage.*
Stage 5	As she is working she finds that although she is learning skills in college, her employer will only let her do the junior's job. She wants to watch and learn from the stylists. *Sophie is now re-entering the evaluation stage, and so it goes on…*

Julie is the department head in a college. It is her job to design the hairdressing **curriculum** to meet local needs.

Stage 1	Julie knows that she needs to meet the needs of full-time and part-time learners. She also needs to offer various levels of the qualification and offer some professional updating courses. *This is the identify need stage.*
Stage 2	She looks at her staff, the size of the training salon and the number of classrooms she has available. She creates a timetable for her full-time students, which can also be dipped into by the part-time students. She decides that the professional updating would have to be done in the evenings when salons are closed and hairdressing professionals can attend. *This is the design stage.*
Stage 3	Julie creates the timetable and allocates it to her staff, playing to their strengths. They then deliver teaching and learning strategies to the groups attending the course. *This is the implementation stage.*
Stage 4	Throughout the year, Julie organises quality activities to ensure that the team are delivering an effective curriculum. The awarding body visits to ensure that the standard matches national provision and teams from within the college audit several parts of the delivery. Feedback from learners also identifies development areas. These result in actions to develop the course and the staff. *This is the assess and evaluate stage.*
Stage 5	Julie uses these development points to create an action plan for future provision. *This re-starts the training cycle.*

Legislation and codes of conduct

As with any area of work, teachers must work within the boundaries of the law and professional values. There are a vast number of laws, directives and professional ethics; they are constantly changing or being updated. Every organisation will have its own policies and procedures relating to these legal aspects and there are some differences in requirements, depending upon the age of learners and the environment.

Whilst this book will endeavour to cover the main aspects, every teacher remains accountable for their own familiarisation with how to remain compliant. Every opportunity should be taken to ensure that you are up to date. Go back to that first rule of teaching – ASSUME NOTHING!

 **ACTIVITY 3**

This may be one of your first development points:

To identify all legislation and codes of practice in relation to teaching (your subject), by:

- Attending your organisation's induction event
- Finding out who the health and safety manager or representative is
- Checking out where the policies and procedures are. They may be stored in paper or electronic formats
- Asking your line manager about particular rules relating to your subject
- Enquiring about the names of key staff to help you
- Finding out if you need a Criminal Records Bureau (CRB) disclosure, and how will you get it.

The main acts and rules

Health and Safety at Work Act (1974)

Everyone has a responsibility for the safety of themselves and others. Therefore, rules must be followed and safe practices adhered to, you should demonstrate a model of best practice, lead by example. There are additional rules relating to taking learners on educational visits following a series of tragic accidents. Do not consider taking learners on visits without seeking advice.

The Management of Health and Safety at Work Regulations (1999)

The legislation seeks to prevent unsafe practices and minimise risk. For example, fire and emergency procedures, first aid at work, safe handling practices, visual display unit codes, risk assessment.

Risk assessment

All activities have an element of risk, some more so than others. It is the teacher's responsibility to assess the level of the risk, establish practices to minimise risk and record such activities.

Child Protection Guidelines

Recent high-profile cases have brought about the necessity to introduce legislation and guidance on protecting children and vulnerable adults against inappropriate behaviour. Each organisation should exercise their functions with a view to safeguarding and promoting the welfare of children (Protection of Children Act, 1999). Mandatory Criminal Records Bureau (CRB) checks are required of teachers working with children and vulnerable adults. The Government holds lists of those deemed unsuitable to work with these groups and organisations should check these before appointing staff. You may also find that groups of learners, for example child care students, are checked before embarking on their course of study. This is 'due diligence' on behalf of the organisation, who may send these learners into work placement in nurseries and the like.

▶

Disability Discrimination Act (1995 and onwards)
This Act gives disabled people the right to employment, education and other services. Part 3 (2004) legislated that businesses must take reasonable steps to modify physical features that may cause barriers. Part 4 (2005) extended this to include educational establishments.

Copyright guidelines
Copyright guidance protects the originators of material against plagiarism and compromising intellectual ownership. Materials includes books, newspapers, journals, material downloaded from the Internet, broadcasts – in fact anything which is not your own original material. It is against the Copyright, Designs and Patents Act 1998, and the subsequent amendment of 2003, to reproduce material in any way without acknowledging the originator. During research this means using a system like Harvard referencing to cite the sources. In order to devise a fair system of paying royalties to originators, the Copyright Licensing Agency (CLA) offers licences to educational establishments so that teachers can photocopy information for their learners. Usually, close to every photocopier there is a charter explaining how much can be reproduced. Your reprographics department will advise on this. Exercise caution when copying anything, as the CLA can carry out spot checks and could go through filing cabinets to check that information is not being illegally copied. Always state the originator's name, even if it is a handout devised by a colleague.

Data Protection
The Data Protection Act (1998) requires any organisation that holds any data on individuals, electronic or otherwise, for more than two months, to register as data users. It restricts the sharing of data. Caution should be taken when holding records associated with learners, staff, or partner companies. It is common sense that you should never reveal personal information about anyone to another person, however convincing the request!

Duty of care
Common, civil, statute and criminal law all apply to teachers. If you are proven to be negligent, then you may have to compensate the injured

party. This applies to individuals as well as a corporate responsibility. Teachers are, in principle, *in loco parentis* to their younger learners. This means they need to offer a safe environment, whilst balancing the need to experiment and develop independence. If you and the organisation have taken all reasonable steps to ensure safety, yet a learner is injured as a result of not following the rules, it is unlikely to be proven that you are in breach of the duty of care. So, if you are using equipment in a workshop, or scissors in a classroom, or taking a group on a visit, you should assess the risk, warn of the safety implications and use protective equipment. Failure to do so is negligence.

Equal opportunity legislation

A series of laws have been passed to ensure that no one is discriminated against, irrespective of gender, marital status, sexual orientation, disability, race, nationality, ethnic origin, age, religion or belief, domestic circumstances, trade union membership, social or employment status.

For the teacher this means ensuring language, handouts and other learning materials are free from bias, and that inappropriate comments are challenged and excluded from the classroom. When advertising courses and delivering learning, a teacher should not stereotype or in any way disadvantage groups of learners. The environment and all support structures should enable access and include facilities to meet all learners' needs.

Disciplinary policies and sanctions

Keeping order in the classroom will in itself provide a safer learning environment. Corporal punishment is illegal and hitting (teachers hitting learners or learners hitting teachers) is criminal assault. Restraint is a difficult one because it relies on evidence of training and reasonableness. Each organisation will have its own policies on discipline and related issues and what to do if things go wrong, which will include **sanctions**, use of force, disciplinary hearings and exclusion. Managing behaviour and problems in the classroom and how to deal with them are further discussed in Chapter 4.

Dress codes

There are some vocational areas that require learners to wear particular things in order to meet professional standards, for example trainee chefs wearing 'kitchen whites', motor vehicle learners wearing personal protective clothing and equipment. Dress codes should, wherever practicable, respect safety issues and respect religious beliefs. Guidance on the wearing of uniform, jewellery and other such rules should be shared and advocated throughout the organisation. You should familiarise yourself with the organisation's rules. In terms of the dress code for teachers, one should remember professional values; there is rarely a uniform, but smart, comfortable and practical should prevail.

Terms and conditions of employment

Every teacher will receive a contract of employment which not only details pay and working hours, but defines the rules of the organisation and what would happen if the rules are breached. You should always read everything in your contract and question things that you are unsure about.

Whilst some of these aspects need only an awareness of context, many will impact from your first teaching experience and therefore require a detailed knowledge. You will need to talk this through with your line manager, your mentor or your union representative. The importance of this cannot be over-emphasised.

Useful online resources

Useful references for further reading about legislation are
Cohen, Manion and Morrison (2004: 85–96)
http://www.hse.gov.uk/services/education/index.htm
http://www.teachers.org.uk/resources/pdf/law-and-you.pdf
http://www.natfhe.org.uk/
http://www.ucu.org.uk/index.cfm?articleid=1738
http://www.rospa.com/safetyeducation/atschool/index.htm
http://www.dfes.gov.uk/

Referral

Knowing the boundaries of the teacher's role is essential to an effective learning environment. It is also important for the teacher to realise that there are some aspects of the learners' expectations that are beyond the role of the teacher. You may also find that experience plays an important part here; you may not know all the answers because you are new to the role and/or the organisation. The teacher should always consider the interests of the learners as paramount. We might like to help, but are we really the most effective person for the learner to consult? Understanding and respecting professional boundaries is essential.

The boundary between the role the teacher has in respect of teaching, tutoring and caring for learners is rarely clear. Each aspect is important and it is equally important for the teacher to learn when their role or help is dealt with more effectively by another trained professional.

Q: *Where does the teacher's role end and the specialist's begin?*

A: If only this were a clear line! The answer really is going to alter given the particular issue the teacher is faced with. The teacher is generally tasked with the front line delivery of learning. Each individual or group of learners will usually be allocated a tutor whose role it is to support learning and academic/vocational achievement. They may also be involved in a certain amount of personal connection, which means learners may confide in them. However, whether or not the tutor has sufficient time or knowledge to problem solve on behalf of their learners is down to position and experience. You should always remember the implications of legislation and duty of care pp. 19–22: thus, if an issue discussed is beyond your knowledge, experience, accountability or responsibility you should refer to your mentor, manager or student support service department.

There are some rules here:

- Back to the first rule of teaching: assume nothing…
- Remember the first rule of customer service: if you promise to do something – do it.
- And finally, the rule of trust and tutoring – integrity and confidentiality.

Q: *Who are the specialists and how do my learners access them?*

A: If you look in the Student Charter, which is usually given to all learners either at enrolment or induction, it will inform them of the support available within the organisation (see Internal support services below). In addition to this, there are various external voluntary bodies who will offer information, advice and guidance for all members of the community (see External support services below).

Internal support services

Whilst this list is not comprehensive, it will give an idea of the mechanisms usually available within an organisation:

- Student Services Office
- Crèche
- Counselling
- Tutoring
- Financial support
- Remission of fees for recipients of means-tested benefits
- Learner support for physical and/or educational support needs
- Dyslexia/dyscalculia (words/numbers) support.

External support services

These are the professionals. Offices and telephone lines are staffed by trained personnel, are usually open 24/7 with phone lines normally free or making modest charges to cover costs. Again, this is not comprehensive, but the main ones are listed.

Samaritans	Confidential emotional support
Drugs line	Information about drugs and solvents for those who use them, or are affected by them
Citizens Advice Bureau	Local community help agency, legal advice and general information on a range of issues
Shelterline	Legal and housing advice line offering independent information and advice
Childline	Helpline for children and young people up to 18 years old in danger, distress or with a problem
Help the Aged – senior line	Welfare benefits advice for older people

▶

Parent line	Support and information for parents and those in a parenting role
National Debtline	Help for anyone in debt or concerned about falling into debt
Lesbian and gay switchboard	Support and information for lesbians and gay men
Victim Support	Emotional and practical support for anyone affected by crime
National Domestic Violence Helpline	Safe accommodation for those experiencing domestic violence
NHS Direct	Confidential health advice
Crimestoppers	Community service which helps to prevent and solve crimes

Use your local telephone directory for contact information.

It is important when working with learners that you respect their wishes and their confidentiality. You might use statements like 'if I were you...', but they are not you and you should remember that. Advice means that you give someone the benefit of your worldly experience; the nature of advice means that nobody has to accept it.

Issues relating to someone claiming they are being abused or supplied drugs should always be referred – even if only to someone more senior; it is your duty of care.

Equality, diversity and inclusion

Whilst **equality** generally means everyone is treated equally and fairly, it is linked directly to legislation and guidelines, which together drive the initiative. **Diversity** goes one step further by valuing the differences between individuals, and by ensuring they are participating, you are including everyone (**inclusion**).

Equality, whilst driven by legislation, should develop the culture and ethic of wanting to meet the needs of all learners. Equality, diversity and inclusion are words associated with implementing the various pieces of legislation into a specialist context. For us that means education, teaching and training.

Each of your learners is an individual who should be treated as an equal and with respect, irrespective of gender, marital status, sexual orientation, disability, race, nationality, ethnic origin, age, religion or belief, domestic circumstances, trade union membership, social or employment status. This means that you should not have favourites, nor should you allow your learners to treat each other with disrespect.

Some of the key documents relating to equal opportunities are:

- Equal Pay Act (1970)
- Rehabilitation of Offenders Act (1974)
- Sex Discrimination Act (1975)
- Race Relations Act (1976, 2000)
- Disability Discrimination Act (1995 and subsequent regulations)
- Human Rights Act (1998)
- Employment Equality (Sexual Orientation) Regulations (2003)
- Employment Equality (Religion or Belief) Regulations (2003)
- Employment Equality (Age) Regulations (2006)

For the organisation, it means setting up a **policy** and codes of practice which ensure staff are aware of the law and are familiar with how to implement it in their job roles. The table below explains how the laws relating to equal opportunities are developed into an inclusive strategy.

Equal opportunities	Diversity and inclusion
Concentrates on removing discrimination	Maximises learner potential
Can be an issue for disadvantaged groups	Is relevant to all learners
Relies on positive action by managers and the organisation as a whole	Relies on implementing policies and practices in context

Adapted from Kandola and Fullerton (1994: 49)

For the teacher this means ensuring language, handouts and other learning materials are free from bias, and that inappropriate comments are challenged and excluded from the classroom. When advertising courses and delivering **learning**, a teacher should not stereotype or in anyway disadvantage groups of learners. The environment and all support structures should enable access and include facilities to meet all learners' needs. 'Political correctness' is a commonly used term at the moment, and is used to ensure that expressions do not cause offence to any particular group of people.

Let us look at some examples:

Material	Watch points
Handouts	Never use 'he' or 'she'. Try to use 'they' or 'their'. Be prepared to photocopy large print versions if necessary
Language	Never use words like 'manpower', 'blackboard', 'craftsman'.
	Relate learning to experiences to aid understanding (anecdotes, analogy). The expression 'thought-shower' is preferred to 'brainstorm'
Advertising/ course leaflets	Do not stereotype. All courses should be accessible and open to all

Written and spoken text	Use clear language, without jargon, explain technical terms. Use dictionaries and vocabulary books to aid understanding of terms
Visual aids	Consider colours and their effectiveness. Write clearly in a legible style of writing. Use expressions such as wipeboard and chalkboard rather than whiteboard and blackboard
Learning aids	Offer alternative formats, i.e. electronic, paper, large print, Braille, whenever possible
Space	Ensure coats, bags, etc. are not left around the room, ensure there is sufficient space for moving around the classroom
Support	Ensure that learners' needs are addressed, which may involve using a specialist team of physical and educational support workers

You can anticipate inclusive learning strategies, but should never assume.

Record keeping

It will not take you long to recognise that part of the teacher's role is that of keeping records. They may be kept electronically or in paper formats. The documents are required for several reasons:

- Auditing purposes
- Information gathering
- Quality assurance systems
- Health and safety management
- Financial accountability.

Some of the documents used at this introductory stage are:

Types of form	Use
Enrolment forms	Gathers personal details and information about declared **learning needs**, marketing information and declarations
Qualification/registration forms	Used to register a candidate with an awarding body, thus notifying them of the intent to certificate following a period of study
Learner needs analyses	Collecting details about preferred learning styles, used by the teacher to devise appropriate classroom activities
Registers	An auditable document recording attendance and punctuality
Individual Learning Plans (ILP)	Personal targets to aid the monitoring and development of learning, used to track progress and support study
Induction records	Used to record what has been explained during induction, training on use of equipment and which documents have been issued
Training and assessment plans	Used instead of, or in support of an **ILP** to plan and track progress through a particular qualification

There are different requirements for recording progress and **achievement**, which are dealt with later.

However time-consuming the paperwork is, it must be completed regularly and accurately. Other departments in the organisation will be relying on you to do this in a timely manner. They will also use these records to inform their workloads, claim funding, ensure examination entries are made at the correct time and allocate appropriate support for learners. Record keeping is part of the contract of employment, and whilst teaching is the more enjoyable part of the job, paperwork is similarly important to the efficiency of the organisation.

Glossary of terms

Academic relating to education, school or scholarships

Achievement meeting learning goals

Awarding bodies the people who devise the qualifications and award the certificates

Curriculum a programme of study

Differentiation catering for the needs of all learners to reduce barriers to learning

Diversity valuing and celebrating the differences in people

Due diligence pro-active investigation to help prevent future incidents occuring

Equality the state of being equal or the same

Ice-breaker an activity used to introduce learners to each other

ILP individual learning plan

Inclusion finding opportunities to integrate all learners

Learning to gain knowledge or a skill; what the learners do during a session

Learning goals what a learner sets out to do

Learning needs things which will help a learner to achieve their goal

Learning styles analysis of how learners learn

Plagiarism to pass off somebody else's work as your own

Policy course of action by an organisation

Qualification a skill that makes someone suitable for a job

Recreational learning a skill for pleasure

Sanction a penalty for disobeying rules

Teaching to impart knowledge or a skill; what the teacher does during a session

VAK visual, auditory and kinaesthetic learners – different ways learners like to learn

Vocational skills related to employment

SUMMARY

In this chapter we set out to achieve the following outcomes:

- Describe your role and responsibility as a teacher within the context of your specialist subject

- Describe strategies which help you to identify how learners learn, how to introduce learners to you and their chosen programme of study, and how learning will progress through a teaching cycle

- Identify the relevant laws, statutes and codes of practice that affect the teaching profession

- Identify the scope of your own responsibilities and recognise when to refer an issue or incident to a specialist

- Describe and review how the learner must be at the centre of the learning experience respecting equality, diversity and inclusion

- List the types of records kept by the teacher required to audit and demonstrate that learners are at the centre of the organisation's values

Your Personal Development

You will have completed an activity which has helped you to identify where you are at the moment in terms of your strengths, weaknesses and experience as a teacher. You should have a list of questions to ask your mentor, line manager or course tutor which should help to set your own personal learning goals.

You will have learned to assume nothing, and that making assumptions about people can be detrimental to their learning.

You will have analysed both your own and your learners preferred learning styles and can explain how this will impact on your teaching. You will use your own learning experiences to create your own list of values that will not be compromised whilst you are teaching.

You will have identified questions to ask the health and safety manager, diversity manager, your line manager and/or your mentor to ensure that you comply with all of the legislation and codes of practice that apply to you whilst teaching in your specialist subject.

You should be able to answer questions relating to:

- your role, responsibilities and boundaries as a teacher in terms of the teaching cycle
- key aspects of legislation and codes of practice related to your organisation and specialist subject
- how you will promote inclusion, equality and diversity within your current and future teaching roles and how to refer learners to meet their needs.

CHAPTER 2 (PTLLS)

Approaches to teaching and learning

EDUCATION PHOTOS / ALAMY

LEARNING OBJECTIVES

The measurable outcomes that you will achieve by reading this chapter and completing the activities are:

- To select appropriate teaching and learning strategies
- To describe functional skills and identify opportunities for learners to gain those skills
- To identify challenges, barriers and attitudes to learning
- To state the importance of the environment in relation to learning
- To identify and select relevant resources

Approaches to teaching and learning

Teaching and learning strategies will vary according to what you want to get out of the session, what the learners are able to achieve within the time allowed, what materials and resources are available to you, the subject matter you are delivering, the needs of the learners and your personal style.

The choice of method will depend on whether you wish to deliver a formal teaching session in which all learners are working on the same topic at the same time, a learner-centred session, where learners are working on the same broad topic but using different methods and resources, or finally a self-study style where learners are working on different aspects of a topic or even different topics, using their own style of learning (Petty 2004: 430).

Factors that influence teaching:

- How learners learn and their preferred learning style
- What the teacher wants to achieve
- The subject matter
- What the learners are capable of achieving
- Time constraints
- Resource implications
- What the learners want to get out of the session
- Where you will teach
- How dependent your learners are

First of all, you should separate teaching from learning in order to understand these influences. In short, teaching is what we do; learning is what your learners will do. Each activity in the classroom will consist of teaching and learning activities. These should be balanced to meet the different needs of your learners (see Chapter 1) and to develop motivation (see Chapter 4). Modern technology allows for a **blended learning** style which incorporates traditional and computer-based methods. This is often referred to as information learning technology (**ILT**) or information communication technology (**ICT**). The use of computer-based technology to enhance teaching methods and resources or develop learner **autonomy** is widely promoted.

The table considers some of the most frequently used approaches and compares them in the context of teaching and learning activities.

Activity	Value to teacher	Value to learner
Lecture (verbal exposition)	High focus on teacher activity Excellent knowledge base required Uses verbal exposition to impart a lot of information in a short time Clarity and tone of voice needs to be clear, interesting and unambiguous Can be used to deliver to large groups easily Is enhanced by visual aids	Requires good listening and note-taking skills Passive learning Limited opportunities to clarify understanding Appeals to auditory learners
Demonstration	Needs to be well organised before session Explains difficult parts of the task when verbal exposition is not suitable Teacher-centred Links theory and practice	Opportunities to see, hear and smell Allows a task to be broken down into smaller chunks Limited hands-on experiences Appeals to visual learners (ensure everyone can see!)

▶

Activity	Value to teacher	Value to learner
Group work	Less teacher-focused Teacher needs to monitor progress to keep on task Takes a long time to extract key points Several different ways of working: **buzz**, **snowball** (**pyramid**), **jigsaw group activities**	Suits kinaesthetic learners Weak and strong learners work collectively
Discussion and debates	Free exchange of ideas on a given topic Needs careful management to ensure range of ideas and to keep on task Can be used to support other teaching methods Develops deeper understanding	Allows ideas to be shared and is an opportunity to value other learners' opinions Suits auditory learners Balanced teacher/learner input
Questioning (Q&A)	Different styles of technique: can be call-out or nominated in style Collects ideas which can be recorded on board Need to ensure everyone participates Good way of introducing or summarising a topic Assesses understanding of topic	Call-out style is not intimidating Challenges learners to think Can develop note-taking skills and increase accuracy of learners' notes Nominated style will ensure everyone is included in activity Instant feedback on response Appeals to kinaesthetic and auditory learners
Experiential	Teacher does not control the learning, thus developing autonomy Teacher is a facilitator	Learners develop their own methods of gaining information Highly learner-centred

Activity	Value to teacher	Value to learner
	Can develop personal skills in communication, number and IT May allow loss of focus	Can stimulate higher ability learners and motivate less able learners Ideal for kinaesthetic learners Ideal for **autonomous learners**
Presentations and seminars	Similar to lectures with added dimension of learner activity Key information presented, then deeper understanding acquired through gathering of further information Highly motivational	Able to gather key information and build upon it through their own research Learners investigate their topics and present back to their peers Develops individual styles Balance of teacher and learner activities Suits all learning styles
Simulation, role-play and practical work	Simulation used for expensive or dangerous activities Builds on previously demonstrated skills Mirrors work place practice Can be costly and time-consuming to organise; needs sufficient resources for all Needs to be carefully managed to ensure skill is practiced accurately Some learners may feel self-conscious Will promote and develop safe and healthy practice	Opportunity to practice skills Ideal for kinaesthetic and visual learners Can experience emotions, feel, taste and smell Reinforces previous learning Can learn from teachers, support workers or peers

▶

Activity	Value to teacher	Value to learner
Games/quizzes	Develops competitive spirit Can be used to open or close a topic Useful to keep as a contingency plan 'if time allows' or 'if you work well'	Fun activity Suits kinaesthetic learners
Research-style activities	Teacher is a **facilitator** or resource rather than leader of learning Promotes independence in learners	Suits visual and kinaesthetic learners
Case study	Develops higher levels of understanding on a topic Develops problem-solving capabilities Develops critical thinking	Enables learners to develop opinions and ideas from a given set of facts 'Safe' analysis which may impact on later application

Your second rule of teaching should be VARIETY

Variety in **teaching** and **learning** will ensure that your sessions are meeting individuals' needs and are addressing different spans of attention, as well as being interesting for you and your learners. By using a balance of teacher- and learner-centred activities you spread the responsibility of learning. Too many new teachers believe that they should 'perform' for the entire lesson; all they do is exhaust themselves to a usually passive (and possibly bored) group of learners. In the same way that you would integrate theory and practice whenever possible, intersperse passive and active learning activities – so that everyone benefits from a rest during the session!

The basic strategy for every session should be a beginning, middle and an end. This will form the structure, and will also help when you come to plan and prepare for your sessions. By following this structure you will be demonstrating an organised approach to teaching and learning. This should be the basis of role modelling for your learners; indirectly it will organise them and this will also help in managing the classroom atmosphere.

Simple structures			
Beginning	The introduction Explain what is going to happen in the session Setting the scene	For example: Verbal exposition (VE) Questioning – to check previous knowledge	Teacher-centred intro. Aims on board and spoken (auditory/visual) Collect any homework. Prompt and organised start, set any rules now Use an **opener activity** to engage learners immediately
Middle	The content Move from the known to the unknown Give clear instruction on how the activity will progress/time allowed	For example: Scenario 1 Demo + practical Scenario 2 VE + discuss + game	Balance of teacher/learner activity. Visual/kinaesthetic Learner-dominated. Auditory, visual and kinaesthetic
End	Assessment of what has been learned Conclusions and summary Future development	For example: Scenario 1 Discussion/evaluation Scenario 2 Quiz or Q&A Ending in VE – prep for next session.	Learner-centred. Opportunity to complete notes Learner-centred. Corrected script provides future notes Teacher-centred. Issue homework now

In order to ensure that you are meeting individuals' needs by using visual, auditory and kinaesthetic teaching and learning strategies, look at the lists below for some ideas for your teaching sessions, remembering to include a variety of techniques:

Visual learning techniques

- Use cards, posters and prompt sheets
- Display session tasks on board
- Write key words on board
- Collate ideas from group activities on board or flip chart
- Supplement verbal exposition with pictures and diagrams
- Ask questions which exploit visual imagination: 'What would it look like?'
- Encourage learners to 'see' words/concepts in their mind
- Use highlighter pens to annotate work
- Use a glossary of terms in a vocabulary book or poster
- Vary colour, font style/size in visual aids in learners' handouts
- Use mnemonics
- Number sentences or bullet points

Auditory learning techniques

- Listen to learners (teacher and peers)
- Talk through ideas on posters, boards, handouts
- Ask questions which exploit auditory skills: 'What does it sound like?'
- Introduce new words through language games
- Give thinking time in group activities
- Use musical connections to words (sing alphabet, use rhyme)

Kinaesthetic learning techniques

- Use breaks/pauses to get learners moving, even within the room
- Locate different activities in different parts of the room
- Use role play or practical activities
- Put words on cards to be sorted into types
- Write letters on cards to make words
- Use Post-It™ notes to record questions in lectures or demonstrations
- Ask questions which exploit kinaesthetic skills: 'What did it feel like?'
- Provide opportunities for learners to do things

Functional skills

Functional skills are a development initiative to standardise qualifications for English, maths and ICT. In the past they have been known by several different names:

- Core skills
- Common skills
- Basic skills
- Key skills
- Minimum core.

Irrespective of the name, functional skills refer to the mastery of English/literacy, maths/numeracy and ICT/information technology. These are the skills that underpin all learning and without them learners will struggle to meet the demands of their qualification, the world of work and life skills. Each of the names listed relates to a style or level of qualification, you will still hear them referred to as such in the staff room. Do not be confused – everyone is talking about the same broad topic; it is usually the method of assessment that determines the small differences. For example:

- *Common/core skills* were attached to academic qualifications, such as General National Vocational Qualifications (GNVQs).
- *Basic skills* are an initiative introduced by government, to raise the standards of literacy and numeracy in the post compulsory sector, usually assessed by a test.
- *Key skills* are basic skills applied to or in the context of a vocational qualification, usually demonstrated by preparing a portfolio of evidence.
- *Minimum core* is what you are addressing, probably at Level 3, in your teacher training qualification. It covers language, literacy, numeracy and ICT. Included within will be the assessment of personal skills and the ability to deliver functional skills to your learners. See also Chapter 10.

Functional Skills Qualifications are not planned to be fully launched until at least 2010. In the interim, existing qualifications will remain and pilot programmes will gradually introduce the new revised qualifications.

Whatever the current name, and there will be others, it is bestowed upon the teacher to develop these skills in their learners at every opportunity. As we noted in the first rule it cannot be assumed (assume nothing) that learners leaving full-time compulsory education (school) have sufficient skills in English, maths and IT to achieve their qualification. The Government sets the target that a learner leaving school should have, amongst others, English and maths at Level 2 (GCSE), and school performance tables reflect their ability to meet these targets. Most post-compulsory providers undertake diagnostic tests with their learners during induction to confirm the level of competence of its new entrants.

The Qualifications and Curriculum Authority (QCA) publish the National Qualifications Framework (NQF). Using this table, all qualifications are aimed at a specific level. The recently developed Qualifications Credit Framework (QCF) will classify qualifications according to level and size (http://www.qca.org.uk/qca_8150.aspx).

National Qualifications Framework (NQF)		Framework for Higher Education Qualifications (FHEQ)
Previous Level (e.g.)	*Current Level (e.g.)*	*Level (e.g.)*
LEVEL 5 NVQ Diploma	LEVEL 8 Specialist Award Advanced Professional Awards	D Doctorates
	LEVEL 7 Diploma Advanced Professional Awards	M Masters Degrees, Postgraduate certificates and diplomas
LEVEL 4 National Diploma Higher National Diploma L4 Certificate	LEVEL 6 L6 National Diploma/Cert Professional Award	H Honours – Bachelors, graduate certificates
	LEVEL 5 Higher National Diploma	I Intermediate – Diplomas of HE/FE, Foundation Degrees, HNDs
	LEVEL 4 Certificate	C Certificate of HE
LEVEL 3 National Certificate/Diploma NVQ A levels/As levels		
LEVEL 2 NVQ GCSEs Grades A*–C Basic/Key Skills L2 National Curriculum Key Stage 6 First Diploma/Certificate		

National Qualifications Framework (NQF)		Framework for Higher Education Qualifications (FHEQ)
Previous Level (e.g.)	Current Level (e.g.)	Level (e.g.)
LEVEL 1 NVQ GCSEs Grades D–G, Basic/Key Skills L1, National Curriculum Key Stage 4/5, Introductory Certificate		
ENTRY LEVEL Entry Level Certificates, Adult Skills for Life Entry 1, 2, 3		

The structure of the NQF, adapted from www.qca.org.uk

This table shows how qualifications are currently structured and will give teachers an idea of the level of functional skills a learner should possess to be able to achieve their main qualification. For example, someone on a Level 2 NVQ in Motor Vehicle Studies should study functional skills at Level 2 – GCSE Grade A* – C or equivalent. A learner on a Level 3 Certificate in Small Animal Care should be working on Level 3 Key Skills in communication, application of number and information technology. There will be variants to this to match curriculum specifications, for example, learners on Computer Programming courses may do ICT qualifications at a higher level, or hairdressers may do communication skills and number skills to an equivalent level of their main qualification and ICT to one level lower. These variants will often be recommendations from the awarding body or may be designed by whoever writes the course programme. It will be informed by the functional skills required to meet the job role and the results of **diagnostic assessment**.

Literacy standards include reading, writing, speaking and listening. Numeracy standards include interpreting information, calculations, interpreting and presenting results. ICT standards include finding and selecting information, entering and developing information and developing presentations. Each level from entry 1 through to Level 3 and above, has progressively more complex tasks and details required to show competence. There are several sources of information on the worldwide web:

Useful online resources

Advice about progress of functional skills qualifications:
http://www.qca.org.uk

Resources and teaching information:
http://www.basic-skills.co.uk
http://www.bbc.co.uk/skillswise

Standards and qualifications:
http://www.city-and-guilds.co.uk
http://www.ocr.org.uk
http://www.edexcel.org.uk

Embedding functional skills into teaching and learning activities

Embedding skills means that functional skills (things like literacy, numeracy and information technology) are taught within the main subject topic in a seamless way. *Integrating* functional skills into your teaching means that you will set activities which meet the literacy or numeracy standards; they may or may not be in context. By incorporating functional skills into every activity they will become embedded. **Embedded** skills are always in context.

Every activity that occurs in a teaching and learning session has the potential to gather information which demonstrates a learner's ability against functional skills – the level of the functional skill will be determined by the complexity of the information. The following table demonstrates some examples of embedded functional skills.

Functional skills are essential; they will help your learners to achieve and succeed in life. By embedding the functional skills

A learner who is *listening to the teacher* at the beginning of a class is listening for and identifying relevant information

In a *question and answer session* the learner will be both listening and speaking, or if it is a written question sheet they will be reading and writing

By *designing a poster* for display in the classroom, in addition to the subject matter the learner will have to:

● calculate the overall size of the poster
● estimate the size of the smaller parts to be attached to the poster
● decide on the ratio and proportion of text, picture and white space
● present information in a visual format
● gather data from a variety of sources – the Internet, books, magazines, or people, etc.
● write text (handwritten or word processed)
● read data sources
● interpret and summarise information
● display images or pictures

A catering learner *baking a cake* will have to:

● read the recipe
● interpret the information into a time plan of work
● calculate the time the task will take
● estimate the size and number of bowls required
● measure the ingredients
● talk to the teacher or support worker for advice and listen to their reply
● talk to other learners, hopefully about the cake!
● solve problems relating to the planned activity

In *reading this* book, you are:

● understanding explanatory text
● inferring meaning
● using reading strategies – skimming, scanning or detailed reading
● summarising information

A *visit to a supermarket* will require the learners to:

- write a shopping list
- calculate the cost of two or more items
- compare the price/weight of similar items
- talk to shop assistants/cashiers
- follow basic instructions
- listen to total cost of shopping and give money
- calculate the amount of change needed

A group of learners, *investigating a topic* and *presenting their findings* to the group will:

- respond to extended questions on a range of topics
- speak clearly and confidently using informal and formal language
- design a presentation using IT software
- present information grammatically correct, in a logical order and proofread the work
- present information in graphical format
- contribute within the group, engage in discussion about findings, arguments and opinions
- summarise information from a number of sources

into the curriculum both you and your learners can overcome the fear of English and maths, which may have been a barrier to earlier success in the subject. Sometimes giving something a different label, whilst confusing to the teacher, may sidetrack the learner into success.

 ACTIVITY 1

....

Personal Development

Stage One
Take an idea or lesson plan to your organisation's Functional Skills Advisor, Teaching and Learning Mentor or your ITT tutor.
Sit with them to map the functional skills that emerge from the activity.
Ask questions like 'why' and 'how' and don't forget to ask 'how can I develop the activity to include . . . '
Deliver the session and note any unplanned functional skills that occurred.

▶

Stage Two
Use a copy of or download the relevant functional skills standards from
an awarding body and repeat the task in Stage One above on your own.
Take the completed mapping exercise to your Functional Skills Advisor,
Teaching and Learning Mentor or ITT Tutor and discuss it.
Make any amendments and deliver the session.
Note any unplanned functional skills that occurred.

Challenges and barriers to learning

Challenges, barriers and attitudes to learning are general
expressions, which mean 'things that hold back' learning. Challenges,
in this context, usually mean 'making learning difficult'; barriers
mean 'things that prevent learning'. Attitudes are feelings and
emotions brought into the classroom by learners. As a teacher we
want our learners to work to the best of their ability, yet we
empathise with factors which from time to time restrict that ability.
Some learners may present themselves in our classes with more
long-term barriers, challenges and attitudes.

Challenges, barriers and attitudes are often the reason (or
occasionally the excuse!) for not learning. 'I can't do this' or 'I've
never been any good at . . .' or 'I hate tests' and any number of
similar expressions can be heard in classrooms up and down the
country. For teachers, this is our learner's 'cry for help'. When
learners say things like this they are demonstrating their lack of
motivation or poor self-esteem. We should think, 'how can I make this
easier to understand?', 'how can I prepare learners for their future
test?', 'is there something else behind that behaviour?' Whatever the
cry, whatever the remedy, few people have a phobia of learning
(sophophobia); many have challenges, barriers and attitudes which
inhibit their learning and so their success.

Remembering some of the challenges, barriers or attitudes to
learning can be made easier by using 'DELTA' to classify them:

Disability, Emotional, Language, Technology, Ability

Disability	Emotional	Language	Technology	Ability
Chronic pain	Behaviour	Accent	Car	Absence
Dexterity	Child care	Basic skill needs	breakdown	Inaccurate
Dyscalculia	Commitments	Communication	Computer	advice
Dyslexia	Concentration	Cultural	skills	Large classes
Hearing	Confidence	differences	Fear of	Motivation
Long illness	Dependents	Foreign	technology	Personal skills
Mental health	Discipline	language	Heating	Punctuality
Mobility	Employer	Pace	Lighting	Resources
Visual	pressure	Rapport	Temperature	Short illness
	Fear of unknown	Terminology	Transport	Study support
	Finance			Support
	Hormones			Teaching
	New			styles
	surroundings			
	Parental pressure			
	Peer pressure			
	Personal			
	problems			
	Poverty			
	Previous			
	experience			
	Returning to			
	education			
	Stress/worry			

Learning to recognise the symptoms of these barriers is essential in attempting to resolve the issues. As many of the barriers arise from emotions, it is difficult to predict how different learners will react, but just recognising that something in the character of your learner is different to their usual behaviour is usually enough. It returns to the idea that we should know our learners. Also, don't forget that people are human before they are teachers or learners and respect, praise and enjoyment are excellent motivators. NB: It is usually a good indicator that you have lost the interest of your learners if you look up and they have gone!

Before it gets that far, here are some things to look out for:

- Limited short-term memory
- Carelessness in work
- Lack of eye contact
- Glazed looks
- Repeated and persistent errors
- Time-management difficulties
- Reactions and side-effects to prescribed drugs
- Poor concentration
- Lack of participation or reluctance to participate
- Constantly demanding attention
- Panic or anxiety
- Tiredness or weight variance
- Poor behaviour
- Hyperactivity
- Poor attention span
- Lateness
- Attempts to sidetrack topic or activity
- Excessive calling out and interruptions
- Loud or demanding behaviour
- Sighing
- Fidgeting
- Putting coats on, or taking layers off.

Before embarking on a one person mission to cure all of your learners' symptoms, you might want to consider using referral agencies such as those discussed in Chapter 1. What you can do something about are your teaching and learning strategies to ensure an inclusive learning environment. See also Chapter 1, Equality, for some ideas. Recommendations include:

- Recognise changes in your learner's behaviour and make time to listen to their concerns
- Include lots of smaller activities to build and develop the topic and praise at each stage of achievement

- Offer one-to-one support during group activities
- Use nominated questions, aimed at differentiating to meet learners' individual levels of ability, to increase self-esteem
- Vary your teaching techniques to ensure a variety of auditory, visual and kinaesthetic activities
- Know your learners
- Use signers, note-takers and support workers to aid those with visual and hearing impairments or learning disabilities
- Allow use of tape recorders; it is difficult to lip read and make notes
- Offer comfort breaks within longer sessions
- Provide additional or extended work for less able or quick learners
- Always start from things that are known before moving to the unknown
- Experiment with different colours of paper for handouts; yellow is good and makes the words easier to read
- Encourage study skills. Stress key words and when to make notes
- Use Post-It™ notes for learners to record issues, areas of difficulty, questions, etc., collect them in, read them and act upon the content
- Ensure writing size on boards is legible: stand at the back of the room before the class and check it out!
- Include images and pictures in handouts, overhead transparency (**OHT**) or PowerPoint presentations
- Provide moments in the class when learners can ask questions and seek clarification
- Offer rewards for good behaviour or good progress.

The learning environment

The learning environment is any area in which teaching and learning takes place. This may be a classroom, a workshop, a lecture theatre or the workplace. The learning environment is not just limited to a space and equipment; it includes the atmosphere that creates a suitable learning setting. Teachers and learners will have experienced a variety of previous situations; those that are traditional in nature, full of teacher-led activities and learners taught in rows. The opposite, and more favourable route, is that of an engaging environment, i.e. that which is less formal, modern and interactive. The table compares these two environments.

Comparison of traditional and engaging learning environments	
Traditional learning environment	*Engaging learning environment*
Passive learners	Active learners
Learners absorb information	Learners interact with information
Insular learning style	Collaborative learning style
Same ability groups	Mixed ability groups
Teacher-centred	Learner-centred
Isolated themes	Integrated themes
Routine and predictable teaching	Innovative and exciting teaching
Discrete provision	Differentiated provision

The learning environment is within the power of the teacher to control. By choosing teaching and learning activities that empower learners to learn, a teacher will motivate learners and as a result they will achieve. Some of these factors are forced upon us due to funding and economic reasons, for example, the need to keep labour costs low results in different ability levels within the class groups, hence the need to meet individual needs in a group. Some factors arise from changes in thinking and technological developments. A teacher needs to accept these challenges and not create their own barriers to teaching (and learning).

The learning environment should meet the needs of individuals and of the chosen teaching strategies. Before the class starts the teacher should consider how they are going to teach during the session and arrange the furniture in an appropriate manner. Some of the options available for a 'taught' session are:

Desks or tables in rows

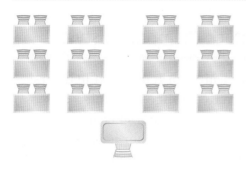

A very traditional arrangement. Suitable for lecture-style presentations, when learners need to focus on the front of the room. Not suited to any session where interaction between learners is needed. When learners enter the room, they usually head for the back row, which may cause problems when delivering a session.

Desks or tables in a U shape

A modern arrangement. Suitable when learners need to see the front but also need to engage in discussion with others. The teacher can easily reach learners to support activities although the tables may still form a barrier. The teacher should be mindful that

learners sitting towards the open ends of the 'u' may be in peripheral vision and therefore may be forgotten! See also Chapter 4, Activity 1.

Desks or tables in a central block (boardroom style)

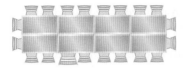

Ideal for group work, or when learners need space to arrange large pieces of work or games. Learners become the focus because the teacher is outside of the group, unless they sit down at the same table and become part of the group.

Desks or tables in small clusters (cabaret style)

Ideal for small group activities, such as discussion or jigsaw sessions, or as a way of arranging different activities within a single room space.

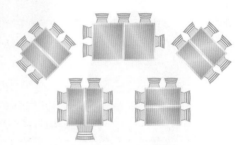

Chairs in a U shape

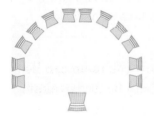

Ideal for group discussions. Suits very informal sessions, such as those in counselling-type discussions. The teacher either forms part of the group or sits outside of the group as an observer. The teacher can refocus the group by using equipment at the front of the room and the absence of tables removes barriers.

Chairs in rows (theatre style)

Very formal in style. Ideal for presentations and lectures where note-taking and discussion is not required. If questions from the floor are allowed, the teacher will have to repeat questions or use a microphone to ensure everyone can hear.

Chairs around the edge of the room (open style)

Ideal when space is required for role play or active learning strategies. Small groups can perform in front of peers.

In all of the room arrangements, the teacher should remember the health and safety of themselves and others. Tables can be heavy to shift around without the help of others, and there is always the matter of what to do with spare furniture when rearranging a room. You should always put the furniture back to its original position at the end of the session, so some teaching time will be lost in the lesson. Also, the teacher should consider where learners are to put their coats and bags, how learners will move safely around the room and how those with mobility problems will cope. You should also remember that those with visual impairment may have learnt the room layout and changes will disorientate them. Whilst changing a layout has advantages and health and safety issues can be overcome, always prepare learners for a change. You can either tell them that the room will look differently next week because … or get them involved in the change, explaining why it is necessary. Do not underestimate the feelings of learners.

The size and shape of the room will impact on how the room can be arranged and the types of learning activity that can be undertaken. Rooms are usually allocated by others in your organisation, but if your learner numbers increase beyond what is acceptable, or the room is not suitable for the teaching activities or resources you need, it is worth asking to change rooms, even if only on a temporary basis.

A learning environment should be suitable for learning. Learning will only occur in a relaxed, familiar surrounding. The teacher must also consider factors such as temperature and light. In a hot room, learners will become sluggish and tire easily. In a cold room, they will be concentrating on trying to get warm. Find out where the thermostat is, or where the remote control for the air conditioning is, or how the windows open. The amount of light needed will vary

EXAMPLE

For many weeks the learners have been attending their session in a particular room, and they will probably have claimed their seat. It will be next to their friend and certainly in a comfortable position. They will always sit there. It is their space!

Move the room around before they arrive and just watch the panic in their faces! They are uncomfortable and do not like it. They will be suspicious and reluctant to participate. If it is an examination period, they will immediately lose any self-confidence they had.

I do this to my groups of trainee teachers – by experiencing their own fears they quickly understand the impact their actions will have on their group.

Maybe not the true meaning of experiential learning – but it works!

according to activity. A beauty salon may need muted light, but the artist needs plenty of natural light. You might need to dim the lights to make visual aids more visible or add light to write notes. Where is the light switch?

Carefully chosen teaching strategies with good resources in a comfortable environment are the key ingredients to a successful and effective teaching and learning session.

Resources

Resources are the equipment and aids that a teacher or learner will use to promote learning. They can be classified in the same way that learner styles are classified and therefore a teacher will be able to choose resources to meet individual needs (differentiated). The more senses a resource affects, the more useful it will be. By linking suitable teaching strategies with professional resources, effectiveness and efficiency of learning will be increased. For example: if doing a verbal exposition, by listing key points on a handout and recording discussion points on a board, or preferably by learners in their handout, most learners' learning needs will be met.

Resources will vary according to the subject, the learners, the accommodation and the skills of the teacher, but they should always be accurate in terms of content, spelling and grammar.

Some examples of resources and their link to the senses

Auditory (using the sense of hearing)

- Tape recordings
- Video, DVD – hearing + sight

Visual (using the sense of sight)

- Boards – chalk, wipe, chart or electronic
- Printed – handouts, overhead projector (**OHP**), posters
- PowerPoint presentation with note style handout (auditory + visual + kinaesthetic)

Kinaesthetic (using the sense of touch)

- Models
- Games

The age of technology has increased the types of resources available and developed existing resources to the advantage of both teacher and learner. A computer attached to a projector enables anything created using a software programme to be displayed and modified in front of the learners; the Internet will become 'live' in the classroom; resources stored on intranet or on virtual learning environments (VLE) (e.g. Moodle, Blackboard, Learnwise) are constantly accessible. Information communication technology (ICT) is also being increasingly used, for example, email to transmit/submit work, mobile phones to send text messages to learners. Text writing is also being used to quicken learners' note-taking skills, but be careful that learners don't prepare their formal work in the same style!

Purpose of using resources

- Increase understanding
- Reinforce key facts
- Create deeper learning
- Motivate
- Variety
- Effective use of time
- Simplify ideas

(Reece and Walker 2006: 157–158)

Boards

Includes chalk boards, white or wipe boards, flipcharts and stands, electronic boards. Chalk boards are a little outdated now due to the dust they create, but may still be found in some teaching venues. More commonly, you will see the dust-free wipe boards or flip charts and stands. On a safety note, beware of the fumes that are given off by some permanent pens. More and more often you will see electronic or interactive boards in rooms (IWB).

Every type of board uses the principle that words and drawings are displayed in front of the learners, using chalk, dry-wipe, permanent or electronic pens to write with. The electronic board has the additional facility that anything written on it can be saved for future use or printed to provide permanent copies. Flip chart paper can be peeled off the stand and displayed in the room to provide a reference point in classes. Unfortunately, chalk and wipe boards have to be regularly cleaned to provide sufficient space, so make sure learners have taken information into their notebooks before erasing board-work. It is essential that words and drawings on the board are clear, accurate and written in a way to encourage note-taking and of course, visible and legible. The way you use the board is generally the same way that learners will create their own notes, so 'meck shure u cheque yor spellin' and learners understand your handwriting and the presentation style.

Using boards	
Advantages	*Disadvantages*
Cheap (except electronic)	Not permanent (except electronic)
Accessible	Teacher has back to room
Easy to use	Can be messy
Can be pre-prepared	Usually fixed position
Always in view	

Hint:

If you accidentally use a permanent pen to write on a wipe board, overwrite it with a dry-wipe pen and it will come off easily.

Ensure that boards are visible to all of your learners. Remember that visibility may be reduced for those sitting at the back of the room – the most popular seats – and things like colour blindness may limit visual impact for some learners.

Projectors

Overhead projectors (OHPs) are used to display overhead transparencies (OHTs). They are common in most areas and there are portable varieties for those working in community-based venues. The skill in the use of the OHP is in the creation of professional OHTs. The modern equivalent is the laptop computer and a portable or ceiling-mounted projector. Both are displayed onto a suitable pale coloured surface. A pen or pencil point makes a convenient pointer to identify a word or phrase.

Single sheet transparencies, which are sometimes called view foils or slides, are useful to display text or diagrams. It is easy to incorporate colour and they are relatively easy to make. They can be handwritten or printed using photocopiers and computer printers, although each type uses different qualities of transparency slides. A transparency suitable for handwriting will melt if used in a photocopier, and printers need slides which absorb the ink, so be careful. Transparencies can be stored for future use in envelopes or clear plastic wallets.

Using overhead transparencies (1)

Reveal technique

A sheet of paper can be used to slowly display facts or information on transparencies, which is a good way of focusing on a fact or pacing the session.

Overlay technique

A series of two or more transparencies placed on top of each other in sequence to build up a picture.

Liquid crystal display (LCD) projectors are used with electronic/ interactive boards, computers or video/DVD machines to display information to learners. They are either portable or ceiling mounted and offer a high quality method of display. They are, however, expensive and not available in all teaching rooms. In order to use them efficiently and connect them correctly, a teacher needs to be trained in how to use the software and associated equipment and cables.

As projectors rely on an electricity supply and electronic components to operate them you should always check that they are working before the start of the session. You are advised to have a back-up plan just in case the equipment is faulty. Your organisation should also check that they are safe to use (portable appliance testing – PAT), and may insist that personal equipment has been safety checked.

Using overhead transparencies (2)	
Advantages	*Disadvantages*
Colourful	Prone to breakdown
Interactive	Slightly noisy to use
Can pace learning	Needs window blinds or dimmed lights to be clearly visible
Versatile	
Easy to use (OHP)	Light from projector can shine in teacher's eyes
Professional	

Hints:

- Use sentence case when preparing slides
- Stand to one side and face learners
- Do not overcrowd slides
- Read from projector not viewing board
- Use legible font style and size

Note: Creating PowerPoint presentations uses similar skills to making OHTs, although it is a more modern and professional style; they can also include animations which add interest. Beware of 'death by PowerPoint.'

Handouts

Handouts are the most commonly used resource due to availability of photocopying and printing facilities. Their versatility makes them useful in the classroom as information sheets, records of key words, *aides-memoire,* question sheets or notes pages. When creating a handout, the teacher should always consider the purpose of the resource:

- Is it to be used to support the session or as additional information?
- Are learners expected to write on it?
- Does it need hole-punching to put into files?
- Would it be better with pictures?
- Does it comply with copyright guidance?
- Is it user-friendly and does it respect **equality of opportunity**?
- Is the writing legible?
- Will learners read it or just file it?
- Would coloured paper or coloured font make it clearer to read?
- Would it be better enlarged onto A3-sized paper?
- Would it be enhanced by borders, bullet points etc.?

There are several different types of handout, the main ones being:

Information sheets. Usually text based, but there is a danger that they will be distributed and filed before being read and understood, thus rendering them useless in terms of learning. If a handout is used in that way it is a waste of paper! It would be better to write key words, maybe using a bullet format and have plenty of white space on the sheet for learners to annotate with meaning, paraphrasing or similar explanations. Or ask learners to highlight key words as you are discussing the topic. Hole punch handouts before issuing to learners – it saves time whilst waiting for the hole punch to follow the distribution and/or saves them falling out of their files on the way home!

Gapped handouts are ideal as a means of differentiating information according to ability. They can be used to aid learning by getting learners to complete them during discussions or as a test to check that a topic is understood. For example:

Text	Level	Strategy
'Resources are the equipment and aids that a teacher or learner will use to promote learning. They can be classified in the same way that learner styles are classified and therefore a teacher will be able to choose resources to meet individual needs (differentiated). The more senses a resource affects, the more useful it will be' (see p. 58).	Difficult	Omit words. 'Resources are … and … that a…. or learner use to … learning. The more … a resource affects, the more … it will be.'
	Average	Omit words – leave correct number of dashes to replace letters. 'The more ------ a resource affects, the more ------ it will be.'
	Easy	Omit words – leave first letter and dashes to replace words. 'The more s----- a resource affects, the more u----- it will be.'
	Very simple	As above but list the missing words at bottom of sheet. 'The more s----- a resource affects, the more u----- it will be.' senses, useful

Help sheets are a means of developing learning by interacting with the learners. By leaving white space on the page, learners can be encouraged to add their own notes. The printing of PowerPoint slides as 'handouts – three per page' is a very professional style of presentation. Add label tags to diagrams so that learners can complete them as you say the words or copy them from the board as you complete them. Just the simple strategy of leaving lines under a question for the learners to answer, helps them to understand how much to write in their response.

Posters and display materials are useful tools to consolidate learning. They can be created by learners, who will, hopefully, be quite proud to display their work, or created by the teacher. A poster displayed in the room will be looked at during the class as eyes and concentration wander; the content is then subconsciously noted. It is a good way of using colour to stimulate learning and is seen as a fun exercise rather than hard work.

Teachers can laminate key handouts to ensure that they are kept in pristine condition; small activities used with learners will also keep longer if preserved by laminating them.

Models and games

These offer visual and kinaesthetic learners the opportunity to see or feel an item, albeit a model. A model is three-dimensional and can be a tactile way of looking at something. Games provide fun activities to experience or practice topics. Think about how different spelling tests would become using word games rather than a pen and paper. However, games and models tend to be expensive and the use of a particularly costly item has to be supervised. There are also problems associated with obtaining and storing such things.

Audiovisual resources

For example, DVD, video, slide shows. These are frequently used resources and offer good ways of visualising an activity or initiating discussion. They are usually of a high standard. If recording items from the television or radio, you should ensure that you have the necessary permissions for use. The teacher should prepare well – it is not usually just popping the thing into the recorder or projector. A good lesson around a video or DVD will have a list of prepared discussion points or questions. This focuses the learner on things to look for during the screening and a basis for a later discussion or question activity. The necessary equipment must be available: this might mean hiring equipment or moving to a room with equipment already in it. In most cases there will be a key involved – who's got it? Where is it? What will I do if it doesn't work?

Again, as with teaching and learning activities, the success of resources will be *variety*: variety in terms of resources used and the way in which the teacher uses them, but also in terms of meeting needs of learners.

ACTIVITY 2

Personal Development

Ask (your mentor) where you can borrow specialist equipment, for example a portable overhead projector.

Practice preparing some handouts/overhead transparencies. Try different types, e.g. a handwritten type, a printed type, and then make them useful for two different ability levels.

Check your spelling and grammar skills by asking a colleague to proofread for you.

Do an assessment to identify your IT skills.

Glossary of terms

Autonomy independence in the ability to learn

Autonomous learner one who requires minimal guidance from the teacher

Blended learning a mixture of traditional and computer learning technologies

Buzz group activities small groups interact with the teacher to gather answers

Diagnostic assessment assessment used to identify capability or skill level

Dyscalculia associated with difficulties in making sense of numbers and calculations

Dyslexia associated with a difficulty in reading or interpreting words and symbols

Embedded fixed firmly in the vocational context

Equality of opportunity legislation and focus on gender, age, culture etc.

Facilitator one who supports or stimulates learning

ICT Information communication technology

ILT Information learning technology

IT Information technology

Jigsaw group activities small groups discuss different themes within a topic, which are collated by the teacher at the end of the activity

Learning to gain knowledge or a skill; what the learners do during the session

OHP overhead projector

OHT overhead transparency

Opener activity a short activity at the start of sessions to set scene, create learning ethos and engage learners quickly

Snowball (pyramid) group activities pairs discuss then form gradually larger groups to gain a consensus of opinion on a topic or subject

Teaching to impart knowledge or a skill; what the teacher does in the session

SUMMARY

In this chapter we set out to achieve the following outcomes:

- Select teaching and learning strategies appropriate to your specialist area
- Describe the meaning of functional skills and identify opportunities to collect evidence to support your learners' acquisition of those skills

▶

- Identify challenges, barriers and attitudes to learning which will impact upon your teaching and learning sessions
- State the importance of the learning environment in relation to the delivery of teaching sessions
- Identify and select relevant resources appropriate to your specialist area

Your Personal Development

You will have had the opportunity to compare many different types of teaching and learning methods and resources and consider how they will be used in your learning sessions.

You will have understood the need for variety to minimise boredom, increase motivation and meet the different needs of your learners and how your teaching, the environment and your resource choices influence this.

You have learned about functional skills and the many ways they are referred to in the staff room and carried out an activity to embed them into your sessions and map them to qualifications.

You can now use DELTA to categorise barriers and challenges to learning and devise ways to use teaching and learning methods, resources and personal skills to minimise them, resulting in learners who are eager to learn.

Finally, you have looked around you to check if the area in which you work is suitable to learning and provides an engaging and stimulating environment.

You should be able to answer questions relating to:

- Explaining ways to embed elements of functional skills in your specialist area
- Explaining why you have made choices of teaching and learning approaches and use of resources, justifying your strategies, and
- demonstrate a selection of teaching and learning approaches to engage and motivate learners in your teaching sessions.

CHAPTER 3
(PTLLS)

Session planning skills

LEARNING OBJECTIVES

The measurable outcomes that you will achieve by reading this chapter and completing the activities are:

- To describe the key features and purpose of schemes of work and lesson plans
- To list the main parts and how to structure the documents
- To state the difference between aims and outcomes
- To write measurable statements
- To explain your choice of appropriate strategies to meet the needs of individuals in your sessions

Planning sessions

First of all the basics: a scheme of work is the overall programme of study. It may last, for example, one week, ten weeks or two years. It is merely a breakdown of the whole programme into smaller chunks based on the frequency of your meetings with learners. A lesson or **session** plan is a detailed description of one of those chunks in terms of how you will deliver the topic to your learners and what learning development will occur.

Neither the scheme of work nor the **lesson plan** is fixed. They should be considered as 'work in progress' and will alter in response to organisational and learner needs.

Scheme of work

This may be called a **scheme of work** (SoW), 'a learning programme', or 'a **programme of study**'. When you start teaching you will probably be asked to take X group in Y room and teach them Z. The first thing you must establish is what 'Z' is. If you are teaching any type of subject that is qualification based, someone, usually the organisation that issues the certificates, will already have determined what has to be taught. This is usually broken down into smaller components and you will have been employed to deliver one of those components, i.e. Z.

This may be described to you as a unit, module, subject or even its title. You should always ask to see the official content of the subject. It is usually called the **syllabus**. Once you have seen the syllabus, then, as a specialist in that subject, you will be able to break it down into smaller chunks. You will include sessions relating to what *must* be known, what *should* be known and what *could* be known (if time allows), thus creating the scheme of work or programme of study. Do not be surprised if this brings on your first panic. New teachers often doubt their knowledge in their specialist area. It is only panic.

Just relax and ask yourself 'What is the first thing a new learner must understand before moving to the next?'

Remember, always move from the *known* to the *unknown* (Chapter 2).

For example, when you learnt to drive, what did you do first? Did you go backwards? No! Did you go forwards? Yes – but I bet you learnt about the controls first!

So on this simple scheme of work the first session would include some information about the pedals, switches and steering wheel. Then you would build on that and start moving off and stopping, then gears and turning, etc.

This would be underpinned by the theory – importance of mirrors, what makes the vehicle go and so on, and learning the Highway Code. Can you see how this is starting to build into a 'programme of study?'

However, you may not be working to a subject which is part of a qualification. You may be delivering a recreational programme or addressing a company's training need. In this case, the strategy is the same as above but the goals (the end result) will either be determined by the learners or by the company's training manager. In this case, it is not a syllabus but specified learning outcomes. The same principles will follow. You must breakdown the **learning outcomes** (or end result) into small chunks of learning. If you are delivering a one-off training session you would not be expected to complete a scheme of work, they only really apply to multiple sessions.

You will usually be asked to write your scheme of work and present it to your line manager. It is also a good idea to present it to your learners. They are also interested in how they will progress their learning.

Why do a scheme of work?

- To identify the smaller stages of learning
- To prepare for planning of sessions
- To give structure to the learning
- To evenly distribute learning
- To identify resource needs
- To ensure variety
- To monitor progress
- To inform learners of the stages of learning
- To record proposals for learning
- To inform line managers of strategy
- To help colleagues if cover necessary
- To assist quality processes

A scheme of work should include:

1   General Information:
    - Who the group is, usually described as a qualification and/or subject. For example: First Year National Diploma, Unit 8; Intro to Watercolours, Washes; Key Skills L1 Communication; Management Information Group, Intro to Software.
    - Location and Duration of meetings. A record of how often, where and how long sessions are. For example: Monday 9.30 to 11.30 (30 weeks – Room LG004); or Wednesday 7.00 to 9.00 Autumn Term – Apple Centre; or 9.00 till 13.00 in the MIS room.

2   Aims and outcomes of the programme. Detail about what the end result of the programme will be, written from both the teacher's and the learners' viewpoints.

3   Content and structure:
  - Brief detail about the content of each session
  - Details about the teaching and learning methods to be used
  - Links to functional skills
  - Information about assessment of learning.

4   Additional information:
  - Examination or assessment practice
  - Revision periods
  - Assessment planning sessions
  - Progress or tutorial sessions
  - Assignment or catch-up workshops
  - Study skills.

AN EXAMPLE OF A SCHEME OF WORK PROFORMA

Programme title:	
Programme area:	Module/unit:
Tutor:	Duration:

Aims and outcomes of programme:

Assessment and qualification:

Wk	Topic	Method	Resource	Functional skills	Assessment method
1					
2					
3					
4					
etc.					

The way you break down the syllabus into smaller chunks will depend on how many sessions you have allocated to the topic, the level of the learners, the complexity of the topic and the needs of the learners. The detail is usually recorded on the session/lesson plan.

The lesson plan

> ## To fail to plan is to plan to fail

(Petty 2004: 422)

The lesson plan, usually abbreviated to LP, is the detail that relates to each session/week on your scheme of work. It states the specific expectations (outcomes) of the lesson, and provides a guide or order of work describing how the teacher will achieve those outcomes. It is the teacher's *aide-memoire*. It will help to provide structure – a beginning, middle and end, remind you of the order you have planned to do things, how you thought to do it and what you have planned and prepared to support you in the session. It will be there in case you forget where you've got to, it will remind you of what is left to do – and provide you with the opportunity to reflect on which bits worked and which bits did not. By timing the activities it will help you to ensure that you have the correct amount of work for the time allowed. This is usually a second period of panic. Have I got enough stuff? Have I got too much? Again, this is perfectly normal – and with practice comes more accuracy in pacing your lesson. If you want a comfort zone then plan an activity that goes in to the lesson if time allows or can come out if you run out of time, i.e. give yourself a contingency plan.

Things to consider when writing a lesson plan

1 What is the purpose of the session?

2 What do you (the teacher) want out of the session (aim)?

3 What do you want/need your learners to get out of the session (outcome)?

4 Who are your learners?

5 How will you differentiate your teaching?

6 What order will you need to teach things in?

7 How will you keep learners interested?

8 What will be the ratio of teacher- and learner-centred activities?

9 How long is the session?

10 How far into the course/programme is this session?

11 What has happened before?

12 How long will each activity last?

13 What accommodation and resources will you want to use?

14 How will you know that learning has occurred?

15 What contingency plan do you have?

Let's think about putting all of those answers into your lesson plan. Here is a typical format, but you will probably find that your organisation has already got a form that is in regular use.

LESSON PLAN

Teacher	Date
Course/level/year of group	

Subject	Time
Number	Age *14–16 16–18 19+*

Previous knowledge

Write here what the learners already know, for example:
key words and similar skills/knowledge. Always remember
to move from the known to the unknown so this section is
your starting point

Aim of session

Should be written from the teacher's perspective, for
example – understand about…, be aware of… know about…

Outcomes of session

Should be written from the learners' perspective, for
example:

By the end of this session, the learner will be able to …
Describe, write, explain, state etc i.e. measurable
statements/verbs
Alternative expression is 'objectives' which means the
same thing

Outcomes assessed by

How you will know that learning has occurred in this session?

Content	Method
Firstly –	List here the teaching
Share lesson outcomes with	and learning methods you
learners	plan to use. Remember
	variety.
Secondly –	
Introduction (x minutes)	
Then –	
Development (x minutes)	
Next –	
Conclusion (x minutes)	
Finally –	
Summary (x minutes)	

Resources	Planned differentiation
List the resources you	How are you going to
need to deliver the session	meet the needs of
	individuals in your session?

Links to next session

What homework or 'bridging' activities will occur between this & the next session; this might be an exercise, a reading, looking at an Internet site, collecting something, etc.

Lesson evaluation

This section would be completed soon after the session, and the teacher would talk about what worked and what didn't work. Was there too much, not enough? Which bit was understood well and which bit might have to be revisited? What would be done differently next time? Were the learning outcomes met?

Aims, objectives and outcomes

In the sections about schemes of work and lesson plans, the expression 'aims and outcomes' has been used repeatedly.

The word **aim** is used as a general statement of intent, usually written from the teacher's perspective. For example 'to raise awareness of the use of filing systems'. As you can see this is really describing the topic: it does not say to what extent a learner should be aware, or the types of filing systems to be included. It is a very broad topic. Other words you may use when writing aims are 'to know about', 'to understand', or 'to appreciate'. These are very general words and can be used to indicate the type of topic or subject that is about to be taught. As it is almost impossible to measure

ACTIVITY 1

Which of these statements are aims and which are outcomes?

1   To appreciate the works of Mozart

2   To list the main components of blood

3   To label a diagram of the heart.

4   To prepare and bake a Victoria sandwich cake

5   To understand the stages of growth

6   To state Pythagorus' Theorem

7   To replace a tyre

8   To test the effectiveness of . . .

9   To demonstrate safe working practices

10   To know how to replace a tyre

Answers: 1, 5 and 10 are aims, the rest are outcomes

someone's knowledge, understanding or how much they value or appreciate something, these words cannot be used as outcomes.

The word **objective** is a smaller chunk or more specific statement relating to how the aims will be delivered; they are written as a measurable statement, usually expressed as an outcome. An outcome would use words – verbs – to describe what the learner will be able to do. For example 'to list the main types of storage systems used in a legal office'. The statement is an outcome because the word 'list' is measurable. You would be able to do an activity to find out (measure) whether or not the students can 'list' or not. Other words that can be used when writing outcomes are:

Analyse, bake, compare, demonstrate, explain, fill in, gather, highlight, identify, justify, knit, list, make, note, outline, plan, question, research, state, translate, use, visit, write, xtract, y, z (you can do the last two for yourself!) See also the command words section in Appendix C: Study Skills (pp. 648–649).

Planning to meet individual needs

The way you choose to teach your sessions will depend on a number of factors, but the primary factor should be influenced by your learners. As teachers we need to ensure that as well as us 'doing our stuff' in the classroom, the learners must be 'learning our stuff' too! This is done by meeting their needs. In the previous two chapters we have considered how we select teaching and learning methods, resources and how previous experiences of learning influence learners and what we need to do to overcome this. In Chapter 7 we will investigate some useful theories to support the need to meet learners' needs. Strategies are varied according to how learners like to learn and the simplest way of ensuring variety is to remember that learners learn using their senses and will respond to things that they can see (visual learners), hear (auditory learners), or do (kinaesthetic learners). In any class you teach, there will be a mixture of these preferred styles and therefore to meet the needs of all of your learners you must mix and match your teaching and resource selections.

Things that appeal to visual learners are:

- Videos/DVDs
- Handouts
- Demonstrations.

Things that appeal to auditory learners are:

- Teacher talk (verbal exposition)
- Lectures
- Tape recordings
- Oral questioning.

Things that appeal to kinaesthetic learners are:

- Work sheets
- Discussion
- Workshop (practical) activities.

When planning a lesson, you need to think about your learners and what you are going to do to meet their needs. Here are some examples of things you may need to plan when preparing your lessons.

Things to write when planning for differentiated strategies on your lesson plan:

- Abigail and Sunita need to complete assignment task three
- Use nominated questioning to challenge learners
- Support learners struggling with activity by doing 1:1 support
- Prepare handouts for William on A3 paper
- Extension exercises in case Peter and Sarah finish quickly
- Give feedback to Iain, Jessica and Faisal on how to improve their assignment grade
- Two learners require large font task sheet
- B needs to have handouts copied onto pale yellow paper
- Arrange learners into ability groups for task 2
- Level 3 learners to work with Level 2 learners in salon
- George, Joseph to library to continue research, Petra away last week needs intro to task, rest continue with task sheet
- Use screenshot handout for Level 1 learners

As you can see, this will only work if you really know your learners and are methodical about recording their progress. However, it is also important to remember that good teachers have been working in this way for many years and it is only recently that there has been a name for this style of teaching. So, continue 'patrolling' your classroom or workshop, pausing to advise or correct learners and working with mixed levels of ability within the same classroom. Nothing new in this respect, but now you can record it on your lesson plan as differentiation.

Glossary of terms

Aim a broad statement of intent

Learning outcome the result of a learning session

Lesson plan a written structure for a session

Objective a specific statement of intended outcome

Programme of study a structured list of sessions

Scheme of work a document listing sessions within a programme

Session a period of learning

Syllabus the structure of a qualification

 SUMMARY

In this chapter we set out to achieve the following outcomes:

- Describe the key features and purpose of schemes of work and lesson plans
- List the main parts and how to structure the documents
- State the difference between aims and outcomes
- Write measurable statements
- Explain your choice of appropriate strategies to meet the needs of individuals in your sessions

Your Personal Development

You can explain the meaning of the expressions 'scheme of work' and 'lesson plan' and describe the key features of the documents. You can explain the difference between an aim (what the teacher hopes the session is about) and an outcome (what the learner gains from the session) and can prepare plans to meet your requirements.

You can state why planning and preparation is important in relation to variety in sessions, and differentiating activities according to the needs of your learners. You should also be aware of some of the expressions used on lesson plans.

You should now be able to create documents relating to:

- Producing learning programmes/schemes of work within a specific subject area and to a particular type of learner.
- Devising lesson plans which include aims and outcomes, planned differentiation and a range of teaching and learning methods and resources appropriate to the subject being delivered, which
- Prepares you to teach in a teaching session.

CHAPTER 4
(PTLLS)

Motivation and inclusion

LEARNING OBJECTIVES

The measurable outcomes that you will achieve by reading this chapter and completing the activities are:

- To analyse and evaluate effective classroom management skills
- To describe the key methods to improve motivation
- To recognise the value of effective feedback
- To describe ways to effectively engage learners
- To list the key factors which initiate successful communication and describe the main methods
- To reflect on your practice and initiate personal and professional development

Managing the learning environment

The teacher is the person in charge of the classroom

This may seem obvious, but you would be surprised to see how often it does not seem to be so. Managing learning is usually associated with behaviour and is therefore referred to when dealing with younger (i.e. under 19 years old) learners. However, managing the learning environment is broader than behaviour. Remembering our rule about assumption, adults also are entitled to and will always demand a well managed environment. The teacher is the one who, as well as teaching in a well prepared, varied, inspirational and exciting manner, addressing the needs of every individual in their group:

- Keeps control of learners
- Maintains the immediate cleanliness and tidiness of the room
- Cleans the boards
- Reports broken or dangerous equipment or furniture
- Ensures a safe and secure learning environment
- Prepares for any/all eventualities
- Is a role model for acceptable standards of behaviour
- Develops learners
- Sets and secures agreement to codes of conduct

- Ensures security is maintained

- Keeps an eye on the clock

- Determines the frequency and duration of breaks

- Offers guidance, support and counselling services.

If all of this happens, the teacher can consider themselves the 'person in charge'. By putting all of this together, the learners will learn in a manner designed to get the best and most efficient learning available. Unfortunately, I witness an increasing culture of blame and despondency:

'It was a mess when I walked in' or 'It was already broken'. Not the cries of a teenager, but a 'professional' teacher.

'The learners are getting worse' – or are they just unsure of the boundaries and nobody guides them into classroom or learning readiness?

'What time can we have a break?' – usually asked within 30 seconds of the learners entering the classroom, and repeated at two minute intervals.

'The management need to see . . .' You might ask yourself exactly what it is you want *them* to see?

And the classic 'I haven't got time to . . .'

The main issues in managing a learning environment can be classified into five sections:

1   managing the classroom;
2   managing poor behaviour;
3   managing punctuality;
4   managing the workload; and
5   creating learning readiness.

Managing the classroom	
Potential issues	*Possible solutions*
Tables and chairs in a mess	Allow a few minutes at the end of the class to put chairs under tables. Set the standard.
Rubbish everywhere	Insist culprits pick up rubbish and place it in the bin. If lesson has created rubbish allow clearing up time at end.
Writing on board	Clean board at end of lesson – set an example.
Something broken or damaged	Ensure danger does not impact on your learners and report issue to the site team, admin staff or line manager. Never assume someone has already reported it.
Coats and bags lying around	Identify and instruct learners to place bags etc. in a particular place.
Ambience of room	Display student work to create a sense of ownership and introduce a colourful area. Change displays regularly. Remove clutter. Keep it tidy and encourage learners to participate in this process.

Hint:

Always leave a room as you would wish to find it.

Managing poor behaviour
'It's war out there'
'They're out to get you'
Sue Cowley (2003: 52, 83)

Potential issues

Learners talking at the same time as you

Confrontational behaviour

Learners refuse to work

Learners don't come to class ready to work

Phones/iPods on etc.

Possible solutions

Remember that learners have opted to behave in this way. You can cope!
Keep calm; be clear about what you expect by setting targets; reward good
behaviour, ignore bad; be consistent; have plenty of short, varied activities;
keep supplies of pens/paper; use silence or counting strategies to gain
their attention, identify sanctions and rewards and initiate them when using
the 'do or else' speech.

There are two stages to dealing with poor behaviour. First you should try:

1 Patience and nurturing. Setting standards by role modelling and
   listening to reasons, yet setting and agreeing targets and rewards.
   For example 'If you write (set amount), you can (listen to music for x
   minutes/go to break/talk).' You may wish to try peer involvement – get
   the group to design and agree the rules and suggest collective
   responsibility for adhering to them.

2 As a last resort start the 'warning cycle'. Issue a warning, then warn
   again with what will happen if non-compliant, a repeat means that
   you should follow through with the sanction (penalty). The level of
   sanction should reflect the seriousness of the misdemeanour.

Never look scared or argue and never shout or swear. Be assertive not
aggressive. Remember 'The Look' – you know the one your mother/partner
used to give you! If you still have problems, ask a colleague to observe
you and offer suggestions.

Managing punctuality

Potential issues	Possible solutions
Learners arrive late	First of all consider the impact this has on you, the late learner and the rest of the group. This will influence the action needed.
Do you set a good example by *always* being in the classroom before the time the learners are expected?	Challenge – why are you late?
	Answer – bus, family, doctors, ugh!
Do you permit the latecomer to disrupt the lesson? Worse still, do you encourage lateness by starting the lesson again, so they can catch up!	The answer determines the action, but you should do the challenge quickly, and not allow the interruption to impact on the rest of the group. Ask the late learner to settle quickly and ignore it until an appropriate time. Then elicit more info and deal with it appropriately.
	Occasional lateness by someone who quietly enters, says sorry and settles just requires acknowledgement and no further action other than an explanation of what was missed and a target to catch up.
	The ugh! is showing disrespect and if continuous and disruptive you need to follow the warning cycle (a warning, warning and sanction issue, then sanction implementation).

Managing the workload

Potential issues	Possible solutions
Coping with mixed abilities in group sessions	Know your learners and plan for differentiation. (**VAK**, varied activities and resources, different tasks.)

Managing the workload	
Potential issues	*Possible solutions*
Time	Prioritise your work and keep a 'to do' list. Set yourself targets and if someone asks you to do something, be realistic in telling them when it will be done. Better to work like this than be known as unreliable.
Session preparation	Allow time to do photocopying, printing etc., always have contingency plans in case an electrical/technological piece of equipment doesn't work.
Marking	If you set classwork or homework, you must be prepared to collect it in and mark it promptly with feedback. Try marking work sheets in the class using nominated questioning, swapping papers or issuing answer sheets to prevent the need to take it away from the room.
Disruptive learners or colleagues	You will never change the behaviour of another person, but you can change the way *you* deal with them. Try using strategies like repeat, recap, writing things down, asking for clarification or further explanation. This helps you to take control of the situation.
Organisation	Keep a diary. Note when you promise to do something. Record when marking needs to be returned or lessons must be prepared. List when deadlines are.

Creating readiness to learn

Potential issues	Possible solutions
Learners do not know how to behave in the classroom. Issues around.	The teacher has to teach these skills (in addition to the content of their subject). Much will be done by role modelling, some by spoon-feeding and some by 1:1 tutorials to set targets.
<ul><li>attendance, punctuality</li><li>meeting targets</li><li>paper and pens</li><li>respecting others</li><li>being responsible for themselves and others</li><li>planning their own learning</li><li>handing in work on time</li><li>listening</li><li>factual comprehension/ retention</li></ul>	Rules and boundaries are important here to set the standard. You may need to bring a supply of paper and pens to stop the disruption of 'I can't do it because . . .'. Guide learners into making notes by devising handouts with white space. Encourage learners to reflect on what they have achieved at the end of the session and target their own learning in workshops.

Strategies to motivate learners

Don't smile till Easter

This was once believed to be the absolute motivator; fair, firm and focused sessions without deviation. However, this is not the 1960s and the current thinking in the post-compulsory sector is empathy, understanding and negotiation. Irrespective of your opinions with regard to these two strategies, the teacher remains the initiator of learning and to do this you need a willing and receptive audience, i.e. learners who are motivated. You the teacher, also need to be motivated; motivated to make a difference in someone's life. **Motivation** is concerned with the learner's desire (or need) to participate in the learning process.

One of the simplest theories associated with motivation that can be applied to learning is the work of Abraham Maslow. In 1954 he investigated the motivation of workers and this can be applied to learners. In order for a worker (or learner in our profession) to achieve their goals and aspirations, they need to go through a development of basic needs, e.g. comfort, safety, belonging and self-esteem. This is Maslow's Hierarchy of Needs. The chart is usually presented as a pyramid, with the pinnacle or goal being self-actualisation, but I would like to look at it in reverse, that is, starting at the beginning . . .

Let us consider the effects of this theory on the learner. In order to be receptive to learning, Maslow's theory suggests that a learner needs to address:

Figure 4A	Maslow's Hierarchy of Needs interpreted to reflect learner needs. The Back to Basics model.

Physical comfort	The basics of hunger, thirst and sleep are met. The environment is adequately lighted and heated making the surroundings comfortable
Safety and shelter	Working in an environment that has clear boundaries and rules to ensure fairness, safety and developing a confidential, trusting rapport and well-being
Love and belonging	Working in a friendly, caring environment, interacting and communicating, having a good rapport with others
Self-esteem	Feelings of pride, respect, achievement, independence, dignity, encouraged through feedback and praise
Self-actualisation	Feelings of fulfilment, encouragement, optimism, and able to transfer skills and knowledge

In the classroom this is applied usually without any conscious decisions, especially at the lower level. As teachers we talk to learners, create rules, encourage respect and value others' opinions. Our learners respond (i.e. become motivated) by doing what should be considered natural in polite society. It could therefore be argued that failure to comply with acceptable standards of behaviour could (and usually does) affect motivation and subsequent learning. Motivation is simply learners wanting to learn.

To improve motivation, the teacher should:

- Ensure that the learning environment is comfortable (temperature, light, furniture), safe and business-like.
- Ensure that breaks are regular to allow food and refreshments to be consumed. It may be worth noting here that parental support may be needed to encourage younger learners to get enough sleep and eat breakfast before commencing their learning day. Note also that some foods and drinks have been proven to have a detrimental effect on learning and behaviour.
- Create a good **rapport** with learners. Learning is a shared responsibility in so far as the learner will allow it to be so.
- Devise classroom rules for attendance, behaviour, conduct and assessment, etc.
- Know your learners. Devise teaching strategies which are of interest to them and are learner-centred.
- Explain the purpose of the lesson, creating an organised and structured learning environment.
- Plan for variety.
- Create short-term targets which are achievable. Consider incentives to reward achievement.
- Make no assumptions.
- Ensure learners are ready to learn.
- Be prepared to help learners with 'how to learn' skills.
- Support those who are struggling; offer challenges to those who are more able. Keep everyone busy.
- Praise success. Give interim feedback in a constructive manner.

- Encourage learners to identify their own goals and have ownership of their own development.
- Recognise that motivation may cause anxiety and that will also need to be dealt with.

By creating a motivational culture, the art of teaching is made easier. However, you must also expect occasional lapses. These barriers have been explained in detail in Chapter 2, pp. 50–53, but in summary will occur when learners are influenced by:

- Peer pressure
- Hormonal imbalance
- Changes in personal or domestic surroundings
- Work/life imbalance.

Motivation can be described as **intrinsic** or **extrinsic**. When a learner is inspired by learning for its own sake, or just wants to do something they are intrinsically (internally) motivated. The opposite are said to be extrinsically (externally) motivated: those learners who are learning because they need to or in order to do something. This reinforces the fact that by knowing your learners you will have an idea of why they are there, and that will result in different motivational strategies. Someone who is intrinsically motivated already has the desire to achieve, whereas the extrinsically motivated learner needs more praise in order to create the desire to continue.

Intrinsic	Extrinsic
<ul><li>Recreational learners</li><li>Career learners</li><li>Self-directed progression</li></ul>	<ul><li>Needs a qualification</li><li>Needs a job</li><li>Needs more money</li></ul>

There will be further opportunities to look at the theories relating to motivation as you progress in your learning.

Effective feedback

A key to successful development of potential, increasing motivation and assessment is concerned with giving feedback. Feedback is part of the learning process, because it tells the learner how they are doing. The quality of the feedback is as important as the quality of the teaching. Feedback should be frequent and meaningful. There are two types.

The praise and criticism model is that which is based on personal judgements and is therefore subjective. The constructive feedback model is objective, because it is based on specifics and related to the assessment against standards or **criteria**. Constructive feedback can be positive, when good practice is praised. The teacher will appreciate and value what has been done and comment on how well it has been achieved. Constructive feedback can be negative when improvement needs are discussed. Giving negative feedback does not mean giving the feedback in a negative (i.e. unsupportive) way. The teacher should not use sarcasm or anger. Be helpful – start with a positive statement and then comment on the improvements that are needed.

The typical feedback conversation:

Feedback should always be planned and thought about carefully.

- State what the standard is or what the assessment was about. Describe what has been observed or reviewed, without sidetracking.
- Make a comment about what has been achieved.
- Offer alternatives like: have you considered . . ., you could try . . . Avoid 'BUT'. This muddles what you are trying to say and confuses the message.

  'It was OK, but . . .' *(Is it OK or not?)*
- Summarise the key achievements. Make and state your judgement – you meet/don't meet the standards, you've passed or you need more practice.

Feedback should be offered on a one-to-one basis and as privately as possible. The feedback should be immediate or at the very least as soon as possible.

If circumstances mean that feedback cannot be immediate, then tell the learner when it will be possible. For example after the shift, when it quietens down a bit, when you get your next break, etc.

A watch point:

Don't get over-enthusiastic with the praise; it is far more effective when offered as a result of something achieved, rather than responding to everything as 'brill!'

Participation and engagement in the learning environment

Participation, and the extent to which all learners participate in the class, is the question that any observer in your classroom will comment upon. The observer, parent or employer needs to know that everyone in the class has an opportunity to contribute.

Some of the strategies for this are:

Nominated questioning

This is teacher-led questioning and aims to ensure that everyone has the opportunity to answer questions. It uses a technique of posing a question, pausing, whilst learners think of the answer and finally nominating a learner to offer the answer.

Differentiated tasks

To ensure each learner can succeed and achieve to the best of their ability

Jigsaw, snowball (pyramid) group work

Different types of activities to encourage everyone to contribute to a discussion point and be listened to. Jigsaw activities are those where different groups have different questions, the teacher then consolidates the discussion and findings to ensure everyone is aware of concepts. Snowball (also known as pyramid) is a group activity which starts in individual thought; shared with a partner; shared with another pair, until a group consensus is formed.

Buzz groups

These activities are used to consolidate individual thoughts which are transcribed, usually by the teacher, onto a board. Use a 'play or pass' strategy with learners each contributing one thought from their list until their lists (thoughts) are exhausted. You could try variations such as a 'graffiti wall', where learners write their ideas on sections of plain wallpaper which is fastened to the wall – they may use words or pictures to express their thoughts. Or try drawing a brick on an A4 sheet and photocopying it, then issue it to learners so that they can write their thoughts onto the bricks. They can then be fastened to the wipe-board as a wall of ideas and discussed by the group.

Gapped handouts and worksheets

Instead of just stuffing a handout into a file, a learner has to interact with it. This helps personal note-taking skills which helps with retention of knowledge. Different types or levels of handout can be designed to differentiate between learner needs.

Quizzes and games

A fun way of learning. Scrabble is good for spelling and competitiveness can be introduced by organising team Scrabble with extra points for a specialist word. Word-searches, crosswords and Sudoku are good as openers, concluders or while waiting for others to catch-up, and help development of functional skills. A paper dice can be made to initiate questions as recap or lesson summaries, far more interesting than a test.

 ACTIVITY 1

....

Ask a colleague or your mentor to analyse your interactions with learners.

A simple mark (/) chart next to a learner's seating position will record the number of times a learner contributes to the class, either by comment, answering a question or asking a question.

For example:

Figure 4B Interacting with your learners

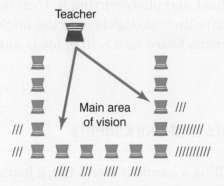

Look at the contact within the main area of vision

Some of the watch points will be:

Those seated in direct eye contact will participate more than those on the periphery of your vision – so make conscious decisions to include those seated on the edges or hiding in the back row by using nominated questioning or by direct **intervention** when organising groups.

Less confident or lazy learners will soon realise that keeping their heads down will not create eye contact and that there is always someone eager to answer questions. Reduce the number of 'open to group' questions and develop nominated questions (i.e., pose the question, pause for a few seconds, then nominate your chosen learner to respond).

Effective communication

REVISION

Teaching is based on an ability to communicate, but you have to know that it is a two way process. There are times when things interfere with that process – revise Chapter 2, Barriers to learning – but generally, learning is a result of effective communication.

Are you sure you are communicating with your learners?

Communication is the art of passing a message. If it is to be effective, the person receiving that message must understand it, and be able to respond to it, usually by sending another message. Think back to times when you have played Chinese whispers. Although that was usually a bit of fun, imagine if all communication became muddled during its transmission. Communication is generally in one of three ways, and within each there are different types:

Written	Verbal	Non-verbal
Long-hand Shorthand Text Images	Spoken: Direct – face-to-face Indirect – telephone	Sometimes called body language Dress Facial expression Proximity Touch

In any communication exchange the teacher should ensure that what has been offered has been understood. The teacher can do this by pausing to summarise things spoken and heard and by asking questions to get feedback from learners to ascertain that they have not only heard, but have understood and comprehended the topic.

Whilst we are on the topic of communication, here are some things to think about:

How much of a piece of writing do we actually read . . .?
It deosn't mttaer in waht oredr the ltteers in a wrod are, the olny iprmoatnt tihng is talil the friot and lsat ltteer is in the rghit pclac.

Text speak.
thx 4 ur help 2day ur gr8
(Thank you for your help today, you are great!)
ijwtk y ur l8 ru ok pcme
(I just want to know why you are late; are you okay? Please call me.)
Text messaging is a new language. It is perfectly acceptable for its intended purpose, or even within personal note-taking, but it is not appropriate in formal work, and it certainly does not aid the development of functional skills. Create rules for its use.

British Sign Language (BSL) is a specialist language for the deaf using hands and fingers to spell and create words. There are significantly fewer words in BSL than in English; sentences are expressed as a whole rather than in a series of words, so ensure that signers in your class receive lesson plans and outline scripts in advance of the session.

Why do people confide in their hairdresser, beautician, doctor, driving instructor?
Answer: because the barrier of proximity/touch is reduced or removed. Caution: these are managed acceptable instances of touch; society in general has an expectation of space around individuals. If you have to 'invade someone's space' always seek permission. Do you mind if . . .?

Spellings opener Tell the learners what the words of the session will be. Ask them to spell them onto the board. Ask each learner for one letter (they could nominate who will go next) and operate a play or pass strategy to reduce fear factor.

'Do you understand me' game? Sit learners back to back. Give one a picture or line drawing, and ask them to describe it to their partner, without saying what it is. The partner should make a replica drawing from the instructions given. This enhances skills of description and use of adjectives as well as creating a team spirit and is good fun!

Barriers to effective communication

Jargon, specialist terminology Demystify expressions by writing specialist or **jargon** words on the board (non-permanent) or why not start a 'new words' chart/poster (semi-permanent and visible) or use vocabulary or personal dictionaries (permanent but not always visible).

Level of language Maturity develops vocabulary. Younger learners haven't learnt the same number of words as more mature learners, nor do they use and understand 'big words'. Be mindful of this when creating handouts or using reference material.

Language and accent Each country or region of a country has its own pattern of words or accent. Some are more easily understood than others. Speak clearly and slowly until learners become familiar with your voice. Illness may also affect the tone and pitch of your voice.

Noise Background noise can be distracting. Computers, extraction units and machinery all give off a constant noise, which to some gradually disappears, but not all have this ability to cut out noise. Those with hearing impairments also have different tolerances to background noise.

Listening and writing Some learners can't do both at the same time. People with hearing impairment cannot lip-read and make notes. Add note-taking time to classroom or workshop activities. Some lessons include writing time and use music as a background . . . when the music stops, teaching starts.

Talking and listening Speech should be at a speed which can be understood, and you may also need to allow thinking time. Time for learners to understand and comprehend – in their own words – between speaking time.

Beware of speaking when your back is turned, for example when writing on the board.

Eye contact is important to effective communication. When to speak (and stop speaking) is very often determined by eyes, pauses and tone of voice.

Summarise Go over what you have said regularly, use your voice to stress key points and pauses to allow thinking time. Tone of voice also adds interest to speech.

Improving your own performance

Recognition that your performance can be improved is accepting that whatever does (or does not) happen in the classroom is in the hands of the teacher. The teacher can, by changing their own actions, influence the behaviours of others. In order to be able to improve your practice, you have got to be able to analyse and evaluate it. This is asking you to really break down what has occurred and check critically if things went well or not.

A checklist is the simplest method of starting the process of reflection or improvement. It may be written after each lesson or a series of sessions or maybe in the form of a log or diary. Another method is to seek comments from a peer. Any feedback about a session is valuable. Sometimes an observer will see things you don't or give you an idea for an alternative method of doing something. Feedback and opinions can also come from learners. You may, for example, ask learners periodically, 'What is the best bit of my lesson?' or 'What was the bit you least enjoyed?'

Hopefully the answer to the first question is not 'the end' and the answer to the second question 'the start'. If it is, then you will need to become reflective and quickly seek advice from your mentor! The important thing is that the teacher gets into the habit of reflection.

EXAMPLE 1

An extract from a simple checklist for a post lesson **evaluation** might be:

Preparation and planning	Did I set outcomes for the session? Did I share those outcomes with learners?

The answers to these types of questions are usually YES or NO responses (i.e. closed questions). Therefore, there is no **analysis**. To analyse this preparation and planning section, you must ask the questions above, but then ask yourself a 'so what?' question or create an open question.

For example:
Did you set outcomes for the session? Answer *YES*
So what? *Because I shared the outcomes with my learners they were clear about the focus of the lesson and what they needed to do.*
OR
What was the effect of preparing measurable outcomes for the class?
It meant that my learners knew what the lesson was about.

Reflection can then occur. Reflection is about trying to improve things or understand cause and effect, i.e. to improve your practice. Taking our previous example, a reflective teacher might say *'and next time I will write them on the board and re-visit them at the end of the class to prove how much they've learnt in the session.'*

EXAMPLE 2

Question	Did you test that learners had learnt something in your lesson?
Analysis	The question sheet at the end of the lesson enabled me to check that learning had occurred
Evaluation	The question sheet was effective in checking learning because the questions were focused and aimed at the different abilities in the group, so that I could check the depth of learning
Reflection	The question sheet was effective and showed that all learners had grasped point A. The second point, however, was not understood by all and I need to recap this in detail next time

The main parts of the lesson that you should reflect on are:

- Planning and preparation
- Teaching methods, participation and differentiation
- Assessment methods and questioning
- Communication
- Resources.

You may also wish to reflect on:

- Tutorials
- Meetings
- Assignments (yours and theirs)
- Reading and research.

These occurrences are collectively known as 'critical incidents' and you will use your professional development journal to discuss and reflect upon them.

A typical **journal** page might look like this:

REFLECTIVE LOG

Incident

Describe the incident or event on which you want to reflect

Questions

What questions or issues does this raise?

Actions

What thoughts do you have to overcome/build on this experience? Who will help you?

Reflection

Reconsider the experience and any actions taken. What is the impact? Is the situation worse, same or better?

Learning to be a reflective practitioner is one of the key development areas for a teacher. It is hard to see things objectively, and it is equally hard to criticise your own practice without making excuses for occurrences. Seek the advice of your tutors, mentors and colleagues and learn to accept feedback as a genuine desire for self-improvement rather than a threat.

Glossary of terms

Analysis a detailed examination

Communication a means of sending and receiving information to share or exchange ideas

Criteria the standard of competence

Evaluation to form an idea about something by measuring its effectiveness

Extrinsic motivation motivation derived from outside the person

Interact to have an effect on

Intervention an interruption

Intrinsic motivation motivation from within the person: natural desire

Jargon language, words or expressions of a specialist occupation

Journal a diary

Motivation enthusiasm or interest

Opener an activity at the beginning of a session

Participation to take part in

Rapport a common understanding

Reflection a considered opinion expressed in speech or writing; thoughts or considerations, developing ideas and thoughts

VAK visual, auditory and kinaesthetic learners – different ways learners like to learn

SUMMARY

In this chapter we set out to achieve the following outcomes:

- Identify factors which influence effective classroom management skills and select strategies to practice within the classroom
- Describe the key methods to improve motivation in learners and relate this to simple theory
- Recognise the value of effective feedback and use a model of giving feedback in a constructive way
- Describe ways to effectively engage learners to participate in learning sessions
- List the key factors which initiate successful communication and describe the main communication methods
- Use self evaluative strategies to reflect on your practice and initiate personal and professional development

Your Personal Development

You have explored how the teacher needs to manage their environment and considered some strategies which may improve your own classroom management. You can explain how poor behaviour impacts on the class and describe some potential solutions. You can describe ways in which you will prepare your learners to be ready for learning.

You can describe how one theorist suggests that motivation can be improved and relate these suggestions to your own learning environment. You can state a number of ways in which motivation can be improved.

You can suggest ways of modifying your teaching and learning strategies to ensure that all learners have the opportunity to participate in your lessons. You may have sought advice from your mentor to analysis how you interact with your group of learners.

You can describe three different ways of communicating and suggest some ideas to improve or develop communication between you and your learners.

You are developing a reflective outlook on your performance and can describe ways that a reflective diary can support your own personal development. You understand the difference between evaluation and reflection and its impact on your performance.

You should now be able to answer questions relating to:

- How you would establish rules to support appropriate behaviour in your classroom
- The importance of developing respect and values
- Collect feedback from peers, learners and tutors to inform your personal development goals
- Use a self-reflection journal/log to evaluate the effectiveness of your own teaching
- Create an action plan related to your development as a trainee teacher and your teaching practice to improve your performance
- Offer constructive criticism to your peers on their performance.

CHAPTER 5 (PTLLS)

Assessment and record keeping

EDUCATION PHOTOS / ALAMY

LEARNING OBJECTIVES

The measurable outcomes that you will achieve by reading this chapter and completing the activities are:

- To identify and describe the main methods of assessment
- To describe the methods used to quality assure assessment techniques and the roles of people involved
- To state purpose of methods for recording progress of learners
- To recognise some simple designs for basic record keeping documents

Types of assessment methods

Methods of assessment

Assessment is the term given to checking that learning has occurred. It may happen at any stage during the learner's progress through their qualification. It will help you to know when a concept is understood and therefore means you can move on to the next topic, or if you need to re-teach a topic. Carrying out an **initial assessment** helps you to plan appropriate sessions for your learners. You may use assessment to identify specific needs of learners and assessment should be an integral component of your teaching and lesson plans.

There are several different ways of assessing. The table below describes the main ones that you will come across. (See also Chapter 13.)

Method	Description
Observation	Used in practical situations when a learner demonstrates their competence (natural performance) whilst being observed by their assessor. This is considered one of the best forms of assessment because there can be no doubts in the mind of the assessor that the learner knows how to do something. The observation should be recorded either on film or on paper. A phone with a camera is quite useful, but ensure that you have relevant permissions before photographing or filming a learner, especially if they or those around them are minors. There may be occasions when the verifier needs observational evidence to verify standards.

Method	Description
Simulation	This is similar to observation, but uses a simulated activity rather than natural performance. The rules associated with observation (above) apply. Whilst National Vocational Qualifications (NVQs) do not generally support this type of evidence, there may be occasions when it is deemed appropriate, for example when using high-cost materials or in dangerous situations. You would not expect an airline pilot to be assessed on his ability to crash land in a natural performance scenario – this is best done under simulated conditions, which should mirror reality. Fire drills and first aid are other commonly simulated assessments.
Project and assignment	These are usually a series of activities which collect together to make a project or assignment. For example, task one may be a written description of something, task two may be a presentation of some findings and task three may be a booklet or poster. Generally, a project is designed by the learner and an assignment is designed by the teacher; both include a 'brief' which is related to the learning outcomes. There may be different assessment methods within an assignment or project depending on the tasks. The assessor will be assessing learning outcomes which relate to the proposed content of the assignment or project and are used during marking. Some qualifications also include levels of understanding, which are reflected in grading criteria.
Written questions	*Essays* A discussion type of question. The assessor will need detailed assessment marking plans to ensure fairness, especially if the essay is around opinion and therefore has no right or wrong answer. The teacher should also

▶

Method	Description
	consider what proportion of marks will be attributed to spelling and grammar, content, structure and argument etc. To be considered fair, these should be shared with your learners. Marking is quite complex.
	Short answer questions
	A series of questions where the answer is usually about a few sentences long. In some (state four reasons for . . .) types of question, only a few words are required. The marking plan should include all possible answers that could be offered by learners. These are quite easy to mark and are suitable for checking learning within a lesson or at the end of a module.
	Multiple choice questions
	A question with (usually) four answers to choose from. The learner has to identify which of the offered answers is correct. As a learner selects an answer there is little opportunity to expand or probe understanding. They are very simple to mark; the awarding body may use computers to scan answer sheets and calculate the number of correct answers. They are quite difficult to write in the first instance.
Verbal/oral questions	These are questions which try to establish depth of knowledge and are a useful assessment tool to complement observation in order to check understanding. For example, 'what would happen if . . .?' questions. Verbal questioning is usually informal and sometimes unprepared in that the assessor sees something during an observation and wishes clarification or further information on a particular issue. Verbal questioning should be recorded on either tape or paper and the learner should sign to confirm accuracy of answers recorded. Good questioning should be of an 'open' type, which means that the learner has to think of the answer, as opposed to closed, where they are offered yes/no or true/false solutions – so could guess the answer.

Method	Description
	Using a nominated style ensures that questions can be offered to learners and pitched at a particular learner's known ability. Nominated style means that the teacher poses the question to the group, pauses so that they can all create their own answer, then nominates (or identifies) the learner to give the answer. It can be made fun by offering play or pass options to minimise embarrassment if learners do not know the answer. You may also try the 'ask a friend' strategy, in which a learner can elicit the help of someone else in the group.
Professional discussion	This is a semi-structured interview where the assessor and the learner discuss an issue and the assessor prompts the learner into answering questions related to subject outcomes. It is very often used to link workplace practice to standards of competence, for example in NVQs. It is an effective tool because an experienced assessor will lead the conversation to ensure all aspects are covered: however, authenticity could be questioned – did the assessor lead in a way that would elicit only correct answers? Is it really the learners own words/actions?
Self-assessment	As an informal strategy it is very common. Reading through a piece of work to ensure everything is covered before handing it in is self-assessment. As a formal assessment strategy it can be used in the format of personal statements or profiling. Both of these assessments require the learner to write down what they did or would do in a given situation; this is then linked to a set of standards or criteria. A student teacher will use this form of assessment to develop their reflective practice. There may be a witness testimony to authenticate the validity of the statements.

Assessment types

Assessment can occur at any time during a programme or course.
Pre-course, initial, diagnostic, formative and summative are the
words associated with assessment and to a certain extent identify the
stage they are used. There is a lot of cross-over and similarity in the
expressions and some differences in how teachers interpret the words.

Pre-course interview This is an interview process to assess
potential or a learner's suitability for a course or programme. Younger
learners may need to refer to schools grades or predicted grades to
meet entry requirements. Adult learners may cite employment
history and experience in the form of a curriculum vitae (CV). The
interview should be a two-way process to ensure that learners fully
understand expectations of the programme before committing
themselves. The pre-course interview is therefore a means of ensuring
that the right people are on the right courses. Accrediting previous
experience, learning or achievement is called **APEL/APL**.

Beginning of course or programme Whether a learner is enrolled
onto a full-time or part-time programme, there should be an induction.
The *induction* provides the opportunity to introduce the learners to
the programme, to each other, to the teacher/s and to the programme
or module. The *initial assessment* will create a **profile** of the learners:

- Why are they there?
- What is their previous knowledge or experience?
- What are their strengths and weaknesses?
- How confident are they?
- Will their personal circumstances influence their progress?
- What is their character?
- What do they enjoy or dislike?
- What are their expectations and aspirations?
- Are they motivated?

It would be very easy to make assumptions at this point and break
the first rule of teaching, the most common assumption being 'they're

here and want to learn'. That may be so, but there will be degrees of desire and these *will* influence the learner! There are some useful yet informal strategies which can be used to find out about your learners. One of these is to use an ice-breaker activity (see Chapter 1). Another even less formal way is to set a simple activity or questionnaire, maybe associated with previous knowledge, skills or experience and whilst the learners are completing it you can go around the room talking to each person on a one-to-one basis to find out something about them and why they are there. The more formal strategies are often collectively known as **diagnostic assessment**. These identify and assess learners' capabilities in order to inform the structure of the programme or scheme of work; they will also identify learning needs and therefore the support needed to ensure progress. Such diagnostic assessments include:

Learner needs analysis	To ensure that teaching methods are suited to individuals
Preferred learning styles	To find out how your learners like to learn
Initial screening	To check basic skill levels to identify level of support needed
Prior learning	To identify previous experience, learning
Skills test	To check current level of competence

As many organisations are measured and funded on their success, it raises the importance of ensuring that the right learner ⟶ is on the right course ⟶ and receiving the right support. This contributes to learners staying until the end of the course and therefore maximises their potential to achieve their learning goal. Effective initial assessment will record plans and development needs in an action plan or individual learning plan.

During the course or programme Assessment during the course is usually *formative*. This means that it is an interim judgement or decision about progress, which is reported to the learner as *feedback*. This enables them to consider what they are good at and build on their strengths, whilst informing them of improvements that need to be made to meet the requirements of the assessment or qualification. There is always 'life after formative assessment'. Careful feedback can motivate, enlighten and provide a vehicle for development. Bad feedback can destroy confidence. Feedback (sometimes called 'constructive' feedback, see Chapter 4) should follow a pattern of identification of what is good or what has been achieved successfully, followed by the 'in order to improve you should' statement and finished with a praise or motivational statement to leave the learner feeling confident and willing to carry out the developments you have identified. The feedback should include the judgement made, for example: pass or refer; satisfactory or needs further development; competent or needs further training or experience, but *never* fail. Formative assessment can relate to a piece of assessed work or as a meeting to discuss progress (a tutorial). Both require skilled practice in feedback and setting of targets.

At the end of the course/module/unit Assessment at this point is usually referred to as *summative*. It is a final decision or judgement about competence or ability. Dependent on the programme, learners may be offered another chance to improve their result, but in the case of examinations it is generally a 'one-opportunity'. It is worth reminding teachers that summative judgements can have a significant impact on learners, hence their learners' apprehension before test periods. The teacher should therefore prepare learners not only by revising content but in how the examination is conducted. Past papers or simulations can provide confidence pre-exam. Some courses have assessment strategies which enable learners to be graded on their work. Clear marking criteria are required, which should be shared with learners – 'in order to receive a merit you need to . . .'.

After the course Some organisations will gather information to provide a statistical picture of their institution. For example the percentage of learners progressing to higher level courses or employment. This may be done at exit interviews or by customer satisfaction questionnaires. It is used to measure the effectiveness of their programmes and their contribution to economic targets.

Effective assessment

The roles of people involved in assessment are related to their part of the process. Some are primary roles, some are roles to proffer reliability and some are for quality assurance and integrity.

Figure 5A Quality assurance – roles and duties

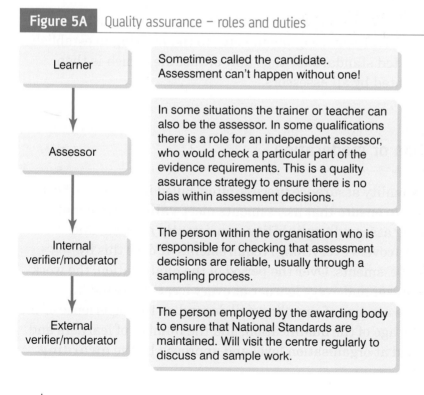

Learner	Sometimes called the candidate. Assessment can't happen without one!
Assessor	In some situations the trainer or teacher can also be the assessor. In some qualifications there is a role for an independent assessor, who would check a particular part of the evidence requirements. This is a quality assurance strategy to ensure there is no bias within assessment decisions.
Internal verifier/moderator	The person within the organisation who is responsible for checking that assessment decisions are reliable, usually through a sampling process.
External verifier/moderator	The person employed by the awarding body to ensure that National Standards are maintained. Will visit the centre regularly to discuss and sample work.

Standardisation

This is a process which is aimed at ensuring all assessment decisions are equal. It ensures that assessors are fully conversant with assessment requirements and consistently make the correct decisions. Periodically, the quality assurance team will convene meetings where everyone involved in the programme meets to discuss the assessment process, identify good practice and support new or weak assessors. Some examples of typical activities would be:

- Every assessor brings one refer, pass, merit and distinction piece of work. They justify to the group why they have marked to that level.
- Assessors submit an unmarked piece of work prior to the event, which is marked by the internal verifier or moderator. Then at the meeting everyone marks the same piece of work, the outcome being that everyone should award the same mark or grade.
- Every assessor involved in a particular unit or module brings ideas or samples of assignments etc., to the meeting to establish the expected standard for that unit or module, which is then implemented by all assessors.

Verification or moderation

This is the quality assurance process, often called internal verification (IV). It aims to ensure that assessments meet **validity** (relevant to what is being assessed), **reliability** (consistently marked) and **sufficiency** (covers everything) requirements. It does this by sampling assessments. Over the period of the qualification, the work of every assessor and every learner at every location should be sampled. The amount of sampling will depend on the experience of the assessor, the age of the qualification, and the number of learners and is determined at organisation level and approved by the **awarding body**.

To demonstrate best practice, for example:

An experienced assessor using an established qualification with a reasonable caseload would have about 10 per cent of their work verified.

An experienced assessor using a new qualification may increase the sample to 25–50 per cent.

A new assessor with an existing qualification might be 70 per cent plus rising to 100 per cent for a new assessor with a new qualification.

Some of the strategies used to quality assure decisions made by assessors include:

- Observing the assessor whilst carrying out a workplace observation
- Observing the assessor giving feedback to a learner about an assessment
- Interviewing assessors
- Interviewing learners
- Reviewing product evidence
- Looking at records of assessment
- Conducting an audit trail of dates.

Every organisation will have their own verification or moderation strategy, which will depend on resources. Internal verification or moderation (IV) should be part of the process of assessment rather than a product of assessment. This means verifying judgements as they occur. The worse case scenario in terms of IV is that at the end of a learner's qualification some inaccuracies are discovered, which causes a lack of confidence in all of the judgements. If this were to happen, the organisation and the assessors would lose their reputation and if this is discovered at external verification the centre is at risk of having sanctions imposed on it. Failure to comply may eventually result in a centre being closed.

One of the quality assurance roles of the awarding body is to comment on the effectiveness of the internal verification/moderation, and it measures its confidence in the organisation accordingly. Organisations will strive for 'direct claims' which means that awarding bodies are confident that they are able to quality assure with integrity, and they are authorised to apply for registrations and certificates without constantly seeking approval from external moderators and verifiers.

Further reading in terms of internal verification can be found in the Joint Awarding Body Guidance which is on most awarding body websites. For example, http://www.cityandguilds.com/documents/ind_generic_docs_policydocs/JAB_GUIDANCE_ON_IV_OF_NVQS.PDF.

Whilst this is aimed at NVQs, the good standards can be applied to many other qualifications. Those involved in assessment and verification of NVQs are required to gain approved qualifications to carry out those roles.

Tracking progress

Advisory note

● Methods of recording assessments will differ according to the qualification type.
● Always use the forms agreed within the organisation.
● Suggestions for improvements should be made through the internal verifier.
● All forms should, at the very least, include the qualification title, names of the assessor and the learner and the date.

Forms below are examples of the format in order to recognise the style. They should not be considered as 'approved' documents.

The forms described, which are examples and not an exhaustive list, are:

- Observations records
- Records of questioning
- Assignment front sheets
- **Tracking** sheets.

Observation records

These forms are most commonly associated with recording of observed evidence when completing NVQs. The purpose of keeping documents relating to observation is to ensure that *what is seen is accurately matched to the assessment criteria*. Whether this is completed by the assessor or the learner will depend on how confident the learner is and how familiar with the criteria they are. In my experience it is usually the assessor's job! The observation record would be a piece of evidence to demonstrate what was seen when and should be confirmed or 'witnessed' by the parties involved – usually in the form of signatures. The most common use of observation documents is to record workplace activities. They are usually descriptive and are written as a chronological record. For example:

2 March 2007 – Reception area of Smith's Engineering, Sometown. At 09.15, Sheila greeted the customer in a polite manner, asking the purpose of their visit and who they wished to see. She then used the telephone to inform the Director's secretary that the visitor had arrived. Sheila gave the visitor's name and the company they represented. Whilst waiting for the visitor to be collected, she issued a visitor's badge and asked the visitor to sign in. Two incoming calls were taken using the standard greeting and directed to the extension required. At 09.20, as the secretary still hadn't arrived to collect the visitor she invited them to take a seat in the waiting area. A package arrived and was signed for; rang to inform addressee of its arrival. She smiled when the visitor left reception with the secretary at 09.25.

When writing up observations, it is useful to have a copy of the assessment criteria to hand and to be mindful of everything that is occurring; even if it is not directly related to the activity, it may have significance to another task or component of the qualification.

An observation record might look like this.

Name of candidate:	Date:
Qualification:	Level:
Location of assessment:	

A description of the event or activity	Links to performance criteria

Assessor's signature:	Date:
Candidate's signature:	Date:

Records of questioning

These documents are more associated with verbal questioning rather than written questioning. Written questions automatically create a record, but verbal questions could just happen. The purpose of the document is to provide evidence of what question was asked and the answer given (whether right or wrong). This should then be linked to relevant criteria. Valid questions are those which are related to theory and underpin a practical activity.

For example, following the observation above, typical questions might be:

- What would you do if the telephone extension had been busy?
- What would you do if the addressee on the parcel had not been a member of staff?
- Why is it important to use a standard greeting when answering a telephone?
- If a visitor is very early for their appointment, what do you do?

At the end of the record of questioning, it is important that both the assessor and the learner sign to say that the document is 'a true record of questions and their responses'.

A record of questioning might look like this.

Name of candidate:		Date:
Qualification:		Level:
Unit/assessment:		
Question		Response given by candidate/learner
Assessor's signature:		Date:
Candidate's signature:		Date:

Assignment front sheets

The purpose of an assignment front sheet is to provide a standardised method of briefing learners on components of the assignment. For example, it will list the tasks to be completed and target dates; it will identify any key/basic or functional skills that are derived from the assessment; it will state the criteria for gaining pass, merit or distinction grades; and usually provide a space for assessors to give feedback on the work. It is customary that the person who designs the tasks should submit the brief to the internal verifier for approval before launching it with their group. This ensures consistency within the organisation and a double check before issuing the assignment to learners.

An assignment front sheet might look like this.

Qualification title:	
Unit title and number:	
Launch date:	Submission date:
Task	Criteria reference including links to functional skills
Feedback:	
Grade achieved:	
Assessor signature:	Date:

Tracking sheets

These are the forms that record progress during a qualification. They may be used so that the teacher can plot achievement of tasks within an assignment, units within an NVQ or completion of homework/class-work activities. It is usual to record the date the unit/task/activity is completed. Best practice models include the date commenced and who assessed the work, with a space to date and initial if the work is internally verified. A similar document can be used to plan internal verification – i.e., identify which part of the qualification and which learners' work are to be sampled.

A tracking sheet might look like this.

Qualification title:									
	Unit, task or activity								
Name	1	2	3	4	5	6	7	8	Etc.
Learner A									
Learner B									
Etc.									

To be effective and meaningful, you should devise a simple marking code to visualise the progress. For example:

- / means a learner has started on the unit/module
- X means they have completed the unit/module.
- Always add a date when completed, together with assessor's initials.
- If verified the verifier could date and initial maybe in a different colour pen.

Glossary of terms

APEL/APL accreditation of previous experience and/or learning

Assessment to make a judgement about something, a measurement of achievement

Authenticity to establish who wrote/owns the subject

Awarding body an organisation that devises qualifications and awards

Diagnostic assessment assessment used to identify capability or skill level

Initial assessment an assessment tool to identify and establish potential or aspirations and discover facts

IV Internal verification

NVQ National Vocational Qualification

Profile an outline of the characteristic traits of a particular person

Reliability a strategy to ensure that assessment decisions are consistent

Sufficiency to check that there is enough evidence to cover the criteria

Tracking a method of recording progress

Validity a strategy to ensure that judgements are made against criteria

 # SUMMARY

In this chapter we set out to achieve the following outcomes:

● Identify the ways that teachers assess learning and competence and describe the main methods

● Describe the key methods used to quality assure assessment techniques and the roles of people in the assessment process

- State appropriate methods for recording progress of learners and the importance of tracking
- Recognise some simple designs for basic record keeping documents

Your Personal Development

You have considered the many methods of assessment and understood how they may be used. You will have identified the different times within a learner's programme that assessment can be used, in particular initial assessment, as well as formative and summative judgements and how these can impact on the learner, the programme of study and the organisation. You can explain how feedback is a valuable tool in developing learning.

You can explain the roles of those within the assessment process and their contributions to the quality assurance processes. You can describe the purpose of standardisation and internal verification/moderation and identify some sampling strategies.

Finally, you have looked at some basic examples of documentation that can be used and clearly explain their purpose.

You should be able to answer questions relating to:

- Explaining different types of assessment and when they are used
- The different ways of assessing and when to give feedback
- The importance of initial assessment in developing potential and preparing programmes of study

Part Two

Planning and enabling learning

(PEL)

This is the second unit in your Diploma in Teaching in the Lifelong Learning Sector (DTLLS) qualification

Learning Outcomes	Assessment Criteria
Understand ways to negotiate appropriate individual goals with learners	● Analyse the role of initial assessment in the learning and teaching process ● Describe and evaluate different methods of initial assessment for use with learners ● Evaluate ways of planning, negotiating and recording appropriate learning goals with learners
Understand how to plan for inclusive learning	● Establish and maintain an inclusive learning environment ● Devise and justify a scheme of work which meets learners' needs and curriculum requirements ● Devise and justify session plans which meet the aims and needs of individual learners and/or groups ● Analyse ways in which session plans can be adapted to the individual needs of learners ● Plan the appropriate use of a variety of delivery methods, justifying the choice ● Identify and evaluate opportunities for learners to provide feedback to inform practice
Understand how to use teaching and learning strategies and resources inclusively to meet curriculum requirements	● Select/adapt, use and justify a range of inclusive learning activities to enthuse and motivate learners, ensuring that curriculum requirements are met ● Analyse the strengths and limitations of a range of resources, including new and emerging technologies, showing how these resources can be used to promote equality, support diversity and contribute to effective learning ● Identify literacy, language, numeracy and ICT skills which are integral to own specialist area, reviewing how they support learner achievement ● Select/adapt, use and justify a range of inclusive resources to promote inclusive learning and teaching
Understand how to use a range of communication skills and methods to communicate effectively with learners and relevant parties in own organization	● Use and evaluate different communication methods and skills to meet the needs of learners and the organisation ● Evaluate own communication skills, identifying ways in which these could be improved including an analysis of how barriers to effective communication might be overcome ● Identify and liaise with appropriate and relevant parties to effectively meet the needs of learners
Understand and demonstrate knowledge of the minimum core in own practice	● Apply minimum core specifications in literacy to improve own practice ● Apply minimum core specifications in language to improve own practice ● Apply minimum core specifications in mathematics to improve own practice ● Apply minimum core specifications in ICT user skills to improve own practice
Understand how reflection, evaluation and feedback can be used to develop own good practice	● Use regular reflection and feedback from others, including learners, to evaluate and improve own practice, making recommendations for modification as appropriate

CHAPTER 6
(PEL)

Negotiating individual goals

LEARNING OBJECTIVES

The measurable outcomes that you will achieve by reading this chapter and completing the activities are:

....

- To state the role that initial assessment has and its value to the teacher, the learner and the organisation
- To list the types of initial assessment currently in use and identify the value of initial assessment
- To describe the difference between a goal and a target and develop use of expressions associated with goal setting

The role of initial assessment

Initial assessment is a term given to that part of the learning process that hopes to combine the learner, the teacher and the curriculum. We know (or are learning about) ourselves and what the teacher does, we know what the curriculum sets outs to achieve, but the biggest variable is the learner, and most of us do not meet that variable until day one, week one. We may know their names and maybe their age, address and phone number, but not what they are really like. As we have already discovered (see Chapter 1), learners are individuals brought together to gain a common **goal**, but they expect and demand respect and individuality within their group setting. **Initial assessment**, therefore, is the first stage in a process designed to create an interesting and relevant programme of study for your learners. As well as finding out about personality, character and behaviour, it also measures attainment and potential and identifies skill gaps, aspirations, support needed and the level of ability. Initial assessment sets out to do quite a lot – but different individuals have come to expect different outcomes from it.

For senior managers it is used to inform strategy and funding, for teachers it identifies the person and informs the scheme of work and resources necessary, and for students it identifies how they will fit in and study.

Figure 6A   Purposes of initial assessment

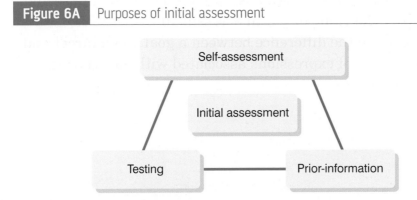

Figure 6A explains how the various components of initial assessment are linked and how collectively they will create the key ingredients required to make your decisions. The process can occur at any stage of the learner's programme. At pre-entry stage it provides the opportunity to make choices, at entry it identifies level of study and needs, and **on-programme** it can inform the type of delivery.

There are many reasons to collect information; there are many uses and equally there are many things which impact on perceived or actual results. In Figure 6B, a **spider diagram** is used to visualise some of the influencing factors.

These ideas are suggestions about what kind of information to collect. Depending on the answers, and they will be as varied as your learners, the results will impact on learners and the learning environment.

Figure 6B Factors that influence initial assessment

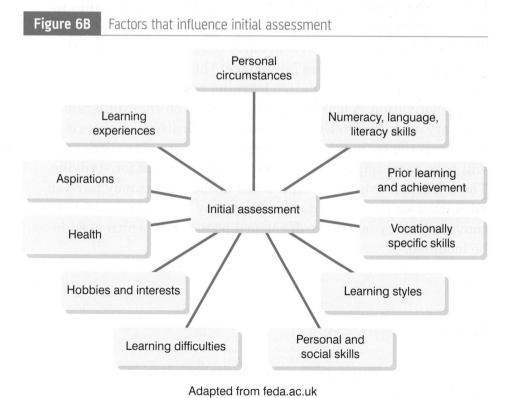

Adapted from feda.ac.uk

Attitudes

Personal circumstances, personal and social skills, hobbies and interests, health, family attitudes to learning may impact on self-esteem, confidence and motivation (see Figure 6B on the previous page). Travelling to and from the learning environment will impact on how settled a learner is at the commencement of a session, or if they can arrive on time. Family commitments and personal health may impact on attendance and punctuality or the ability to meet deadlines. Temporary illness may impact on the impression someone gives at their first meeting. If a learner has a long-standing interest in the subject it will improve motivation.

Ability

Numeracy, language and literature skills, prior learning and achievement, vocationally specific skills – a learner's ability in literacy and numeracy (and ICT) will impact on their ability to cope with the course (see Figure 6B on the previous page). There may be required levels of entry prior to commencing the programme and if learners fail to meet these required levels they may have to choose alternative learning routes. This in turn may affect motivation. A learner's ability to cope on their programme will vary according to their previous qualifications or experience. Work experience, previous employment or learning experiences will have some impact, as will the learner's reason for studying. Those learners who have experience in the subject may have an advantage on the programme as they may have more confidence; conversely, they may have developed poor habits which need to be modified.

Needs

Learning styles, learning difficulties, aspirations, learning experiences – discovering how learners prefer to learn and why they are there is an essential part of establishing how to make learning more effective, as is finding out about any other type of support needs. Trying to establish how learners got on in school, training or previous study will help a teacher to understand and overcome any barriers to learning (again see Figure 6B).

Once a teacher understands what is making their learners tick then progress can begin. It is also important that previously unrecognised traits or weaknesses are identified so that appropriate actions can be taken to support the learner.

Methods of initial assessment

The process of initial assessment (IA) can be formal or informal. The method of assessment and the way it is administered will influence the formality of the process. The teacher should consider the purpose of the IA and what benefits are sought. In The Chief Inspector's Report (2003), the Adult Learning Inspectorate (ALI) found that 'many providers are using a screening test but not following this up . . . the results of the assessment are not being used to inform the ILP', and continued 'different types of learners require different types of initial assessment'. This research proves that although used, initial assessment is not always effective. Much has improved since that report, but it nevertheless begs the question of purpose; if you are going to use IA, then use it well with careful consideration of what you are trying to achieve by doing it. Unless this is clear, it becomes another tedious process in **induction** from which no-one benefits, although it would 'tick a box'. Effective initial assessment is not a one-off activity but the start of an ongoing informative process.

Initial assessment should:

- Aid direction to the right course
- Help to remove barriers
- Help learners to belong
- Reduce anxiety

- Gather information about learners, their aspirations and abilities
- Identify learning needs
- Inform others about progress
- Ensure legal and moral requirements are identified, planned and implemented
- Aid the planning of an inclusive learning programme
- Inform the structure of the programme.

It may involve:

- The student
- Parents
- School teachers
- Careers Advisors
- Employers
- Former lecturers or trainers
- Carers.

It should take place:

- In comfortable surroundings
- In confidence
- In a familiar place or relaxing atmosphere.

It can be gathered using tools (or methods) which are categorised as:

1　Written tools:
   - Paper exercises
   - Application forms
   - Questionnaires
   - References – school, employer, previous course tutor
   - Screening tests – Basic Skills Agency (BSA), Key Skills Builder, Cambridge Training and Development (CTAD)
   - Self-assessment
   - Free writing

- Aptitude tests
- Tutorial records.

2   Electronic tools:

- Diagnostic screeners (literacy, numeracy)
- Learning style questionnaires
- Psychometric tests.

3   Spoken tools:

- Interviews
- Professional discussion
- Informal discussion.

4   Visual tools

- Observation
- Skills tests – mapped to National Standards.

The initial assessment should result in either an individual learning plan (ILP), the basis of a discussion to negotiate goals and targets, or planned differentiated strategies on your scheme of work.

Initial assessment in practice

Look at this scenario and, using a highlighter pen, pick out the many strategies the teacher uses to start the initial assessment of learners.

ACTIVITY 1

- Identify the initial assessment methods.

- List the information gathered before Jamil and Fiona stated their course. How does this help to prepare them for learning and college life?

● List the information gathered during their induction to their course. How does this help their tutors to differentiate their learning?

Jamil and Fiona want to go to their local college when they have finished school. They ring up their local college and ask for a list of courses. Jamil wants to do Business Studies and fills out the application card in the prospectus to apply for a place. Fiona is not so sure: she doesn't know whether to do Tourism or Administration. She knows she wants to do something in an office, because that is the advice she got from her parents and her Careers Officer. She may also do Business Studies so that she can stay friends with Jamil. She decides to go to the open day to have a chat with teachers; her Mum comes along to find out about computer courses.

Jamil has now received a letter inviting him for an interview, which he attends, and is offered a place on the BTEC National, subject to his GCSE results. The Admissions Officer applies to the school for a reference. Fiona settles on Administration Level 2 because, following her chats, she decided that it was the most general course and her Mum says they will be good skills for whatever she wants to do.

In September they go along to the induction sessions for their chosen courses. They were surprised that they had to do some tests to check their English and mathematics. Jamil went into a blind panic: he thought he'd finished tests with his GCSEs and was very wary, especially with the English. He thinks he will not be allowed on the course if he fails. Fiona didn't see the point – she got a B in English and a C in maths in her GCSEs so gave the certificates to the teacher; she was told she didn't need to do the tests.

During this first week, they met lots of teachers and some played games to relax them. They also learned each other's names and where they came from. One teacher made them write about what they wanted to gain from going to college. Sometimes the teachers seemed to just listen and watch, at other times they sat down with each of them for little chats. Fiona said 'they tried to find out what we liked and what we wanted to do when we left college'. In some classes the teacher gave them a programme of what they would do each week, others said that they would give them more details in a few weeks. Jamil said that he preferred some teachers to others, because they were friendlier.

When they bumped into each other on Friday lunchtime, Jamil and Fiona compared notes; they had been asked to complete a questionnaire about their first week in college. They thought that there were bits that were like school, but other bits that were more grown up, they both felt as though most of their teachers were interested in them, but thought that some things weren't explained well – for example why Fiona didn't do the tests and why Jamil did, but was enrolled onto a different Business Studies group. Although Jamil enjoyed the 'getting to know you' sessions, Fiona felt very self-conscious. In general, they felt happy and looked forward to the following week.

Suggested answers to this activity can be found at the end of the chapter on page 148.

Some things you should consider. Do you know:

- Why they chose their course?
- What their previous experience of learning is?
- How self-confident they are?
- If they have any previous experience or interests that are relevant?
- If they need any support?
- How they fit into their groups?
- What their preferred learning style is?
- What their expectations are?

How can you use the information to help Jamil and Fiona?

Initial assessment is a complex process involving pre-course assessment, diagnostic assessment and may continue throughout the programme with constant monitoring and reviewing to fine-tune needs. It results in accurate identification of individual needs, i.e. the planning of differentiation. Suggest some strategies to differentiate the learning programmes. How do you make your initial assessment work for you and your learners?

Evaluating your initial assessment

In order to gain the most from your initial assessment, it makes sense to evaluate the process. Some questions that you may ask yourself to do this are:

- What information or data comes out of the initial assessment?
- Does it impact on the programme or ILP?
- Is the information transmitted to others?
- What does the IA lead to?
- Is it collecting the right information?
- What does the data tell you?
- Who needs the information?
- Does it diagnose existing skills (e.g. basic skills)?
- Does it find out about preferred learning style?
- Does it analyse the person against the skills they require to study, learn, work or progress to higher education?

In summary, initial assessment is aiming to get the best match between your learners and their learning. It should be both backward- and forward-looking.

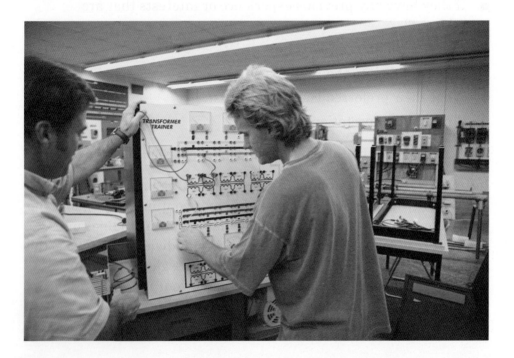

Planning, negotiating and recording learning goals

A goal is what a learner plans to achieve within a course or period of learning; a **target** is a smaller step to help learners achieve their goals. Small, achievable targets are more easily met than longer-term goals and therefore encourage a feeling of accomplishment. Effective targets are those small, achievable outcomes that enable students to experience early success. They are not vague and they are always in context, relevant and understood by everyone. In this context goals and targets are used to refer to learners' ambitions and aspirations rather than aims and outcomes used by the teacher in sessions.

> **If you don't know where you are going you will probably end up somewhere else.**

Laurence J. Peter, 1919–90, Canadian Academic and author of
The Peter Principle (1969)

Our learners arrive in post-compulsory education with many goals:

- Gaining qualifications to prepare for work or further/higher education
- Gaining qualifications to accredit existing skills
- To enhance or update skills
- For personal development or enrichment
- To achieve social integration.

They may also come:

- To meet parental/school targets
- As an alternative to school/work/unemployment benefit.

The motivational aspect of why learners enter post-compulsory education (**intrinsic** or **extrinsic**) will impact on the provision, the methods and on the relationships that emerge (see also Chapter 4). In order to exploit or capitalise on the motivational factors, teachers will need to set goals that are:

SMARTER

There are several different words associated with the **acronym**, but the meaning is clear:

Specific	Goals that clearly refer to what is expected
Measurable	Goals using verbs and phrases that can be judged
Achievable **A**greed	Goals that can be succeeded A more powerful expression because it appears contractual
Realistic **R**elevant	Goals that are reasonable, practical and logical Goals that are appropriate and important (Avoid using achievable and realistic because they mean broadly the same thing.)
Time-bounded	Goals that express when things must be done by
Exciting **E**njoyable **E**thical	Goals that are stimulating Goals that are pleasurable Goals that are fair and decent
Reviewed **R**ecorded	Goals that are revisited to check progress Goals that are written down

Goals are set for achievement over given periods which are usually expressed as:

- Long-term – career plans, ambitions
- Mid-term – programmes of study, assessment targets, learning outcomes
- Short-term – what to achieve in each session.

Goals are the building blocks of progression. They aim to move someone (in this instance a learner) forward. The size of these goals varies, and good teachers know their learners well enough to know how large or small a target or goal needs to be to ensure achievement. Some like the big picture; some are daunted by too large a goal and are motivated by lots of smaller targets and thus achievements. Whether large or small, a goal needs to be expressed in a statement that the learner understands and the goals need to be stated in the context of the overall ambition.

Expressions you may hear:

- *Goal-oriented* – this means that a learner responds to knowing what can be done now that couldn't be done before.
- *Negotiated* – this refers to a discussion about how the learner wants to achieve their goals, for example: in what way, by when.
- *Medal/mission* – a method of motivating and praise associated with setting targets and rewarding achievement (Petty 2004: 65).

ACTIVITY 2

Convert these targets into 'SMARTER targets'.

For example 'improve writing skills' could be written as 'always use capital letters for family names when filling in forms'.

- Hand in assignments on time
- Come to lessons ready to work
- To revise for the exam
- To pass your driving test

Discuss this activity with your mentor.

Goals and targets, usually recorded on the ILP, are best negotiated. This will aid ownership of the targets and create useful discussions to inform the most appropriate targets for the learner.

Glossary of terms

Acronym an abbreviation or series of initial letters which together make a word

Extrinsic motivation motivation derived from outside the person

Goal an aim or desired result

Induction a formal introduction to a programme/role

Initial assessment an assessment tool to identify and establish potential or aspirations or discover facts

Intrinsic motivation motivation from within the person; natural desire

On-programme a term to describe a period of learning

Spider diagram a visual form of note-taking to collect thoughts

Target an objective or focused path towards a specified outcome

 ## SUMMARY

In this chapter we set out to achieve the following outcomes:

● State the role that initial assessment has and its value to the teacher, the learner and the organisation

● List the types of initial assessment currently in use and identify the value of initial assessment

- Describe the difference between a goal and a target and develop use of expressions associated with goal setting

Your Personal Development

You will have further developed the skills and knowledge acquired through the PTLLS stage of your qualification and built on skills associated with initial assessment.

You have investigated the various stages and methods of initial assessment and the reasons why teachers need to collect and use the information. You have completed a case study to identify what initial assessment looks like in the context of induction and considered how information can be used to benefit learning. You have evaluated your own initial assessment strategies by completing a self-assessment questionnaire and adapting your practice in the light of your discussions with a mentor. Finally, you have practiced writing SMARTER targets for learners.

You should be able to answer questions relating to:

- The role and purpose of initial assessment
- Negotiating with learners
- Initial assessment strategies
- Agreeing goals and targets.

You should be able to demonstrate use of initial assessment in your planning of programmes and lessons.

Suggested answers to Activity 1

Information gathered by Jamil and Fiona	
ring	ask for a list of courses
fills out the application card	prospectus
advice	Careers Officer
stay friends with	open day
a chat with	Mum comes along
letter inviting him for an interview	offered a place
reference	Mum says
induction sessions	some tests
allowed on the course if he fails	didn't see the point
didn't need to do the tests	they met lots of teachers
played games	learned each other's names
gain from going	listen and watch
sat down with	tried to find out what we liked
programme of what they would do each week	more details in a few weeks
were friendlier	compared notes
questionnaire	were interested in
weren't explained well	getting to know you
felt very self-conscious	happy and looked forward to the following week

CHAPTER 7
(PEL)

Planning for inclusivity

SALLY AND RICHARD GREENHILL / ALAMY

LEARNING OBJECTIVES

The measurable outcomes that you will achieve by reading this chapter and completing the activities are:

- To describe what is meant by inclusion and how to implement an inclusive environment
- To recognise the importance and key components of a scheme of work
- To recognise the importance and key components of a lesson plan
- To identify ways that you can adapt programmes and lessons
- To state the impact of delivering in an inclusive learning environment
- To list key roles that support an inclusive delivery
- To describe how to collect information and to respond to learners' feedback

Establishing and maintaining inclusive learning environments

Providing opportunities for everyone in the community is not a new idea; equality of opportunity appeared in the 1970s and Helena Kennedy QC wrote about widening participation in 1996 (Further Education Funding Council 1996). Several revisions, in the format of legislation and government reports, have culminated in the current notion (or label) of inclusivity. In this context, we are looking at educational inclusion, specifically in post-compulsory education, rather than social inclusion. Organisations have to plan strategically to deliver equality, diversity and **inclusion** and are being inspected against their ability to provide opportunities. This has resulted in active marketing towards groups that would not normally enter FE. At the classroom level, every teacher has a responsibility to ensure that everyone is included.

The opposite of inclusion is exclusion; not something that happens regularly or without a great deal of anxiety, but in FE one of the changes recently introduced is the delivery of learning to those who have been excluded from compulsory education.

In a report initiated by the Scottish Funding Council (2006: 4), one senior manager in an FE college said:

> There are people here who would not have been here five years ago. Their circumstances have not changed. They are still living difficult lives; still living in poverty; still have a serious disability or health issue. We can't change these things but we can adapt what we do to help them get here, turn up, feel okay about what they are learning, and leave with what they aspired to.

He continued:

> Good learning does not reinforce previous negative experiences and may remove many barriers.

When inclusion is effective it will:

- Motivate by celebrating success and inspiring learners
- Develop and maintain positive attitudes
- Foster interest
- Encourage reflection
- Offer small chunks of learning with progressively more challenging goals
- Create positive relationships between teachers and learners
- Create an effective transition towards employment or relevance to further study
- Use individual learning plans to plan and record progress
- Offer a wide range of provision, delivered at times and locations to meet learners' needs.

When inclusion is not effective, it will:

- Provide poor use of modern technologies to enhance learning
- Offer a narrow range of teaching approaches
- Have insufficient assessment of learning or lack effective feedback
- Withhold development of functional (basic) skills
- Lack adequate methods to collect data or feedback to develop learners or provision.

Inclusion, therefore, is about creating interesting, varied and inspiring learning opportunities for *all* learners; ensuring all learners contribute and are never disadvantaged by methods, language or resources. This is described in other ways such as **differentiation** or 'meeting individual needs': both of these terms tend to refer to the mechanics of inclusion.

ACTIVITY 1

Reflective practice

How do you ensure an inclusive learning environment for your learners?

Think about the actions you take in planning, delivery, support and assessment.

Devising schemes of work to meet learner needs

REVISION

In Part One (PTLLS), we looked at schemes of work and how important it is to create a logical sequence of learning. We examined why planning and preparation of the content of the programme is essential and considered what needed to be included in the document. A scheme of work (or programme of study) includes a general description of who the group is and the timing of the sessions, it states the aims and outcomes of the programme and gives a brief breakdown of the topics to be covered in each session with an indication of how assessment will occur. For a complete review, refer to Chapter 3.

When devising schemes to meet learner needs, the teacher needs to consider the outcome of any initial assessment that has been carried out. In many cases the scheme is devised before the learners commence their course and the specific details to meet learner needs are implemented in the session or lesson plans. However, there are some things to think about which mean that you can both forward plan your programme and be proactive in meeting the outcomes of learner needs identified in your initial assessments.

Remember that a scheme of work is a broad outline of the overall programme and should be considered a working document. I would challenge anyone who maintains that it is a final statement, and especially someone who wheels the same document out year after year, to justify how it can possibly be a working, responsive

ACTIVITY 2

When planning your programme you may want to consider the following questions:

What are you comfortable with?

What are your own strengths?

What do you perceive the difficulties to be?

What do you want your learners to learn?

What resources are available? Can you use them?

Do you know where to get equipment from if it is not already in the room?

Do you know how to prepare the type of resource?

What are the physical surroundings like?

How much material do you need to cover (think about what learners must know, could know, think would be nice to know)?

Can you negotiate learning or is it already set?

Do you understand the curriculum requirements?

How does it fit with other learning on the course?

document aimed at creating the best learning opportunity possible. At the very least, technology changes, curriculum content, current practice and legislation are updated, and good teachers take the best of what has happened before and make improvements!

The questions in Activity 2 will give you an idea of the way you are able to teach your subject, plus broad ideas about methods and resource needs. By asking a few additional questions (Activity 3) or considering a few other points you will begin to be able to create a more learner-responsive programme.

 ## ACTIVITY 3

How will the teaching methods, resources and assessments you have chosen meet individual needs?

Is there something in every lesson for visual, auditory and kinaesthetic learners?

Is the environment suitable for all types of activities in terms of furnishings, accessibility and mobility?

Is there a balance of teacher- and learner-centred activities?

Have you included an introduction to the course, your module or this subject?

How ready are your learners to learn? Do you need to create the rules, set standards and identify boundaries?

How will you know that learners are learning? Build in time to do reviews, tutorials, catch-up sessions and revision.

By preparing your scheme in this way, you will have made significant progress in (generally) meeting everyone's needs and hence be able to concentrate on the specific needs of learners.

There will always be unforeseen factors, but see them as challenges and face them confidently knowing that your scheme is fluid enough to cope with them, rather than a tablet of stone which cannot be moved.

Devising lesson plans to meet learner needs

REVISION

In Part One (PTLLS), we looked at lesson plans and how important it is to specify the fine points of your proposed teaching and learning strategies. We looked at why the planning and preparation of the content of the lesson is essential and considered what needed to be included in this *aide-memoire*. A lesson plan includes details about the group – how many, date of lesson, etc. It states the aims and outcomes of the lesson and gives a detailed breakdown of the topics to be covered, how they will be delivered and an indication of how you will know whether the learners have learned the topic. For a complete review, refer to Chapter 3.

In your lesson plan you will identify the session outcomes, content, resources and assessment methods. You may also annotate it to justify choices made, for example stating methods against visual, auditory and kinaesthetic (VAK) learning styles, or teaching/ learning styles (e.g. active (learner-centred) /passive (teacher-centred), listening, note-taking, speaking etc). When you are teaching you are using differentiated strategies, but sometimes these just happen, they are not planned. By matching what you know about your learners to the topics being learned, you will be able to improve your teaching and thus the effectiveness of the learning experience.

What can you differentiate?

- Learning outcomes
- Tasks and activities
- Teaching methods
- Resources
- Group work
- Assessment
- Support

Amended to suit specific individuals or groups.

These are very broad statements, so let us break them down into actual things that can be done. Some examples of strategies used to differentiate include:

1 Learning outcomes:
   - ILP targets
   - Varying targets.
2 Tasks and activities:
   - Balanced VAK activities
   - Varying complexity of task/s
   - Providing for gifted and less able learners.
3 Teaching methods:
   - Nominated questioning
   - Language and expression, communication styles
   - Changing seating positions
   - Supporting learner readiness to learn/study/work etc.
4 Resources:
   - Enlarging handouts
   - Altering font types and sizes
   - Assistive technology – keyboards, mouse alternatives etc.
   - Introducing visual images
   - Using modern technology, e.g. the Internet, virtual learning environment (**VLE**), intranet.

5 Group work:

- Pyramid group activities.

6 Assessment:

- Questioning techniques
- Complexity of written questions.

7 Support:

- 1:1 support
- Peer support
- Use of support assistants for reading, writing and comprehension
- Memory aids, recording devices or note frames.

 ACTIVITY 4

How do you maximise your learners' potential?

Make a list of some of the things you do in the classroom to meet your learners' needs. Keep this to hand when planning future sessions and prepare to differentiate.

Be proactive and reactive!

Being *proactive* means that you prepare for all eventualities: being *reactive* means that you will listen to your learners and modify accordingly.

Adapting plans and schemes

Adapting plans and schemes means modifying your teaching and learning activities to meet the needs of those assembled in your group. Teaching 'mixed ability groups' is not new; it is another instance of labelling. Differentiating or adapting is usually modifying or doing something differently, maybe changing the way

REVISION

In Part One (PTLLS), we looked at planning to meet individual needs (Chapter 3) and different ways of teaching that will meet those needs (Chapter 2). We discussed how learners have different ways of learning (Chapter 1). We can therefore conclude that effective teaching and learning responds to the individual needs of learners and this is expressed as an idea in the scheme of work, as an intention in a lesson plan and demonstrated in the delivery of learning.

you (usually) deliver something, or it can be about a specific action you make for an individual or small group. Adaptations in sessions are usually by task, by outcome or by support. Each is responsive to the ability of your learners. The adaptations or differentiation are always about what is in the best interests of the learner. Yes, it does take more time to prepare for everyone in the session, but this will be rewarded when your lessons are interesting, keep everyone occupied and don't become a fraught battle of wills. Time will fly because learner-centred activities are more exciting and although they may take longer to achieve the final goal than teacher-centred ones (because they may involve more group exploration and experiential learning), the learners are active so they don't get bored, and you don't become exhausted. Before you know it the lesson is over and outcomes are achieved successfully. Learner-centred activities are invaluable in creating learner autonomy, developing study skills and the skills of critical analysis and reflective thinking.

To bring in some theory, Benjamin Bloom (1913–1999), created a classification of learning which he called a 'taxonomy'. Further work by Bloom, David Krathwohl and R. H. Dave extended this work. Particularly in respect of the third category (psychomotor domain) you will see variations. For example, Elizabeth Simpson and Anita Harrow have both extended Bloom's original work and devised their own terminology. Each has in common a progression leading from basic actions to standard or habitual practice. The theory can be usefully applied when devising differentiated outcomes, because the classifications provide levels of learning. It was originally devised as a means of explaining 'mastery' in tasks, but has been used widely in educational terms in a variety of ways. Although published around 50 years ago, it is timeless and has become one of the classic models of theory.

The first stage of the classification is associated with three skills or **domains**:

- **Cognitive** (intellectual or thinking skills)
- **Affective** (attitudes, beliefs and values)
- **Psychomotor** (physical, practical and co-ordination skills).

Bloom (and others) advocate that all learning can be classified into these three domains. He then subdivides them, which is where it starts to become useful to the teacher.

The **low order** skills are usually those in the short-term or shallow memory. If you tell your learners a fact or opinion today, they will be able to remember it tomorrow; they won't be able to do anything with the information or transfer its meaning to another context, but they can call to mind the basic fact or recall the skill. This is **shallow learning**.

With the **high order** skill, the learner truly understands the fact – the learning is deeper, they can apply it in different situations and argue its worth against other peoples' thinking. It represents second nature. This is **deep learning**. For the teacher, this theory means that you can develop learning and understanding either in a phased way (using Bloom to structure learning development in your scheme of work) or by ability (using Bloom to provide different levels of task according to the capabilities of your learners). You can stretch learners to meet their full potential. Assessment and questioning can be differentiated using Bloom's theory, either to offer appropriate questions according to ability or to challenge more able learners to think and apply their knowledge. Bloom's Taxonomy, therefore, is a useful tool.

Cognitive domain

Level	Taxonomy	Learners will be able to:
Low order skill	Knowledge	State, list, recognise, draw,
	Comprehension	Describe, explain, identify
	Application	Use, apply, construct, solve
	Analysis	List, compare, contrast,
	Synthesis	Summarise, argue, explain
High order skill	Evaluation	Judge, evaluate, criticise

Based on Bloom (1956).

EXAMPLE

Map reading. At its lowest level a learner can recognise a red line on a map as a road.

At the next level they can identify the red roads and maybe see that other roads are blue and yellow; the next level would be to use a map to work out what road goes from A to B. The next level would have the learner using a map to plot a route between locations, listing alternative options.

At the higher levels learners would be able to plot locations using grid referencing and scale and finally apply their knowledge to other map formats to evaluate the difference between the formats.

Affective domain

Level	Taxonomy	Learners will be able to:
Low order skill	Receiving (being aware)	Choose, describe, use, select
	Responding (reacting)	Answer, discuss, perform, write
	Valuing (understanding)	Demonstrate, argue, debate, explain
	Organisation and Conceptualisation	Compare, contrast, generalise, modify
High order skill	Characterisation (behaviour)	Acts, displays, practices, solves, verifies

Based on Bloom and Krathwohl (1964).

EXAMPLE

Health and safety. At its lowest level, if I say 'don't run' a learner slows down to a walk. At the next level, they usually walk along corridors; in the next level the learner realises why running is not allowed; at organisation level they probably tells others around them about running versus walking in corridors, and finally at the highest level they would probably be putting up notices warning others about running in corridors!

Psychomotor domain

Level	Taxonomy	Learners will be able to:
Low order skill	Imitation	Repeat, copy, follow, replicate
	Manipulation	Re-create, perform, implement
	Precision	Demonstrate, complete, show
	Articulation	Solve, integrate, adapt, modify
High order skill	Naturalisation	Design, specify, invent

Based on Dave (1967).

EXAMPLE

Driving a car. At its lowest level, when the instructor says 'brake and clutch', that's what the learner driver does; at the next level, the learner driver repeats the process without always being told, say at traffic lights; next the learner confidently brakes, probably without stalling the car.

At 'articulation', the learner driver can control the speed of the car using brakes, gears and acceleration and finally, as second nature they drive in any situation without thinking, clutch control in a traffic jam or on a hill are examples of that.

Useful online resources

http://www.learningandteaching.info/learning/bloomtax.htm
http://www.nwlink.com/~donclark/hrd/bloom.html
http://www.businessballs.com
http://www.teachers.ash.org.au/researchskills/dalton/htm

ACTIVITY 5

In order to help you think about differentiating to meet individual needs, look at the following scenarios and decide how you might aid that individual's learning. You may find it advantageous to revise from Part One and the previous sections in this chapter before trying this activity.

1   Susan has difficultly in concentrating in group activities

2   Carly struggles with note-taking

3   Shara and Petra were absent last week

4   Matthew has a visual impairment

5   Everyone calls out answers to questions at the same time

6   Barney is dyslexic

7   Four of the group are doing Level 1 within the Level 2 computer class

8   Leroy gets bored but always produces really good pieces of work

9   The transport bus is always late which means learners turn up in dribs and drabs for the first 10 minutes of the morning class.

How would you plan to differentiate for these learners?

Possible solutions (these are my offerings, you may have others):

1   Susan – ensure that there are plenty of short activities in the lesson. Research suggests that even the most highly motivated learner starts to lose concentration after about 10 minutes, so that should be the length of these short, snappy activities. When working with others, help her to remain on task by preparing a 'focus sheet' or writing frame giving ideas, with plenty of room to write and some questions or prompts. Maybe she could be the scribe for the group.

2   Carly – you need to find out how she likes to make notes. Does she like everything neatly arranged in a linear format, or does she like bullet points? Does she like themes with brief notes (nuclear) or a thought pattern style e.g. a spider diagram or clouds? (See Appendix C on Study Skills). Once you've discovered her preferred way of making notes you can help her with pre-prepared note sheets. If she is meticulous and struggles because she really likes you to speak at dictation speed, then I recommend she either uses a tape recorder or other recording device, or you prepare handouts from your notes to offer to her at the end of the session. A support assistant could make notes on her behalf. Perhaps during induction you should talk through note-taking styles and make it part of your initial assessment, rather than waiting for it to become a progress problem for one of your learners.

3   Shara and Petra – obviously you can't repeat the lesson for them, but you do need to get them up to speed. When they arrive, give them an **opener** type of activity to complete whilst you are setting off the rest of the group in a recap or similar activity. An opener can be a quiz designed to recap previous learning, or a word search, crossword activity or a brain gym activity (http://www.braingym.org). You could ask them to read through your teaching notes or handouts from last week (or another learner's notes). Whilst the remainder of the group are completing their activity, you can do a 1:2 session with Shara and Petra to get them to the same level as the rest. You really can see why differentiation should be planned in this scenario; there is no way that you could do this kind of session without preparation.

4   Matthew – this is quite an easy one to deal with, yet Matthew should be respected in terms of which one of the following he is more comfortable with. You can either ask Matthew to move closer to the front so that other learners' heads aren't bobbing about in front of him; however he may prefer to remain where he is. Therefore you would need to copy handouts or presentation notes in a **font** style and size that is legible for him and offer them to him for his use in class. Dependent on the degree of sight impairment you may have specialist support staff accompanying him, in which case you should brief them at the beginning of the class about what help you need.

5   Questioning – this is about how *you* ask the questions. If you are asking questions generally to the whole group it is not surprising that there is a mass answer. The learners don't know that you only want one person to answer! You need to change your approach to a nominated style, but in doing so you must also teach your learners to use the same style, because again they don't know what you are trying to do. A nominated style is discussed in more detail in the assessment unit, but basically it involves you asking your question, allowing time for all learners to think about the answer and then you nominate one person to share their thoughts with the rest of the group. This is called pose, pause, nominate. I've also heard it called pose, pause, pounce – but that sounds a little aggressive! This is a great way of differentiating because you can pose questions at the level you know your learners can cope with, perhaps using Bloom's theory to devise your questions.

6   Barney – has Barney been officially assessed as dyslexic or is
    that what he says? If an assessment has been done, the
    Statement will give you clear guidance about what the dyslexia
    professional considers relevant to aid Barney's learning. You may
    need to check with another teacher or his tutor to find out what
    diagnostic assessments have been done. If you suspect dyslexia
    then seek guidance about how to organise an assessment, again
    through his tutor if appropriate. If it is Barney's own opinion
    then you should be a little more suspicious about what is wrong:
    he may be correct – an assessment will confirm this, but he may
    be covering another barrier to learning, so that needs
    investigating. Some of the strategies to support dyslexia might
    involve use of coloured paper or overlays, font type, reading
    ability level guidance, specialist support, time allowances etc.

7   Mixed ability – this involves some compare and contrast research
    as part of your planning. You must look at the levels of
    qualifications offered within your class and see where the
    similarities are. It could be the level of explanation that is given can
    be amended, i.e. giving your Level 1 learners info sheets or **screen
    shot** worksheets to enable them to carry out the tasks. It may be
    that you have access to a support assistant, in which case brief
    them on the level of support you want them to offer, which would be
    enhanced with a subject specialist support (very rare, but maybe
    possible to organise – if you don't ask . . .). You may have to structure
    group work in such a way as to differentiate tasks or use peers to
    support or integrate learners. In some qualifications it is part of the
    curriculum that Level 3 learners have to 'supervise' Level 1 or 2
    learners in order to prepare them for working within industry.

8   Leroy – he is obviously able if he is submitting good work, unless
    he is copying from someone else or getting family help. This needs
    to be checked out. A few questions about the topic in a one-to-one
    meeting will tell you whether he knows his stuff or whether his
    work is someone else's. His boredom is probably down to one of
    two problems; either your lesson *is* boring, in which case think
    about alternative teaching and learning methods, or Leroy is very
    intelligent, grasps things quickly and you are not challenging or
    stretching him enough, in which case you need to think about
    alternative teaching and learning methods. A clear case for some
    reflection about what you are doing here.

9   Transport – the same answer as number 3, using openers to give you some breathing space, but this time everyone does the activities or recaps as they arrive, with the main class topic being introduced when everyone has got there. The danger with this is that those learners that are there on time will gradually get later, so something relevant must happen in the class from the official start time. If transport is late then so be it. You may wish to report this to the group tutor, or the person who organises the transport. If it is public transport, then you could suggest an earlier bus/train! You could always talk about this in a team meeting: does it happen in every morning lesson? Are the affected learners 'cause for concern'? Should the start time of the class be delayed? (See also Dealing with punctuality in Chapter 4.)

Delivering inclusive learning

In terms of teaching and learning, this is where we are **empowered** to most effect. We can control what we do and to a certain extent what our learners do and can achieve. In the previous section, we

considered how to plan for inclusion, but we can also modify our teaching style and methods, our resources and our assessment techniques either as the programme or lesson progresses or to become routinely inclusive. Some general inclusive learning strategies that you can try are:

Teaching and learning styles

Ensure that every lesson includes methods that appeal to visual, auditory and kinaesthetic learners. Follow a structured style – introduction, middle and an end, with a balanced amount of teacher talk and plenty of things to look at and do. Look out for who is making the contributions in the class and make a conscious effort to ensure that all learners take part in the class. Support your less able learners and stretch the imagination of the gifted ones. Vary activities and make learning fun! Use different outcomes and/or assessment activities to differentiate need.

Resources – paper-based learning aids

If you have to do a lot of talking create a handout for your visual learners to follow. Better still, make it interactive for your kinaesthetic learners by requiring words to be inserted or questions to be considered. I once saw an interactive PowerPoint presentation – the teacher's presentation included all of the facts, but the learners' printed handouts had a modified copy with words, numbers etc. missed out, so although they were following teacher talk, supported by PowerPoint, they also had something to do – therefore meeting all VAK types. Other paper-based activities include self-study packs that provide either catch-up, extra help for those that need help or those that can extend learning or revision uses. Resources to use as openers, fillers or closure activities include word search, crossword or quiz-word or matching games.

Resources – font type and presentation

Use at least a 14 pt font, larger in display formats such as
PowerPoint or overhead transparencies. Use a clear font style such
as Arial, **Berlin Sans**, Tahoma, or Comic Sans. These plain *sans serif*
styles are good. Fonts such as Harrington, *handwriting styles*, or
Old English are not very legible, because they are too fussy. I
particularly like fonts that represent the letter a as 'a', because I
think it is easier on the eyes. Whilst on the subject, blue print on
pale yellow paper is quite easy on the eyes – but I appreciate that
photocopiers are not generally set up for this, so you may wish to
experiment, especially if a learner is suffering from eye strain. Avoid
a **justified text** as it distributes words unevenly across the page.
When developing study skills with your learners you should also
advocate a similar set of rules for when your learners present their
word processed work to you for marking – it helps your eyes as well!

The Royal Institute for the Blind publishes a Clear Print Guideline,
which is very informative and is available at http://www.rnib.org.uk/
xpedio/groups/public/documents/publicwebsite/public_printdesign.hcsp.

Accommodation

Prepare the room for the activities to be completed in the session,
think about what you will be doing and what your learners are
expected to do. Different types of group work require alterations to the
room layout (see Chapter 2). You may need to include provision for
wheelchair users – which could be height adjustable benches, tables or
workstations or just space to move around safely in the classroom.

Support

Differentiation is not just the ability to provide support in the form of a
Learning Support Assistant, but can include documents to support
study. The most common types are assignment frames, writing frames
or research frames. Each of these 'frames' has the ability to set

questions which will help focus learners ideas and structure work. They are especially useful when supporting independent learners. (See Appendix C: Study Skills.)

Assessment

In the same way that teaching and learning is differentiated to meet everyone's needs it follows that assessment must also do so. It is too easy to forget that this is also something which needs to be considered, especially as many assessments are prescribed or preset by the awarding bodies. Any learner receiving learning support can usually apply for special arrangements in any kind of test or timed examination.

Some further ideas include:

- Verbal questioning can be differentiated using nominated styles;
- Written question sheets can include a mixture of multiple-choice questions, yes/no type and short answer type in the same test.
- Homework and class-work assessments could be varied to include things for all learner types:
  - *Visual learners* like to write in bullet points and use images; labelling things; making posters or booklets.
  - *Auditory learners* like to verbalise their answers; write essays; do research.
  - *Kinaesthetic learners* like to make things; do role play; presentations.

Using classroom support workers

Generally, there are three types of support workers that you will come across, but there are as many different job titles as there are organisations in which they work. You will need to find out what the titles and associated job roles are within your organisation. Some of those titles are:

Classroom Support Assistant

Classroom Assistant

Learning Support Assistant

Learning Assistant

Basic Skills Support

Support Assistant

Support Tutor

Support Lecturer

Care Assistant

Student Support Worker

Type one is there to support the physical needs of learners. They will help learners with personal care needs and at mealtimes: in the classroom they will help by holding things or fetching and carrying to ensure a safe learning experience. Together with the learner they will identify and control what they do.

Type two is there to support the academic learning needs of an individual or group of individuals – probably functional skills support. They will help learners to make notes, recall facts and comprehend information, write things down, help with literacy and numeracy needs. They are not usually a trained teacher, although they may be trained in supporting the work of teachers or be volunteers or paid employees. They are a group of people that are most valuable in the room, yet very often they are undirected and therefore their value is not fully utilised. The more experienced they are or the longer they work with a particular teacher or group, the more self-sufficient they become.

Type three is there to support vocational and academic learning needs or behavioural support. They are probably a trained teacher, perhaps from the same subject specialism and assist the teacher, probably team teaching at times. If they are qualified and from the same subject, they can very much pre-empt what the teacher is trying to achieve and are usually an effective support mechanism.

Whatever the type of support worker, communication is the key to the effectiveness of that support. I would suggest that when a teacher plans their lesson they consider how they want the support worker to work with the learner. If this is annotated onto the lesson plan and offered to the support worker then the support worker will be able to see what is going to happen, how you think it will be done and what outcomes you are expecting and use their skills and experience to help you make it happen. Too often I have seen support workers either doing very little, because they do not know what is expected of them or the activities aren't clear so they are unsure of how to support their learner, or in some cases they just do everything for the learner, who forgets to learn how to do things for themselves. A support worker cannot support unless they know what you are trying to achieve; telepathy is not yet in their job description! In an ideal world it would be good to have a conversation about what support is required before the lesson and de-brief on how it went afterwards, but rarely is that feasible. A shared coffee break occasionally is not too demanding though!

Support workers can make valuable contributions:

- in consultations about causes for concern
- when used in an advisory capacity to think about appropriateness of resources and teaching strategies
- in team meetings
- at reporting periods
- as a resource
- when embedding functional skills
- to differentiate teaching.

Who will benefit from support worker assistance?

- learners with mobility, hearing or visual impairments
- learners with special educational needs (SENs)
- learners identified with weak literacy and/or numeracy skills
- teachers with very large or diverse groups
- teachers of learners with behavioural problems.

Research carried out in 1997 found that 'students on learning support were more likely to achieve than those who did not need the support in the first place' (Petty 2004: 513). Accessing learning support and working with support workers must be seen as an opportunity and not as something which confirms that a learner is not very good. This is a cultural shift and is changing positively as teachers, learners and managers see the resulting value. Unfortunately, those of you working in the community or the workplace may not have such staff to support you. However, if you are experiencing situations which regularly need support arrangements you should discuss this with your line manager. Because you work in more isolated situations you may not be familiar with procedures for accessing support or not realise that funding and mechanisms are available. Support, in any circumstance, is not usually systematically employed unless demand or need is assessed.

The role of the tutor

The class tutor plays an important role in supporting learning.

A tutor provides a link between the learner's academic progress and any other concerns or issues they may have. A tutor will have the opportunity to talk – probably on a one-to-one basis about how a learner is doing on the programme. They will review their achievements regularly and aid progress by setting goals and targets for further development. By creating a professional relationship based on trust and openness, the tutor will understand the learner, their motivation and aspirations and engage in discussions with them and others in the teaching team. The relationship should always be based on support towards achievement; a good tutor (and learner) will respect the boundaries of their role.

A full description of the role and associated qualities of a tutor are presented in Chapter 21.

Disability Discrimination Act 1995 (c50)

The Act gives disabled people the right to employment, education, access to goods, facilities and services, and access to buying or renting land or property. Part Three (which was amended in October 2004) requires businesses and organisations to take reasonable steps to modify physical features that act as a barrier to disabled people who wish to access their services. Part Four (which was amended in September 2002) specifically relates to education and states that providers should take steps to ensure that the disabled are not treated less favourably than other students.

The primary instruction is that colleges, training providers and other organisations make 'reasonable' adjustments to include everyone, for example:

- by installing ramps or lifts to replace steps
- ensuring facilities assist access
- creating signage appropriate to needs
- improving toilet facilities
- ensure rooms are accessible
- undertake health and safety risk assessment
- create plans and progress towards accessibility
- publish disability statements and entitlements
- provide support, for example – sighted support, sign language interpreters, note-takers, specialist equipment, rest breaks
- prepare for assessment to ensure that testing is fair and accessible for all. This may involve negotiating extra time in written examinations to meet specific needs, or offering one-to-one support, or providing scribes for written work
- Assistive technologies – a range of equipment can be purchased to make a more comfortable or ergonomic environment, for example, arm supports, pen grips, voice recognition devices.

Useful information

The Open University provides an extensive list of ideas at: http://www.open.ac.uk/inclusiveteaching/pages/inclusive-teaching/learning-environments.php.

In summary, delivering an inclusive learning package means considering what is appropriate and needed. It is a balance of activities, using support staff and guidance to ensure that everyone who wants to access learning can do so that and those who do not usually feel comfortable in accessing learning are confident that your organisation will meet their needs and aspirations.

Acquiring and responding to learners' feedback

There are a number of informal and formal methods of collecting views of students. Learner responsiveness is another of the current buzz words.

The purpose of all of these methods is to collect information and feedback from learners. The Post-It™ notes, for example, mean that learners can make a comment at the time it becomes apparent, without interrupting the flow of the lesson (things like 'I don't understand that' will be written on the Post-It™). The discussion will have an emerging agenda, usually initiated from a single question and then moving on in whichever direction the conversation develops. Focus groups are similar, except that they are slightly more managed and the interviewer has a clear idea of what they are trying to find out and will lead questioning in that direction.

Informal	Formal
Post-It™ notes	Surveys
Discussion	Evaluation sheets
Verbal Q&A	Questionnaires Focus groups

Covert feedback:
    Attendance
    Behaviour
	Tutorials
	Complaints cards

Most organisations delivering training use 'happy sheets' to capture the first reactions to the course or training activity. They are useful to a certain degree. (Did the course match its publicity? Did you achieve your planned objectives? How do you propose to use the learning gained?). However, in terms of evaluating the effectiveness of the learning it comes too soon: learners have not had the opportunity to use the learning or discuss it with anyone. Surveys are another frequently used part of the curriculum to establish student satisfaction. There are companies that carry this task out for an organisation and then match performance to other organisations it works with; this helps to **benchmark** performance against other providers.

Whatever the method of collecting information, it is of no use and would be a waste of time unless something is done about what is gathered from the information. You must close the loop.

You may collect information for a number of reasons:

1   To confirm that learners are happy on their chosen programme of study
2   To audit that processes have occurred, for example: induction paperwork completed, assessment processes are completed
3   To find out if learners' own objectives have been met
4   To check that differentiated learning methods are suitable
5   To inform quality assurance processes – course review, self-assessment, internal verification, satisfaction surveys
6   To confirm understanding.

The final stage of collecting information and receiving feedback from learners is to use it to the benefit of the organisation, the teacher or the learners.

ACTIVITY 6

Look at the following results from learner feedback strategies. What would you do if this came to your attention?

- You find out from class Post-It™ notes that three learners did not understand a key theory you were trying to explain.

- The induction review form shows that not all learners received copies of the Student Charter.

- The course evaluations from today's course confirmed that many learners thought the course would give them ideas to use when they returned to their own establishment.

- The annual student survey said that 37 per cent of learners felt that the prices in the café were too expensive, 87 per cent would recommend their programme to someone else and 67 per cent said that they thought the staff delivering on their programme were helpful and friendly.

- The attendance during Miss B's lesson is rarely above 40 per cent. Other teachers of that programme have attendance averages of 80–100 per cent.

Glossary of terms

Affective concerned with emotions and values

Benchmark a standard or point of reference to compare performance

Cognitive concerned with thinking skills

Deep learning learning which is memorised and fully understood

Differentiation catering for the needs of all learners to reduce barriers to learning

Domain an area or section of learning; a classification

Empowered given responsibility for something

Font a type or style of lettering in a printed document

High order most thorough level of learning

Inclusion finding opportunities to integrate all learners

Justified text even distribution of words across the page within fixed margins

Low order a superficial level of learning

Opener an activity at the beginning of a session

Psychomotor concerned with physical, practical and co-ordination skills

Screen shot a visual image from a software program reproduced into a document to support understanding

Shallow learning learning which is retained for a short period

Taxonomy a classification

VLE virtual learning environment

 SUMMARY

In this chapter we set out to achieve the following outcomes:

- Describe what is meant by inclusion and analyse the importance of implementing an inclusive environment within your own teaching area

- Recognise the importance and key components of a scheme of work and state how schemes are written to meet individual need

- Recognise the importance and key components of a lesson plan and state how plans are written to meet individual need
- Identify ways that you can adapt programmes and lessons to meet needs, and explain the theory behind the processes
- State the impact of delivering in an inclusive learning environment, with reference to disability, teaching and learning and support for learners
- List key roles that support an inclusive delivery
- Describe the mechanisms which collect information about learners and express ideas to respond to their feedback

Your Personal Development

You will have learned about inclusion – what it is, why we do it and what you can do as a teacher to ensure an inclusive environment. You have understood about differentiation and what this means to both the teacher and the learner and the importance of differentiating to create high-quality learning experiences. You have completed activities that develop your ability to create schemes of work; reflected on how to select activities deemed to support inclusion and maximise learners' potential; made suggestions about how to differentiate in a range of situations; and finally, considered the impact of learners' responses and how they may affect your actions.

You should be able to answer questions relating to:

- The use of different delivery methods, resources and adapting session plans to create an inclusive learning environment.

In your teaching practice this will develop your ability to:

- Prepare schemes of work and session plans which meet individual needs and demonstrate inclusive learning strategies.

CHAPTER 8
(PEL)

Using inclusive strategies

LEARNING OBJECTIVES

The measurable outcomes that you will achieve by reading this chapter and completing the activities are:

- To identify learning activities and list factors that motivate learners
- To describe how motivation and inclusive learning enthuse learners
- Analyse the advantages and disadvantages of using a range of resources and how they contribute to effective learning
- To describe new technologies which support learning
- To explain the terms equality and diversity
- To evaluate your own methods and compare them to standards, identifying strategies for improving practice
- To state the importance and use of functional skills
- To suggest ways of modifying resources to meet individual needs of learners

Designing inclusive learning activities which motivate and enthuse learners

Inclusive practice, reviewed in the previous chapter (Chapter 7), concentrated on the necessity of differentiating to meet individual need. To a certain extent this will increase the motivation and therefore make the learning session more rewarding for learners. It is not, however, a rule. As the teacher, you may have devised various activities, resources and assessment tools to meet everyone's needs, but notice that there is still something missing. So what is it? Well, it is likely to be that you have overlooked the fact that people have characters; they have moods, distractions and emotions. Whilst you may be able to deal with changes in these if they are ongoing, if they emerge during your lesson, it relies upon you to 'think on your feet'. It may or may not be possible to sort out the issue or modify your lesson, and in my experience when you can get around to dealing with it – i.e. for next lesson, everything has changed anyway! Younger learners in particular do have quite sudden changes in their behaviour as a result of mood swings and adults may be concerned about other facets of their lives, for example work or family, which temporarily distracts them. So the advice is that you need to understand what motivates and remember the importance of knowing your learners.

REVISION

In Part One, you identified a variety of relevant teaching and learning activities (Chapter 2) and how they are used to meet individuals' needs in your curriculum area. This was also described as differentiation. You also looked at Maslow's opinions on motivation, how to engage learners (Chapter 4) and identified ways to improve motivation in the classroom.

Types of learners – some expressions you may hear:

- VAK – visual, auditory and kinaesthetic learners – different ways learners like to learn

- Disaffected learners – no longer satisfied with the learning environment

- Disengaged learners – detached or not involved in learning

- Dysfunctional – unable to deal with normal social behaviours

- Gifted and talented learners – highly skilled or adept in particular things

- SEN – special educational needs

- **ADHD** – attention deficit hyperactivity disorder

We will look at the different needs of these types of learners later.

Motivation theory

Motivation theory, described by Abraham Maslow (1970), focuses on needs, arguing that basic needs must be met before a learner can enter a state of mind in which to learn. This is not the only theory relating to motivation; all describe ways of trying to find out why someone wants to learn and how best to make it happen. (See also Chapter 4.)

Intrinsic and extrinsic motivators Everyone is motivated in one of these ways. Those said to be intrinsically motivated are developing because they want to; they have an inbuilt desire to progress and want to learn because they can. Those who are extrinsically motivated are developing because somebody or something wants them to or they need to. Maybe they have the offer of financial reward or better job prospects. Whatever the reason for the motivation, it is necessary and it is crucial that the teacher knows what their motivational driver is. If, for example, someone is extrinsically motivated they will improve their motivation if their work is displayed on the wall, or other similar outward expression of their achievement: equally, someone intrinsically motivated will get satisfaction from study time to research a topic. Once again, the teacher should play to the strengths of the learner when trying to raise enthusiasm in learning.

ACTIVITY 1

Why are you doing the Diploma in Teaching in the Lifelong Learning Sector qualification/course?

List the reasons and decide whether you are intrinsically or extrinsically motivated.

What would help you to become more motivated?

Why does reflecting on your own levels of motivation enable development?

Discuss your answers with another member of the course.

Medals and mission This is a goal-oriented theory, based on the desire to be rewarded for achievement. A learner is given a clear direction or task and when it is reached there is a reward. The reward may be money, for example a pay rise on gaining a qualification, it may be a certificate, which could be proudly displayed or it could be acknowledgment from a colleague or teacher in a statement indicating 'well done'. The 'mission' can be a series of small targets or a single target, depending on the preferences of the learners. The 'medal' may also be phased.

Vicious and virtuous circles As the name suggests, this focuses on the fact that when things start to happen (positively or negatively) a learner enters a circle. The vicious circle is spiralling downwards; conversely, the virtuous circle is spiralling upwards. In motivational terms, if you start to achieve things you are more likely to want to continue. A learner enters a Can Do – Will Do mindset.

Turner (1990) promoted a model demonstrating the need for praise to promote a better standard of performance:

Figure 8A   Motivation in training

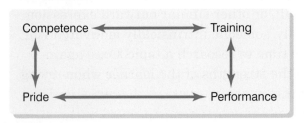

Petty then adopted Turner's model to show how success forms the motivator to further achievement, creating a virtuous circle (Figure 8B); this is the upward spiral.

Conversely in the vicious circle, the statements are in the negative and so the motivation lessens because as a learner fails they are not inclined to progress or do more work.

Figure 8B   The virtuous circle (Petty 2004: 47)

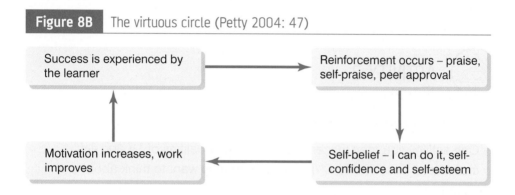

Bandura and self-efficacy Albert Bandura (1994) suggested that an individual's belief in themselves and their ability is related to what they can achieve. The mindset here is 'if I believe I can, then I must be able to.' This is self-efficacy, which in this context means that belief in yourself will aid motivation. When you apply this in the classroom it concerns how you address the learner who says 'I can't do this'. This learner needs to be encouraged to try, you will re-explain the topic and through coaching and reassurance you will enable that learner to achieve.

Herzberg's Satisfaction Theory Frederick Herzberg (1959) was one of the early writers on motivation. This was originally associated with the workplace, but can be attributed to learning. He suggested that people need personal growth and interest and that a person's level of satisfaction determines how motivated they are. This is a 'needs' model in that everyone needs the right conditions, status and security in order to develop.

Positive and negative reinforcement These ideas come from the behaviourist theories originally suggested in research on animal behaviour (Pavlov's dog responding by salivating). In learning terms this is about offering positive or negative rewards to motivate. The motivation has a value. Positive reinforcement is rooted in the desire to seek a reward for achievement or good work. Negative reinforcement works on the threat or fear factor of not doing well.

The two examples that come to mind are: 'If you complete the work you may go to break' or 'If you don't complete your work, you can't have a break.' Both phrases suggest the same outcome, but the method of delivering is totally different. Pay bonuses work on this theory, as do the bonus payments in EMA (The Educational Maintenance Award).

ACTIVITY 2

How to learn about motivation

One activity you may try centres on the personalities of TV and film characters. Some video/DVD scenes you may want to think about are:

David Brent in *The Office*
Basil Fawlty and Manuel in *Fawlty Towers*
Caine and Walters' relationship in *Educating Rita*

How does each of these people motivate their staff or protégés?
List the positive and negative methods each uses and relate those ideas to motivational theory. What can you learn by these examples?

The teacher should consider the advantages of using positive reinforcement as a motivator. Remember, though, that what you offer (or threaten) must be carried out, or it becomes empty reinforcement.

Useful online resources

en.wikipedia.org/wiki/motivation
http://tip.psychology.org/motivate.html
http://www.businessballs.com/maslow.htm
http://webspace.ship.edu/cgboer/maslow.html
http://changingminds.org/explanations/theories/
http://www.geoffpetty.com/downloads/WORD/reinforcement.doc

A simple search through a search engine using the following key words will reveal a lot of information: motivation, Maslow, intrinsic, extrinsic, Herzberg, Petty.

Specialist areas of motivational need

There are groups of learners who have particular issues. Whilst not wishing to stereotype needs, a teacher should be mindful of the support these groups may need to offer to improve motivation. If you follow your own rule of assuming nothing, yet seek to find out how individuals access useful learning strategies, you will create an inclusive environment.

Attention deficit hyperactivity disorder (ADHD). Some learners may be diagnosed with ADHD. If you have such a learner in your class you should seek advice on their particular needs, but in general learners need to be in a position where they cannot be distracted or distract and see positive role models around them. You should not play to their need to gain your attention, but remember that they easily lose focus and their attention span is poor, so planning is essential when preparing lessons to meet their needs.

In lessons, try to:

- prepare material that is of interest
- create responsibility for their own learning
- initiate peer support systems
- design short, sharp activities
- use plenty of varied activities
- maintain a routine in the classroom
- create clear concise handouts
- offer reminders and praise.

Gifted and talented learners These are a group of learners who need to be motivated in the same way as every other learner, although it is tempting to 'assume' that because they are able and usually intrinsically motivated they are OK left to their own devices. This group is at risk of becoming bored by learning that lacks challenge in the same way that any other learner lacks motivation; the teacher needs to respond and act upon it by differentiated teaching.

'Gifted' refers to those learners who excel in core subjects, whereas 'talented' usually refers to those skilled in more practical or artistic subjects. More recently 'gifted and talented' has become a general term for those learners who demonstrate high abilities in a number of areas.

Characteristics of **gifted and talented learners**:

- Quick thinking
- Methodical
- Creative
- Flexible
- Communicative
- Dexterous
- Team players.

Strategies to challenge the group:

- Offering opportunities to investigate and research
- Setting high order objectives (Bloom, Chapter 7)
- Using open questions to seek opinion or argument
- Question opinions and ask what if . . . ? questions
- Providing opportunities to negotiate own targets
- Develop learner and learning **autonomy**.

Specific language needs groups There are groups for whom education is needed to support the ability to either become employed in the UK or work effectively in the UK. These are groups who are not native English speakers. They may struggle to comprehend the language and it must not be assumed that they possess some specific educational need. There are differences in academic ability as with any group of learners; their need is for language support to enable the groups to participate fully in education. The groups that come into this category include asylum seekers, English as a foreign language (EFL) and English for speakers of other language (ESOL).

The motivation for this group will come from activities in the classroom that are appropriate to their academic level, yet mindful of their ability to understand the **concept** in a different language.

In lessons, try to:

- prepare material that relates to hobbies or the learner's vocational area

- create responsibility for their own learning
- initiate peer support systems
- maintain a routine in the classroom language
- create clear concise handouts, using images
- use personal dictionaries.

Motivation and generating enthusiasm are the most challenging tasks that a teacher is faced with. My suggestion is always to go back to basics: assume nothing and find out what makes your learners tick. Remember that things happen around us and that will change how learners feel about their surroundings, targets and aspirations. Respond logically, encourage and remember that it is easier to criticise than praise; we all like a 'well done' or 'thank you'.

Resources – strengths and limitations

REVISION

In Part One, Chapter 2, you listed the types of resources available to teachers, for example: boards, projectors, paper-based, games and audiovisual resources, and justified and evaluated their use in your lessons.

The resources most commonly used in the classroom are:

- Wipe board
- Flip chart
- Interactive board
- PowerPoint presentation
- Handouts
- Overhead transparencies
- Games
- Models
- Video/DVD.

Resources generally enhance the verbal (auditory) teaching methods by providing a visual stimulus. Some resources can engage learners when being used so they meet kinaesthetic learning preferences.

Resource	Strengths	Limitations
Wipe board	Role models note-taking skills, notes key words and spellings, can be colourful, widely available, easy to use, can pre-prepare headlines, visible, cheap, doesn't break down	Non-permanent record, need to keep cleaning board to make space, slippery surface may make handwriting illegible, sustained use makes them difficult to keep clean, fixed position, encourages teacher to have back to room
Flip chart	Paper can be distributed around learners for interactive group work/display, moveable, can double as small wipe board, pads can be pre-prepared	Paper not always available, bulky if moved any distance, small writing space
Interactive board	Writings can be saved/printed, modern, professional, versatile as write-on board or display board, anything visible on computer screen can be displayed in a group setting and retrieved at a later date	Semi-permanent record, very expensive to purchase, not widely available, training needed before effective use, needs a special pen to write with, writing looks odd
PowerPoint presentation	Updated version of overhead projector and slides, graphics and animations aid interest, speed of use can dictate pace of lesson, modern, professional delivery with large audiences	Projection equipment needed which is expensive and noisy, tends to be over-used or poorly used, reliant on hardware which may not work, not widely available in community or workplace environments

Resource	Strengths	Limitations
Handouts	Easy to create, copy and use, versatile, wide variety of formats, permanent record to take away, printed versions make good quality editions, can be laminated to preserve, easy to adapt for differentiation, wide range of styles and uses	Overused at times, learners don't always read them fully, can get tatty when continually reproduced, especially copying from copies or reusing, need to consider copyright when copying from texts
Overhead transparencies	Widely available, portable, can build up pictures and diagrams, colourful, relatively easy to create, can be retained for future use if stored in dust-free area, can be used to pace lesson, good with large audiences	Slightly outdated, slides difficult to keep in pristine condition, different types of transparency needed for write-on, copiers and printers, projector is noisy and relies on power source
Games	Fun activities, tabular/text formats can easily be made into games for group work	Time-consuming to create or expensive to purchase
Models	Three dimensional, either life-sized or scale versions, good to feel/see/smell, ideal in 1:1 or small group settings, ideal to use/prepare for dangerous or expensive situations	Difficult to store, expensive to purchase or difficult to make
Video/DVD	Good method of aiding comprehension, appeals to all age groups, visual	Display equipment required which is expensive, not widely available and reliant on power sources

Resources are used either to aid teaching or to aid learning. The most effective resources stimulate a number of senses, are versatile and easy to use, achieve what they set out to achieve and are simple. There is no single resource that is purely advantageous to prepare and use, so the teacher must weigh up the strengths and limitations, and consider their learners and the environment in which they work. Then they can make informed decisions about what resources they should use.

New and emerging technologies

Most new and emerging technologies are associated with either computers or microchip technologies. It is obvious that teachers will use these (sometimes) labour-saving devices to appeal to their modern learners.

However, there is still a place for tried and tested methods and the key to successful teaching is a blended approach, that is, complementing traditional and modern technologies to aid effective learning. The interaction between the modern and the traditional adds variety, meets different needs and doesn't compromise the skills of the teacher. Inspectorates such as Ofsted advocate that poor learning is linked to lack of use of modern learning technologies (Ofsted, Annual Report 2004/05).

Some of the modern technologies, very often referred to as ILT (information learning technology) or ICT (information and communication technology), are listed below:

- World Wide Web (www)/Internet – a vast array of useful (and useless) information. Learners can be directed to sites for further reading or research or the sites can be downloaded (displayed) for use in class and for learners to engage with the activities contained within the sites. Copyright laws apply to how the Internet is used and transmitted. The teacher should be cautious about its use: a web page can be written by anyone and there are no guarantees about the accuracy of the information they contain; sometimes a very innocent word used in a search engine has different connotations – check it out first, especially with younger or vulnerable learners. Use of 'cut and paste' sometimes incites the learner to plagiarise work by inaccurate referencing

- Intranet – organisational-based web pages, similar to the Internet. Specific readings or information pages can be uploaded (put onto the intranet) to support learning

- VLE – (virtual learning environment) provides alternative learning strategies, without the need for direct contact. Brands commonly seen are Moodle, Blackboard, and LearnWise etc. They can support distance learning packages, support material, tracking systems, chat areas and email functions. Usually accessed and protected through password protection software

- Mobile phones – to text, email or surf the Internet, make video clips

- Digital cameras – a permanent record of practical activities

- Presentation software – PowerPoint

- Interactive boards – used as a board or display screen, touch or mouse-controlled through a PC or laptop or with a DVD player

- Electronic voting systems – an up-to-date version of multiple choice questioning seen on TV as audience-interactive answer systems

- Weblogs (blogs) – personal diary and chat facilities. Their educational use is not yet proven, although it has potential, it is not reliable in terms of content or accessibility.

Resources needed to facilitate the use of modern technologies:

- A computer (PC or laptop)

- A screen

- A projector

- Speakers

- Peripherals (devices associated with a computer: keyboard, mouse etc.)

- Software.

When incorporating ILT or ICT into your teaching you should bear in mind how it is accessed. Not everyone has a computer, nor does every learning environment support the use of modern technologies. Thus a totally ILT/ICT-based learning medium would not be inclusive. This further supports the earlier suggestion of a blended approach. By all means offer it as an alternative means of learning and include it in teaching if you can, but remember that it doesn't suit everyone, nor is every teacher comfortable with its use and by offering both traditional and modern strategies you will be able to differentiate and vary your teaching.

Promoting equality, supporting diversity

Equality and **diversity** are terms which are expressed quite frequently, yet usually without a clear explanation of what the terms mean. So, here goes . . .

Equality means more about compliance with the law than diversity. It pre-empts discrimination by adhering to a systematic policy approach to ensure organisations stay within the boundaries of the legislation. It covers gender, race, disability, age, religion and sexual orientation.

REVISION

In Part One, Chapter 1, we looked at the legislation brought into being to support equality and diversity. We also considered some of the things that the teacher can do in the classroom to enhance their practice.

Society is diverse. Some people are old, some are young. Some are disabled, some black, some have children, some are male – everyone is different but everyone is valued and respected.

Some stats:

By 2010 only 20 per cent of the UK working population will be white, male, able-bodied and under 45.

Ethnic minorities make up 7.9 per cent of the population; in London it is 31 per cent.

National Council Voluntary Organisations – Defining Diversity
http://www.ncvo-vol.org.uk – accessed 30.06.07

Diversity recognises and celebrates differences; it supports equality by respecting rights, valuing individual talents and advocating that everyone's skills are fully utilised. Failing to promote diversity has an expensive outcome; there is a risk of litigation by dissatisfied customers, there is a risk that funding by public bodies will be discontinued and there is the possibility that the organisation's reputation may be harmed.

The equality agenda is more about conformity to laws and policy interpretations. It helps to ensure that the organisation supports equality by advising staff, learners and other stakeholders about its standards. The diversity agenda, in seeking to celebrate the differences in society, looks at the culture of the organisation to check that it promotes equality throughout its business practices.

- Expressed beliefs – that practices do not stereotype or make assumptions
- Cultural forms – that books and media are appropriate and jokes are not biased
- Knowledge systems – that learning resources and the curriculum offer is relevant and appropriate.

It will operate at three levels:

1   Individual – checking for verbal, physical abuse and discriminatory acts
2   Organisational – that practices, policies and procedures are *in situ*
3   Structural – that buildings support an inclusive regime.

Equality and diversity not only affect teachers' practices, but require the teacher to advocate equality and diversity in their learners. For example, comments of an unfair nature must be challenged rather than ignored and, irrespective of the **demography** of the learning environment, learners are prepared for the national balance.

ACTIVITY 3

Self-evaluation: How equal and diverse is your practice?

How well do you do in terms of equality and diversity? Use this evaluation table, but try to avoid yes/no answers by making a comment that discusses how it is and/or how it ought to be.

Have you attended equality and diversity training?	
How diverse are your learners?	
Can your learners explain about bullying and harassment?	
Do the placement providers that you use have equality and diversity procedures in place?	
What is the demography of the community you serve?	
Do you monitor applications, retention and achievement in terms of gender, age, ethnicity etc.?	
Is your course generally taken up by a particular group of people?	
How are complaints dealt with?	
Do social and enrichment events celebrate the diverse society?	
Are all religious festivals recorded on the business calendar?	
Do your resources and teaching methods promote equality and diversity?	

From your answers, you should now write down ideas about how you can develop your inclusive practice to ensure equality and diversity.

Identifying functional skill abilities of learners

In 1998, the Moser Report highlighted the poor basic skills in society, saying that one in five people were functionally illiterate. The Leitch Review in 2006 stated that one-third of adults do not have basic school leaving qualifications. **Functional skills** are a key element of the 14–19 reforms as set out in the 14–19 Education and Skills White Paper (DfES 2005), which defines functional skills as:

> Core elements of English, mathematics, and ICT that provide an individual with essential knowledge, skills and understanding that will enable them to operate confidently, effectively and independently in life and work.
>
> 14–19 Education and Skills: Implementation Plan
> (Feb. 2005) www.dfes.gov.uk

The Basic Skills Agency (2001) writes:

> The ability to read, write and speak English and to use mathematics at a level necessary to function and progress at work and in society in general.
>
> http://www.basic–skills.co.uk

REVISION

In Part One, Chapter 2, you were introduced to the meaning and purpose of functional skills, reviewed their location within the National Qualifications Framework (**NQF**), and looked at how functional skills could be embedded into the curriculum.

In the post-compulsory sector, we are constantly faced with meeting the people these reports refer to. The reasons behind these levels of ability are varied and subjective, but suffice to say, they are real and may inhibit our learners' abilities to achieve their potential. It may be appropriate here to describe what a learner should be expected to be able to do at the various levels as a means of setting the benchmark for identifying the skills required of learners entering your specific career or vocational area.

Literacy	Numeracy
At Level 1, someone can:	
● Take part in an interview for a job or course or follow a simple procedure in a manual ● Fill out an application form for a driving licence or passport	● Read bus and train timetables correctly ● Follow direction to mix, dilute substances in proportion ● Estimate distances using scales printed on a map
At Entry 3, someone can:	
● Obtain information or advice from a telephone helpline ● Read a job advert in a local paper or job centre ● Write a short letter to a family member or friend	● Understand price labels on prepacked food ● Check the receipt and money when paying for goods ● Use a map to find a location, e.g., for an interview
At Entry 2, someone can:	
● Respond to a question and know when to ask for help ● Follow simple instructions on a vending machine ● Fill in a simple form	● Understand measurements and sizes on labels ● Use simple measuring equipment, e.g., scales ● Understand expiry dates and renewal dates, e.g., food labels, road tax
At Entry 1, someone can:	
● Follow a one-step verbal instruction ● Understand common signs in their local area and at work, e.g., toilets, no smoking ● Write their own name and address on an official form	● Select the correct numbered button in a lift ● Count the correct number of drinks for visitors ● Key in a telephone number

http://www.advice-resources.co.uk/adviceresources/general/guides/bsa/bsa.pdf

ACTIVITY 4

In the context of your subject, what functional skills do learners of that subject need in order to be proficient?

It may help to break those skills down:

Literacy:
Speaking
Listening
Writing
Reading

Mathematics:
Numbers
Measurement and shape
Handling data

You should think about the skills required to achieve technical or knowledge abilities AND skills to aid learning.

People need functional skills for different reasons:

1   Those who need a quick update to get their skills to the required level
2   Those who need minimal support in functional literacy or numeracy
3   Those who need specific targeted help to develop their skills.

There is a fourth group who may need support and that is those whose first language is not English. In this group they may be literate and numerate in their mother tongue but not able to transfer those skills into a second language.

Identifying problems in functional skills

Screening The obvious thing to do as part of your enrolment or selection process is to check that your learners have the minimum requirements for entering your programme. For example: entry to a

National Diploma requires 5 GCSEs at C or above (or equivalent). It is the 'equivalent' that usually causes problems, but the NQF (see Chapter 2), guides you to academic and vocational equivalents and a CV will help you decide about the skill levels of mature learners.

Initial assessment The next check is likely to be at induction. You can observe and/or interview your learners. You can look at set pieces of writing and ask questions to identify ability levels. Learners with poor functional skills, especially the more mature ones, are adept at disguising those skills. Some things that may alert you to problems are:

- 'I forgot my glasses, so I can't do it'
- 'I'm in a rush, can I take it home and do it later?'
- Patchy completion of the enrolment or application form.
- Distracting conversations or behaviours.

Some strategies that help to reassure learners about why you need to do these initial assessments include:

- Talking about improving skills rather than poor skills
- Raise self-esteem; motivate by looking at values and reasons
- Explanations
- Discussing outcomes and support.

Diagnostic The final method of checking ability is usually either a routine strategy of induction or a response if you suspect that there may be inadequacies in functional skills. There are a range of tests, both paper-based and online, to ascertain the level of ability. Some learners with poor functional skills benefit from computer-aided resources. It is highly likely that learners will have what is called a 'spiky profile'. This means that they are good at some aspects and weaker in others, causing them to be at different levels on the NQF.

Useful online resources

http://www.basic-skills.co.uk/resourcecentre
http://www.learndirect-advice.co.uk/helpwithyourcareer/jobprofiles/
http://www.move-on.org.uk

Adapting resources

Adapting resources to meet needs, both yours and your learners, is similar to adapting methods of presentation and assessment to benefit learners. Resources are not only the equipment and paper you take into the classroom, but you and your support mechanisms. A resource is anything which aids either the teaching or learning. There are some very simple rules when making sure that your resources are fit for purpose:

- Keep it simple, both in its creation and use.
- Ensure purposefulness – why create a resource that does not offer any value to the learning process?
- Be confident – practice how you will use the resource, especially if using it for the first time.
- Equipment – have you got access to what you need to use your resource?

REVISION

In Part One, Chapter 2, you reviewed a range of resources and were able to identify how to use them in the context of your own teaching subject.

Why do we use resources?

- To create interest
- To explain things visually
- To provide information
- As a memory aid
- To collect information
- To create active learners
- To promote autonomy
- To offer variety
- To promote equality
- To communicate
- To differentiate.

The adaptations that are made depend on what resources you use, how you use resources, and when you use resources. Earlier chapters and sections within this chapter have detailed some ideas about adapting resources. These involve considering your learners, what they are studying, how they are studying and all the variables that emerge as you get to know your learners. Some of the simplest and more common adaptations that can be made are:

- To include white space – learners can add notes during your presentation, thus engaging with the resource
- To include images – to enhance visual appearance and create interest
- To word process handouts and OHTs, with appropriate font styles and sizes
- To miss out words – again to engage learners with the handout or PowerPoint
- To address inclusivity (paper/print colour, size, language, expression, etc.)
- To slow down your speed of writing on the board which helps to improve legibility
- To use reveal and overlay techniques to create pace in the lesson
- To use key points or bullet points rather than lots of text.

To consolidate this section, try this activity to analyse one of your resources:

 ## ACTIVITY 5

Adapting resources

Take one handout or print out from a PowerPoint presentation or web page (or similar text-based resource) that you have used in the last few weeks.

Analyse the following:

What percentage of the resource is white space?	
Is it read-only or is the learner required to interact with the resource?	

How many images are in the resource?	
What is the presentation style?	
Is the resource prose, subtitle/ text, bullet point or key word?	
What is the balance between the presentation style (same/varied)	
What is the font style and font size?	
How do you know if the information contained within the resource is understood?	

How can you improve the resource to meet the needs of:

● Visual learners?
● Kinaesthetic learners?
● ESOL learners?
● Entry Level learners?
● Level 3+ learners?

Is the resource fully referenced?

Are there additional links to further information or websites?

Can the resource be effectively used as:

● A teacher's aid?
● A learning aid?
● A revision tool?
● An assessment tool?

Review the resource and *adapt* it accordingly. Keep before and after versions to show your personal development, and *reflect* on this activity with a colleague or tutor.

Glossary of terms

ADHD Attention deficit/hyperactivity disorder

Autonomy independence in the ability to learn

Concept an idea

Demography a study of population trends

Diversity valuing and celebrating the differences in people

Equality ensuring fairness

Functional skills basic skills of literacy and numeracy

Gifted and talented learners highly skilled or adept

NQF National Qualifications Framework

VLE virtual learning environment – a modern teaching and learning style using computer technologies

 SUMMARY

....

In this chapter we set out to achieve the following outcomes:

- Identify learning activities and list factors that motivate learners

- Describe how motivation and inclusive learning sessions link to provide opportunities to enthuse your learners and encourage them to meet their full potential

- Analyse the advantages and disadvantages of using a range of resources and how they contribute to effective learning

- Describe some of the new technologies which support learning and analyse how they enhance learning

- Explain the terms equality and diversity and why these agendas are required

- Evaluate your own methods, comparing them to standards and identify strategies for promoting and improving practice ▶

- Compare and contrast the functional skill abilities of your learners with the functional skill needs of your curriculum
- State the importance and methods of identifying functional skills in both contexts and how to develop literacy, numeracy and information communication technology skills
- Suggest ways of modifying resources to meet individual needs of learners and to suit curriculum requirements whilst maintaining an inclusive learning environment

Your Personal Development

You will have looked at motivation theories, considered your own level of motivation and reflected on how this affects your learning and what could be done to improve motivation.

You have reviewed a range of resources and compared the advantages and disadvantages of their uses, commenting on how they can be adapted in order to be fit for purpose. You have analysed a resource, commenting on possible adaptations. You have evaluated and reflected upon how new technologies are appropriate and relevant in the learning environment.

You have developed your awareness of equality and diversity and how and why it is important. You have undertaken a self-assessment of your own practices, identifying areas for development and improvement.

In the final section, you have revisited functional skills needs and started to explore how functional skills are important in your specific curriculum area in preparing your learners for study and work.

You should be able to answer questions relating to:

- Equality and diversity in the classroom
- Adapting resources for inclusive learning
- Development of functional skills.

And demonstrate:

- Appropriate selection of resources in your teaching situations.

CHAPTER 9
(PEL)

Effective communication skills

LEARNING OBJECTIVES

The measurable outcomes that you will achieve by reading this chapter and completing the activities are:

....

- To state the main theoretical ideas surrounding communication models and describe methods that create effective communication
- To express ideas which will enhance communication skills in your learners and yourself
- To state why communication is not always effective and describe the effects this has on learning
- To describe the role and communication lines between the various stakeholders in the education process and state the importance of liaison

Communication methods

In Part One, Chapter 4, you discovered that **communication** is the art of passing messages and can occur mainly by written, verbal and non-verbal methods. You also considered how some things will turn out to be a barrier to **effective** communication.

Communication theory – Shannon and Weaver model

One easy to understand model of communication was suggested by Shannon and Weaver in 1949. This is a basic model in which they say that all communication needs:

- An encoder – the means of sending the message (speaking/writing)
- A message – something to say
- A channel – a way of sending the message
- A decoder – a means of receiving the message (listening/reading)
- A receiver – the person to send the message to.

They further add that communication is hindered by noise.

This model is satisfactory in so far that it explains how communication is transmitted; however, it does not suggest how messages need to be understood in order to be effective. Nor does it address how individuals put their own interpretation on messages and that those interpretations sometimes confuse the issue.

Remember our first rule of teaching
ASSUME NOTHING

| Figure 9A | Communication model – Claude Shannon and Warren Weaver 1949/ David Berlo (1960) |

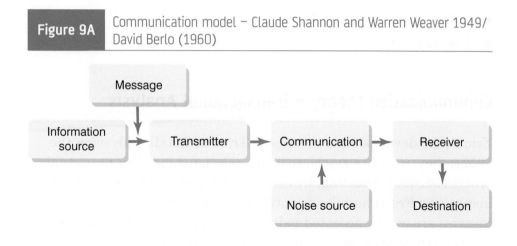

Just because we have said or written something, it does not mean that it has been received and understood. This leads us to consider the many skills required when communicating.

- *Listening* – The ability to hear what is being said
- *Comprehension* – The ability to understand what is being said
- *Speaking* – The ability to express thoughts and messages clearly
- *Writing* – The ability to express thoughts and messages legibly
- *Negotiating* – The ability to agree or compromise with others in discussions
- *Reading* – The ability to understand written text
- *Empathising* – The ability to understand and share feelings and emotions
- *Using numeracy* – The ability to use numbers to express ideas
- *Persuading* – The ability to reason or argue your beliefs in discussion
- *Networking* – The ability to work in a group to share ideas
- *Assertiveness* – The ability to be forceful and confident
- *Sharing information* – The ability to contribute to or take part in discussions
- *Speaking and writing in a foreign language* – The ability to express ideas to those whose language is different to your own.

This is critical to:

- Workplace harmony

- Effective teaching and learning
- Productivity.

Communication theory – Transactional Analysis

Eric Berne developed his theories of Transactional Analysis in the 1950s; they are more associated with relationships than the actual process of communicating, which offers another perspective. He was inspired by Freud and the scientific developments of the era. His theories are widely accepted today, but are being modified to meet the modern environment. You will find that they are applied in a wide variety of contexts including medical research, personality analysis and management development as well as communication theory. Not surprisingly, he ascertained that communication was at the centre of human relationships and that communication was natural. He argues that it is a stimulus: thus, we will always speak when spoken to. He does quantify this by saying that those responses will vary according to our 'alter ego states'. Each person is made up of three alter **ego** states: parent, adult and child.

Parent ego state This is our voice of authority, very often typified by tried and tested statements, learned from our parents, For example the parent would say: 'under no circumstances', 'always', and advocate values such as don't lie, cheat etc. The **body language** may show impatience and the verbal language includes patronising expressions.

Child ego state This is our dependent state. This is typified by us seeking assurances, or at its worse displaying immature behaviours. It may display temper tantrums, whining voices, baby talk, excuses and big words used incorrectly.

Adult ego state This is our independent state; the ability to think and act responsibly and maturely. The physical appearance is attentive and non-threatening. Sentences include reasons and negotiated styles.

The styles are not limited to words and also include non-verbal expressions.

Berne states that effective communication is when the states are equal. For example, when someone in the parent state talks to someone in the child state, it is only effective if it is returned in the same style, i.e. the child accepts they are communicating with a parent. Thus the dialogue with younger learners who may be seeking guidance and reassurance as they enter post-compulsory education is usually a parent–child type. As learners mature you are more likely to see adult to adult communications. In short, Berne argues that effective communication is more about relationships than the act of sending and receiving messages.

 **ACTIVITY 1**

Scenario

It is the beginning of a new term and the inexperienced teacher is working with a group of 14-year-olds in a vocational setting. Communication is failing and as a result creates a poor behaviour management situation. The teacher thinks that they cannot teach or manage this group and becomes confrontational.

Using Berne's theories of Transactional Analysis, explain the underlying causes of this communication problem. How could the teacher improve this scenario?

The teacher probably made the assumption that the learners wanted to learn the subject, would be motivated and probably enjoy an environment different to that of the methods seen in schools. Using Berne's theory, you may be likely to see the teacher initially trying to communicate in an adult–child position. Unfortunately, this was the first mistake. Younger learners have to learn how to communicate in an adult way. From the day they were born, they (the learners) have communicated in parent–child positions and this is mirrored in schools. In a confrontational situation a child–child position emerges and usually goes nowhere! It is part of the transition between compulsory and post-compulsory education that a parent–child style is maintained and as trust and maturity develop, then a more adult–adult position can be adopted.

Communication in teaching

Communication occurs in every teaching and learning interaction.

- *A presentation* – speaking, listening, reading and writing occur in the preparation and delivery of every presentation. Both learners and teacher present information during their programme.
- *Assignments* – learners will communicate to you through their writing and they will have engaged in communication throughout the gathering of information. The ability to express themselves accurately in their written work is essential to language development.
- *Questioning* – either verbal or written; teachers and learners have to speak or write and listen or read in order to understand and respond to the question.
- *Verbal exposition* – teachers are offering information, learners are listening, comprehending and hopefully rephrasing into their own notes. Again accuracy in spelling, grammar and punctuation is essential to ensure meaning and correct interpretation.
- *Feedback* – teachers and learners need to be able to communicate effectively in order to support learning.

Modern communication channels Teaching and learning is being modernised as communication develops and evolves using modern technologies. We email each other frequently, our learners text us to let us know they will be late, we can receive and mark work online, learning programmes can be 'taught' remotely using distance learning and self-study packs, possibly linked to virtual learning environments (VLEs). Increasingly we blog and chat about things in our lives and participate in forums to ask questions and discuss issues. We need not now attend meetings (or lessons!) if we can use video conferencing, web cams and conference calls. Our learners might even catch up with missed lessons by downloading a webcast or podcast! Whilst these technologies continue to improve and become more interactive, there is nothing which beats a blended approach to learning. So don't get too carried away yet, there is still considerable value in communicating face to face and of course, we should not disadvantage those learners who are technophobes or simply do not have access to such resources.

Authenticity In communicating with learners and other stakeholders it is essential to validate the authenticity of what is spoken and written. Whilst it is easy to identify whose thoughts are being expressed when using direct assessment methods such as observation and questioning, it is not so easy through some of the other assessment methods, for example assignments and essays. Unfortunately, whilst the Internet is valuable to research, it is also easy to express other people's ideas and claim them as your own. This is plagiarism. See Chapter 29, pp. 601–602 and Appendix C: Study Skills, p. 648.

Improving communication; barriers to learning

REVISION

In Part One, Chapters 2 and 4, you discovered that there are numerous reasons for communication not to work. Using DELTA (disability, emotional, language, technology and ability) classifications and considering language tone and style you discovered that you are able to modify your teaching to overcome these barriers.

Improving communication

Negotiating is one of the keys to effective communication. Finding out why learners want to do something (or not), and establishing compromise is when and how a more favourable environment will emerge; a more adult relationship. This will not occur overnight, just because a 16-year-old has started college and thinks they are grown up, it does not necessarily follow that they are adult. This maturity may take up to six months (or longer) to develop before that 16-year-old starts to understand the needs, language and behaviours associated with post-compulsory education. Try not to give up too soon!

Communication is essential in the learning environment and it becomes more effective when enhanced by active learning strategies:

Oral skills can be developed by talking in class, discussions and questioning. By offering learners time to 'solo free write' you are giving all of them time to consider their answers, and this will develop how they participate in constructive talking by increasing their confidence in speaking. Similarly, allowing pair time or small group time to discuss issues and then a feedback slot improves knowledge and thus confidence.

Writing skills can be enhanced by note-taking, class and homework exercises, written assessments. In any activity that you do you should encourage writing skills, even if the writing is in note form. It could be a handout where the learner has to complete missing words, or ideas expressed in writing using note, report and essay formats.

Listening skills can be enhanced by discussion groups, role play activities and teacher talk sessions. These sessions develop listening skills by creating opportunities during which learners have to listen to other ideas; those ideas can be consolidated into their own evaluative work. Asking learners to present mini seminars about a subject will result in them responding to questions posed by others in the group, which results in comprehension activities. ICT skills may also be developed if presenting information using software packages.

Reading skills can be enhanced by paraphrasing, case studies and comprehension activities. By giving a learner something to read and asking them to do something as a result, it demonstrates their understanding of the subject.

These active learning ideas both develop the basics of communication as well as creating lively things to do in class. Even the most passive activity of listening can be enlivened by asking learners to do something with the information just received. The responses from learners will confirm the effectiveness of your communication – that is: is the message received and understood?

How do you know if communication is effective?

There are some simple watch points:

- Facial expressions
- Loss of attention
- Noise level rises
- Leaning back on seats.

There are some simple checks:

- Ask open questions
- Gather feedback
- Recap asking for explanations
- Listen to conversations in group activities.

By watching out for change you will soon pick up vibes about effectiveness.

CHECKLIST FOR COMMUNICATION EFFECTIVENESS	
Language used was clear and used tone and expression to create mood	
Technical words and jargon terms were explained	
Learners' body language demonstrated interest in the speaker	

▶

CHECKLIST FOR COMMUNICATION EFFECTIVENESS (*continued*)

Facilities created for writing, listening and effective recording of information	
Questions were relevant and were open in style (demanding answer – not yes/no response)	
Clarification was sought if unsure about intended meanings – by teacher, by learner, by support assistants	
Feedback was unambiguous	
Activity and learning summaries were clear and highlighted key issues	
Suitable communication strategies were used to ensure all learners participated	
Background noise is minimised	
Communication assessment How was communication effectiveness assessed? By self, peers, learners, tutors, other: _____	
Reflections about how communication can be improved:	

Barriers to learning

Petty explains communication as a chain of events, in which a message is developed, transmitted, heard and comprehended. He expresses this as:

> What I mean → what I say → what they hear → what they understand.

> (Petty 2004: 38)

He refers to the game of Chinese whispers as a means of proving that communication as a messaging system can sometimes go a little awry. This, however, is a linear model, a one-way process: effective communication is formed from a two-way process. That is, there needs to be some form of check to ensure that what is said has been understood.

Just because you are a good teacher and everything around you is conducive to learning, it does not necessarily follow that your learners will be able to learn. Sometimes, their previous experiences in learning will form a barrier which will prevent learning occurring; with widening participation in learning comes a variety of behaviours which, if inappropriate, can interrupt or constrain the learning process, resulting in **disengaged** learners and problems with attendance and punctuality. Additionally, staff may be reluctant to meet the new challenges in the curriculum, and be expected to cope with learners who bring their many characteristics and individualities. These obstacles must be managed.

Some of the main issues that you will see in learners are: lack of confidence; lack of vocational/basic skills; lack of understanding about expectations and ineffective transition from the previous to the current learning programme. These can be overcome by:

● Access to preparatory courses
● Learning at a level/pace relevant to need
● Modes of attendance to meet need
● Negotiated learning
● Targeted learning
● Supported learning
● Structured tutorials.

Increasingly, the principle of putting the learners first when designing programmes is being demonstrated in schemes and session plans. This can be achieved by:

● Delivering topics practically before underpinning with theory;
● Designing the curriculum to meet learner needs rather than staffing needs;

- Addressing deficiencies on functional skills by differentiating, discrete provision, flexible learning materials, learning support, but always embedding the skills and supporting the development of learners;
- Using **holistic** learning strategies to minimise repetition in programmes;
- Preparing learners for learning;
- Spreading out assessment over duration of course;
- Assessing with consideration of other commitments of learners.

Equally, you might not be good at getting the message across, in which case you need to review your methods and adapt your strategies accordingly.

Liaising with learners, peers and other stakeholders

Liaising means to co-operate. It is important that everyone in the educational **context** is working to the same outcome, even if they are motivated by different drivers. Let us consider the various people (the stakeholders) involved:

The learner

The learner wants to achieve their learning aim or ambition. There are sometimes periods when this is not their primary goal (other factors may influence their progress), but generally they are enrolled to reach a specific goal. They will liaise with their teachers and employers – or if under 18, their parents.

The learners' parents or guardians

Learners aged below 18 remain the responsibility of their parents or guardians. As such they care about the progress of their wards and may contribute to that process (to varying degrees). They will liaise with teachers and learners.

Teachers or tutors

They are involved in the process of helping their learners develop. They will be a team of people, each responsible for a specific part of their curriculum. They will liaise with learners, parents or employers (dependent upon age of learner), other teaching staff and managers.

Management teams

They oversee the work of teachers and undertake quality assurance arrangements. They will liaise with teachers, governors and funding bodies.

Governors/board of directors

They have overall responsibility for the running of the organisation. They will liaise with the management team and funding bodies.

Employers

Employers will either send their staff for training or receive people at the end of their training and education. They want to ensure that training offered in either case is relevant to their needs and is up to date. They liaise with learners and teachers and funding bodies.

Funding bodies

They provide the money to pay for courses and training and therefore want assurances that the monies are well spent. Funding may be from public or private sources. They will liaise with employers, managers and the governorship or directorate.

Other people in the process are:

- Corporate services (finance, personnel, admissions),
- Careers, employment agencies
- Awarding bodies, regulatory bodies
- Inspectorates
- Government bodies, and
- Care and support services.

Whilst each has a valuable role, their contact is usually restricted to one of the group of primary stakeholders, listed above.

The co-operation between all of these groups of people is vital to the smooth running of the organisation. Communication between the parties ensures that learners receive the most **efficient** and effective learning that can possibly be provided. The learner is at the **hub**. Without learners, teachers wouldn't have anyone to teach, parents and employers would not need or be able to promote training as a means of economic survival, funding bodies would not need to support learning and managers and governors would not have organisations to strategically direct. Therefore, it is not surprising that most educational initiatives are responsive to learner needs, yet oddly they (the learners) are very often the smallest voice in educational development, although this is changing with the emergence of 'Learner Voice' strategies.

By representing this sequence visually, you will see the possible reason for the learner voice not having a strong impact on how education happens. It may be a cynical viewpoint, but the people who control education have the least dealings with those who participate in it, which means it befalls the teacher, who has a greater role in the liaising between those involved in the process of education, to ensure meaning and value are provided for all stakeholders. So, whilst the learner is the centre of the education, the teacher is the centre of the communication.

Figure 9B Communication channels

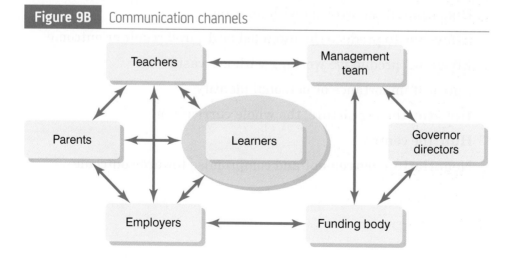

Whilst discussing stakeholders, it may be appropriate to mention 'the learning contract'. It is becoming more and more frequent that learners are asked to sign documents committing to achievement, attendance or compliance to rules.

Arguments for:

- Learner is clear about expectations
- Learner commits to a learning agenda.

Arguments against:

- Value to learner or organisation
- Legal requirement or moral value.

It is quite acceptable that these documents are used; however, how binding they are remains an issue.

Glossary of terms

Body language using conscious or unconscious gesture to express feelings

Communication a means of sending and receiving information to share or exchange ideas

Context the setting in which learning occurs

Disengaged uninvolved with learning

Effective to produce the intended or desired result or outcome

Efficient productive working without waste

Ego self-importance or personal identity

Holistic the big picture; the whole curriculum

Hub the centre

Negotiation agreement and compromise towards outcome

SUMMARY

In this chapter we set out to achieve the following outcomes:

- State the main theoretical ideas surrounding communication models and describe methods that create effective communication
- Express ideas which will enhance communication skills in your learners and yourself
- State why communication is not always effective and describe the effects this has on learning
- Describe the role and communication lines between the various stakeholders in the education process and state the importance of liaison

Your Personal Development

You will have looked at theories of communication and seen how they can be applied to the dialogue between teacher and learner. You have considered ways that communication can be made more effective and the impact that effective communication has on the learning process. Finally, you have reviewed the roles of people associated with learning and identified how they must liaise with each other to improve the learning environment.

You should be able to answer questions relating to:

- Effective communication
- Methods of communication
- Communication theory
- Active learning to develop communication
- Efficient liaison between stakeholders.

CHAPTER 10 (PEL)

The minimum core

LEARNING OBJECTIVES

The measurable outcomes that you will achieve by reading this chapter and completing the activities are:

- To develop competence in language, literacy, numeracy and information communication technologies (ICT)
- To identify opportunities to develop your skills and understanding of literacy, language, numeracy and ICT
- To demonstrate your progress through referencing teaching and learning activities and your personal development to the standards

Overview of the minimum core

This chapter considers the ways in which you can develop your skills of **literacy**, **language**, number and information and communication technologies. It should be read in conjunction with the latest guidance from the Lifelong Learning UK (**LLUK**) skills council about literacy, language, **numeracy** and **ICT** (**minimum core**) standards. This is available from http://www.lluk.org.

One of the first things that should be done as part of your qualification is to find out your current ability in the minimum core themes and then identify how you will develop them. This will probably be done by initially asking you to produce any previous certificates in the subjects, for example, GCSEs, O levels, A levels or adult literacy or numeracy tests. If you do not have such certificates, or can't find them, you may be asked to sit **diagnostic assessments** to confirm your level of competence. This information will then be transferred to your individual learning plan (**ILP**). Most providers of teacher training will specify the minimum level of competence required to enter their programmes. Generally, if you do not hold at least a Level 2 qualification in English or literacy, you will struggle to meet the requirements of the assessment of the programme and risk not being confident to teach or assess your learners. You should seek additional support should this be the case.

Summary of the minimum core elements

Language and literacy:

- Personal, social and cultural factors influencing language and literacy learning and development
- Explicit knowledge about language and the four skills: speaking, listening, reading and writing
- Personal language skills.

Numeracy:

- Personal, social and cultural factors influencing numeracy learning and development
- Explicit knowledge about numeracy communication and processes
- Personal numeracy skills.

Information and communication technology (ICT):

- Personal, social and cultural factors influencing ICT learning and development
- Explicit knowledge about ICT
- Personal ICT skills.

Each section of the minimum core requires you to have both the skills and understanding to develop the functional skills of your learners and your own personal functional skills. In Preparing to Teach in the Lifelong Learning Sector (PTLLS) there is no requirement to meet the minimum core, although you may find that it is at this point that your own skills are first analysed. In the first year of the Diploma in Teaching in the Lifelong Learning Sector (DTLLS) the focus is on the development of personal skills. There will not be any assessment other than for the purpose of proving that development. Your programme will include opportunities to develop the skills either embedded into the programme, as part of your teaching experience, within a continuing professional development programme or as a stand-alone class.

The second year of the Diploma in Teaching in the Lifelong Learning Sector (DTLLS) will include both personal skill development and developing knowledge and understanding elements. This will be reviewed regularly and targeted developments made. The minimum core is initially to be assessed through **self-assessment**. Whilst in its introductory stage there are no formal assessment requirements. It is anticipated, however, that external testing will soon be introduced to measure the development and outcomes.

Note: The coding system used within the standards below is unique to this publication and is used to link the suggested activities with the standards.

Some of the activities listed below are more effective when carried out under the supervision of a literacy, numeracy or ICT specialist.

Developing literacy and language skills

In the same way that you may be developing your learners' functional skill needs, your own personal skills may benefit from a similar exercise. For the teacher these skills will be development from Level 2 skills (at entry) to Level 3 skills (on exit). These skills are known as the *minimum core*. That means the standard of literacy, language, numeracy and ICT required of teachers. There is still much national development in this subject in so far as it will apply to teachers – are the skills embedded and evidenced through the role or is there a need for testing? It really is watch this space at the moment, but this section concentrates on developing skills as part of the role, rather than attempting to 'teach' Level 3 functional skills in literacy, language, numeracy and ICT.

Listed below are the standards of competence required of teachers. They will probably seem complex and confusing at first – it is normal to think that. Your tutor will guide you through the process by creating an individual learning plan to identify exactly what you need to do to develop the skills. This may vary according to the skills you possess as you start the programme and changes in policy and assessment of functional skills.

The minimum core standards (literacy)

Part A   Knowledge and understanding

Personal, social and cultural factors influencing language and literacy learning and development

- The different factors affecting the acquisition and development of language and literacy skills (LAK1)
- The importance of English language and literacy in enabling users to participate in public life, society and the modern economy (LAK2)

- Potential barriers that can hinder development of language skills (LAK3)
- The main learning disabilities and difficulties relating to language learning and skill development (LAK4)
- Multilingualism and the role of the first language in the acquisition of additional languages (LAK5)
- Issues that arise when learning another language or translating from one language to another (LAK6)
- Issues relating to varieties of English, including standard English, dialects and attitudes towards them (LAK7)
- The importance of context in language use and the influence of the communicative situation (LAK8)

Speaking

- Making appropriate choices in oral communication episodes (LAS1)
- Having a knowledge of fluency, accuracy and competence for ESOL learners (LAS2)
- Using spoken English effectively (LAS3)

Listening

- Listening effectively (LAL1)

Reading

- Interpreting written texts (LAR1)
- Knowledge of how textual features support reading (LAR2)
- Understanding the barriers to accessing text (LAR3)

Writing

- Communicating the writing process (LAW1)
- Using genre to develop writing (LAW2)
- Developing spelling and punctuation skills (LAW3)

Part B   Personal language skills

Speaking

- Expressing yourself clearly, using communication techniques to help convey meaning and to enhance the delivery and accessibility of the message (LBS1)
- Showing the ability to use language, style and tone in ways that suit the intended audience, and to recognise their use by others (LBS2)
- Using appropriate techniques to reinforce oral communication, check how well the information is received and support the understanding of those listening (LBS3)
- Using non-verbal communication to assist in conveying meaning and receiving information, and recognising its use by others (LBS4)

Listening

- Listening attentively and responding sensitively to contributions made by others (LBL1)

Reading

- Find, and select from, a range of reference material and sources of information, including the Internet (LBR1)
- Use and reflect on a range of reading strategies to interpret texts and to locate information or meaning (LBR2)
- Identify and record the key information or messages contained within reading material using note-taking techniques (LBR3)

Writing

- Write fluently, accurately and legibly on a range of topics (LBW1)
- Select appropriate format and style of writing for different purposes and different readers (LBW2)
- Use spelling and punctuation accurately in order to make meaning clear (LBW3)
- Understand and use the conventions of grammar (the forms and structures of words, phrases, clauses, sentences and texts) consistently when producing written text (LBW4)

Some activities that will develop your knowledge, understanding and skills:

A case study

Identify an individual or group of individuals and identify their educational and cultural backgrounds, their barriers to learning and any specific learning need relating to literacy (LAK1, LAK2, LAK3, LAK4, LAK7). What are their aspirations and how does literacy form part of their development? (LAK2, LAK8).

The lesson

Conduct a typical lesson and map it to the minimum core.

Alternatively, observe a session and comment upon the speaking, listening, reading and writing activities of the teacher and learners (LBS1, LBS2, LBS3, LBS4, LBL1, LBR1, LBR2, LBR3, LBW1, LBW2, LBW3, LBW4).

Reference the objectives or outcomes of the session/s to literacy (and numeracy) national standards (Core Curriculum Entry/L1/L2).

This activity is also effective when the analysis is related to learning styles and teaching methods, thus (hopefully) demonstrating a balanced, inclusive style (e.g. visual, auditory, kinaesthetic; active/passive).

Understanding material

Analyse a handout, worksheet or assignment task in relation to the complexity of the language, the activities it requires (writing something or reading and comprehending etc.), and reference it to national standards/core curricula (LAR1, LAR2, LAR3, LAW1, LAW2, LAW3).

Comprehension – research

Interview someone whose first language is not English, and find out how they cope with learning and teaching in a second or foreign language How has their language choice changed and are there external influences on language choice (LAK2, LAK3, LAK5, LAK6, LAS1, LAS2, LAS3, LAL1, LBS1, LBS2, LBS3, LBS4, LBL1).

An alternative activity is to listen to about five minutes of a person speaking in a foreign language. Then discuss your feelings, and identify if you understood anything through expression or gesture (LAL1, LBL1, LBS4).

Another similar activity is to attempt to decode some text using a different alphabet system, shorthand or Wingdings font (LAR1, LAR2, LAR3, LAW1, LBR2).

Shadow drawing

Two people sit back to back. One person (A) has a simple picture; the other (B) has a blank sheet of paper and a pen. (A) gives instructions to (B) in the hope that (B) will replicate the picture. (B) is allowed to check the instructions, but may not look at the original picture (LBS1, LBS2, LBS3, LBL1).

Colour – action research

- Use a range of coloured overlays and place over the top of white handouts.
- Experiment with coloured pens on boards and overhead transparencies.
- Select a different colour when writing on the interactive board.
- Photocopy handouts onto different coloured paper.
- Print handouts using a different font colour.

Compare and contrast the clarity of the colours and decide which are more easily read. This strategy of colour clarity is particularly useful in supporting learners with **dyslexia** (LAK3, LAK4, LAR2, LAR3, LAW1, LAW2, LBR2).

These activities will demonstrate your understanding of literacy and language (and in some cases numeracy) and how it impacts on learning. It will show that you are aware of barriers which impede language and literacy development. In writing the reports your own skills of reading and writing will be developed, especially in terms of spelling, grammar and punctuation and paraphrasing. (LBW1, LBW2, LBW3, LBW4). When interviewing or speaking to learners to elicit the information, your own oral communication and listening skills are developed (LBS1, LBS2, LBS3, LBS4, LBL1).

Developing mathematical skills

The minimum core standards (numeracy)

Part A   Knowledge and understanding

Personal, social and cultural factors influencing numeracy learning and development

- The different factors affecting the acquisition and development of numeracy skills (NAK1)
- The importance of numeracy in enabling users to participate in, and gain access to, society and the modern economy (NAK2)
- Potential barriers that can hinder development of numeracy skills (NAK3)
- The main learning difficulties and disabilities relating to numeracy skills learning and development (NAK4)
- The common misconceptions and confusions related to number-associated difficulties (NAK5)

Communication

- Making and using judgements about understanding (NAC1)
- Communication processes and understandings (NAC2)

Processes

- A knowledge of the capacity of numeracy skills to support problem-solving (NAP1)
- Making sense of situations and representing them (NAP2)
- Processing and analysis (NAP3)
- Using numeracy skills and content knowledge (NAP4)
- Interpreting and evaluating results (NAP5)
- Communicating and reflecting on findings (NAP6)

Part B   Personal numeracy skills

Communication

- Communicate with others about numeracy in an open and supportive manner (NBC1)
- Assess your own, and other people's, understanding (NBC2)
- Express yourself clearly and accurately (NBC3)
- Communicate about numeracy in a variety of ways that suit and support the intended audience, and recognise such use by others (NBC4)
- Use appropriate techniques to reinforce oral communication, check how well the information is received and support the understanding of those listening (NBC5)

Processes

- Use strategies to make sense of a situation requiring the application of numeracy (NBP1)
- Process and analyse data (NBP2)
- Use generic content knowledge and skills (NBP3)

- Make decisions concerning content knowledge and skills (NBP4)
- Understand the validity of different methods (NBP5)
- Consider accuracy, efficiency and effectiveness when solving problems and reflect on what has been learnt (NBP6)
- Make sense of data (NBP7)
- Select appropriate format and style for communicating findings (NBP8)

Whereas dyslexia is associated with a difficulty in interpreting words and symbols, **dyscalculia** is associated with difficulties in making sense of numbers and calculations. Some people just seem to panic when faced with maths, whereas others really enjoy working with numbers. Hence there seems to be emphasis in the numeracy standards on 'supporting' and 'sensitivity'.

A case study

Identify an individual or group of individuals and identify their educational and cultural backgrounds, their barriers to learning and any specific learning need relating to numeracy (NAK1, NAK2, NAK3, NAK4). What are their aspirations, and how does numeracy form part of their development? (NAK2, NAK5).

Data-related activities

Many of the things a teacher is required to do will relate to analysing numbers. How many passed their course (**achievement data/success rate**), how many stayed until the end (**retention**), what is the average pass mark etc. You need to learn how to follow these simple formulas and present your own statistics.

For example, look at the following register:

	Week number										%
	1	2	3	4	5	6	7	8	9	10	
A	/	/	/	/	/	0	0	/	/	/	80
B	/	/	0	0	0	/	/	0	0	0	40
C	/	0	/	/	/	/	/	/	/	/	90
D	/	/	0	/	0	/	0	0	0	0	40
E	0	0	/	/	/	/	0	/	/	/	70

A has attended 8 out of 10 sessions. To calculate the percentage: 8 ÷ 10 × 100. This will give you 80 per cent. The **formula** is always the number of sessions attended, divided by the number of sessions possible, multiplied by 100.

What else does this table tell you?

- The average attendance is 64 per cent.
- There were 60 per cent of learners who completed their course.
- E started late; did this impact on achievement?
- What happened in week 7?
- Is there a link between the absences of B and D?

Analyse the attendance at your classes in number and percentage format.

What is the average (mean) attendance?

(NBP1, NBP2, NBP4, NBP7, NBP8)

Numeracy ice-breaker

Using five or six random numbers and the basic mathematical signs of add (+), minus (−), divide (÷) and multiply (×), make a given number. You do not have to use every number or sign, but may only use any number once. Give a time limit of 20–30 seconds. For example:

4, 10, 3, 7, 8. Make 559.

(Based on *Countdown*, Channel 4).

(NBP2, NBP3)

Discussion about how you felt when presented with a calculation should conclude this activity. Did you understand the instructions? What is the link between communication and number?

(NAK3, NAK4, NAK5, NAC2, NBC1, NBC4, NBC5)

Answer: $(7 \times 8 = 56 \times 10 = 560)$. $(4 - 3 = 1)$, $560 - 1 = 559$

Interpreting and evaluating results

Carry out a survey with your learners. Use a questionnaire that responds to questions in a quantitative way. For example, yes/no, strongly agree/agree/disagree/strongly disagree, true/false. Analyse the results and present the findings as 'x per cent of students agreed that . . .' etc. What does the information tell you?

(NBP1, NBP2, NBP3, NBP5, NBP7, NBP8)

See also mean, median and mode activity in Chapter 16.

Developing skills in information communication technologies

The minimum core standards (information and communication technology – ICT)

Part A   Knowledge and understanding

Personal, social and cultural factors influencing ICT learning and development

● The different factors affecting the acquisition and development of ICT skills (IAK1)

- The importance of ICT in enabling users to participate in, and gain access to, society and the modern economy (IAK2)
- Understanding the range of learners' technological and educational backgrounds (IAK3)
- The main learning disabilities and difficulties relating to ICT learning and skill development (IAK4)
- Potential barriers that inhibit ICT skills development (IAK5)

Communication

- Making and using decisions about understanding (IAC1)
- Communicating processes and understandings (IAC2)

Processes

- Purposeful use of ICT (IAP1)
- Essential characteristics of ICT (IAP2)
- How learners develop ICT skills (IAP3)

Part B   Personal ICT skills

Communication

- Communicate with others with/about ICT in an open and supportive manner (IBC1)
- Assess your own, and other people's, understanding (IBC2)
- Express yourself clearly and accurately (IBC3)
- Communicate about/with ICT in a variety of ways that suit and support the intended audience, and recognise such use by others (IBC4)
- Use appropriate techniques to reinforce oral communication, check how well the information is received and support the understanding of those listening (IBC5)

Processes

- Using ICT systems (IBP1)
- Finding, selecting and exchanging information (IBP2)
- Developing and presenting information (IBP3)

Technology is moving so quickly that it is sometimes difficult to keep up to date, both with equipment and skills. Teaching involves using technology to aid learning. Handouts are clearer when freshly printed. Interactive boards can save what you write on them and print off copies for learners. But have you ever 'lost the will to live' in front of a poorly delivered PowerPoint presentation? Using ICT needs to present a balanced approach and therefore every teacher needs to know and develop their skills in ICT.

A case study

Identify an individual or group of individuals and their educational and cultural backgrounds, barriers to learning and any specific learning need relating to ICT (IAK1, IAK2, IAK3, IAK4, IAK5). What are their aspirations and how does ICT form part of their development? (IAK1, IAK2).

The lesson

Conduct a typical lesson and map it to the minimum core.

Alternatively, observe a session and comment upon the ICT activities of the teacher and learners (IBC3, IBC4, IBC5, IBP1, IBP2, IDP3).

Group or individual activities or discussion points

List the ways that computers, the Internet and email influence our lives (IAK2).

List the resources that include technology (IAC2, IAP1, IAP2).

How comfortable are you with ICT? (IAK2, IAK5, IAC1, IAC2, IAP1, IAP3).

What is legal and what is not in terms of accessing and using material on the Internet? (IAK1, IBP1, IBP2).

Are learners disadvantaged in any way by the use of ICT? (IAK4, IAK5).

Self-assessment

Can you use: a word processing package, a presentation package, a spreadsheet application, a database package, a publishing package, an email application, a search engine?

For each would you consider that you are proficient, acceptable, OK with the basics, or nor very good?

Can you open, save, print and retrieve documents?

Do you know what all the icons mean and what shortcuts there are?

Do you understand terms like virus, spam, surfing, download, blogging? (IAC1, IBC2, IBP1, IBP2, IBP3)

Recording progress of the minimum core

It is important that you are able to demonstrate your progress against the minimum core standards. It is not sufficient that you 'think' the tutor has done this, so 'it must be covered'. Here are some suggestions about how you may record (sometimes called tracking, referencing or mapping) your progress.

Idea 1

Use this column to either write the standards in full or use a coding system as suggested above for each of the literacy, numeracy and ICT standards	Use this column to explain how you have met the standard
EXAMPLE Part B Personal language skills SPEAKING Expressing yourself clearly, using communication techniques to help convey meaning and to enhance the delivery and accessibility of the message (LBSI)	I communicate to my learners verbally, through handouts and through my PowerPoint presentations. I use body language to express my feelings and to interpret theirs. I communicate to my peers and managers using spoken and written formats, which include email. My lessons are structured to have a clear beginning, middle and ending and each session progresses from the previous; I use recap to show explicit progress. Whenever I can, I relate the subject to examples from my own experience and try to engage learners in discussions about their own experiences. I have used visual images in handouts and have created models to demonstrate the topic.

Idea 2

Standard	Task 1	Task 2	Task 3	Task 4	Task 5	Task 6	Task 7	Task 8	Etc.
	Each task should be described								
Write the standards or use a coding system	Use a ✓ to show when done								
LAK1	✓	✓		✓					
LAK2	✓			✓					
LAK3		✓	✓	✓					
LAK4	✓		✓						
LAK5	✓		✓						
etc.									

Sources

1   *Addressing literacy, language, numeracy and ICT needs in education and training: defining the minimum core of teachers' knowledge, understanding and personal skills. A guide for teacher education programmes,* June 2007, The Sector Skills Council for Lifelong Learning.

2   *Addressing literacy, language, numeracy and ICT needs in education and training: defining the minimum core of teachers' knowledge, understanding and personal skills. A guide for teacher education programmes,* July 2004, Lifelong Learning UK/Further Education National Training Organisation (**FEnto**).

3   *Including language, literacy and numeracy learning in all post-16 education: Guidance on curriculum and methodology for generic initial teacher education programmes,* March 2004, Further Education National Training Organisation/National Research and Development Centre for Adult Literacy and Numeracy.

Glossary of terms

Achievement data the number of students who achieved their qualification, usually expressed as a percentage of those who completed

Diagnostic assessment assessment used to identify capability or skill level

Dyscalculia associated with difficulties in making sense of numbers and calculations

Dyslexia associated with a difficulty in reading and interpreting words and symbols

FEnto Further Education National Training Organisation

Formula a mathematical rule

ICT information and communication technology

ILP individual learning plan

Language written or spoken communication

Literacy the ability to read and write

LLUK Lifelong Learning (UK) Sector Skills Council

Minimum core standards of competence in language, literacy, numeracy and ICT

Numeracy the ability to use numbers

Retention the number of students who complete their programme

Self-assessment an organisation's ability to monitor and quality assure its provision

Success rate the number of students who complete and achieve their qualification, usually expressed as a percentage of those who commenced

SUMMARY

In this chapter we set out to achieve the following outcomes:

- Develop competence in language and literacy
- Identify opportunities to develop your skills and understanding of literacy and language
- Demonstrate your progress through referencing teaching and learning activities and your personal development to the standards
- Develop competence in numeracy
- Identify opportunities to develop your skills and understanding of numeracy
- Demonstrate your progress through referencing teaching and learning activities and your personal development to the standards
- Develop competence in information communication technologies
- Identify opportunities to develop your skills and understanding of information and communication technology (ICT)
- Demonstrate your progress through referencing teaching and learning activities and your personal development to the standards

Your Personal Development

You will have looked at the overview of the standards and matched some of the jobs you do as a teacher to those standards. You have also had an opportunity to complete some exercises which meet the standards. Finally, you will have created a system of recording your progress towards completion of the standards and presented these to your mentor or tutor for assessment and guidance.

Assessment of the minimum core is through self-assessment. Many of the activities, essays, presentations and discussions you have done in class will demonstrate and provide opportunities to collect evidence of competence. The sessions you have with learners and conversations with peers and managers will also provide evidence.

Note:

The numbering/coding system used in this chapter is unique to this publication and therefore may not be widely recognised.

CHAPTER 11
(PEL)

Reflection, evaluation and feedback

JENNY MATTHEWS / ALAMY

LEARNING OBJECTIVES

The measurable outcomes that you will achieve by reading this chapter and completing the activities are:

- To explain reflection and describe some of the theories that underpin reflective practice
- To describe direct and indirect strategies for acquiring feedback
- To evaluate formal and informal processes which lead to personal development
- To explain the effects of reflective practice
- To describe personal development and how this can benefit the teacher

Reflection and reflective practice

Is reflection a benefit or a chore?

Reflection means learning from experience, mistakes and success. It is a process of self-awareness, through **critical analysis**, leading to informed decisions about development. The ability to reflect must be learned; a teacher must learn to be honest, constructive and remain impartial when reflecting. It may not be a systematic, intuitive personal skill. If it is too critical, too congratulatory, too shy, or too confident it will not answer the key question when reflecting: 'How was it for you?'

When analysing yourself or receiving feedback from a colleague, it is important not to feel threatened. All judgements are made for a purpose, and for you, the recipient, the purpose is to improve, develop and become a better teacher. A reflective practitioner does not operate in a blame culture; they wonder about the impact of their actions and what they can do or change to make things easier, better, more efficient and more effective. The important emotions are not concerned with failure but with how to regard each experience as a learning opportunity.

It is important to remember on what and why a teacher reflects, and that is the core business value: the learning process.

What can be reflected upon?

- Lessons – methods, resources, assessment etc.
- Communication
- Behaviour
- Success and **attainment**

- Self: skills and knowledge
- Learners.

In fact any event or occurrence is worth reflection.

How does reflection occur?

- Questioning
- Discussions and chats
- Questionnaires
- Interviews
- Observation
- Observing
- Feedback.

When does reflection occur?

Never or always.

That seems an odd answer, I hear you say. Reflection is something that good teachers engage with and coasting teachers don't bother about. The choice is yours! The argument here is the nature–nurture debate. Is good teaching natural or is it developed?

Theories associated with reflective practice

As with any other part of teaching, there are a number of models, created by **philosophers** and research, which help to explain the process of reflection and the reasons why it is important.

John Dewey wrote about reflective thinking in 1933. He suggested a five-stage model that takes someone through a problem to a solution. It broadly follows a route of:

- Identifying the problem,
- Thinking about answers, and
- Experimenting with solutions.

In this simplified version, it expresses the notion of 'thinking about answers' in order to create the reflection, and thus identify a solution.

One theorist, David Kolb (1984), is used frequently to explain learning processes. He describes how people learn from their experiences, using trial and error. In this way, he explains how **reflective practice** builds upon things that happen (concrete experience) and develop through understanding why into a 'have another go' scenario. This, he suggests, is a logical cycle of development which constantly (through repetition) leads to better practice.

Figure 11A   Kolb's learning cycle (1984)

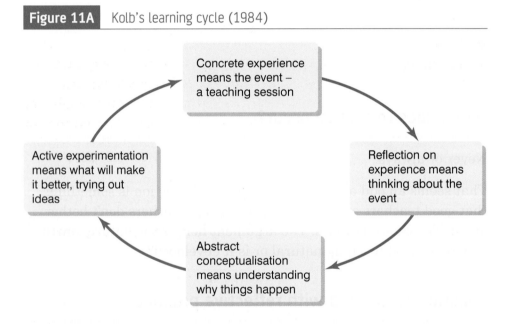

The year before this, Donald Schön (1983) had categorised theory into two types:

1   Official theory – tried and tested strategies, passed down through the ages,

2   Unofficial theory – personal ideas used to problem-solve.

This was developed further when he considered reflection and suggested that reflection also occurred in one of two ways:

1   In-action – when thoughts (reflections) are made immediately and adjustments are made which react quickly to a problem. That

is, those which could be described as thinking on your feet or, more cruelly, winging it!

2   On-action – when considerations (reflections) are made after the event. A more analytical and thought-out process in which future practice is amended. This is very similar to Kolb's opinions.

In 1985, Stephen Brookfield added his contributions to the beliefs of others. In his theory, Critical Lenses, he thinks about how we respond to assumptions. He states that what we are told can work (in theory), but that it may differ in practice. The analysis of this reminds us that a teacher's development is influenced by that which is around us, by the assumptions we make and by the events we experience. Do we always see what is in front of us?

More recently, David Boud (1995) adds to the theories, suggesting a clear link between self-assessment and reflection; learning only occurs as a result of both processes. This is similar to the thoughts of motivation theorist Bandura (1994) (see Chapter 8), who said that in order to develop, someone must want to do so. Applying this back to Boud, in order to learn (and improve), you have to be sufficiently motivated to want to analyse your own performance and spend time thinking about improving.

Further references to theories are included in CPPD Chapter 22.

Using feedback

Feedback will come from a variety of sources:

Direct:

- Self-assessment
- Peer assessment
- Performance assessment
- Student feedback.

Indirect:

- Diaries and logs
- Action research
- Professional development planners.

Self-assessment is a way of analysing the thoughts you have either at the time or later: it may be a very informal process. It may be that on the journey home at the end of the day you wonder why Jodie reacted like that in the session, or wondered how you could have delivered that bit of information in a better way, because it was clear that it wasn't fully understood, or how you could improve your use of a particular resource to make it more interactive – lots of things may go through your mind. It is important to realise, however, that you did what you did because it seemed right at the time, but with hindsight you could have . . . . It may be that you did what you did because that's all you knew; you may not know what else you could do.

To develop your performance using self-assessment and reflection, especially in the more informal style described above, it is important that you move towards a more formal style in order to make it more valuable. To do this, it is better to write things down so that you can look at them later, in the cold light of day, perhaps with someone. List the facts, be descriptive, write down your immediate thoughts, feelings, reactions (i.e. start the evaluation) and then close the book until later.

In a more formal self-assessment process, you may decide to consider each part of your lesson systematically. You will certainly be asked to do this frequently as a student teacher or newly qualified teacher (**NQT**). It is part of the way you will learn teaching skills.

A suggestion for a self-assessment checklist to use after a lesson:

Session:	
Date:	Time:
Group:	
Planning and preparation Documentation, outcomes, variety, timing	
Delivery Methods, differentiation, resources, balance, structure	
Learning Engagement, participation, motivation	
Environment Room layout, safety, temperature, facilities	
Rapport Communication, behaviour, discipline, attendance	
Assessment Variety, achievement of outcomes, Q&A style, homework	
Overall comments	

Remember that checklists like this are to remind you about events; they will aid later reflections and enable adaptations for future sessions. Look at how this might be completed:

Session:	
Date: February	Time: 10 – 12
Group: ND Second Year Level 3	
Planning and preparation Documentation, outcomes, variety, timing I had a written copy of my plan on the desk. I found it useful there because at one point I forgot where I was,	

▶

and had to refer to it to get me back on track. The timings were mixed, I allowed too much time to introduce the topic but when we went into the discussion group it was longer than I expected. Never imagined that the feedback would be so detailed, everyone wanted their say, even though others had said the same things. My writing of outcomes is much better now, maybe move them now to differentiated ones for some students.

Delivery
Methods, differentiation, resources, balance, structure

I followed the advice of my tutor and used a very structured approach (had a beginning, a middle and an ending). In the main body of the lesson I introduced the topic with teacher talk and I didn't really do another teacher bit until the end. The middle was a mix of group activities using pyramid and jigsaw group strategies. The pyramid got a little manic, I don't think I managed it very well, especially as the groups got bigger. I remembered to photocopy my notes for AB, but then others wanted them – I think they may want them to prevent making notes themselves. Must speak to their tutor – do they know how to take notes? My ending was not good, because I had run out of time.

Learning
Engagement, participation, motivation

They seemed to like this way of learning, plenty of time to think about answers to problems. I think everyone joined in, but can't be sure.

Environment
Room layout, safety, temperature, facilities

I'm used to this room now, so I know what it's got and how to use everything. Wasted time setting out room when learners were in, I could have got in earlier (it is empty during the break). Didn't put it back when I'd finished cos I'd run out of time - should I? Noticed the OHP is missing.

Rapport
Communication, behaviour, discipline, attendance

Some good discussions going on, this must be useful in their communications class. I asked them to write key words in their personal dictionaries. No problems with behaviour this week - was that because I did more group work? Archie was off again today.

Assessment
Variety, achievement of outcomes, Q&A style, homework

Didn't really assess today, I listened and I think that they all met the outcomes because they took part in the discussion groups and we all got the same information from the groups.

Overall comments

I was happy with the lesson, although the timing was still not right. Need to copy notes in case Archie is in next week. Group work was good.

 ## ACTIVITY 1

If this was your lesson evaluation, what reflections would you make?

How would you change the session if you had to repeat it?

What feedback would you give to the teacher if you had observed this session?

Peer assessment is another feedback tool. It will be used during the early parts of your teacher training to support micro-teaching sessions. In this case you will deliver a small teaching session to your peers and ask for their comments. According to what they write or say, you will make decisions about future practice. As you develop as a teacher, you will initiate support and comments from other teachers, or mentors. The chances are that they will use a document similar to the one used for self-assessment and together you will discuss the things that emerge. You may ask someone to come in and help you because you are struggling with a particular issue, or it may be part of your organisation's procedures that colleagues engage in peer assessment in order to initiate useful conversations about teaching and learning. It may be part of your development that you work with a mentor.

The conversation that follows a peer observation, which is not judgemental, is called feedback. It is the same thing as the feedback you give to your learners to develop their skills and knowledge. The feedback itself should consist of comments, personal opinions, advice and suggestions. As with all feedback, it is up to you what you do with the suggestions and advice. Hopefully it will give you ideas, but good feedback will 'listen' to your justifications and together develop ideas for improvement.

Performance assessment is something that will probably occur either as part of your assessment on a teacher training qualification or as part of your organisation's quality assurance processes. In Appendix D: Teaching Observations are described some of the things you should do before and during an observation. A performance assessment will make a judgement on your abilities. If it is an observation from your tutor, then the purpose, whilst assessing your competence, will also be to initiate conversations about skills and give developmental feedback. The outcome will probably be 'satisfactory' or 'needs further practice' – the wording may vary, but they are the usual outcomes of a teacher training assessment.

If the assessment is part of the quality process by an inspection team, then the feedback is probably going to be more of a judgement than feedback. You will be told your particular strengths and weaknesses, from which you should be able to ascertain your grade. The observers are making judgements about the learning experience, to which you contribute, but may not control. Not all observers will tell you your grade and any feedback may last only a few seconds. The grades in this process are likely to be:

- *Grade 1 outstanding.* There are many strengths and few, if any, weaknesses, much of the teaching is exceptional and promotes a positive learning experience for all learners.
- *Grade 2 good.* The strengths outweigh the weaknesses. The learning experience is sound with many examples of good practice.
- *Grade 3 satisfactory.* There are a balance of strengths and weaknesses, leading to satisfactory learning experiences.
- *Grade 4 inadequate.* The weaknesses outweigh the strengths, resulting in learners who do not succeed in their goals and targets.

These grades are used by internal and external inspection teams to make judgements about the organisation's performance.

Student feedback is one of the most valuable, yet least used feedback tools. Who better to ask about the quality of the teaching than those in receipt of it? Feedback from learners can be gathered through questionnaires or interviews, formally and informally.

 **ACTIVITY 2**

List the ways you do/could collect information from learners about:

- The teaching
- Their course or programme
- The learning environment
- The support they receive.

ACTIVITY 3

Devise a questionnaire to use with a group of learners to find out if they enjoy and learn in your lessons. Note in your journal when you issued it, and undertake a self-assessment of the lesson.

Analyse the results of the questionnaire, writing the results in your journal.

Compare your self-assessment with the analysis of the student questionnaire.

Complete a table like this:

Main self-assessment outcomes:	Main student questionnaire outcomes:
List the main points you thought were good/bad in the session.	List the main points your learners thought were good/bad in the session.

State the similarities between your self-assessment and the student questionnaire _____

State any differences between your self-assessment and the student questionnaire _____

Comment on the perceptions of your learners' experiences and compare them to your own _____

Reflection:

Justify why any differing opinions have occurred. Make suggestions about how your performance could be modified in the light of these findings.

Diaries, logs and journals

These are means of recording events. They are used with a self-assessment process to help you to remember what happened. A suggestion for a log is offered in Chapter 4. Although an indirect form of feedback, it creates the opportunity for feedback through records. The feedback comes when you re-read the logs. One of the advantages of keeping logs, particularly about **critical incidents**, is that the reasons for things happening may not be explained until much later. If a student is playing up in class, you may think at the time 'oh, that's unusual', but carry on nevertheless. It may not be until weeks later that you find out about something that happened in that learner's life that caused the unusual outburst. The reflection may be that next time you might initiate an 'are you OK' discussion (at an appropriate time). Just remember that they may say 'Yes', which wouldn't move anything forward at the time.

Action **research** is quite a detailed investigation into something. It is when you undertake a systematic trial of a new or different strategy and analyse the effects – thus giving you feedback on future development.

Professional development planners are a means of recording your development and learning, but may tell you about what else you need to do. For example:

Activity	Learning outcome	Future development
19 May 2009 Attended event in B149, to learn how to access data about how many learners pass their course. Organised by MIS team. 2 hours cpd.	Learned how to use the management information system to find out how many learners started, stayed and completed course. I now understand the importance of completing forms and responding to requests about numbers.	Found out that retention was not very good, especially for learners who start late on their programmes. Need to work with team to create an online induction to support late starters and ensure through tutorial and initial assessment that they settle into their course. Discuss at team meeting next week. Talk to lead tutor and student services.

From this chart several things can be noted:

- Events attended
- Number of continuing professional development (**CPD**) hours
- What you got out of the development activity
- What further training is required.

The feedback in this instance is concerned with the teacher finding out that there is a retention issue on the course; probably during the course the trainers were able to give ideas about why and this enabled the teacher to plan some more development to overcome this secondary discovery.

Proactive personal development

In Part One, Chapter 4, we looked at some self-evaluation strategies and how they might be used to develop personal and professional development. We focused on how to write in an evaluative, rather than descriptive, style in order to prepare for reflection. Earlier in this chapter we looked at reflection and how this is used to develop practice.

It is suggested that there are links between theories associated with reflection and those of motivation; a teacher must have the desire to develop themself. This is demonstrated as a development model, in which the teaching life is mapped.

A non-reflective practitioner:

Figure 11B Model showing decline resulting in lack of development

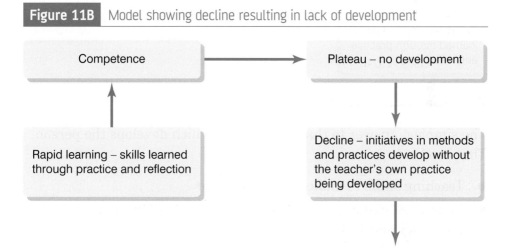

The second model (Figure 11C) shows how someone enters into constant improvement and development, thus keeping up-to-date with everything around the sector, through engagement with reflective practices.

This reinforces the point that development is determined by the individual teacher: thus it is within the power of the teacher to state when that development will occur. Does the teacher wait until they need to develop or do they develop to prepare themselves for what is to come? To a certain extent, this decision has been taken out of the hands of the teacher by the introduction of legislation demanding that teachers engage in continuous professional development.

| **Figure 11C** | Model showing improvement as a result of reflection |

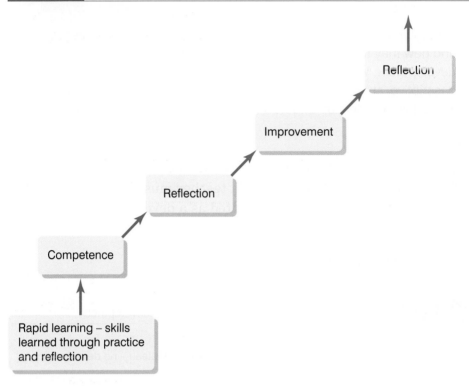

What constitutes personal development?

The simplest answer to that is: anything which develops the person. That can be:

- Teaching skills to make a better teacher
- Functional skills to support minimum levels of literacy, numeracy and ICT
- Study skills to enable efficient learning
- IT skills to enhance skills in using computers
- Tutor skills to support learners' development
- Assessment skills to improve the reliability of judgements
- Theoretical skills to improve understanding of roles
- Character skills, time/stress/relaxation, to support the teacher under pressure
- Legislation updates to ensure compliance
- Research skills to maintain up-to-date practice and knowledge.

There are probably other categories. In short, development = progress.

Progress will then lead to efficient and effective teachers, which in turn will lead to a successful learning environment – which is our key priority.

Recommended reading

Hillier, Y. (2005) *Reflective teaching in further and adult education.* London: Continuum.

Glossary of terms

Attainment reaching the goal or qualification aim

CPD continuous professional development

Critical analysis a detailed examination resulting in an opinion or argument

Critical incidents events that have a significant effect

Direct feedback/communication clear and unambiguous link

Feedback verbal or written comments about the assessment intended to bring about improvement

Indirect feedback/communication a link via a secondary method

Justify explain and prove something

NQT newly qualified teacher

Philosopher someone who studies theories, attitudes or beliefs

Reflection a considered opinion, expressed in speech or writing; thoughts or considerations, developing ideas and thoughts

Reflective practice thoughtful practice to develop skills

Research an investigation

 SUMMARY

In this chapter we set out to achieve the following outcomes:

- Explain what reflection is and describe some of the theories that underpin reflective practice
- Describe direct and indirect strategies for acquiring feedback in order to support skills in reflective practice
- Evaluate formal and informal processes which lead to personal development
- Explain the effects of non-reflective practice and efficient reflective practice
- Describe the types of personal development and how this can benefit the teacher

Your Personal Development

You will have considered what reflection is and how to use it to develop your own practice. You have looked at the theory associated with reflection. You have carried out self-assessment of your own teaching, practicing reflection and feedback skills. You have developed your ability to question learners in order to find out about their learning and used the answers to develop your own practice. You have improved your skills in using personal development to improve your teaching, stating the importance of using a positive approach to development.

You should be able to answer questions relating to:

How and why you should evaluate and reflect on your performance and, following your teaching sessions, will demonstrate an ability to make reflections and prepare your development plans, in order to improve your practice.

Part Three

Enabling learning and assessment

(ELA)

This is the third unit in your Diploma in Teaching in the Lifelong Learning Sector (DTLLS) qualification

12 Concepts and principles of assessment
13 Types of assessment
14 Analysis of assessment
15 Feedback and questioning in assessment
16 Recording progress and achievement
17 Evaluating effectiveness

Learning Outcomes	Assessment Criteria
Understand theories, principles and applications of formal and informal assessment and their roles in learning and evaluation	● Analyse the application of theories and principles of assessment in relation to practice in own specialist area ● Analyse the role of assessment in evaluation and quality processes
Understand the significance of equality and diversity issues for the assessment of learning	● Critically discuss the implications of equality and diversity issues in assessment for teachers and learners
Understand and demonstrate how to plan/design and conduct formal and informal assessment to enable learning and progression	● Plan and/or design and use assessment schemes, methods and instruments that are fair, valid, reliable, sufficient and appropriate for learners, using new and emerging technologies where appropriate ● Justify the selection and/or design and use of formal and informal assessment methods and tools used in own specialist area ● Establish and maintain an appropriate environment for assessment to maximise learners' opportunities for success ● Record, and report on learner progress and achievement, using organisational and/or awarding institution protocols and procedures as required
Understand and demonstrate how to give effective feedback to promote learner progress and achievement	● Justify and use appropriate skills and approaches in giving verbal and written feedback to learners ● Justify and use appropriate skills and approaches to negotiate targets and strategies for improvement and success for learners
Understand and demonstrate knowledge of the minimum core in own practice	● Apply minimum core specifications in literacy to improve own practice ● Apply minimum core specifications in language to improve own practice ● Apply minimum core specifications in mathematics to improve own practice ● Apply minimum core specifications in ICT user skills to improve own practice
Understand how to evaluate and improve own assessment practice	● Evaluate and improve the design and effectiveness of formal and informal assessment procedures, methods and instruments, using feedback from learners and appropriate others and referring to relevant theories of learning ● Evaluate own approaches, strengths and development needs in relation to assessment ● Plan and take up appropriate development opportunities to improve own practice in relation to formal and informal assessment

CHAPTER 12 (ELA)

Concepts and principles of assessment

LEARNING OBJECTIVES

The measurable outcomes that you will achieve by reading this chapter and completing the activities are:

- To describe the meaning of words associated with assessment
- To explain the main concepts (ideas) and principles (values) relating to assessment
- To define the rules associated with assessments to ensure valid, reliable and accurate assessments
- To state the legal responsibilities and ethical values of assessment

Concepts and principles of assessment

This chapter also links to:

- Chapter 16, The purpose of assessment section.

Assessment basics

Assessment is the term given to the process of checking that learning
has occurred. It is the way teachers know whether or not they have
been effective in their sessions.

> Assessment is the process by which evidence of student
> achievement is obtained and judged. Ecclestone (1996)
> points out that assessment requires two things: evidence
> and a standard or scale.
>
> Gray et al. 2005: 50

Some of the first things you need to grasp in assessment are: how, what,
when, where, why. You cannot assess somebody or something without
telling them about it or setting the standard. The standard may be role
modelled, industry-based, competence-based or theoretically driven.
Whichever applies, the standard should come from the syllabus.
However, in recreational courses there is unlikely to be a syllabus,
so the **standard** becomes the teacher's and/or the learner's goals.
Therefore standards and goals are the keys to successful assessment.

> ## If you know where you are going, you'll be able to tell when you've got there.

The output of assessment is 'evidence'; evidence is the confirmation that assessment has occurred and the way it is proven. To summarise, assessment in educational terms usually means 'a method of confirming learning'.

Why assess?

Look at the table in Activity 1: it notes key parts of the learning process and asks you to think about your current practice by using how and why statements.

ACTIVITY 1

Where are you now in terms of how you assess learning?

Key stages of learning	How do you currently assess this stage?	Why do you do this? (Self, learners, managers)
Initial assessment of skills at entry to programme		
Getting to know your learners		
Planning learning for groups: for individuals:		

▶

Key stages of learning	How do you currently assess this stage?	Why do you do this? (Self, learners, managers)
Check that the content of the lessons is learned		
Check that the content of the topic/module/unit is learned		
Learning is understood and can be transferred to other contexts or situations		
Dealing with emerging issues and needs		

The purpose of this exercise is to see where you are now.

Assessment is an essential part of learning, and you can use this initial self-assessment to think about where you need to develop. You may refer to this in a reflective journal or diary.

The language of assessment

Assessment can be carried out before recruitment (at interview), at commencement (diagnostic and initial assessment), during and at the end of the lesson and at the end of the module, unit or programme. It may be pertinent at this point to look at how qualifications are structured, as this will lead us to the points at which assessment should occur.

Programme of study

A collection of qualifications usually associated with full-time attendance which create a framework or course: the curriculum.

Qualification

A certificated qualification, endorsed by an awarding body and approved through the National Qualifications Framework (**NQF** – see Chapter 2, pp. 45–46), for example:

C&G Cert in Teaching

BTEC First Dip in Health and Social Care

NVQ Level 1 in Hairdressing

NCFE Cert for entry to the Public Services

HND in Business Studies

Level 3 Application of Number

A qualification consists of the standards of performance, ability or competence i.e. the syllabus

Unit/module

The smaller subsections of the qualification which focus on a particular aspect. There will usually be several units or modules in a qualification. Each unit or module will have its own specified outcomes and evidence requirements. Some qualifications have a further breakdown of the unit/module which is called an element.

Content/performance criteria

Each unit, module or element will have statements relating to what has to be covered in order to achieve the unit. These statements about content are written in terms of what the learner will know or do at the end of the unit/module/element.

In NVQs these are called performance criteria (PC): statements of competence – what the learner will be able to do at the end of the unit/module/element.

Lessons are arranged around these frameworks: thus you may be employed to teach a particular unit or module or you may work within a team of people to train towards a whole qualification. Whichever strategy is used, the teacher will have to assess whether learning has occurred. In some qualifications this learning is referred to as demonstrating competence.

Unfortunately, assessment is such a wide topic and the qualification frameworks so varied that many different terms are used (assessment **jargon**) and it sometimes takes a while to learn the words; usually when you do discover their meaning it is broadly the same as another similar word used by a different qualification team. Let us look at some of those terms.

Term	Alternative expressions
Qualification	Standards, specifications, course, syllabus
Learning outcome	Objective, range statements, content, statements of competence
Evidence requirements	Assessment guidance, evidence, portfolio, assignment, assessment criteria
Grading	Grading criteria are the level at which the outcomes are met – e.g., pass merit/credit or distinction
Verification	Moderation, standardisation
Assessment	Test, exam, evidence (proof)

 **ACTIVITY 2**

Make a list of any similar jargon terms you use in your lessons when explaining the subject or how it will be assessed.

- ●
- ●
- ●
- ●
- ●
- ●

- ●
- ●
- ●
- ●
- ●

Consider:

Wording in assignments or instructions to complete question sheets.

Development point:

Create a dictionary of terms that your learners may find helpful.

See also Appendix C: Study Skills, Command Words pp. 648–649.

Concepts of assessment

A concept is an idea, in this instance, about assessment. The concepts that you will commonly see are:

- Norm referencing (or normative)
- Criterion referencing
- Ipsative assessment
- Formative assessment
- Summative assessment.

Norm referencing is when learners are assessed against each other. It is quite an old fashioned concept. For example, if you were to set a test where the top 10 per cent were able to progress to a higher level or rewarded in some way, and the lowest 10 per cent were penalised in some way, perhaps by going down a **grade** of class, then this would be norm **referencing**. The learner's ability is measured (and compared) against other learners. This is very common in educational establishments, when learners are split into classes according to ability rather than year or house groups. The percentiles can also be varied: for example if there were a lot of students who gained high marks in their test, but you only had reward spaces for half of them, it is possible to raise the pass mark to match the figure of 'top 10 per cent of learners,' equally if the tests were very difficult, you can lower the pass mark to reward the 'top 10 per cent'. In this way, you will consistently have a top 10 per cent, although their pass marks may have been different.

Criterion referencing is when a learner achieves a standard, they either can (or can't) do the task, question or competence. They can continue in their attempts until the criterion is achieved (plural is criteria). Therefore in this style of assessment it is measuring what a learner can do. Whilst it is generally associated with a 'can do–can't do' (pass–fail) assessment, it may be linked to a grading scale which determines how well a learner can do something. In this strategy a learner can pass, pass with credit or pass with distinction.

Ipsative assessment is relatively new in assessment concepts. It is used within self-assessment when an individual is matching their performance, knowledge or ability against a set of standards. It is a useful way of undertaking an initial assessment or, alternatively, a way of summarising learning; it can also be used whilst learners are on their programme of study to encourage reviews of progress. **Profiling** is a method of recording **ipsative** assessment.

If you were to measure your performance as a teacher against the 'New overarching professional standards for teachers, tutors and trainers in the lifelong learning sector' (LLUK 2006), you would be undertaking an assessment using an ipsative model.

For example, this is an extract from Domain E – Assessment for Learning, using criteria related to professional practice (LLUK 2006: pp. 11, 12).

Assess your own performance against the statements of competence:

EP1.1	Use appropriate forms of assessment and evaluate their effectiveness in producing information useful to the teacher and the learner
EP1.2	Devise, select, use and appraise assessment tools, including where appropriate, those which exploit new and emerging technologies
EP2.1	Apply appropriate methods of assessment fairly and effectively
EP2.3	Design appropriate assessment activities for own specialist area
EP3.2	Ensure that access to assessment is appropriate to learner need
EP4.2	Use feedback to evaluate and improve own skills in assessment
EP5.3	Communicate relevant assessment information to those with a legitimate interest in learner achievement, as necessary/appropriate

In the boxes on the right you will write statements, make lists, justify your choices and opinions, describe strategies and give examples of instances when the competence is demonstrated. In ipsative assessment, as it is usually a self-assessment and therefore only an individual's opinion of their ability, the judgements will usually be supported by other assessments.

Formative assessment is an interim judgement. It is also known as 'continuous assessment'. It has the advantage of being an ideal opportunity to tell a learner how they are progressing and giving them the chance to improve. This type of assessment is very motivational because it is seen as a review rather than an assessment. It helps learners to progress and maximise their potential. There is life after **formative** assessment! One of the disadvantages of formative assessment (although significantly outweighed by the advantages) is that continuous assessment may feel like *continual* assessment. Kolb's learning cycle (see Chapter 11, Figure 11A, p. 248) advocates the concepts of formative assessment and feedback within the cycle, indicating their value in personal development and progression. Formative assessment aids learning.

Summative assessment is usually associated with tests and exams. It aids the assessment of learning and is quite formal. In **summative** assessment styles, a learner progresses through their qualification until the time comes that learning is complete and they are tested on their knowledge or skills. A judgement is made, which is then expressed on a certificate. If a learner wishes to improve they usually have to 'sit' the examination again. This does put enormous pressure on learners as the outcomes may determine their future, however with teaching that prepares a learner well for their test, such apprehension and anxiety can be lessened.

Principles of assessment

A principle is a rule that you will follow; it is an underlying standard that you will not compromise. Some of the principles that you should advocate are:

- Consistency. You will always ensure that the methods and timeliness of your assessment are at a level standard, making certain that irrespective of how and when your learners are assessed, the outcomes are constant.
- Accessibility. You will always ensure that all of your learners are able to access your assessments and follow systems of equality and inclusion.
- Detailed. You will always ensure that your assessments cover your curriculum or unit fairly and evenly, leaving no part undecided.
- Earned. You will always ensure that your learners have achieved their qualifications with rigour and others will respect the integrity of the assessment.
- Transparency. You will always ensure that everyone involved in the assessment is crystal clear about its purpose and meaning.

These principles form the **acronym** CADET.

C	Consistent
A	Accessible
D	Detailed
E	Earned
T	Transparent

So, these are the values and principles that you follow when preparing, implementing and evaluating assessment. It will be these values that will help to determine the effectiveness of your assessment.

It should be remembered that assessment is not merely something which occurs in a modular format or end of year test. In every lesson that you do you will set learning outcomes, deliver your topic and then close the lesson. You must remember that to truly know if you have achieved the learning outcomes you must set an assessment activity. If the close of your lesson is: 'Well, today folks we've looked at x y and z, is everybody clear now?' you may be able to claim that you have 'taught' your topic, but you cannot claim that your learners have learned anything! You must, therefore, include small assessment activities in the structure of your lesson, to help you confirm learning. The easiest to prepare are verbal or written questions – but make sure everyone contributes and remember that you can use similar activities in the next class to recap, before moving forward to the next topic. In the next chapter we will review the different ways that this can be achieved.

The rules of assessment

Assessment rules

Once you have sorted out the basics, you can get down to the actual assessment. There are a number of different ways of assessing, but all rely on the fact that you need something to measure against. These are usually written by awarding bodies but there are some courses where you may have to devise your own standards, for example non-qualification courses or recreational programmes. Some words of caution here: *never* substitute your own standards onto qualifications which are approved within the NQF, however well intentioned. These are National Standards and approved as such by bodies charged with the remit to create a standard across the country. By doing so you may disadvantage your learners, because you are creating your own qualification, which will not be recognised within your professional area.

The first task when planning assessment is to gain sight of the awarding body's specifications for your unit/module or qualification. In it you will find a series of paragraphs telling you what a learner will know/be able to do/demonstrate at the end of the unit or module. Again, there are variants here: some qualifications/units will tell you that you need to collect two of this, a report on that or an observation for the other, but more often it will be up to you to decide on the appropriate assessment task and the method, usually under the supervision of the moderator or verifier. There are some rules that will help you make informed choices. You should ensure that your assessments are:

- Valid/relevant: assesses what it is supposed to, according to the curriculum, in an appropriate manner
- Reliable: assesses in a consistent manner to the expected standards, regardless of who makes the judgement or when the judgement is made

- Authentic: is able to be attributed to the learner
- Current/recent: is up-to-date and recently written
- Sufficient: is enough to cover the content/performance criteria
- Power of discrimination: a balance of easy and difficult questions, so that learners are not disadvantaged
- Objective: judgements made are not personal opinion, which means that marking criteria need to be clear and not open to interpretation.

Some of the problems associated with assessment are concerned with the issues listed above. For example:

- Poor wording of questions and assignments leads learners in a wrong direction, causing their assessment to be completed inaccurately.
- Future criticism of competence, usually from future employers, because learners have not been tested sufficiently across the breadth of the syllabus.
- Ambiguous or inaccurate marking by staff who do not communicate well leads to different standards of competence of learners.
- Assessors inventing their own standards that can lead to varying degrees of competence.
- Poor research skills leading to inaccurate citation and/or **plagiarism**.

To overcome these issues you should follow the rules of assessment by:

- Always ensuring that your learners are prepared for their assessments
- Devising tasks that test what you have taught
- Telling learners how, when and where assessments will happen
- Offering study skills to support presentation of research in work
- Asking colleagues (or an internal verifier) to review the task before submitting it to learners (when devising assessments)
- Creating varied assessment tasks to give good coverage of material and opportunities for differentiation.

The rules of assessment associated with ethics are concerned with confidentiality and authenticity.

Confidentiality

This section is for guidance only; it does not constitute legal advice. Organisations will have their own codes of practice and teachers should always seek advice from colleagues or managers.

Most teachers automatically respect that the information they have and keep about their learners is confidential, but this will be on two tiers. There are those issues which are confidential to the organisation and those issues that remain in confidence between the learner and the tutor.

There are laws and guidance to support this issue:

1   Data Protection Act (1998). Protects personal data which should only be used as stated, never disclosed (unless there are criminal implications), kept only for as long as is required and must be held securely. Individuals have the right to see the information you keep about them. However, we must remember that it might also be necessary to report things, even when mentioned in confidence – e.g. issues around child abuse and illegal acts.

2   Freedom of Information (2000). The public's right to know. It states that individuals can request information held about them and about the organisation. Organisations must declare information about performance etc.

3   Human Rights. As far as education is concerned this is mainly associated with equality and welfare.

Authenticity

We must ensure that all work submitted for assessment is the work of the individual learner, equally, we must ensure that learners do not copy (plagiarise) the work of others. We should do this by addressing skills of referencing and advocating study methods and research strategies that do not leave a student vulnerable to accusations of plagiarism. Unfortunately, one of the downsides of the Internet is the apparent ease with which people can download information and cut and paste it into their work, or even acquire whole assignments.

How to spot plagiarism:

- Different writing style or writing level to that seen in classwork
- Variants in fonts and font size within text
- American spellings
- Different referencing to that which has been taught
- Word processed work when handwritten is usual
- Obscure references or sources of information
- Different opinions/context to those made in class or textbooks.

If you suspect something, you don't need fancy software tools to detect it. Just type the sentence, without the smaller words (e.g. of, and, the, etc.) or key words that seem obscure, into a search engine – like Google – and generally, it will appear verbatim in the list of 'hits' that appear as search findings.

In terms of authenticity, it doesn't hurt to get learners into the habit of signing and dating their work:

> I confirm that this [assignment/essay etc.], is all my own work.
>
> Signed: A. Learner
> Today's date

This does not stop plagiarism, but it enters the learners into a contract concerning ethics.

Glossary of terms

Acronym an abbreviation or series of initial letters which together make another word

BTEC Business and Technology Education Council; a qualification title part of Edexcel; an awarding body

C&G City and Guilds; an awarding body

Competence the knowledge of or ability to do something

Formative continuous assessment

Grade a level or degree of competence

HND Higher National Diploma

Ipsative self-assessment against standards of competence

Jargon language, words or expressions of a specialist occupation

Level 3 a position within the NQF indicating the value of a qualification

NCFE Northern Council for Further Education; an awarding body

NQF National Qualifications Framework

NVQ National Vocational Qualification

Plagiarism to pass off somebody else's work as your own

Profile how information about a thing or person is recorded

Referencing a source of information

Standard an agreed level of competence

Summative final or summary assessment

SUMMARY

In this chapter we set out to achieve the following outcomes:

- Describe the meaning of words associated with assessment
- Explain the main concepts (ideas) and principles (values) relating to assessment
- Define the rules associated with assessments to ensure valid, reliable and accurate assessments
- State the legal responsibilities and ethical values of assessment

Your Personal Development

You have completed a couple of activities to identify your starting points in understanding assessment and developed your knowledge of assessment in the context of current curriculum. You have looked at the main concepts of assessment and what is meant by the terms norm and criterion referencing, ipsative, formative and summative assessments.

You have investigated the rules of assessment: validity, reliability, authenticity, currency, sufficiency, objectivity and the power to discriminate with reasons as to why problems occur if the rules are not followed. Confidentiality is also discussed with mention of related legislation.

Finally you have looked at principles of assessment and decided on the values you advocate when carrying out assessments.

You should be able to answer questions relating to your understanding of:

- Concepts and principles of assessment.

CHAPTER 13 (ELA)

Types of assessment

LEARNING OBJECTIVES

The measurable outcomes that you will achieve by reading this chapter and completing the activities are:

- To describe the advantages and disadvantages of each assessment method and make informed decisions about which to choose
- To make decisions about your choices of assessment and identify what makes assessment effective

Methods of assessment

In Chapter 5 you looked at the methods of assessment more commonly used in the post-compulsory sector – these were observation, simulation, project, assignment, written questions, verbal questions, professional discussion and self-assessment. Each method was described with some instances of how it might be used.

In this chapter, we are going to extend your knowledge of assessment methods so that you are able to make decisions about which methods to choose for your purposes.

Methods of assessment can be classified into two main types:

1   **Direct** – evidence of the learner's work
2   **Indirect** – evidence or opinion from others

Assessment method	Advantages	Disadvantages
Observation Direct	Primary assessment method for practical skills	No permanent record of performance
	Able to see naturally occurring practice	Expensive
	Ideal opportunity to see if theory is applied in a practical situation*	Needs to be verified to confirm judgements
		Can be intrusive
	Can be used formatively or summatively	Can't check theory or underpinning knowledge
	'Can do' or 'can't do' outcomes	Detailed preparation and organisation required
		May be subjective

Assessment method	Advantages	Disadvantages
Simulation Direct	Can be used to assess when circumstances involve dangerous or expensive resources Can be used formatively or summatively	Does not match the real thing in terms of senses and emotions
Project and assignment Direct	Can be used formatively or summatively Allows individual creativity to develop Develops research skills Collection of tasks which can be differentiated easily Assesses wide range of skills and knowledge*	Confused in meaning – project is learner-derived, assignment is tutor-derived Poorly used – preparation only concerned with single subject, whereas it may be applicable across a broader range of topics Time-consuming
Written reports/ case studies Indirect/direct	Less formal than an essay Allows description, comprehension and analysis of facts* Opportunity to answer 'what if' scenarios Aids reflection Can include personal values and opinions	Need detailed marking grids
Written questions Direct	**Essays** Assesses understanding and high order cognitive skills* Can gain insight to opinions/arguments relating to an issue Can assess literacy Can be closed (no reference), open book, or open (later submission) styles	**Essays** Takes time to write and mark No single answer Easy to prepare Limited coverage of the subject/syllabus Prone to subjectivity in marking

▶

Assessment method	Advantages	Disadvantages
Written questions Direct (*continued*)	**Essays** (*continued*) Can bo uocd formatively or summatively Appropriate as exam or a stand alone pieces of work	
	Short answer Versatile – ideal as introductory, plenary, homework or exam questions Used to reinforce learning Ideal when information needs to be remembered as opposed to recognised* Assesses comprehension* Quick to mark Can be used formatively or summatively Can be used as one word, simple sentence or extended answers	**Short answer** Answers can lack depth unless extended answers are requested
	Multiple choice Good way to check facts Low to high order cognitive test* Checks recognition and recall* Can test a lot of things as questions are short Answers are easy to mark Outcomes are reliable Questions can be 'banked' and selected to make different tests each time they are used High level of objectivity in marking Can be used formatively or summatively	**Multiple choice** Answers may be sorted to get a 50/50 guess scenario Difficult to prepare

Assessment method	Advantages	Disadvantages
Oral questions Direct	Can be used formatively or summatively Informal in style Supports theory in practical situations Responsive to needs Open questions probe knowledge	Sometimes difficult to devise questions May be posed as closed questions
Professional discussion Direct	Generally used supported by other assessment methods Allows for description, evaluation and reflection* Structured discussion allows for gaps to be covered	Expensive as it is 1:1 Can be too leading Can be disjointed; learners need preparation time to ensure logical flow of ideas Recording of discussion needs to be prepared (audio/writing)
Self-assessment Indirect	Generally used supported by other assessment methods Enables evaluation and reflection* Allows learners to develop responsibility for own learning Learning logs can record progress and aid reflection	Judgements made by self rather than an expert Difficult to be objective Limited to the extent of the profile document
Peer assessment Indirect	Generally used supported by other assessment methods Gathers ideas and emotions from similar people Informal feedback Aids reflection	Peers may not know the standards and so compare with what they do

Assessment method	Advantages	Disadvantages
Accreditation of Prior Learning (APL) Indirect	Generally used supported by other assessment methods Values previous learning, achievement and experience	Need to validate all claims May not cover current competence Difficult to prove Time-consuming to analyse Needs specialist staff
Group activities Direct	Motivational as tasks are shared Less intimidating Individual strengths can be played to maximise results Can be used formatively or summatively	Difficult to attribute results to an individual or particular skill Weaker learners can hide
Witness testimony Indirect	Able to collect information from work or other activities to support studies Generally used supported by other assessment methods	Reliability of witness can not be guaranteed
Products/ artefacts Direct	Items generated outside of the classroom can be used to support demonstration of competence Generally used supported by other assessment methods Links the importance of classroom and work-based assessment	The authenticity (ownership) of the product is not without doubt

*References are related to Bloom's Taxonomies of Learning (see Chapter 7/pp. 158–162).

Effective assessment

If assessment is to be seen as a valuable tool and respected by learners, colleagues and other stakeholders, then it must be seen to do what it purports to do, i.e. it must be **effective**. Effectiveness means producing the intended or desired result. Therefore, the first thing you should establish is what you intend or want from the assessment.

- To demonstrate practical skill (psychomotor skills)
- To recall knowledge (cognitive skills)
- To value or appreciate an opinion (affective skills)

In this example, Bloom (1956, 1964, and Dave 1967) is used to identify the desired outcomes (see PEL Chapter 7). Once you have established what you want, then you should select methods of assessment which will deliver the products of assessment you need in order to make the **judgement**.

To make decisions about effectiveness you should consider:

- the desired **outcome**
- the methods of assessment
- justify the choices you make
- gather evidence – the products which demonstrate competence?

The products of assessment are:

- Documents – letters, printouts
- Photos
- Portfolios of evidence
- Essays, reports, presentation notes,
- Artefacts, artwork, finished items
- Models and diagrams
- Testimonials, references
- Personal statements, CVs

- Certificates
- Observation reports.

There are various ways to achieve confidence in your assessment and thus promote effectiveness. One of the easiest is to **triangulate** judgements: this means using more than one assessment method to confirm competence. For example, would you allow (believe) a student who presented a photograph or product and told you it was their work? It is more likely that you will check this out by asking some verbal questions to elicit information about how they did it. You may add to this by considering previous classwork activities they have done or by setting another practical task to confirm their ability. If the results of all of these assessment methods say the same thing then you can confirm competence. Each method is therefore contributing effectively to produce an assessment that is reliable and authentic.

Another easy method of delivering effective assessment strategies is that of variety. By testing learners in different ways, not only does it add interest, but it also appeals to different learning styles and in the same way as triangulation, it provides confirmation that decisions are accurate and consistent.

Communication aids effectiveness. By agreeing, sharing, negotiating, and discussing plans, methods and outcomes, the teacher (or assessor) will be able to justify and evaluate their assessments. It will also aid some 'joined-up thinking' – many requirements contained in standards are common across a range of units or modules. Communication about these common factors will lessen the assessment load on learners by consolidating tasks to cover more than one unit or module (a holistic approach). This can also apply to key and basic skills – why can't presentations be assessed for communication skills as well as content?

Finally, in trying to establish effectiveness, the assessor should consider the values, ethics and safety of the assessment. The values (**CADET** – see ELA Chapter 12, p. 274) should not be compromised when aiming for effectiveness: the ethics concerning **confidentiality** and **integrity** in assessment are paramount and we should never forfeit standards of safety when creating or carrying out assessments.

ACTIVITY 1

How do you know everyone has learned the topic?
Quite simply, you don't unless you assess.

Give two examples of how you might assess each item in the list below.
State why you think your chosen examples are the right ones:

Discuss the effects of the Second World War on the economy of Britain.
Identify road signs for crossroads, T-junctions, speed restrictions etc.
Using a photocopier.
Baking a cake.
Reviewing and evaluating teaching methods.
Comparing and contrasting two issues.
Preparing for a job interview.
List the correct flag for a list of countries.

How will you know if your assessments are effective?

Qualifications for assessors

Awarding bodies will set the standards required of people who
undertake assessments in relation to their qualifications. One of
the most obvious is that of personal **competence**. Assessors are
required to be competent in their subject themselves to at least a
level higher than that which they assess. Government guidelines
recommend that this is a minimum of Level 3 (A level on the NQF)
and between 3 and 10 years' experience* in the field of expertise.
Where there are no appropriate Level 3 qualifications available,
lower levels are acceptable, supported by relevant industrial or
commercial experience. Second, they look for competence in
assessment. Depending on the type of qualification this may be a
generic teaching qualification, which includes modules on
assessment, or, in the case of NVQs, there is a requirement for a
specialist assessment unit from the Learning and Development
NVQ. You may hear these called D32, D33, D34 or the up-to-date
versions, A1, A2, or V1.

Additional information

....

LLUK – regarding standards and regulations for teachers

ENTO – regarding Learning and Development NVQs

C&G – regarding qualifications for teachers and assessors

*Sector Skills Councils – for information regarding occupational competence

Glossary of terms

APL accreditation of prior learning

CADET consistent, accessible, detailed, earned, transparent

Competence the knowledge of or ability to do something

Confidentiality secrecy of information

Direct assessment evidence of the learner's work

Effective assessment to produce the intended or desired result or outcome

Indirect assessment evidence or opinion from others

Integrity having values and principles

Judgement a decision about an assessment

Outcome result or consequence of assessment

Triangulate measuring by different perspectives

 # SUMMARY

....

In this chapter we set out to achieve the following outcomes:

● Describe the advantages and disadvantages of each assessment method and make informed decisions about which to choose

● Make decisions about your choices of assessment and identify what makes assessment effective

Your Personal Development

You have investigated a wide range of assessment methods and looked at the advantages and disadvantages of each. This will enable you to make better choices about the assessment methods you plan to use and to justify your selection. You have further considered what makes assessment effective and how you will know when your assessments are producing the results you expect. Finally, you have looked at how the competence of assessors will aid effectiveness by adding confidence in assessment strategies.

You should be able to answer questions relating to choosing and justifying assessment tools to gain purposeful assessment outcomes. In your teaching practice you will demonstrate successful choices and increase the effectiveness of assessment and assessment systems.

CHAPTER 14
(ELA)

Analysis of assessment

LEARNING OBJECTIVES

The measurable outcomes that you will achieve by reading this chapter and completing the activities are:

- To develop the insight gained about inclusive practice in Planning and Enabling Learning (PEL chapters 7 and 8)
- To apply that knowledge to assessment practice
- To describe some examples of relevant use of peer and self-assessment

Matching assessment to the needs of learners and the curriculum

REVISION

In Part Two, Chapter 7, you established what inclusion meant and how to create inclusive teaching and learning sessions to meet the needs of all of your learners. You discovered that inclusive practice enhances motivation, and impacts on all aspects of teaching and learning, from planning through delivery and resourcing to supporting learning. In this chapter we will extend this process through to assessment.

Inclusion simply means 'available to all'. Inclusion begins when you first hear about your learners, even before you meet them, and we will discover that the routines you practice will not end until after your learners have left your care towards the next stages of their development, be that further education, training, higher education or employment.

A lot of the focus associated with inclusion centres on planning for differentiation. This starts in the classroom when you prepare outcomes to suit your learners whilst remembering that the curriculum should also be covered. It therefore follows that checking that those outcomes have been met will vary according to the type and depth of knowledge or skill learned. Hence it is easy to see that assessment must suit both individual needs and the curriculum.

Differentiating formative assessment

It is far easier to adjust assessments for formative purposes than for summative assessment. This is because generally formative assessment is devised by the teacher and therefore it is controlled.

EXAMPLES OF RELATIONSHIPS TO THEORY

Kolb's (1984) learning cycle states that assessment is a factor that is necessary to keep the cycle a circle. Something is done: a concrete experience which can be thought about (self-assessment). Try to understand it (questioning) and experiment with solutions (observation, peer assessment, more questions and an evaluation) which leads to . . .

Bloom's taxonomies (1956–1967) which can be used to differentiate the learning outcomes which will indicate the types of assessment methods. Low order cognitive skills suit multiple choice questions, high order cognitive skills and affective domain skills suit essays and short answer questions, psychomotor skills suit observations.

Differentiation in this case is all about planning and preparation. If we know our learners we can enable them to access their assessment, however learners do not have to disclose their requirements. We should be watchful for their needs.

Some ideas:

- Nominated questioning at the end of the lesson to check progress
- Written question sheets with a mixture of short answer and multiple-choice questions
- Group activities resulting in collective decisions
- Tutorials or 1:1 progress reviews
- Self-assessment questionnaires
- Peer assessment following presentations
- Different command words used in homework or class activities
- Varied font type, size, paper colour
- Ask learners if they need assistance
- *Varied* adds interest and meets all needs, known or unknown
- *Differentiated* is inclusive, relevant, motivational
- *Balanced* is never too much of one type, so meets varied needs.

Differentiating summative assessment

Differentiating for summative assessment is more difficult than for formative assessment. This is because you will probably need special permission from awarding bodies to deviate from the agreed type of assessment. Difficult, yes, because these things have to be agreed in writing prior to the events, but not impossible. Awarding bodies will always accommodate those with specific needs: however, they respond to needs, not wants!

You are advised to seek help from examinations administrators, support staff and external moderators (EM) or verifiers (EV). This is essential as you will need the following support in order to differentiate:

- From support tutors you will need professional statements declaring the need and specific allowances that should be made.
- From the examinations office you will need to confirm special arrangements and they will arrange/organise resources, accommodation and **invigilation**.
- From the EM/EV you will need their written consent, so that they are aware of what is occurring and therefore will expect different assessment products at their visit.

Under no circumstances should you modify a test date or time, or permit additional resources in an examination room without prior, written consent.

Variations to summative assessment are usually only applicable to those with a specific need or disability. The learner who always has to do the school run will have to amend their day to cope with an exam that starts at 09.00, whereas the learner who has difficulty in writing due to disability will be allowed extra time. In a formative assessment you may differentiate to cope with the *wants* of individuals, but in a summative assessment only *needs* are addressed.

If a learner has enrolled and completed their programme of study or course they must be able to access assessment. Some of the specialist arrangements include:

- Signers or lip readers
- Scribes (writers)
- Speakers/readers

- Viva (oral examination)
- Time – related to time allowed or date of test
- Location
- Specialist equipment and software.

These recommendations will be advised by support tutors or professionals, and are based on extensive assessment of need; typically these are those with physical or mental needs, hearing or sight impairment or dyslexia.

A teacher can support summative assessment by helping learners to prepare for their exams, tests, questions etc. This can include teaching study skills: note-taking, reading, researching, essay preparation, presenting work or referencing. You may talk through what will happen during observations or examinations, and perhaps use classroom role play or video/DVD to help learners prepare for their assessment.

ILT in assessment

ILT is used increasingly as a teaching tool; it therefore follows that it will be seen as an assessment tool also. For teachers and learners who enjoy this style (but remember this doesn't include everyone), it is merely a continuation of their learning when they are assessed in this way. Some of the ways in which ILT/ICT can support assessment are:

- word processing work,
- using presentation software, e.g. PowerPoint, for presentations,
- using interactive boards in question sessions,
- using the Internet for research,
- using forums for ideas and questions,
- using databases and spreadsheets to track progress,
- using email to submit and return work
- storing evidence in portfolios
- online screening or diagnostic assessment
- course material uploaded to virtual learning environments (VLEs)
- questioning using electronic voting systems.

The Qualifications and Curriculum Authority (**QCA**) has expressed a commitment to the development of **e-assessment**. It requires that awarding bodies develop opportunities for online assessment and on-demand assessment.

Advantages to e-assessment:

- Learners can take tests as they become confident/competent
- Immediate feedback and results
- Objective marking, especially when computer marked
- Less requirement for paper records, results stored electronically
- More inclusive.

Disadvantages to e-assessment:

- Expensive technology and specialist software necessary
- Reliant on power – what if this is not available due to location or supply?
- Not everyone is comfortable with technological advances
- Difficult to assess values and attitudes, typically presented in essay format
- Overuse of 'cut and paste'.

Progress around ILT in assessment needs to be concerned with a **blended learning** approach. This will offer alternatives according to levels of confidence in using computerised technologies and provide changes in style (as opposed to death by computer technologies). E-assessment should be offered as an acceptable alternative rather than a required option.

Peer and self-assessment

Both peer and self-assessment generally lead to reflective practice. Both are concerned with the ability to judge oneself and involve a critical analysis of the individual learner. It is useful when trying to develop a learner's evaluative and feedback skills. Peer assessment is based on learning from each other and is therefore a good way to share ideas and best practice.

The assessment strategy usually starts with some carefully posed questions, ideally devised by the learner although teachers can guide them to reach solutions and standards. The questions should be open and probing.

EXAMPLES OF RELATIONSHIPS TO THEORY

Kolb (1984). His learning cycle relies heavily on concepts of reflection – which involves self-assessment.

Schön (1983). Reflective practices in-action and on-action rely on self-assessment to influence changes in behaviour.

Boud (1995). Expressed his beliefs that learning and development will not occur without self-assessment and reflection.

Some ideas to include self- and peer assessment in teaching and learning:

● *Student presentations* – at the end of the presentation ask observers and presenters to assess themselves against some criteria – for example, content, communication, contribution and professionalism.

● *Micro-teach sessions* – as presentations, but ask observers to comment on whether the teaching appealed to their learning style and if they learned anything.

● *Tutorials* – specific questions such as which part of the course/assignment was the most difficult? How do your key skills lessons support your main qualification?

● *Profiles* – ask learners to describe their abilities against occupational or academic standards, or at the end of the course ask them to describe the key things they have learned and where their development now lies.

Glossary of terms

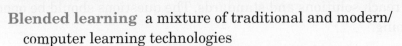

Blended learning a mixture of traditional and modern/ computer learning technologies

E-assessment electronic versions of assessment

Invigilation supervision of examination candidates

QCA Qualifications and Curriculum Authority

SUMMARY

In this chapter we set out to achieve the following outcomes:

- Develop the insight gained about inclusive practice in Planning and Enabling Learning (PEL Chapters 7 and 8)
- Apply that knowledge to assessment practice
- Describe some examples of relevant use of peer and self-assessment

Your Personal Development

You have considered inclusion through differentiated assessment at both formative and summative levels. You have reviewed ideas about how to differentiate assessment to suit needs and strategies to support special assessment needs in summative assessment. The role of ILT in assessment is analysed and suggestions made regarding appropriate use.

Finally, you have reviewed peer and self-assessment and their importance is described with suggestions for relevant use.

You should be able to answer questions relating to:

- The importance of rules in assessment
- The purpose of inclusion
- Differentiated assessment
- Values of peer and self-assessment in learning.

CHAPTER 15
(ELA)

Feedback and questioning in assessment

LEARNING OBJECTIVES

The measurable outcomes that you will achieve by reading this chapter and completing the activities are:

- To identify the value of feedback, especially relating to assessment and progression, the methods of feedback
- To describe the skills required to provide effective feedback
- To compare and contrast a variety of different questioning techniques
- To consider the strengths and weaknesses of each and make informed decisions about selection of questions

Feedback in assessment

Feedback is the conversation between teacher/assessor and learner. It aims to celebrate strengths, give constructive advice on weaknesses and identify areas for further development. It is essential in the assessment process, and its main purpose is to let learners know how well (or not) they are doing. (See also Chapter 4, pp. 96–97.)

Feedback skills

Giving feedback is not easy; it is particularly difficult at the opposite ends of the feedback spectrum. If observed practice or an assessed piece is particularly good, it is difficult to identify development suggestions, or, conversely, it is difficult to feedback to learners without destroying confidence when their assessment is not up to standard. Giving effective feedback will test your own skills in listening, objectivity and explaining. It will improve the confidence of your learners and develop their potential, but it takes time to get it right. The hint here, although you will be encouraged to give immediate feedback, is that in the early days you may wish to consider what you want to say before diving in – so give yourself a few minutes to think and plan what you are going to say.

Feedback should:

- Be delivered promptly after the assessment, preferably immediately, especially after observation or verbal questioning sessions
- Be a two-way process – you can always ask the learner to say how they think it went and get an idea of their understanding, checking their ideas for development
- Be motivational – feedback increases confidence and self-esteem and therefore potential attainment
- Be specific – feedback should only be about the assessment; it should be unbiased, without opinion, unnecessary digression or imposing your own standards

- Offer choices and solutions – this develops potential
- Only comment on things that can be changed – e.g. behaviours or values, not appearance or inner character
- Positive – use strategies that will encourage a learner to develop
- Be constructive – use a balance of positive and negative comments.

Constructive feedback

Constructive feedback is the title given to a form of feedback which is helpful and supportive. It is motivational in that it neither gives false descriptions of a learner's ability nor does it destroy their self-esteem, but aims to develop and fine-tune skills. Whether produced verbally or in writing, this effective style of feedback follows a distinct pattern of:

1   A positive opener
2   A developmental statement
3   Motivational close

also known as . . .

'the feedback sandwich'

By starting with a positive statement, you will reassure and relax the recipient of the feedback. Always identify something good, even if it is only the fact that they turned up on time! The comments you make should always link to the standards being assessed. The feedback should always be about the individual and you should never compare their performance with any one else or anything other than the standards expected.

Developmental statements are the point at which you should make comments about things which need to be improved. It is good to get contributions from the recipient of the feedback. Using open questions will aid this process and together you will formulate your future plans.

Some questions you might wish to consider are:

- IIow do you think that the customer felt when you . . .?
- What would you do if . . .?
- What alternatives are there to . . .?
- Why did that happen?
- At what point in the process would you think about . . .?

If there is going to be a 'but' the person giving the feedback should build up confidence (i.e. discuss the positive aspects of the work) before delivering the shock. The word 'but' should also be used cautiously.

'It was alright but it wasn't very welcoming' is not particularly helpful. It seems to suggest a negative outcome. An alternative suggestion might be: 'I liked the way that you welcomed the customer and believe it would be improved if you'd stood to greet them.' This is of the same flavour but not as hard as a 'but' statement. In the second statement the 'but' is delivered as an 'and'. Therefore, is not as critical and more developmental.

Ending the feedback in a motivational way will incite the learner to take on board recommendations and leave them feeling positive about their performance, even if they are not ecstatic about the outcome. Ideally in a feedback session, you should try to get the recipient to identify their own way forward. This ownership of the actions needed to improve will result in a high level of motivation. It is at this point that you can develop reflective skills in your learners.

Assessment decisions

Following an assessment and the resultant feedback, you will have to make a **judgement**. The decision will be a summary of what you saw that was good, the standard achieved and how much further development is needed. There will usually be parts of the assessment that are satisfactory, but there may be others that were not so good – and this may be reflected in the grade or pass mark. In NVQs, all **performance criteria** (PCs) must be met, which is why an assessment may consist of more than one method of assessment to cope with the things that don't naturally occur. Depending upon the type of qualification, purpose of assessment and level of formality in the assessment, the decision will either be:

- **Pass or Fail** – the assessment either meets or doesn't meet the standard required.
- **A graded result** – **pass**, merit [credit], distinction which describes how well a learner has achieved, but your feedback needs to explain the development between levels.
- **Marks** – out of 10, 20, 100 etc., usually expressed as percentage.

The teacher should be quite clear in stating the outcome of the assessment. Saying the words 'you've passed' is very often the thing that is forgotten at the expense of creating good feedback. Also, sometimes the feedback is so positive that a learner can misunderstand the outcome, maybe thinking that they've passed or achieved a higher grade than they actually have.

The 'F' word

The word **fail** is rarely used. This is because it is highly demotivational. Rarely is everything so bad in an assessment that the teacher cannot comment positively on some aspect. If an assessment is not at the required standard, i.e. *fails*, you should consider alternative expressions such as 'needs further training' or 'not yet competent' or simply 'refer'.

In discussing feedback, it is worth noting the research of Professor. John Hattie of Auckland University (1999 and 2003). He investigated the effects of feedback on achievement and the ability of teachers to influence learning.

Having dissected the factors associated with teaching and learning and categorised them into responsibilities, he discovered, not surprisingly, that the teacher has a significant influence on learning. This furthered his earlier research which identified the extent to which feedback impacts on achievement, all of which supports the current beliefs in assessment *for* learning rather than the assessment *of* learning. This concept is discussed further in Chapter 16. In summary, effective feedback is more effective in developing learner progress than merely providing grades. This is generally because if a learner is told 'that's a pass' or 'it's a grade B' they are more likely to accept that outcome without seeking development or improvement. When given feedback, most learners will attempt to develop future work. In combination they are able to meet both learners' values and aspirations.

Additional reading

....

Additional reading on this research is widely available on the Internet using Hattie, feedback and assessment as key words in a search engine.

Questioning in assessment

REVISION

In Part One, Chapter 5, you looked at questioning as one of the methods of assessment and discovered what the main purposes were. In Chapter 13 the methods of assessment were analysed in more depth to identify advantages and disadvantages of their use. In this chapter, we focus on questioning and look in more detail at some aspects of questioning techniques and their benefits.

One of the most successful and versatile assessment methods is that of questioning. The variety of methods within the category of **questioning** is large and the way it can be used to differentiate, motivate and develop learners is very broad. Equally, it is the assessment method that is most criticised and open to inefficient and ineffective use.

1 Essay type

Description	A structured, semi-structured or unstructured piece of writing on a topic.
	The level of structure is determined by the question posed.
	May also be called **extended questions**.
Main uses	Depth of subject knowledge is tested.
	Tests values and opinions and argument.
	Academic/research investigative pieces.
	Creative, evaluative or descriptive writing.
	Unsuitable as oral questioning.
Designing questions	Very easy, questions can range from unstructured, when learners decide upon their own topics as in dissertations, to semi-structured, when broad topic titles are given, to structured when learners answer a series of questions making up the topic title.
	Categorised as supply type of questions.
Making judgements	Difficult to mark – detailed assessment criteria required to allocate set marks for specific component of essay (e.g. 10 marks for . . ., 50 marks for . . ., etc.).
	Difficult to mark objectively so results may lack consistency.
	Generally marked as a percentage or grade.
Assessment rules	Formative or summative applications.
	May cover only a small aspect of the curriculum so impacts on validity and sufficiency.
	Open to plagiarism and cheating thus questioning authenticity.
Differentiation	Assesses understanding and cognitive skills.
	Assesses literacy skills (and numeracy when data collection requirements are included).
	Can be intimidating for learners, as essay writing is a skill in itself.
	Level of high order skills makes them highly suitable for learners at Level 3 and above.

▶

2 Short answer type

Description	Specific questions on a single or multiple topics, requiring a few paragraphs of text as an answer.
Main uses	Very versatile style of questions, which can be oral or written, requiring one-word, sentence or extended answers. Tests cognitive skills and either depth of knowledge or breadth of knowledge – dependent on questions asked. Good homework questions as they do not take too long to complete. Requires learners to remember information. Ideal as extended oral questions. Often called 'open' questions. Very effective when used orally in a nominated questioning style, so that questions are linked to learner ability.
Designing questions	Fairly easy to design using words such as How? Why? When? Where? What? Create open questions, requiring responses covering fact, opinion. Can design should/could/would options in questions. Categorised as supply type of questions. Can be one-word or sentence/paragraph length responses.
Making judgements	Marking grids are required as answers will vary. Objectivity increased due to more focused responses. Weight of questions is usually reflected in number of marks available for each question.
Assessment rules	Formative or summative applications. Covers a wider range of topics in the curriculum and improves sufficiency in coverage. Widens opportunities to collect valid, reliable and qualitative responses. When questions are asked verbally it is absolutely authentic – unless the question is posed in advance and answered at a later time.

Differentiation	Less frightening than essay type questions.
	Develops essay writing skills, therefore ideal for learners progressing to or aspiring to higher academic levels.
	Degree of difficulty can be varied to support different needs of learners.
	Less analysis and argument needed, questions usually relate to fact or opinion, which makes them more suitable for Level 1 and 2 learners.
	Can be used to probe deeper into a subject to ascertain levels of understanding.
	Opportunity to collect ipsative/profiling information.

3 Multiple-choice type

Description	A question with (usually) four possible answers, which requires learners to identify the correct answer.
	Sometimes called **restricted response** or expressed as multiple-choice questions (**MCQs**).
Main uses	Requires learners to recognise information.
	Possible as oral questions if planned in advance.
	Very often used in summative tests.
Designing questions	Very difficult to prepare.
	Questions (the **stem**) have a correct answer (the key) and several (usually 3 or 4) incorrect answers (distractors). The **key** and distractors are collectively called 'options'.
	Learners call them multiple guess questions as once the obvious **distractors** are removed; it usually leaves two possible answers. C is the most common correct answer so the test needs to be tested so that correct answers are evenly distributed.
	Categorised as selection type questions.
Making judgements	Very easy to mark as only one answer will be correct.
	Computerised marking software can be used.
	Learners can participate in marking if given answer frames.
	Very objective way of testing.
	Opportunities to vary levels of questions to test range of ability – power of discrimination.

▶

◄

Assessment rules	Questions can cover a large part of the curriculum.
	Large numbers of questions can be asked in a relatively short space of time.
	Can be used to gather **quantitative** data in larger research studies.
	Can be used formatively or summatively.
Differentiation	Questions can vary in level of difficulty.
	No test of writing skills, but good to develop reading and comprehension skills.
	Questions can be 'banked' and reused at a later date.
	Generally MCQs test recall rather than comprehension, however, more complex questions can be formed to test higher order skills.

4 Alternative answer type

Description	Either yes/no, true/false answers to specific questions resulting in very restricted responses.
Main uses	Requires learners to recognise information by giving limited answers.
	Very little depth of knowledge required.
	Tendency to guess, therefore low order cognitive skills are tested.
	Used in questionnaires to gather data.
	Often called 'closed' questions.
Designing questions	Simple to answer and prepare.
	In more complex questionnaires, avoid an odd number of responses as this allows people to remain undecided (sitting on the fence), which may not be helpful in eliciting data.
	Categorised as selection type questions.
Making judgements	Easy to mark, learners can participate in marking.
	Objective method of marking, but limited reliability due to guesswork.

Assessment rules	Doesn't test reliably due to chance of guessing answers correctly.
	Due to lack of reliability, they are more suitable to formative assessment.
Differentiation	Does not test writing skills.
	50 per cent chance of correct answer.
	Use of Likert scale can bring in more responses (strongly agree, agree, disagree, strongly disagree).

5 Matching answer type

Description	Two lists of data or facts are written which have to be matched.
Main uses	Used to match, for example: events and dates; terms and explanations; facts and figures; etc.
	Can be used with individuals or groups.
	Unsuitable as oral questions.
Designing questions	Average ease to design, but messy to answer; answers tend to be lines drawn from one correct answer to the corresponding fact in other list, so may need to prepare answer sheets.
	Categorised as selection type questions.
Making judgements	Easy to mark, although answer sheets may be difficult to read.
	If one question is wrong it may limit opportunities to get all other answers correct.
	Very objective in scoring/result.
Assessment rules	Valid and objective method of testing factual data.
	Difficult to include the power to discriminate because of limited answer frameworks.
	Ideal formative assessment for low order skills.

▶

Differentiation	Suits fun activities and opener/closure activities.
	Very few literacy skills assessed.
	Can test whether learning outcomes are met.
	Covers wide curriculum or can link separately delivered topics to create learning links.

6 Completion type

Description	Text or diagrammatic sheets in which key words are omitted. Sometimes called gapped handouts.
Main uses	Can be used for recall tests at beginning and end of lessons or to create interaction during class time.
	Can be used as oral questions if planned in advance.
	Useful to create *aides-memoires* for learners.
Designing questions	Any document can be adapted to become a completion-type test.
	Cloze technique (missing out letters in regular patterns) can be used to determine reading ages and comprehension levels.
	Categorised as supply type questions.
Making judgements	Objective as there should be only one correct solution.
	Marking is usually correct responses out of maximum.
Assessment rules	Valid, in that tests are usually about current topics being taught in the curriculum.
	Formative strategy to check classwork progress.
Differentiation	Can be used with or without answer options to differentiate between abilities.
	Can test spelling and comprehension of technical terms.

General hints and tips about questioning

● Make sure that learners know how to answer the questions – special answer sheet, black ballpoint pen or pencil, style (essay, report or bullet points), word count.

- Make questions short and precise.
- Avoid negatives in questions – 'which of the following is not . . .' and multiple correct questions – with questions like 'which is the main reason for . . .'. If these *must* be used then highlight the command word using **bold**, *italics* or <u>underline</u> formatting.
- Arrange questions logically and avoid repetition in subject type.
- If suggesting a word count, it is usually acceptable to add a '+ or – 10 per cent' rule, before marks are deducted for too few or too many words.
- The more unstructured the question the more creative and diverse the answer because of the freedom of ideas allowed.
- Reduce misinterpretation of questions by avoiding words like 'some', 'a few', 'a range'. How many *is* a few?

Glossary of terms

Constructive a term used to imply helpful feedback

Distractor incorrect answer choices in MCQs

Extended question a question that involves a long answer

Fail an assessment decision; not at pass standard

Feedback verbal or written comments about the assessment intended to bring about improvement

Judgement a decision about an assessment

Key the correct answer in a MCQ

MCQ multiple choice question

NVQ National Vocational Qualification

Pass assessment decision relating to satisfactory performance

Performance criteria standards of required competence

Qualitative data relating to opinions or thoughts

Quantitative data relating to statistics and number

Questioning queries inviting responses

Restricted response limited choices in answers

Stem the term given to a question in a MCQ

SUMMARY

In this chapter we set out to achieve the following outcomes:

- Identify the value of feedback, especially relating to assessment and progression, the methods of feedback
- Describe the skills required to provide effective feedback
- Compare and contrast a variety of different questioning techniques
- Consider the strengths and weaknesses of each and make informed decisions about selection of questions

Your Personal Development

In this chapter you have analysed the meaning and purpose of assessment in the context of questioning and feedback. You can recognise key terms relating to feedback and questioning. You have identified strategies to offer and deliver feedback and reflected on the possible outcomes of assessment.

You have reviewed several types of questioning techniques and can distinguish between the main types of questioning, considering their value to both teacher and learner in achieving valid and reliable data about progress.

You should be able to answer questions relating to the importance of feedback and justifying choices about appropriate assessment methods, whilst ensuring that they are fit for purpose.

CHAPTER 16
(ELA)

Recording progress and achievement

PHOTOFUSION PICTURE LIBRARY / ALAMY

LEARNING OBJECTIVES

The measurable outcomes that you will achieve by reading this chapter and completing the activities are:

- To describe the purpose of assessment in terms of measuring achievement and progress
- To specify procedures and documents relevant in the planning, implementation, feedback and judging of assessments
- To explain the quality assurance practices that provide reliability in assessment
- To describe the need for record keeping
- To describe how and why progress is reported

The purpose of assessment

Purposes of assessment

Assessment is a key function in teaching and learning; it informs the reasons for teaching and collects information regarding the results of that teaching; this makes assessment integral to the process of learning. In their research, Black and Wiliam (1998) suggest that assessment together with constructive feedback will bring about raised levels of achievement. This has reformed the way assessment is perceived in the classroom, bringing about a subtle change from 'assessment *of* learning' to 'assessment *for* learning' (Assessment Reform Group 2002, Craig and Fieschi 2007).

Much is written about assessment; in many of the key texts that you will read, assessment is defined as:

> [to] judge a learner's performance against identified criteria.

> Fawbert 2003: 247

> The process of obtaining information about how much the student knows.

> Reece and Walker 2006: 35

> Assessment equates to testing: if a learner is being assessed, then he or she is being tested.

> Tummons 2007: 4

There are three stages of assessment, which associate with its purpose:

1   Obtaining information
2   Forming judgements
3   Making decisions.

The first part, obtaining information, refers to the various methods of collecting the information, but more importantly, the teacher should ask 'why do we collect information?' (see Chapter 13).

You can gather information that relates to:

● learners' progress
● levels of motivation
● perceived and actual levels of attainment
● the effectiveness of teaching methods and practices
● diagnosing the needs of learners
● identification of the support needs of learners
● the confirmation of acquired learning outcomes
● start and end points of learning
● the amount and level of feedback needed to progress learning
● previous learning, experience or qualifications.

This collection of information enables you to make a judgement (assessment) about ability, competence or levels of knowledge and understanding. You can also use these outcomes to ascertain the effectiveness of your teaching. Assessment should be the tool to celebrate achievement and identify development. In reality it is all too often used as a negative tool to criticise poor achievement or failing standards and, therefore, it is very often seen in a threatening way, because we all fear failure.

Inside the Black Box

Prof. Paul Black and Dr. Dylan Wiliam (1998)

Assessment For Learning: Beyond the Black Box (1999), University of Cambridge, School of Education

A four-year study, commissioned by the Assessment Reform Group (funded by the Nuffield Foundation) to review the research available on classroom assessment. Their finding was that informal assessment in the classroom, with constructive feedback, raises achievement.

Subsequent research suggested that increasing the amount of assessment does not enhance learning, rather it is using assessment effectively that raises achievement and potential. It recommended strategic and political changes to implement the change from assessment of learning, designed for grading and reporting processes, to assessment for learning, designed for development and progress.

Budge (2005), citing Black and Wiliam (1998), summarises the research and writes:

What works:

- regular classroom testing and the use of results to adjust teaching and learning rather than competitive grading;
- enhanced feedback between teacher and pupil which may be oral or written;
- the active involvement of all pupils;
- careful attention to pupil's motivation and help in building their self-belief;
- self- or peer-assessment by pupils, discussion in groups and dialogue between teacher and pupils.

. . . and what doesn't

- tests that encourage **rote** and superficial learning;
- over-emphasis on the giving of marks and grades at the expense of useful advice to learners;
- competitive teaching approaches that de-motivate some pupils;
- feedback, testing and record-keeping that serve a managerial function rather than a learning one.

David Budge, TES, Tasting the assessment soup. 18th February 2005.

The Association for Achievement and Improvement through Assessment (AAIA), sets out ten principles, devised by the Assessment Reform Group (ARG), as:

Assessment:

1 is part of effective planning

2 focuses on how students learn

3 is central to classroom practices

4 is a key professional skill

5 is sensitive and constructive

6 fosters motivation

7 promotes understanding of goals and criteria

8 helps learners know how to improve

9 develops the capacity for self-assessment

10 recognises all educational achievement.

www.aaia.org.uk/pdf/AFL_10principlesARG.pdf (accessed 30.09.07)

These principles advocate the assessment *for* learning instead of assessment *of* learning. The Learning and Skills Council (LSC) still requires measurements in terms of **success**, i.e., collecting data about outcomes (assessment of learning). This requires teachers to prove their performance in terms of targets, arguing that learner's performance, whilst born through **nurture** and tutoring (assessment for learning), is a contributory factor to the final result. Current research and trends seem to argue that it should be the leading role and are therefore pushing for significant policy changes (ARG 2002).

The links between outcome and purpose of assessment and the timeliness of assessment may not be absolutely clear. The following table attempts to make that link explicit.

	Pre-enrolment	Initial assessment	Diagnostic assessment	Formative assessment	Summative assessment
Increasing the motivation of learners	✓			✓	
Diagnosis of functional skills needs			✓		
Establishing understanding of topic				✓	✓
Demonstrating ability			✓	✓	✓
Identifying support needs	✓	✓	✓		
Assessment of unit or module outcomes					✓
Statement of competence					✓
Previous attainment	✓	✓			
Forward planning				✓	
Effectiveness of teaching and learning				✓	

Assessment procedures

Procedures are defined as 'the official way of doing things'. These
routines are usually specified or informed by legislation or in this
case by codes of practice. There are procedures associated with the
planning, implementation, feedback and judgements of assessment.
NVQ qualifications have specific codes of practice relating to the
delivery, assessment and quality assurance of programmes and the
qualifications of assessors and verifiers. Guidance exists to ensure
that learners, teachers, trainers and assessors, delivery and

assessment institutions and awarding bodies are clear about strategy, method and role and that practices are able to stand up to scrutiny by **inspectorate** and audit teams.

Awarding bodies will also provide information on quality assurance (**QA**) processes. In particular, see:

NVQ Code of Practice
Ensuring Quality
Guidance on Internal Verification

Planning

Assessment needs to be planned. In the same way that teaching is planned in order to meet need, produce variety and structure, so assessment should be organised similarly. Some of the reasons for this include:

- Learning outcomes need regular assessment to ensure learners are on target to achieve their goals;
- Assessments in the workplace need to be arranged with supervisors, to minimise disruption to the business;
- Recreational courses will have learners working on their own projects, so the teacher needs to liaise closely to ensure learners goals are recognised, realistic and monitored;
- Special arrangements may need to be made – access to specialist equipment and resources;
- Complex programmes of study need to have all assessments plotted to ensure even distribution across the programme.

Planning, especially for one-to-one assessments, needs to be recorded and agreed. The candidate should have clear guidelines about what they are expected to do and what the outcomes are likely to be. In some, particularly vocational courses, assessment strategies require a number of successful formative assessments of practical skills, before a summative assessment of practical skill or knowledge tests. A suggestion is:

SUMMATIVE ASSESSMENT PLAN	
Name:	Date of proposed assessment:
Planned activity:	
Expected outcomes/criteria/evidence:	
Plan signed/dated by assessor:	Plan agreed, signed/dated by candidate:
Feedback following assessment:	Actions for development:
Outcome: Pass ▢ Needs further training ▢	Assessor signature: Candidate signature: Date:

In planning for more academic subjects, the teacher should consider the total number of assessments (which may consist of a number of tasks) and plot these into a calendar to distribute them across the programme of study. This involves liaising with other teachers on the team, whilst working within awarding body deadline dates. A suggestion is:

Unit	September	October	November	December	January	February	March	April	May	June	July
1		✗									
2				✗							
3						✗					
4							✗				
5									✗		
6											✗

In modular or unitised programmes, for example National Diplomas, then assessment will take the format of an assignment which includes a number of tasks, which relate to criteria and the demonstration of key skills. In this instance, an assessment plan may follow this style:

Unit title:			
Task	**Interim due date**	**Links to criteria**	**Links to key skills**
Task one *Description of what a learner must do or present for assessment*		*e.g. P1, P3, M1*	*Communication, Applications of Number, ICT and wider key skills links*
Task two *Description of what a learner must do or present for assessment*		*e.g. P2, M2, D1*	*Communication, Applications of Number, ICT and wider key skills links*
Task three, etc *Description of what a learner must do or present for assessment*		*e.g. P4, P5, M3*	*Communication, Applications of Number, ICT and wider key skills links*

To achieve a pass, the learner must:

This section will specify the P criteria using command words such as describe, identify, etc.

To achieve a merit, the learner must:

This section will specify the M criteria using command words such as analyse, etc.

To achieve a distinction, the learner must:

This section will specify the D criteria using command words such as evaluate etc.

The completed assignment must be handed in by:

Signatures: *Teacher and Quality Assurance Coordinator*

Implementing

The processes involved when implementing (doing) the assessment are related to ensuring that the rules of evidence are being met (Chapter 12). You should consider what type of assessment it is (Chapter 13), whether or not it is formative or summative (Chapter 12), and what you need to achieve in terms of outcomes and the time/location available.

Some of the things you may need to consider during formative and summative assessments are:

- Is the learner sufficiently prepared for the assessment?
- Do you have access to **registration** numbers; have you confirmed the eligibility to enter the assessment process?
- Do you and the learners have access to sufficient, adequate resources for the assessment?
- Does the arrangement of furniture facilitate equality and honesty?
- Has there been an accurate briefing of expectations and statement of proposed outcomes – shared planning?
- Is there a quiet area for oral questioning (if necessary)?
- Are you able to identify individual progress within the group?
- How will the assessment be recorded?
- Does the assessment need third party intervention (an invigilator) to ensure impartiality?
- Can you guarantee accuracy in timing of assessment – start and end times, a visible clock, adherence to specified durations?
- Have you checked the authenticity of candidates – are they who they say they are?
- Have you considered how the results of the assessment are to be conveyed?
- Do you need a feedback session afterwards?

Judgements

The procedures relating to judgements are associated with marking schemes, grading **criteria** and hand-in dates. These must always be clearly stated before the assessment. It might be a good idea to double check these during the planning processes.

A *marking scheme* may look like this:

ESSAY TITLE: Describe the importance of communication in a specific retail environment	
Definition of communication	One mark
Definition 'specific' retail environment	One mark
Theories associated with communication	Two marks
Links between communication and retail environment	Four marks
Stated factors of importance	Four marks
Coherence of expression	Two marks
Accuracy of spelling and grammar	Two marks
Structure of essay	Two marks
Bibliography, referencing and accuracy of citation	Two marks
Total marks available	20

In this example it is quite clear from the weighting of the marks (60 per cent) where the emphasis of the work should be. Yet marks can be lost, for example if the skills associated with essay writing (40 per cent) are not met. There may also be a stated requirement to achieve a pass standard – for example 10 out of 20.

Grading criteria relate to the quality and depth of the work. For example you will see grids written into many of qualification guides that specify what learners have to do to achieve a pass, merit and distinction grades. The information contained within the **grading** grids enables the teacher to challenge learners to aspire to a level greater than that which may be predicted or expected. It helps the learners to clarify what is expected of them in their assessment and hopefully stretch themselves.

For example:

To achieve a pass grade, learners must achieve *all* pass criteria. To achieve a merit grade, the learners must achieve all of the pass criteria and all of the merit criteria. To achieve a distinction grade, the learner must achieve all of the pass and merit criteria and all of the distinction criteria.

The processes involved in stating and achieving hand-in dates are going to be very specific to each qualification and/or organisation. Some will notionally suggest dates by which work should be submitted, probably using the individual learning plan to negotiate these; other qualifications may specify an absolute, non-compliance means a sanction, type of situation. You and your learners should be fully conversant with which applies and what, if any, sanctions are administered if pertinent.

Quality assurance

Quality assurance (QA) increases the levels of confidence in the value of assessment and the decisions made during assessment; they are mechanisms or policies for ensuring reliable, effective assessment, i.e. guarantees of quality. The purpose of QA is to assure the integrity of product nationally, to set entry and exit standards that are equal so that all stakeholders know, regardless of where the qualification was achieved, the standards are equal. This is one of the main differences between qualifications and unvalidated company training.

Qualifications have to be seen to be of a specific standard, whereas company training is designed to meet the unique requirements of a particular organisation. Both assure quality of provision, but company training certificates are less transferable between other sectors because the training is being designed around individual company practices.

The basic duties of assessors and moderator/verifiers have been clearly stated in the PTLLS (Chapter 5), but when it comes to quality assurance, you may find other personnel or functions involved in assessment.

For example, there is an increasing requirement to use independent assessors. This is to support the accuracy and reliability of assessment decisions. As many assessors are also involved in the delivery of training, it is difficult to assure objectivity when an assessor and learner have built up a successful learning and training rapport. By building another tier into the assessment, the quality of the assessment decisions are made more robust. Independent assessment usually means that a particular component must be assessed by someone not previously involved in the training, learning or assessment process. It is not validation of an assessment decision as this remains the role of the verifier or moderator.

Advantages:

- Assessors are protected from accusations of unreliability by using a third party to make certain assessment decisions
- Learners are guaranteed unbiased judgements.

Disadvantages:

- Another tier of assessment means additional costs.

Language of quality assurance

Standardisation (Chapter 5) relates to the consistency and agreement of expected standards or content. It can occur before assessment to set unified expectations or afterwards to agree the standard of marking.

Moderation refers to checking the marks and grades awarded by the assessment team.

Verification relates to checking that assessment processes are reliable.

Second (and *third*) *marking* refers to a process similar to standardisation, when one piece of work is independently marked by another person to (hopefully) get the same result.

Approval is the process involved with seeking permission to run particular programmes, under the guidance of an awarding body. Awarding bodies, who **certificate** the programmes, are required to meet stringent audits by the Qualifications and Curriculum Authority (QCA) to ensure their quality assurance practices are sound.

Recording assessment

REVISION

In Chapter 5, you saw examples of record keeping at an individual level for the purpose of tracking progress. You learned that records are an essential part of the assessment process by providing evidence of achievement and competence. In this section we extend that to the wider purpose of assessment and achievement records for organisational purposes.

The part of the job associated with record keeping often seems bureaucratic and repetitive. It sometimes takes longer to prove you did the job than it took to do the job in the first place. These feelings are quite common and you should not feel guilty about having them, although to move on you need to see the value in the process, so here goes . . .

Paperwork: The necessary evil or the answer to your prayers?

The need to record assessments or in fact any other aspect of the role is essential to you, your learners, your colleagues and your managers. Completing the necessary paperwork on time and distributing it to those who need it is essential for efficient and effective working practices.

Record keeping is best done in smaller chunks and not all left to the end of a programme, this ensures a distribution of the workload and timely completion of records which ultimately saves time. Records help you to remember what has occurred and act as a guide to others in case you are not available. A filing system suits methodical workers but not spontaneous types and so it is something that may need personal development time to fine tune. Records need to be kept in a logical sequence; **chronological**, alphabetical, by name, by programme or any combination of those. They may be stored as a paper record or saved electronically.

Who needs them and why:

Who	Why
Learners	To provide records to evidence achievement, progress and support needs. They will need support in storing their information.
Teacher	To replicate progress records of learners (in case of loss), inform reports to others, inform reflective personal and professional practice. To know who has done what and when. To vary assessment methods, to raise awareness of the overall assessment strategy of a learner.
Colleagues	To support team members in their absence, to share in team meetings and self-assess the effectiveness of their programmes. They need records to be assembled logically and accessible.
Managers	To monitor performance; plan for responsive provision, make strategic and financial decisions.
Quality unit	To generate comparative analysis across the organisation and compare performance with benchmarks.
Parents	To inform about the progress of their child on the programme. Learners may not communicate well with their parents and so this is the only link. Don't rely on learners giving reports to their parents, especially if they are anticipating less complimentary reports.
Schools	To create a link between vocational and academic studies and develop a standardised approach to a learner's development.

▶

Who	Why
Employers	To inform about the progress of their employee on the programme. As the financial sponsor, they require accurate and reliable progress information. To inform their business processes.
Awarding bodies	To register and certificate achievement, to action and record external quality monitoring processes, to inform responsive development.
Auditors	To check funding claims are legitimate and business processes are legal and above question. To scrutinize accountability and responsibility.
Inspectorate	To quality assure performance at organisation level against national standards, to justify appropriate use of public funds.

What are the consequences of failure to keep records?

● The learner's progress is haphazard and unstructured;

● Mistakes and trends are not noticed so they continue to impact on practice, possibly in a downward spiral;

● There is a lack of accountability with no-one taking the lead on responsibility to learners and other stakeholders;

● Learners don't gain their qualifications, or if they learn the required elements they will not be accredited through a recognised body;

● Public confidence is reduced, which results in lower enrolments, which leads to fewer classes, fewer jobs, and eventually the demise of the organisation.

Hints and tips for record keeping

● Keep copies for third parties.

● Write in an appropriate style for the reader – the learner, parent, awarding body etc.

- Keep notes about informal processes – development needs and actions, late work, resubmission dates, problems, etc.

- Documentation should give an overview rather than record every 'if, but and maybe'.

- Documents should be fit for purpose.

- Keep records relating to the process and product of assessment.

- Records may be self-devised or devised by the organisation – ask what is in use before going your own way.

Minimum core numeracy – averages in assessment

You may be asked to prepare statistical information to record assessment, achievement or progress. You may wish to analyse the results of your own assessments for similar reasons. One way of doing this is to identify norms or standards, either to identify trends or compare data with other sets of data. To do this it is advantageous to present data in percentages or using averages. As part of your personal numeracy development, you need to be clear about the expressions mean, median, mode and range and how these can help you analyse results (see Chapter 17).

The *mean* is the average score; it is the easiest of the averages to calculate. It is done by totalling the scores and dividing by the number of learners.

Learner	Score
Jake	19
Sam	18
Phil	12
Sian	15
Sarah	17
Chloe	19
Adam	20
Rafiq	18
Mo	14

In this example:

The scores total $152 \div 9 = 16.8$. This means that the average score is just under 17 out of 20. This can be represented as a percentage – the average score is 85 per cent.

The *median* is the exact middle of the data set. Using our example above, first you should write them in ascending or descending order:

12, 14, 15, 17, 18, 18, 19, 19, 20. The median is 18 because there are 4 figures below and 4 figures above the middle value.

The *mode* is the number that appears most often. In our example there are two modes: 18 and 19.

The *range* of scores is calculated by taking the lowest score from the highest score. In this example 20 is the highest score and the lowest is 12.

$20 - 12 = 8$. The range therefore is 8.

Reporting progress

Much of this was covered in the previous chapter, but whereas that was concerned with record keeping, this part is about sharing those records with others in order to initiate a development. This is the move discussed earlier: record keeping is associated with assessment *of* learning, progress reporting is concerned with assessment *for* learning. As we have already seen, the benefits to the learner when the focus of assessment is changed from measurement to development impacts significantly on the learner's achievement.

Why does progress need to be reported?

Quite simply, because common sense (and current research) says it is the best way to develop potential. If the teacher tells the learner how they are doing, they can engage in a discussion to move forward, rectify mistakes and build on their strengths. It is highly motivational for the learner to be told how well they are progressing. Equally, with constructive feedback, it is equally valuable to know what isn't going so well, and, perhaps through motivational interviewing, you will come up with strategies to overcome this.

Parents are also interested to know how their child is performing in the classroom. It is increasingly important that the learning ethos is shared between home and the learning organisation. If homework is being set, it is good to know that parents are helping to ensure it is done.

Employers are interested because they have identified training needs in their employees and have contracted with learning organisations to realise those goals. They need to know that their employees are getting value for money and that they are attending and contributing to learning.

How and when is progress reported?

- One-to-one reviews – regularly throughout the programme
- Feedback – with all marked work
- Reports – usually once or twice a year
- Employer forums – usually annually
- Parents' evening – usually annually.

The timing of reporting is only a suggestion; it will be determined by cost and availability of resources and staff. It is hoped that informal chats will be almost weekly and progress will be reviewed through feedback every time a piece of work is marked.

Who reports progress and about whom?

The teacher reports to the learner and may also report to either the parent or employer, dependent upon the age of the learner.

ACTIVITY 1

Why do these learners need to know how they are progressing?

Case Study 1

From a younger learner's perspective . . .

Being aged between 14 and 19 is very exciting; the social life is getting better and relationships are being made and broken in a regular cycle; getting paid for work or through a grant or bursary is great – oh yes – there is that classroom stuff but so long as it is interesting and we get plenty of breaks and it doesn't get boring it is not too bad! However, along come teachers and parents who want us teenagers to gain a qualification and then talk about us as though we care, life is for now, not the future. There's plenty of time for that.

Case Study 2

From a mature learner's perspective . . .

I am doing this because I want to, I need to change jobs/get a qualification/earn more money/update my skills and I want the teacher's undivided attention to enable that to happen. I am motivated and want challenge, but I also want to come away from class with loads of notes, ideas and things to do. I want reassurances that I can do the things I have to, because it's been quite a while since I was last in study.

Recommended reading

The following documents and downloads relating to assessment procedures and quality assurance processes can be provided by the relevant awarding body.

NVQ Code of Practice
Ensuring Quality
Guidance on Internal Verification

Glossary of terms

Approval permission to deliver qualifications on behalf of an awarding body

Certificate a recognised outcome of a programme of study

Chronological in date order

Criteria the standard of competence

Grading the degree of competence, pass, merit, distinction

Inspectorate e.g. Adult Learning Inspectorate, Ofsted

Nurture development of characteristics, beliefs or attitudes

QA quality assurance – an official system to establish the quality of something such as an assessment

Registration an official list of entrants on a qualification

Rote teaching by repetition, e.g. learning multiplication tables

Success recognition of achievement

 SUMMARY

In this chapter we set out to achieve the following outcomes:

● Describe the purpose of assessment in terms of measuring achievement and progress and developing potential

● Consider the impact of moving from assessment of learning to assessment for learning

▶

◀

- Specify procedures relevant in the planning, implementation, feedback and judgement stages of assessment, giving examples of appropriate documents and strategies to support the procedures

- Explain the quality assurance practices that provide reliability in assessment

- Describe the need for record keeping at individual and organisational level

- Describe how and why progress is reported, to whom and about whom

Your Personal Development

You have discovered the difference between assessment *of* learning and assessment *for* learning and are able to describe the subtle difference between the two concepts. You can recognise and describe terms associated with development of learning through assessment. You can state the difference between assessment and progression, by listing the principles that underpin development and improvement.

You have investigated procedures of assessment and can explain them, giving examples of relevant documentation to be used during record keeping. You have developed an awareness of the need for marking grids, and how to use grading criteria in order to challenge and motivate learners as well as preparing for assessment.

In terms of quality assurance you are now able to express the purpose of QA in assessment and describe some of the terminology.

Regarding recording and reporting progress, you are able to justify why these processes are essential to business practices and developing a learner's potential. To develop your ability to provide data, you have looked at how averages are calculated and the different types of presenting 'average' statistics.

Finally, your learning is consolidated by engaging in a case study activity to explore why particular groups, albeit stereotypical formats, need to engage in progress development activities.

CHAPTER 17 (ELA)

Evaluating effectiveness

LEARNING OBJECTIVE

The measurable outcomes that you will achieve by reading this chapter and completing the activities are:

- Identify how you can use assessment outcomes to develop the way you assess in the future
- Analyse the effectiveness of your teaching strategies
- Inform your personal development plan

Using assessment outcomes to develop yourself

The expression **assessment**, which means 'to measure achievement', and **evaluation**, which means 'to measure effectiveness' are synonymous. This means they are interchangeable, but in academic language there is a distinct difference. For the teacher, assessment is gathering the information, and evaluation is making sense of that information. The results of assessment will obviously tell us how well our learners are progressing in their programme or how much information they have understood; it may tell us how well they can transfer knowledge or skills into different situations. It is essential that we look at assessment outcomes and try to analyse what they are telling us. This evaluation will open up issues which can then be addressed. Tummons starts this process off by saying:

> Evaluation of the assessment is about judging the extent to which the assessment does what it is supposed to do.
>
> Tummons 2007: 87

A reflective practitioner will take this one stage further and comment about what those results mean to them and endeavour to improve their own performance. For example:

Extract from reflective diary

I set some short answer questions to do as part of the summary of the lesson. There were five questions collectively covering the learning outcomes I set at the beginning of the session, with a question about some 'nice to know' information that I covered immediately after break. I put the 'nice to know' question in to challenge the learners and I'm really pleased that they all answered it very well. In fact they all did very well in the test, mostly getting 4 out of 5. When I looked in more detail I found out that a lot of them (6 learners out of 17) generally went wrong on the same question.

I looked at my teaching notes later and checked that I had covered the topic; it was done by talking it through in some detail. I told the group to take notes and checked that they were writing, so I really can't understand why the question was poorly answered. In fact, I distinctly remember that it was just before break and that straight after break I covered the 'nice to know' bit which they did well in.

If you were reflecting on this event, what conclusions would you make?

Evaluation

In this situation the teacher has not made the link between the teaching style used, the time within the lesson that the topic was covered and the outcome of the test question. Perhaps there is also a link between those that got the question wrong and their learning style; the topic was ideal for auditory and kinaesthetic learners, but not good for visual learners. Add to this that it was just before break and things like tiredness and low attention spans may have an impact on the learners' ability to retain information. The topic may have been one of those parts of the subject that is quite complicated and so has to be explained in detail to be understood. The teacher may have believed that the information was important so had to be delivered by verbal exposition, but that can be boring, because it is a passive activity.

Reflection

What would you do next time if you were the teacher?

What can assessment tell us?

Progress. A test can reveal how well, or not, a learner is progressing. This information can be used in tutorials to offer additional help in the topic, perhaps by directing attention to self-study packs or by advice to attend support workshops. It could be that the learner needs additional training in the skill before attempting another practical test. Do you need to arrange additional sessions, more practice or support?

Effectiveness of teaching. As in the reflective practice exercise above, if it was clear that a large number of learners had not grasped a topic that topic should be revisited. It also reinforces the need to ensure that the questions or observations cover as much of the topic or curriculum as possible. If you don't ask the question, you won't know the answer! Do you need to change the way you teach a particular topic?

Effectiveness of assessment. Were all of the questions valid and reliable (see Chapter 12). Did the questions produce the expected answers? Were you able to mark them objectively? Was there a good coverage of topics/**syllabus**? These questions will establish how good your questions were in testing knowledge. If you were observing performance, you need to think about how useful this activity is in generating evidence for what is being assessed. Do you need to redesign certain aspects of the assessment? Look at the self-assessment checklist below and use the right-hand column to comment upon whether or not the assessments you use follow the rules.

ACTIVITY 1

Checklist to evaluate your assessment techniques.

Think of an assessment activity you have done recently. It could be something you've done at the end of the class to check learning, a module assignment, a unit task or programme end test.

Answer the questions fully. The more detailed the answer, the better your analysis will be.

Validity

How do the questions or tasks relate to material covered in class or in syllabus requirements?

State how the assessments are balanced to reflect the (importance/ significance of the) topics.

Is the language or expression clear, unambiguous and understood?

How do learners know what is expected of them?

Reliability

Describe the purpose of the marking guide or sample answer sheet.

Describe how consistency in marking is to be achieved.

Describe the format of the assessment. Is this the most effective way of gathering evidence (proof of competence)?

Sufficiency

How does the assessment cover aspects of the syllabus:

- In its entirety?
- Over a number of assessments?

Authenticity

How do you guarantee that it is the learners' own work?

Relevance

Describe how the assessments fit into the overall programme.

Describe how they are related to industry/commercial standards.

◀

Recording

State how the outcomes of the assessment are reported and recorded:

● To other tutors
● To learners
● To stakeholders.

Review how all aspects of the assessment were effective:

● Were there hard bits?
● Were the tasks successfully achieved?
● Were there tasks suited to all learners?
● Do the results show an even distribution of correct responses/competence?

What do you think were the key strengths of the assessment?

What do you think were the key weaknesses in the assessment?

Administering the tests. Sometimes the answers can reveal how well we carried out the assessment. Things like too little time to complete fully, classroom activity could not guarantee that everyone completed it independently, homework activity was not completed by everyone, proximity of learners meant that copying occurred, similar question/s not being answered or answered incorrectly. Do you need to review the timing or resources?

Statistics and outcomes. What do the results show? You can look at average scores to identify how easy or difficult the test was, if there are similarities or trends between correctly and incorrectly answered questions. What does it tell you about the way you wrote the test, delivered the topic or distributed easy and hard questions?

The evaluation is 'How well have you taught?' If you consider that imparting knowledge is a key role and the measure is the recall, application or **mastery** of knowledge and skills, then you have to ask yourself, 'If the measure is not achieved, do I assume that the teaching is poor?' Not necessarily: it tends to mean that you have not taught in a way the learner can learn. In summary, teaching in a differentiated way is known to support the needs of everyone in your class, and therefore, assessment results will confirm the effectiveness of your differentiation.

Assessment and emotions

Assessment brings about many different feelings. The teacher can alleviate these emotions and thus help learners to do their best in assessments.

ACTIVITY 2

Reflection

Think about the last time you were assessed. What were the emotions you experienced? How did your teacher prepare you for the assessment?

Consider:

- O/A Levels, GCSE exams
- Driving test
- Job interview
- University or college tests – dissertation, exams, assignments, NVQ observations
- Classwork and homework activities

Describe your emotions in two lists:

1 Positive emotions – for example: excitement, relief, ambition
2 Negative emotions – for example: fear, anxiety, nerves

How could the teacher overcome the negative emotions?

How has the assessment developed since you did it?

In this activity you will find that the positive aspects of assessment are fewer than the negative aspects. Some of the things that can be done to help learners prepare for assessment include:

- Explaining what will happen
- Visits to assessment centres or rooms
- Practice tests
- Feedback to support strengths
- Practice form filling
- Imitate style of assessment

- A **SWOT** – strengths, weaknesses, opportunities, threats – analysis to show collective emotions
- Motivational interviewing.

Evaluating and reflecting on the assessments you use in the classroom and at the end of the programme will facilitate a positive move forward in your own development.

Glossary of terms

Assessment to make a judgement about something, measurement of achievement

Evaluation to form an idea about something, to measure its effectiveness

Mastery comprehensive ability

Reflection a considered opinion expressed in speech or writing; thoughts or considerations, developing ideas and thoughts

SWOT analysis of strengths, weaknesses, opportunities and threats

Syllabus the structure of a qualification

 SUMMARY

In this chapter we set out to achieve the following outcomes:
- Identify how you can use assessment outcomes to develop the way you assess in the future
- Analyse the effectiveness of your teaching strategies
- Inform your personal development plan

▶

Your Personal Development

You have compared the terms assessment and evaluation and how they apply to your development. You have used your skills learned to date to engage in an activity/case study which requires you to link assessment outcomes with teaching performance.

You have completed a self-assessment to investigate a specific assessment method you have used. You have then analysed the information to identify key strengths and weaknesses in that assessment.

In a final activity you have explored the emotions that surround assessment and how you might overcome negative feelings.

You should be able to use ideas and checklists to identify your own strengths and areas of development, with the aim of improving your assessment techniques.

Part Four
Theories and principles for planning and enabling learning
(TPPEL)

This is the fourth unit in your Diploma in Teaching in the Lifelong Learning Sector (DTLLS) qualification

18 Principles and theories of learning and communication
19 Applying the theories and principles of learning and communication
20 Developing own practice in the context of the theories and principles of learning and communication

Learning Outcomes	Assessment Criteria
Understand the application of theories and principles of learning and communication to inclusive practice	● Identify factors affecting learning and explain the potential impact of these on learner achievement ● Explain ways in which theories and principles of learning and communication can be applied to promote inclusive practice
Understand how to apply theories and principles of learning and communication in planning and enabling inclusive learning	● Justify the selection and use of teaching and learning strategies with reference to theories and principles of communication and inclusive learning ● Apply up to date knowledge of own specialist area to enable and support inclusive learning, following organisational, statutory and other regulatory requirements ● Use and justify a range of inclusive activities and resources, including new and emerging technologies, to promote and maintain an inclusive learning environment ● Use and justify a range of skills and methods to communicate effectively with learners and relevant others in the organisation
Understand and demonstrate knowledge of the minimum core in own practice	● Apply minimum core specifications in literacy to improve own practice ● Apply minimum core specifications in language to improve own practice ● Apply minimum core specifications in mathematics to improve own practice ● Apply minimum core specifications in ICT user skills to improve own practice
Understand and demonstrate how to evaluate and improve own practice, with reference to theories and principles of learning and communication	● Evaluate own strengths and development needs in relation to the application of theories and principles of learning and communication ● Identify ways to adapt and improve own practice with reference to theories and principles of learning and communication drawing on feedback from learners ● Plan and take up opportunities to develop and improve own performance in integrating theory into practice

CHAPTER 18
(TPPEL)

Principles and theories of learning and communication

LEARNING OBJECTIVES

The measurable outcomes that you will achieve by reading this chapter and completing the activities are:

- To state the difference between a principle and a theory
- To list the main schools of theory
- To identify the main factors influencing principles and theories
- To establish the links between principles and theories
- To analyse how principles underpin the planning and delivery of learning
- To evaluate the impact of principles in relation to inclusive learning and communication

Principles and theories

Every time you walk into the classroom you have a set of values and beliefs that you aspire to achieve. These maybe as simple as always stating your aims and outcomes at the start of the class, always allowing time at the end of the lesson to consolidate what has been achieved or maybe you will always give verbal feedback or praise to learners after they complete an activity. These, and many others, are what we call **principles**. They are the core priorities in your teaching life; you will not deliberately compromise your delivery if it means that your principles cannot be achieved. There are no right or wrong ideas when it comes to values and principles. The detail of the principle will change; the curriculum, the type of learner, the time of day will vary the idea but generally the main ethos will remain.

There are Principles *for* Learning which relate to accessibility of learning, diversity, inclusion, personalised learning and developmental learning. There are Principles *of* Learning – which are the usual values a teacher takes into the classroom – as described above.

A **theory** is something which either attempts or has been proven to explain something. Some of the theories we've seen before include Kolb, Maslow and Berne. These will be revised in this section as they are used to explain some of the principles of learning and communication; you will be introduced to some new ones. Many of the theories we still find valuable today were developed in the last century, some as long as one hundred years ago. They remain useful to the teacher as a way of developing an understanding of why and how things we do today work. Some teachers do what they do because it seems the right thing to do at the time; they are **intuitive**, some need to understand the meaning of things to effectively and confidently review their practice. This difference (between the teacher's style), can also be linked to theories, particularly those associated with **learning preferences**.

In a nutshell therefore, a principle is a value, belief or ethic relating to something you do and the theory is that which explains why it works.

The learning theories

The **psychology** of learning is very complex, this overview is simplified for the purpose of trying to compare, contrast and understand the ideas in the context of teaching and learning in today's classrooms. There are three main schools of theory relating to the study of human behaviour, in this case, teachers and learners.

The **Behaviourist** School

The **Cognitivist** School

The **Humanist** School

Others you may come across are:

- **Neo-behaviourists** – modern theorists advocating behaviourist theories, but adding that the learning must be driven by goals and targets.
- Gestaltists – The main thrust of Gestaltist thinking in terms of learning is that it is based on the notion of insight. The school advocates understanding the whole in order to have a better perception; Gestaltists like to see the big picture in order to assimilate information and therefore like to learn with large or long-term targets. Founded by Wertheimer (1880–1943), Köhler (1887–1967) and Koffka (1886–1941), they are an off-shoot of the Humanist school, totally rejecting behaviourist theories.

Each 'school of thought' attempts to explain why people behave in a particular way. It is not, however, without fuzzy edges. Rarely does one person, teacher or classroom scenario fall completely within one particular school of thought. It is therefore useful to have an overarching awareness of the theories in order to make sense of what is going on in the here and now.

Behaviourist School This school of thought believes that people respond to things around them. Behaviour is learned from things seen around them or from the environment, or that individuals respond to stimuli and that learning and the ability to learn requires a change in behaviour. Learning is mechanistic. The behaviourist school, however, does not explain things like problem-solving. Other critics also comment that the early research was based on animal behaviour and that humans are not animals, they are more complex. Others criticise the belief that humans just respond, they believe that humans will think. A behaviourist's belief seems to relate to a passive learner who merely reacts to teaching rather than a trait that responds and contributes more actively. Some of the early behaviourist researchers are listed here.

Main exponents of the Behaviourist School:

I. P. Pavlov (1849–1936) – a Russian whose research into the digestive system revealed that dogs could associate food with a sound and respond by salivating, thus was initiating the idea of 'classical conditioning'.

S. Freud (1856–1939) – instigated the suggestion of intuitive behaviours and opened up research into personalities and development.

J. B. Watson (1878–1958) – an American who challenged Freud's opinions and produced a further work associated with 'classical conditioning' which stated that people are not born with instincts and will react in a particular way to something through reflex actions. Things that don't work will not be repeated but successful actions will be. He gave rise to the concept of 'trial and error': that human reactions are the result of experiences.

E. L. Thorndike (1874–1949) – produced his 'Law of Effect', which stated that satisfaction serves to strengthen responses to stimuli. He extended the work of Watson and found that animals sought effective outcomes to achieve their goals. He made a significant contribution to the school of behaviourist theories.

Neo-behaviourists include:

B. F. Skinner (1904–1990) – is well known for developing the notion of 'operant conditioning' in which behaviour is a response to previous experience, praise or punishment. Again, this research was carried out with animals and applied to humans. In 1971 he stated the idea that free will is an illusion, it is the stimulus that causes the reaction or in teaching terms, learners need to be trained to achieve desired or appropriate behaviours. Using Skinner, learning is phased into smaller chunks. He sparked recent controversy by arguing that cognitive and humanist theories were contributing to the poorer performance in American schools and that 'teachers must learn how to teach' (Skinner 1984). His work was instrumental to the development of programmed learning and it could be argued as a rationale and justification for the emergence of resource-based learning, now more commonly known as e-learning.

A. Bandura (1977) – developed behavioural frameworks and linked behaviour to cognition, moving from the idea of 'trial and error' to 'observation and imitation'. The notion of observation and imitation led into his work concerning influences that shape a person's self-efficacy (effectiveness) and the critical nature of this in terms of self-confidence and **motivation**.

From our examples of principles, listed in the first paragraph, 'you will always give verbal feedback or praise to learners after they complete an activity', is an example of a principle which would be proven to be effective using behaviourist thinking. This is because the repetition of the task will consistently apply, therefore learners will wait (and expect) the feedback and ultimately will work better at the merest hint of feedback from the teacher, or because they know if they do work hard, they will gain their reward of feedback.

Cognitivist School The cognitivists believe that learning is a process of acquiring knowledge though thought, senses and experience. This school challenges the behaviourist's beliefs, not just because most of the behaviourist's research was based on animals, but because the cognitivists felt that 'knowledge' was missing in a stimulus model. They argue that humans have a more complex **psyche** and that the research is limited because it assumes that the laboratory research with animals is able to be automatically attributed to humans, without further investigation into human **idiosyncrasies**. Cognitivists recognise that humans follow mental processes – they think, remember and process information, and that this information is stored for future use in both the short and long term memories. Sensory models such as 'brain-theory' and 'brain-gym' have emerged from the cognitivist school. These models attempt to explain the impact that the different sides of the brain have on learning and how knowing which side of the brain is dominant can influence learning. The left-brain provides a focus on logical thinking, analysis, verbal skills and accuracy. The right-brain provides a focus on perceptions, musicality, aesthetics, feeling and creativity. There has also been recent analysis on the effects of diet and hydration on learning (Department of Health 2005) which concluded that drinking water has a positive effect on learning.

Some of the researchers associated with cognitivism are shown below.

Main exponents of the Cognitivist School:

J. Dewey (1859–1952) – one of the founder philosophers and psychologists who lived in an era when many were espousing their beliefs. He believed that education was borne from reflection and understanding of surroundings and recognised that people had different reasons underpinning the desire to learn (early differentiation, circa 1933). He further reinforced the teacher's influence on learning.

W. F. Brewer (in 1972) – who made a comparison between conditioned responses and co-operation, arguing a more controlled approach to actions and learning.

J. Piaget (1896–1980) – who is widely known for his work in analysing the various stages of child development.

E. C. Tolman (1886–1959) – claimed by both neo-behaviourists and cognitivists. In 1932 he made links between behaviourist and cognitive schools, by arguing that particular scenarios demand a type of response which will vary according to the situation, resulting in purposeful learning and behaviour.

J. Bruner (b. 1916) – stated that there are stages in cognitive behaviours and learning; first a person gains a piece of information, then, learns if it is transferable to other situations and finally, checks how useful it is before storing the information (1966). He stated some rules for instructional teaching.

D. Ausubel (b. 1918) – advocated **discovery learning**. He totally disagrees with rote learning describing it as inconsequential.

H. Gardner (b.1943) – defined 'multiple intelligences' used to explain learning preferences. He says that teaching and learning should focus on one of seven particular forms – linguistic, logical/mathematical, musical, kinaesthetic, spatial, interpersonal and intrapersonal.

R. W. Sperry (1913–1994) – an American neuro-psychologist famous for split-brain experiments; he developed a greater understanding of left- and right-brain models of understanding cognitive learning. He earned the Nobel Prize in 1981.

C. Hannaford (1985) in the publication *Smart Moves,* initiated the brain gym concept.

From our examples of principles, listed in the first paragraph, 'allowing time at the end of the lesson to consolidate what has been achieved' is an example of a principle which would be proven to be effective using cognitivist thinking. This is because the act of consolidating the lesson enables the thinking processes to kick-in. It enables learners to decide where they are going to use or store this information for future use.

Humanist School This is the most recent area of research and differs from others because it is the one that relates most closely to the varied behaviours of human learning. It is the least scientific of the schools, recognising the complexity and instability in life. Humanist theories argue that people need to search for meanings and need personal goals in order to develop **autonomy**, returning the learner to the centre of learning. There is a lot of focus on motivation, hence many of the theorists are better known to teachers for their work in motivation theory. Humanists put the 'art' into teaching, and advocate a very active, participative style of teaching. Teachers in a humanist school facilitate learning in a conducive learning environment.

Main exponents of the Humanist School:

C. Rogers (1902–1987) – a founder of the humanist school who advocated that humans grow and become independent; they like to be accepted for who they are and valued as people. He contributed to the work on **experiential learning** and considers that the teacher is a **facilitator** of learning. His approach to student-centred or 'autonomous' learning is based upon his ideas concerning the concept of the development of the self; that individuals construct a subjective view of what they are like based on their interactions or experiences.

A. H. Maslow (1908–1970) – considers that once basic needs are addressed people will reach their full potential and designs a model of motivational theory which impacts effectively today: Maslow's Hierarchy of Human Needs 1970.

D. Goleman (1995) – Emotional Intelligence. He argues that western learning cultures place an emphasis upon 'intellect' but should also take into consideration a person's emotional characteristics. This can form the basis of current arguments relating to the management of behaviours.

From our examples of principles, listed in the first paragraph, 'always stating your aims and outcomes at the start of the class', is an example of a principle which would be proven to be effective using humanist thinking. In this instance, letting learners know what the whole lesson is to be about enables them to prepare themselves for learning and feel that they are involved in that process. If they know where they are going, they see the big picture and therefore understand the purpose (Gestaltist theory).

Recommended reading

For further detailed readings about Learning Theories see Child (2004: 124–132), Fawbert (2003: 114–121), Curzon (2003: 35–121).

In the model below (Figure 18A), the three schools of theory are displayed to show how the teaching styles that dominate each area shift from a very **teacher-centred** methodology within a behaviourist school to a very **learner-centred** approach in a humanist school of thought. This introduces the relationship between theories, principles and the practice of teaching.

Figure 18A The relationship between theory schools and teaching styles

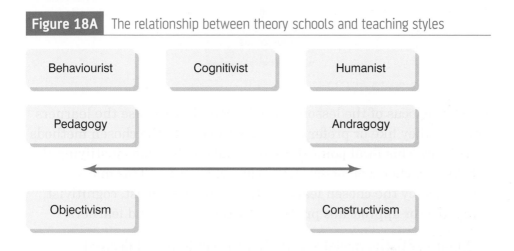

Factors influencing principles and theories of learning

The factors that influence learning are broadly split into:

- The model of learning (objectivism, constructivism)
- The type of learning (pedagogy, andragogy)
- The level of learning (Bloom, Gagné, surface/deep learning

Models of learning

In teacher-centred models of learning the content is the focus of the learning. How the teacher is going to impart the subject material will lead to the ways that the content will be delivered. In a learner-centred

Figure 18B Teacher-centred model

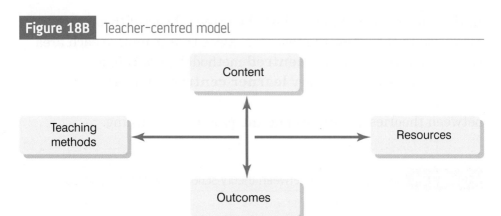

model the focus of the lesson is the learner. In this case the learners and how they like or prefer to learn is the key to the chosen methods of delivery. This focal point therefore leads to decisions justifying the selection or choice of models (or styles) of teaching. This may also be influenced by the chosen learning theory (behaviourist, cognitivist, humanist) or approaches preferred by the teacher and learners.

In Figure 18B, the model shows that the content and desired outcomes influence the methods seen in the classroom and the resources that will be used. In this instance the resources are more likely to be teaching aids, in order to consolidate learning. Factors that may influence choice of this method will be time and amount of content. In the model below, Figure 18C, we see a different approach:

Figure 18C Learner-centred model

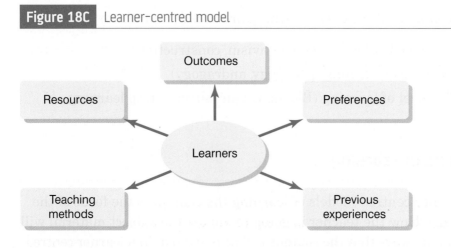

In this model, the learner is at the centre of the lesson and is the most important person in the learning process. The methods, resources, starting points all consider the learner. It is in this style that you may see experiential and discovery types of learning.

Objectivism This is the name given to the concept that advocates a teacher-centred approach in which the teacher transmits knowledge in the form of rules and seeks for mastery in practical tasks. **Rote** learning (that of repetitive learning, for example: the alphabet or the times tables, to a point at which they are known automatically) typifies objectivism. The teacher takes the role of an **instructor**.

Constructivism In the context of teaching, this is a learner-centred method of delivery which focuses on learning that has meaning, explanations and interpretations; it develops through a continual process, modified through experience. The teacher takes on the role of a facilitator. In its truest form, individuals create their own learning; ideas are not given, they are made from experiences. This **laissez-faire** approach (a non-interference teaching/learning style) is the ultimate student-centred strategy.

Types of learning

The type of learning will influence and is influenced by the type of teaching and therefore the choice of activities you and your learners do in the classroom or workplace. The choices you make when deciding how to deliver your session are broadly linked to teaching styles and learning preferences.

Pedagogy This is the name given to the skill or ability of teaching. It is predominantly concerned with teacher-centred methods and historically these passive methods of learning have been related to learning being seen as a chore. These previous poor experiences of teaching may still form barriers to learning in current times.

Fortunately, most teachers now firmly believe in a more learner-focused strategy, although the name pedagogy is still attributed to teaching, especially that of teaching children. In its purest, but old-fashioned meaning, pedagogy infers an **authoritative** or **autocratic** style of teaching.

Andragogy This term is synonymous with teaching adults, although it can apply to all age groups. It means teaching in a learner-focused style using guided learning techniques and thinking skills (Dewey 1916), which are self-directed. The learning is a very active process in which the learner participates fully with their learning. The two-way shared responsibility of learning models itself on a **democratic** approach to teaching. It is mid-way between the autocratic and laissez-faire styles previously mentioned.

One of the most significant writers on adult learning is Malcolm Knowles (1913–1997). He made five assumptions:

- Adults move from dependency to autonomy
- Adults gain experience (in life)
- Adults are ready to learn
- Adults move from 'need to learn' to 'want to learn'
- Adults mature and become motivated.

He suggests that adults need to know why they are learning, are very self-directed, responsible, experiential and motivated. Equally, they may be slower at grasping new information or recalling existing facts, more set in their (learning) ways, and display varying levels of self-confidence. Knowles (1984) suggests that teachers 'assist' adults to learn as facilitators rather than 'teachers'. He was influenced by Rogers' humanist school of thought.

The notion of teaching adults raises an interesting debate about when a child becomes an adult. Is it measured by age, maturity or is it a particular point in the lifecycle? Whatever the answer, adults are usually life experienced, opinionated, and generally work autonomously.

Levels of learning

The next influencing factor relates to levels of learning and will impact on the planning and delivery of your sessions. In Part 2, Planning and Enabling Learning, Chapter 7, Planning for Inclusivity looked at Bloom's Taxonomy of Learning, which is summarised below.

Bloom, and a number of other people who worked with his ideas, categorised levels of learning into three distinct areas: Cognitive (thinking skills), Affective (attitudes, beliefs) and Psychomotor (co-ordination skills). He called them Domains. He then sub-divided them into levels, for example, simple recall or imitation type of levels (low order) through to refined, complex and transferable skills (high order). The tables demonstrate how the skills move from being low order to high order and provide some adjectives to describe the depth of learning involved at each level within the domain (Wilson 2008).

Cognitive domain These are the thinking skills, at the lowest level based on being able to recall previously taught facts, moving towards thorough understanding leading to considered opinions:

Level	Taxonomy	Learners will be able to:
Low Order Skill	Knowledge	State, list, recognise, draw,
	Comprehension	Describe, explain, identify
	Application	Use, apply, construct, solve
	Analysis	List, compare, contrast
	Synthesis	Summarise, argue, explain
High Order Skill	Evaluation	Judge, evaluate, criticise

Based on B.S. Bloom (1956).

Affective domain This relates to the attitudes or behaviours a learner develops. Again it moves from just being aware of a particular belief to a higher level in which the belief is defended and explained in detail:

Level	Taxonomy	Learners will be able to:
Low Order Skill	Receiving (being aware)	Choose, describe, use, select
	Responding (reacting)	Answer, discuss, perform, write
	Valuing (understanding)	Demonstrate, argue, debate, explain
	Organisation and Conceptualisation	Compare, contrast, generalize, modify
High Order Skill	Characterisation (behaviour)	Acts, displays, practices, solves, verifies

Based on Bloom and Krathwohl (1964).

Psychomotor domain The domain looks at the practical or motor skills involved in the learning process. Childhood development is a good example of seeing how actions are developed from copying to automatic reactions:

Level	Taxonomy	Learners will be able to:
Low Order Skill	Imitation	Repeat, copy, follow, replicate
	Manipulation	Re-create, perform, implement
	Precision	Demonstrate, complete, show
	Articulation	Solve, integrate, adapt, modify
High Order Skill	Naturalisation	Design, specify, invent

Based on R. H. Dave (1967).

In this theory (Taxonomy of Learning), Bloom argues that there are levels within a task and that the teacher can use this theory to pose questions, set learning outcomes, prepare resources or assess ability which ultimately will recognise that within any group there will be a mixture of learners who grasp the topic at different levels.

In terms of planning this could mean creating a series of lesson outcomes, for example:

- By the end of the session, all learners will be able to . . .
- By the end of the session, most learners will be able to . . .
- By the end of the session, some learners will be able to . . .

In assessment, you will frequently see Bloom demonstrated in the types of verbs used to express outcomes. Some awarding bodies use pass, merit and distinction criteria and each one is progressively more complex. For example at pass level you may see words such as explain or describe. At merit you may see analyse and at distinction you may see evaluate. This also links to the depth of knowledge required of a topic.

In questioning you might ask one learner to state a date or particular fact, yet another learner might be required to explain what it means, or another might analyse the effect it has. The questions are posed to learners, whose abilities you are familiar with, to ensure they all contribute to sessions according to their ability or are challenged to stretch or gain higher grades. This leads us to the concepts of surface and deep learning.

Surface learning This is knowledge of a topic or skill which is quite shallow. It is probably based on imitation, repeating or re-writing. There is very little understanding of the topic and usually learners can only repeat what they have been told or shown. They cannot apply the knowledge to different contexts nor argue its value against other ideas or opinions. Rote learning which might be considered surface, due to the repetitive nature of the learning, may be the exception. If I said '9 times 5', there would be a lot of shouts of 45, thus proving the value of those endless chants. The fact that those multiplication tables are then used widely in a number of more complex numerical actions, implies that the depth of knowledge is increased. Surface learning should not be confused with the academic level of learning; it is possible to learn some very complex tasks superficially.

Deep learning This is a phrase used widely to express the notion of a more complete understanding of a topic; the opposite of surface learning. It requires a greater depth of knowledge. Deep learners are usually well read in their topic. They can explain it in many different ways and argue its worth against others' opinions. Activity 1 provides an opportunity to analyse how teachers learn aspects of their craft at different levels.

Hopefully, you will discover that you have a surface learning level in all aspects of teaching, maybe with some depth in one or a few topics. The varied way in which we learn and retain information and the difference in how well we know and understand facts or information within a topic is called a 'spiky' profile. This **spiky profile** of knowledge is very typical of all learning and knowledge.

Biggs (1987), suggests that we use both deep and surface learning according to how much time we have, the complexity of the task and even the content of the subject. He further suggests that the quality of teaching has a direct impact on the depth of learning.

'Jack of all trades, master of none!'

We do not need (or use) everything there is to know about everything, but we do need to know a little bit about a lot of things and some things we need to know a fair bit more about hence we all have a 'spiky' profile with regard to what we know and can do.

There is also an idea that in 'profound learning' the learning is so deep that behaviours become intuitive and are used effectively to problem-solve. West-Burnham (2005: 35) describes this as the 'why' level.

Robert Gagné in 1974 added further theories to the concept of levels of learning; however, whereas Bloom created three main divisions, Gagné suggested five main stages, devising a model of progressional

ACTIVITY 1

In this table you will see a number of activities that the teacher engages in; all are part of the curriculum for initial teacher training (ITT).

Using the column titles, analyse the depth of knowledge you have in the areas listed.

	Can recall main points of topic	Can explain many key areas of topic maybe with prompts	Can use topic in a different context or apply in a different situation	Can argue value against others' opinions; well read/ researched
	Surface ←————————————————————→ Deep			
Planning and preparing lessons				
Teaching and learning methods				
Assessment strategies				
Differentiating to meet learner needs				
Codes of conduct for teachers				
Reflection to improve own practice				

learning, relating to different outcomes of learning. Rogers (2002) gave the following explanation of Gagné's work:

> ● 'motor skills which require practice; verbal information – facts, principles and generalisations which when organised into larger entities become knowledge; intellectual skills – the 'discrimination, concepts and rules' that help in using knowledge; cognitive strategies – the way the individual learns, remembers and thinks, the self managed skills needed to define and solve problems; and attitudes' (p. 87).

These stages are not as distinctive as Bloom's theory suggests, because Gagné suggests that they are sequential and inter-relate; thus they are the 'conditions of learning' required to result in changes in behaviour. He also suggests that low order skills must be understood before entering his cycle of learning. Gagné follows the neo-behaviourist school's beliefs; Bloom's work links more closely to the cognitivist's views. However, together they form a platform for constructing lessons. This is because both agree and value the stages of learning development:

● move from known to unknown;
● simple to complex;
● example to principle; and
● concrete to abstract. (Kolb)

In this way learning develops from unnatural or stilted attempts to a natural or automatic behaviour.

The motivation theories

Whichever school of thought (Learning Theory) you are able to relate your teaching incidents to, whatever you advocate as your abiding principle, it is widely recognised that all of them will work better when the learner wants to achieve or succeed, i.e. they are motivated. Increased motivation occurs when the teacher makes a conscious decision to remove all of the barriers to learning that a learner may erect. Teaching, therefore, is a factor that influences motivation. Strategies to improve motivation and the more commonly used theories have already been described earlier in Part 1, Preparing to Teach in the Life Long Learning Sector and Part 2, Planning and Enabling Learning, see Chapter 4 and Chapter 8 respectively.

These are summarised as:

Maslow (1970) presented his Hierarchy of Needs. In this theory he stated that in order for a person to fully achieve their goals they need to satisfy a series of needs; then, and only then, will learners be in a frame of mind which is conducive to learning:

Figure 18D   Maslow's Hierarchy of Needs (1970)

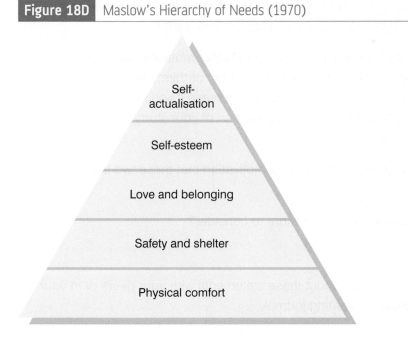

The arguments and agreements relating to this model are those centred around **intrinsic** and **extrinsic motivation**, i.e. the factors that influence the desire to learn.

ACTIVITY 2

Discussion Question.

Learner A

Let us imagine that you are studying for your Diploma because you have to, not because you want to; you are a reluctant learner. You are extrinsically motivated – this is because an external influence (your manager) has told you to do the course, maybe with some kind of sanction if you don't complete it.

Learner B

Let us imagine that you have signed up to complete your Diploma because you love teaching and want to find out everything there is to know about it. You are intrinsically motivated – this is because you have a personal desire to complete and value the benefits of the discussions you have with colleagues about teaching and learning.

According to Maslow, you will be more highly motivated and enthusiastic especially if you are not hungry or thirsty and you are in comfortable surroundings. This would increase if you knew that your tutors were happy to see you, you felt part of your study or peer group and you felt valued.

Is there a difference in the level of motivation that these two learners would have?

Is Maslow correct or is there more to consider?

Why?

Discuss your feelings about these statements with your peers or in your personal/reflective learning journal.

There are a number of theories associated with rewards. In the earlier chapters you will have looked at a model of 'medal and mission' and 'vicious and virtuous circles'. In these models there is a belief that if you receive praise and reward when you do well and you have a clear idea of the next goal you will be motivated to continue. Similarly, learners who receive '**positive reinforcement**', may be in a behaviourist type of situation, are motivated to a greater degree than those who constantly receive '**negative reinforcement**'. Another theory associated with this type of model of motivation is McGregor's Theory X and Theory Y (1960). In this model, originally researched around the management of a workforce, McGregor argues that the teacher will make one of two assumptions about their learners' motivation levels. The learner (Theory X) will avoid work whenever possible, will need to be persuaded to work and probably has little ambition; the teacher, therefore, acts to de-motivate just by being in the same room as this learner and trying to get him or her to work by controlling and threatening. Alternatively, the learner (Theory Y), wants to learn, is eager to take responsibility for their learning and contributes positively in the classroom. In this case, the teacher acts as a motivator to realise the aspirations of a learner. It could therefore be argued that the teacher's attitudes to learners and motivation are equally as relevant as those of the learners; a teacher's perceptions will influence how they act in the classroom. An example of this is when the teacher assumes that the learners will not do any work, and is not disappointed when they don't. To overcome this, the teacher must not make assumptions (about their level of motivation) and must believe that every learner has the potential to achieve something, albeit to different levels.

There are three models of theory associated with the person which result in motivated learners. One, discussed earlier in the course, was Herzberg's Satisfaction Theory. His 'hygiene' factors are the basic requirements on which to build motivational theory. People need status, job security, good working conditions, etc. and then they will be more motivated, especially in conjunction with achievement, recognition, growth and interest. He believed that a learner needs to be satisfied with their work (or learning); that it is in the right environment and that they are confident of the purpose and benefit of the learning. The second is Bandura's 'Self Efficacy' model. In this model, motivation is dependent on the amount of self-belief or confidence a learner has in his or her own ability. It is the belief that a learner will aspire to the level they (the learner) thinks they can achieve, or conversely, if a learner doesn't believe they can do something then the chances are that they won't be able to! Finally, David McClelland argues that those with a need for achievement have a greater level of motivation when they are allowed to solve their own problems, rather than gaining chance results. The learner is in control of their learning and gets a 'buzz' from working out and finding solutions. This is midway between the learner who learns by chance – a gambling type of situation – and the 'conservative' learner who does not participate in any learning opportunity unless the outcome is predictable. McClelland (1988) further suggests that learners with a high need for achievement will attain better results, because they respond well to feedback as they know that this helps them to succeed.

All of these theories have the same result; they broadly mean the same thing, although each advocates a different purpose. Motivation is a desire and that desire is met through:

- Need
- Drive
- Goals
- Satiation.

(Curzon 2003: 225 and Rogers 2002: 95–99)

The link between the classroom and the theory

The learning and motivational theories continually suggest that what happens in the classroom, how the sessions are planned and delivered, impact significantly on the principles that the teacher advocates. In order to make the links between what happens in the classroom and the theories, it might be useful to consider the following:

Experiential learning

Experiential learning is a trial and error model. In its absolute form there is no teacher present in the process. Learning from things that happen and mistakes that are made is promoted by Kolb (see Chapter 11 p. 248) and Rogers – a humanist school of thought. Dewey, a cognitivist, didn't agree that this type of learning was always effective, referring to it as 'mis-educative'. He thought that sometimes failure is due to poorly chosen methods of learning rather than the inability to learn, although he did advocate that learning is based on experience. Experiential learning will be seen in role-play and case-study activities.

Discovery learning

In a discovery learning model, the learner is allowed to find out things for themselves in order to be able to put them into meaningful patterns. The new information is learned in the context of previous learning. This type of learning therefore is a cognitivist view. Ausubel and Bruner are the main exponents, but with slightly different viewpoints. Ausubel talks about effective experiential learning being meaningful, whereas Bruner argues that not all learning is meaningful, but agrees that learners need to organise their own knowledge and build on things they already know. Discovery learning will be seen in practical situations and research activities.

Sensory learning

In a **sensory learning** model, the teacher recognises and exploits the learner's natural abilities in sight, hearing, touch, etc. Dugan Laird argued that learning is more effective when the senses are stimulated.

75% is learned through seeing

13% is learned through hearing

12% is learned through touch, smell and taste.

Laird (2003: 114)

Sensory learning will be seen in demonstrations, video/DVD studies, and situations where models or artefacts are investigated.

Group learning

Most of the learning that occurs in educational settings will be in large groups. Workplace learning is generally one-to-one or small groups. This is because most learning is funded, either publicly or privately and cost efficiency demands that groups of learners seeking similar outcomes are collected and taught together. The challenge then for teachers is respecting and valuing the individuals within the group, meeting their needs and creating a cohesive learning environment. **Group learning** is more than just seating people in various combinations; it is about building a team ethos to ensure that group work is shared and learners are willing to work together. There are two theorists associated with group dynamics. Belbin (1993) suggested that people take on a particular role within a group, yet they are all needed to create a team. Again this is derived from the workplace but can be attributed to an educational setting.

- Implementer – does things in the group, turns ideas into actions
- Team worker – keeps the group together
- Co-ordinator – organises the team, sets the goals
- Plant – puts in ideas and suggestions, the creative one
- Completer – keeps the pace to ensure the job is done
- Monitor – provides opinions and checks progress
- Resourcer – brings in the wherewithal to do the job
- Shaper – directs the team
- Specialist – provides the knowledge and expertise to do the job.

Belbin (2001) www.belbin.com

Secondly, Tuckman (1965), in Fawbert (2003: 188), identified the stages of team development:

- Forming – the individuals are brought together
- Storming – they jointly consider the task in the context of their abilities
- Norming – they start to work together to develop their objectives
- Performing – they work well together and achieve their aim.

Tuckman later added:

- Adjourning – also described as deforming and mourning, which is when the group recognises and accepts their success and maybe feels a sense of loss as the group disbands.

Group work is not without arguments as individuals offer their ideas and opinions, but hopefully teams will settle. Only when the group is poorly formed ('too many chiefs and not enough Indians') will it implode.

Communication theories

In this last section, you will find an overview of communication theory, although these have been discussed in earlier chapters (see Chapter 4, pp. 101–104 and Chapter 9).

Communication is the act of passing a message from one person to another; effective communication ensures that the message is understood. Communication is a basic skill. It involves listening, responding, speaking, writing and comprehending. As well as these overt methods, there is also the importance of non-verbal communication – the secret messages relayed by the body which help the process. Communication forms part of current educational initiatives such as Every Child Matters and the Diversity agenda. Both require communication to be appropriate, relevant and respectful to the individuals or groups concerned.

> # A definition of communication is:
> # An interaction between one or more people.

The theories

Transmission types include the Shannon and Weaver (1949) **linear** model, described in Chapter 9, Effective Communication Skills, as a means of sending a message from one person to another. Whilst it recognises that there may be factors that cause the message to be confused, it is presented in a linear style and therefore infers a one way process. It is a method of passing information, therefore in a teaching context you would use this style of communication to express facts, to lecture or deliver content using verbal exposition. It does not allow for any measurement of understanding.

Another transmission type, also linear in style, is David Berlo's SMCR Model (1960). This is based on the Shannon and Weaver model. In an SMCR model:

> # Source → Message → Channel → Receiver

the source, also described as the 'encoder', sends a message (information, facts, etc.) using a channel (communication method) to the receiver, described as the 'decoder'. The main communication channels used by the encoder are speaking and writing, whilst the decoder uses listening and reading skills. Berlo adds 'thought and reasoning' which he says is 'crucial' to the communication.

The Lasswell Formula (by Harold Lasswell, 1976) is very similar to the Shannon/Weaver and Berlo models although his wording is different. Lasswell's adaptation to the model is the inclusion of 'an effect'. This is starting to recognise that unless the message is understood it cannot be assumed that it has been correctly received.

Osgood and Schramm, in McQuail & Windahl (1993) provide us with a circular model in order to add 'interpretation' to the communication process. They further confirm that transmission types are teacher-centred whereas a circular model allows for more application and feedback.

Another alternative communication theory (see Chapter 9, Communication theory, pp. 208–210), devised by Eric Berne, centres on the relationships in communication, rather than the process. In his Transactional Analysis, he suggests that people enter 'ego states'. It is his opinion that there are three main 'states' that apply: Adult, Parent or Child. Looking at each communication scenario:

In the first example, the person sending the messages is doing so in an adult style. This adult-adult situation is ideal; both are equals, which Berne says is the best scenario. However if it is an adult conversing with a parent or child, then the recipient of the information is not a peer. In both adult–parent and adult–child scenarios the recipient of the information is not matched; the parent wants the controlling role and may rebel against being instructed and the child is too passive and compliant to respond appropriately. The teaching of adults (andragogy) is an example of adult-adult communication working in practice. Adult–adult leads to effective communication because both are equal and therefore will respond appropriately.

EXAMPLE 1

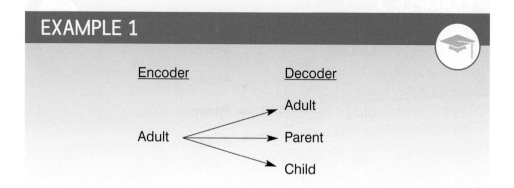

In the second example the parent is leading the communication. In this situation the parent will dominate the adult who wants a negotiating role, two parent styles would respect each other and the parent would domineer the child. In some teaching situations, the parent–child scenario is required, for example, when teaching younger learners who need to learn how to communicate, so initially the teacher takes on a parent role in order to nurture their learners.

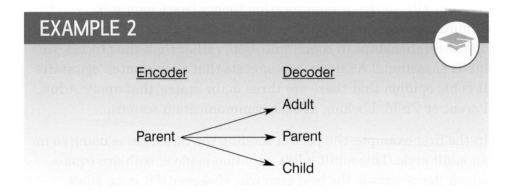

EXAMPLE 2

In the final example the child is initiating the communication. This is the least effective scenario, because the child does not have the maturity to cope with the role. The only time when this would be effective is a child–child match; again, because they are equals the communication would work. This would be the relationship of two young learners discussing a topic in the classroom.

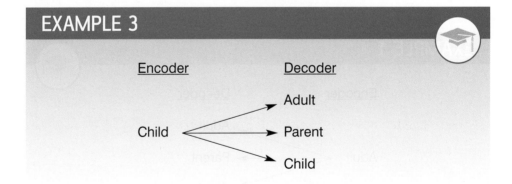

EXAMPLE 3

Berne's model can explain some of the teaching dialogues and show how like ego states are the best method of achieving sensible, effective communication.

In the final part of this section, to review and develop your communication style, consider this:

ACTIVITY 3

List the ways that a teacher can improve communication to ensure that it is effective:

- ●
- ●
- ●
- ●
- ●

- ●
- ●
- ●
- ●
- ●

Now list the ways you communicate with your learners:

- ●
- ●
- ●
- ●
- ●

- ●
- ●
- ●
- ●
- ●

Following this activity, and the theories discussed, identify four improvements that you will make to your communication strategy and how these will develop your principles of learning.

- ●
- ●
- ●
- ●

Principles of learning in practice

There are significant relationships between teaching approaches and learning preferences. Many teachers endeavour to meet the needs of their learners, but find it difficult to do so all of the time. This is why the teacher needs principles to underpin and set their own standards. Obviously the sector has its professional values (Overarching Professional Standards for teachers, tutors and trainers in the Lifelong learning Sector – 2006: 2). An example is listed below:

Domain A

The practice of teaching is underpinned by a set of professional values that should be observed by all teachers, tutors and trainers in all settings. The domain sets the standard for these values and their associated commitments.

Teachers in the lifelong learning sector value:

1. All learners, their progress and development, their learning goals and aspirations and the experience they bring to their learning.

2. Learning, its potential to benefit people emotionally, intellectually, socially and economically, and its contribution to community sustainability.

3. Equality, diversity and inclusion in relation to learners, the workforce and the community.

4. Reflection and evaluation of their own practice and their continuing professional development as teachers.

5. Collaboration with other individuals, groups and/or organisations with a legitimate interest in the progress and development of learners.

They are committed to:

1. The application of agreed codes of practice and the maintenance of a safe environment.

2. Improving the quality of their practice.

The teacher's own individuality will impact on the planning, delivery and assessment of learning as will the learner's ability to learn. Personalities, such as:

- extroverts/introverts
- dependency/autonomy
- confidence/reservations

will influence choices made, but they should not compromise the principles set.

Some principles that may be set:

- I will systematically value the experience my learners bring to their learning
- I will plan my lessons to include learner-centred activities for all members in the class
- I will encourage learners to set their own learning goals
- I will always introduce the session with a clear statement of what is to be achieved during the lesson

- My lessons will be structured with an introduction, development of skills/knowledge and a summary of learning
- I will always assess the learning achieved in the session and give feedback designed to progress the learners
- I will create an environment conducive to effective learning
- I will set ground rules for the standards of acceptable behaviour
- I will value the diversity of learners' backgrounds and challenge instances of discrimination
- I will structure group work to maximise the potential of the learners.

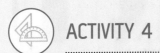

ACTIVITY 4

Look at the principles that are recorded above. Alternatively list TEN of your own principles.

For each principle,

- identify which learning, motivation or communication theory best applies to your principle

- list the theorists who are commonly associated with the idea

- list three teaching or learning strategies that you will use to ensure you meet your principle

- identify any legislation or codes of conduct that influence your principle

Collect session plans, resources, etc. which demonstrate your ability to achieve your principles. Save these in your teaching file, discussing them with peers, mentors or tutors.

Reflect on the effectiveness of your ideas.

Glossary of terms

Affective domain concerned with emotions and values

Andragogy how adults learn

Authoritative a self-confident or assertive method of teaching

Autocratic a domineering approach to teaching

Autonomy independence in the ability to learn

Behaviourist a school of thought associated with responses to stimuli

Cognitive domain concerned with thinking skills

Cognitivist a school of thought associated with thinking processes

Constructivism a learner-centred model of learning

Deep learning learning which is memorised and fully understood

Democratic a style of teaching based on negotiation and shared values

Discovery learning finding things out through research, investigation and discussion

Experiential learning learning by trial and error

Extrinsic motivation motivation derived from the outside of the person

Facilitator one who supports or stimulates learning

Gestaltist a school of thought associated with the whole learning process

Group learning collaborative learning techniques

Humanist a school of thought associated with meeting all human needs

Idiosyncrasies a particular way of behaving

Instructor direct or commanding delivery of information

Intrinsic motivation motivation from within the person; natural desire

Intuitive instinctive; apparently natural behaviour

▶

◀

Laissez-faire a non-interference model of teaching; learner-devised; a laid-back approach

Learner-centred the learner dominates the learning environment

Learning preferences the individual's favoured way of learning

Linear in communication, a message following a direct line

Motivation enthusiasm or interest

Negative reinforcement feedback that inhibits practice and lessens motivation

Neo-behaviourist a school of thought which believes learners are driven by goals

Objectivism a teacher-centred model of learning

Passive learning in which the learners accept teaching with little or no active response

Pedagogy the skill or ability of teaching

Positive reinforcement feedback that enhances practice and improves motivation

Principle a set of values or beliefs promoted by the teacher

Psyche the human mind or spirit

Psychology the study of the human mind or behaviour

Psychomotor domain concerned with practical skills

Rote teaching by repetition, e.g. learning multiplication tables

Sensory learning learning which relies on the five senses

Spiky profile mixed levels of learning within topic

Surface learning shallow understanding of topic

Taxonomy a classification

Teacher-centred the teacher dominates the learning environment

Theory an explanation or proof of an idea

Transmission type in communication, a message passing from one to another

SUMMARY

In this chapter we set out to achieve the following outcomes:

- state the difference between a principle and a theory
- list the main schools of theory
- identify the main factors influencing principles and theories
- establish the links between principles and theories
- analyse how principles underpin the planning and delivery of learning
- evaluate the impact of principles in relation to inclusive learning and communication.

Your Personal Development

Initial paragraphs in the chapter explain the differences between theories and principles and provide sections covering each of the learning theories – behaviourist, cognitivist and humanist. Each section describes the beliefs of the school and the main people associated with the theory.

In figure 18A, the relationship between the theories and teaching styles is explained. The factors influencing principles and theories of learning are categorised into three types – models of learning, types of learning and levels of learning, each introducing the main theory and principle exponents.

Activity 1 proves that a learner's understanding of a topic will vary and produce a 'spiky' profile of ability and this will impact on the teaching and learning.

In the section on motivation, which summarises key theories and revises previous learning on the subject, activity 2 offers an opportunity to explore the different emotions involved with motivation, which again impact on teaching and learning.

The choices relating to how learning is planned are categorised into the main types of classroom activity: experiential, discovery, sensory and group learning. Each is described together with reference to theories and activities.

In the section on communication, which again summarises key theories and revises previous learning on the subject, you will be more familiar with how effective communication will be achieved using the models suggested. In activity 3 you are asked to review your communication methods and how these could be developed in the hope that this knowledge will help you to achieve some of the principles and values you set yourself. How the teacher communicates has a direct impact on learning.

Finally, there is a section which puts all of the ideas learned in the chapter into practice. Activity 4 invites the reader to make the links between principles, theories and teaching and learning strategies, resulting in a thorough understanding of the chapter content.

CHAPTER 19
(TPPEL)

Applying the theories and principles of learning and communication

LEARNING OBJECTIVES

The measurable outcomes that you will achieve by reading this chapter and completing the activities are:

- To justify teaching and learning strategies in the context of theories and principles
- To demonstrate justifications in your planning documentation

Applying the theories

In this chapter we shall think about the principles and theories and consider how this is evidenced as part of your Diploma in Teaching award. Most of the practical application of the theory will be observed by your tutor or mentor in the way you deliver your session, but we can look at the documents to support your **rationale**. In order to set this chapter into context, you should read an explanation of the difference between a **principle** and a **theory** and a summary of the main theories in the previous chapter.

The table below attempts to link why we need to be aware of what goes on behind the teaching. You would not be alone in thinking: 'why do I need to know about theories?' I concede that some of you do

The links between principles and theories and teaching practice			
Summary of previous chapter:			*Impact on practice*
Principles	These are your personal **values** and the professional values advocated by **LLUK**. They may also include **codes of conduct** set by your organisation to address legislation		Behaviour codes Dress codes Attitudes Relationships Personal actions Planning and delivery
Theories	*Learning:* Behaviourist Cognitivist Humanist	*Communication:* Transmission Relationship	Initial assessment Diagnostic test Tutorials Planning and preparation Support strategies Referral systems Delivery of sessions
	Models of learning Types of learning Levels of learning Motivation		
Teaching methods	Experiential Discovery Sensory Group		Choice of activities Resources selected Assessment methods Modern technologies Delivery of sessions

what you do in the **learning environment** because it seems right, but it does help to confirm your confidence if you understand why that was a good idea. As part of your Initial Teacher Training you are required to '**justify**' your actions to prove you are not only a successful teacher but that you realise the consequence of your actions and how they **impact** on others.

On the left of the table you will see the principles and theories covered in the previous chapter and the right hand column links to things that you will do with your learners as part of your teaching role. It is not an absolute classification in that many things could apply across all teaching and learning activities carried out in the post-compulsory sector; it lists the main impacts that the particular values and theories will have.

In the previous chapter, we listed some principles which defined our values in the learning environment. Using some of these, I will explain the links and the practical application, noting some of the potential changes that could impact on practice and therefore change the session focus; these may be considered areas for development.

The ten suggested ideas are:

- I will systematically value the experience my learners bring to their learning
- I will plan my lessons to include learner-centred activities for all members in the class
- I will encourage learners to set their own learning goals
- I will always introduce the session with a clear statement of what is to be achieved during the lesson
- My lessons will be structured with an introduction, development of skills/knowledge and a summary of learning
- I will always assess the learning achieved in the session and give feedback designed to progress the learners
- I will create an environment conducive to effective learning
- I will set ground rules for the standards of acceptable behaviour
- I will value the diversity of learners' backgrounds and challenge instances of discrimination
- I will structure group work to maximise the potential of the learners.

Principle: *I will set ground rules for the standards of acceptable behaviour*

Theories: This principle is embedded in a *behaviourist* school, because it is very mechanistic and demands an automatic type of response, If I say x – you do x – without question – or else. It is *autocratic*. It relies on the belief that learners will follow good examples. The motivation factor meets *Maslow's* suggestion that learners will ultimately feel safe and confident in their environment and therefore will become more motivated; it is *extrinsic* motivation. In terms of communication it tends to exact the *linear models* and would be a *parent–child* relationship within Berne's Transactional Analysis. The principle is a *pedagogic* approach due to the teacher-led approach. Dave Vizard (www.behaviourmatters.com) offers practical solutions to managing challenging behaviour.

Development: By involving the learners in the decision about what is and is not acceptable behaviour, you could move it towards a democratic humanist approach. This more intrinsically motivated approach with a shared responsibility is developing a mature learning environment and moves younger learners towards an adult way of learning and acting.

Principle: *I will plan my lessons to include learner-centred activities for all members in the class*

Theories: This principle relates to a *cognitivist* approach because it is creating opportunities for learners to consolidate and compartmentalise their learning, developing their knowledge. It can also follow Humanist (Rogerian) theory concerning autonomy in learning. It is a *democratic* approach because the teacher remains in control of the environment but includes and probably values the learner's abilities to find out things for themselves. It follows a *constructivist* model of learning in which the learner is considered first allowing the teacher to become a *facilitator* of learning rather than an initiator. The inclusion of the word ALL in the principle means that the teacher will be differentiating learning to address different levels of ability in the group, and would probably use *Bloom's taxonomy* to state the different outcomes. Motivation theory is *McGregor's Theory Y*, because of the teacher's beliefs in the learners.

Development: This can become a humanist approach by ensuring the learners understand the purpose of the activities in the context of their whole learning programme. This is a Gestaltist way of thinking. By ensuring that the activities are designed to apply or analyse previous learning, you would be encouraging high-order learning which will create a deeper understanding of the topic. These developments may optimise the learning for intrinsic learners.

 ## ACTIVITY 1

Look at the principles advocated in the example below and identify relevant theories in the same way as suggested above. There are two versions according to how confident you are in analysing theories and relating them to principles . . .

Version A:

Principle: *I will always introduce the session with a clear statement of what is to be achieved during the lesson*

Theories:

▶

Principle: *My lessons will be structured with an introduction, development of skills/knowledge and a summary of learning*

Theories:

Version B: hints and prompts . . .

Principle: *I will always introduce the session with a clear statement of what is to be achieved during the lesson*

Theories:

This principle is Behaviourist/Cognitivist/Humanist because . . .

The teaching style used to create this principle is Autocratic/Democratic/ Laissez-faire, which would make the type of learning pedagogic/ andragogic and the learning teacher/learner-centred. The session could be differentiated using ....'s theories to create surface/deep learning. The principle is an example of developing motivation by . . . [describe] . . ., re-creating ....'s theories of motivation. Communication is linear/ circular and follows B....'s theory of T...... A..... using ..../......... ego states to describe the relationship between the teacher and the learner.

Principle: *My lessons will be structured with an introduction, development of skills/knowledge and a summary of learning*

Theories:

This principle is Behaviourist/Cognitivist/Humanist because . . .

The teaching style used to create this principle is Autocratic/ Democratic/Laissez-faire, which would make the type of learning pedagogic/andragogic and the learning teacher/learner-centred. The session could be differentiated using ....'s theories to create surface/deep learning. The principle is an example of developing motivation by . . . [describe] . . ., re-creating ....'s theories of motivation. Communication is linear/circular and follows B....'s theory of T...... A..... using ..../......... ego states to describe the relationship between the teacher and the learner.

As a further example, in the next activity we will look at when we use these theories and principles. The main document that you use in teaching which would demonstrate how you apply principles and use the theories is your planning document – the Session Plan. The Session Plan below has been annotated to show where the theories appear and where principles are advocated. You may wish to complete a similar activity using your lesson planning form and include it in your teaching file:

Programme:	BTEC ND in Uniformed Public Services (Year One)
Module:	Unit 5, Understanding Discipline in the Uniformed Public Services
Subject:	Intro to authority and discipline

Class size: 17	**Age of Learners:** 16–18	**Class layout:** group tables

Lecturer: **	**Date:** ** November 20** **Time Allocated:** 2 × 2 hour sessions (Wed/Thur)

Aim: To introduce ideas of discipline and authority and consider how and why they impact on UPS

P1 – the need for and role of discipline in UPS, M1 – analyse need, D1 – evaluate impact

P6 – explain nature of authority in UPS, M4 – explain importance & consequences of lack of

Principle: I will always set the context of the learning within the bigger picture – Humanist Theory. Progression from low to high order cognitive skills – Bloom's Taxonomy

Outcomes of the lesson: *Principle: I will ensure that the learning outcomes meet every learner's ability, Theory – motivate by providing opportunities for achievement (virtuous cycle). Outcomes are developmental – Bloom.*

All learners will be able to:

- define the specific terms associated with this unit (discipline, self-discipline, authority, obedience, conformity and compliance)
- describe the purpose of discipline in the context of a public service sector
- identify the rank system of a chosen UPS

Most learners will be able to:

- apply research into a poster recording levels of authority
- commence an investigation into the nature of authority in a chosen uniformed public service

Some learners will be able to:

- link the rank systems to the need to create discipline and authority in UPS
- evaluate the importance of discipline and authority

SESSION PLAN DETAIL Introduction/recap; Development; Assessment; Conclusion (recap on objectives); Homework (prep for next session)	PROPOSED METHOD OF DELIVERY/ STUDENT LEARNING	POSSIBLE RESOURCES
Introduction: Share outcomes. (Principle: I will always tell learners what lesson is going to be about) Discipline plays an important role in the public services; it affects effectiveness and efficiency. Discipline is usually part of a hierarchical command system. 5mins	Verbal Exposition (VE) Teacher-centred pedagogy Cognitive school Principle: Although essential to pass key information I will keep teacher-centred activities to a minimum.	Text books: GRAY & CULLINGWORTH www specific service Principle: I will strengthen learner's ability to learn by preparing them for learning and developing study skills.
Six terms associated with discipline: <ul><li>DISCIPLINE</li><li>SELF-DISCIPLINE</li><li>CONFORMITY</li><li>COMPLIANCE</li><li>AUTHORITY</li><li>OBEDIENCE</li></ul> 15mins intro + 35mins activity Learner-centred pedagogy, words are known.	Write each word on board; ask learners to thought shower words or expressions associated with each. Split group into six (friendship gp) – give each a piece of flipchart paper and ask them to define one of the terms. Nominee to share and explain, with examples the definition with other groups, put sheets on wall for reference. Text book research Humanist in activity – teacher = facilitator	Note taking sheets Spare pens Wipe Board/Pens Electronic board (if available) Give handout to support notes at end of activity

▶

Hierarchy of Public Services Discuss what 'hierarchy' means. Discuss 'rank system' Impact of discipline/authority in ranks of UPS 15mins intro + 45mins activity + 5mins summary *Development from known to unknown*	Nominate a sector, e.g.: Armed Services, Police, Fire & Rescue etc. Get into those groups. Investigate the rank structure in your chosen service. Devise a poster showing the rank insignia in ascending order and explaining authority and levels of command. Start preparing the poster. Internet research *Constructivist – Discovery learning*	May need to re-arrange room or sub split large groups. A4 and A3 size paper to facilitate photocopying for each student's file. Poster materials box – pens, crayons, felts, coloured paper, card, rulers
Session Two		
Recap work in previous session 5 mins	Nominated Questioning – students to say one short thing about the words explained yesterday (DSCCAO).	
Why do we need rules? Why do people need to follow orders? What happens if people don't follow orders? 10mins intro + 15mins group work + 20mins feedback & consolidation *Humanist thinking – developing learners' ideas and opinions*	VE Intro *(Autocratic – teacher centred)* Group activity – about 4/5 in each group then nominated group response to teacher *Changed to democratic – learner-centred – discovery & group learning)* Extend Q give each member a sub question: *(Bloom – High order skills to challenge distinction level students)* Give THREE rules that you have to abide by in college or work – who issued them, why do you think it is a rule, do you conform? What punishment could you expect if you are found to be disobedient?	Board/pens – spider diagrams Note making sheets/pens Split D level students within groups

Continue with the poster project (assignment task 1) 45mins Ensure that spelling and grammar used is correct and cite all sources of information	Tour classroom – feedback and comment *Facilitator role – Feedback develops self-esteem – Maslow/Bandura* Extend Q: analyse how do rank systems help discipline and authority *(Bloom)*	Poster materials box Dictionaries Harvard Ref sheet
Summary Review flipcharts used to create definitions 5mins Ask each group who is lowest/highest rank in their chosen service Issue question sheet – collect in and keep in assignment file 20mins	Questions – Why does the person in the lowest rank need to receive his orders? Why does he obey them? Who does the person in the highest rank receive his orders from? Extend Q – why is respect important?	Question sheets

Details of Differentiation (meeting the needs of individuals):	**Assessment of learning outcomes:**
Students progressed from BTEC first should have an awareness of rank systems from last year so nominate them to lead discussions *(Principle: I will always value the experience that some learners bring to the group)* W, X, Y, Z working towards Distinction criteria – split between groups Nominate questioning to mirror p, m & d criteria as relevant *(Principle: I will strive to provide challenging opportunities for learners who aspire to high levels of achievement)* A, B need extra support – no support assistant available on Wed; keep a close eye – team A with X. Split C, D, E – need to keep focused Support Assistant (Thu) – Work with A. Help to make notes and file in folder. Help to keep focused by rephrasing q repeatedly *(Principle: I will provide support for those learners that need the extra help)* 1:1 in group activities *(Principle: I will provide opportunities to develop team building skills by devising group activities)*	Observation of performance in lesson – behaviour, content development, outcome Question sheet Work contributes to summative assessment by assignment *Principle: I will always check that learners have met session outcomes. Motivation Theory – sense of achievement aids learning. Praise and reward. Humanist school – aware of own learning*

You will notice that the lesson does not include one particular style of teaching throughout the lesson. This is because as the teacher **differentiates** and includes variety into lessons so the style of teaching will change. It is important to make these adjustments: it reduces boredom and adds interest; it shows how you respond to your learners; and creates a learning environment based on respect and shared responsibility. You may also find that something occurs in the session that requires you to be responsive to learner needs, which sees you having to change your teaching style or methods. As we already know, it is perfectly acceptable to change your plan during a session – the evaluation will explain the justification (or rationale) behind the change. The important factor is that the change should not compromise your principles.

Glossary of terms

Code of conduct a set of standards governing professional values

Differentiate catering for the needs of all learners to reduce barriers to learning

Impact an effect; an influence

Justify explain or prove something

Learning environment general term for where learning occurs

LLUK Lifelong Learning (UK) Sector Skills Council

Principle a set of values or beliefs promoted by the teacher; a rule or moral code

Rationale the reasons for an action

Theory an explanation or proof of an idea

Value something which is important

Verbal exposition teacher-talk

 SUMMARY

In this chapter we set out to achieve the following outcomes:

- Justify teaching and learning strategies in the context of theories and principles
- Demonstrate justifications in your planning documentation

Your Personal Development

This chapter is demonstrating that what occurs in the classroom, usually quite naturally, has got a theoretical justification. This means that our actions can be explained by theory.

First, there is an overview of the main theories of learning and communication and instances in teaching and learning where they may occur.

Second, there is a list of 10 principles which you may advocate in your role and two of them are explained, again, using the theories seen in Chapter 18. This is followed by an activity in which the reader is invited to carry out a similar exercise on two further suggested principles.

Finally, a session plan is used to further explain the links between theory and practice. It is hoped that this final example consolidates the theories, principles and how the teacher uses them in their everyday teaching life.

SUMMARY

CHAPTER 20 (TPPEL)

Developing own practice in the context of the theories and principles of learning and communication

LEARNING OBJECTIVES

The measurable outcomes that you will achieve by reading this chapter and completing the activities are:

- To evaluate your own practice against theories and principles of learning and communication
- To identify ways of adapting and improving own practice
- To develop an action plan to meet development needs

Developing your practice

REVISION

In Chapter 11, Reflection, evaluation and feedback, you learned about what **reflection** was, looking briefly at some of the theories associated with reflection (Dewey, Kolb, Schön and Brookfield). You were introduced to some of the documents that form the basis of recording reflective practice and the methods of identifying improvements. You will use some of these skills in this part of the unit, which is concerned with developing your practice in the light of your new awareness of the theories of learning and communication.

Evaluating your current practice

In any **evaluation** it is necessary in the first instance to know where you are now. Although you have this new knowledge of the theories, you have always had principles in respect of your teaching standards – although they may not have had the label 'principle'. Remember, there are no right or wrong answers.

ACTIVITY 1

Devising principles

This first activity requires you to think about what those principles are. By using a **self-assessment** questionnaire to **identify** your current beliefs and then a few questions which require an honest **critique** of your practice you will be able to reflect on the answers.

In the left hand column you will see questions which are designed to help you think about four basic principles – one around planning, one relating to the structure, another about differentiating activities and finally, one looking at assessment. In the right hand column are some suggested responses. They may not be exact, but the exercise is to prompt ideas from which you will be able to design your own statements.

Question	Is your response?
How does session preparation help you in your teaching role?	As I know my subject inside out I don't feel I need to do session plans, but I know what I'm doing.
	I have an idea of what I'll do and make sure I've got copies of handouts, etc., so that I've got everything I need to deliver the topic.
	I have to write a script, if I don't feel in control.
	I feel my session plan gives me confidence and ensures I appear professional.
What is the usual structure of one of your sessions?	I tend to 'go with the flow'; I take my lead from my learners.
	It is structured with 'military precision'.
	I have a beginning where I introduce the topic, a middle where we add new stuff and an ending in which I summarise what's happened.
	I start with what I know my learners know, and build on it from their experiences and ideas.

▶

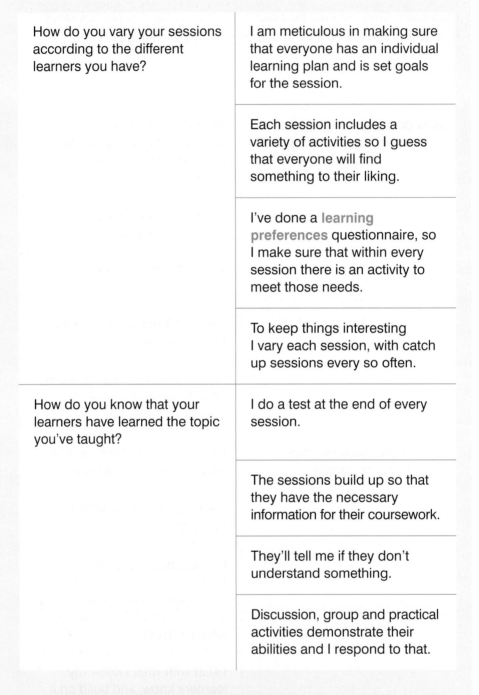

How do you vary your sessions according to the different learners you have?	I am meticulous in making sure that everyone has an individual learning plan and is set goals for the session.
	Each session includes a variety of activities so I guess that everyone will find something to their liking.
	I've done a **learning preferences** questionnaire, so I make sure that within every session there is an activity to meet those needs.
	To keep things interesting I vary each session, with catch up sessions every so often.
How do you know that your learners have learned the topic you've taught?	I do a test at the end of every session.
	The sessions build up so that they have the necessary information for their coursework.
	They'll tell me if they don't understand something.
	Discussion, group and practical activities demonstrate their abilities and I respond to that.

You may of course wish to modify one or more of the answers to make it more representative of your teaching – you can. This activity is to help you identify *your* principles not inflict principles on you!

From your answers, can you identify what your underlying principles are for

- planning lessons?
- structuring lessons?
- meeting learners' needs?
- assessing learning?

Each principle will generally start with 'I will always . . .'.

You should now have four principles, relating to planning, structure, differentiation and assessment; these are the values that you currently take into your learning environment.

You now need to analyse each one:

- Is it accurate in terms of *all* the sessions you run?
- Do you adhere to all of them without compromise?
- Is that what you want, or is it a 'best shot' ideal?

The ultimate test of your principle is . . .

How would you defend your principle if challenged about it by a colleague?

To answer this you need to think about the theories you explored in the first part of this chapter. Whatever your principle, it will be correct if you can justify it against the theory. If other people don't agree, it is probably because they are exponents of different theories, not that they are necessarily correct.

ACTIVITY 2

Justifying principles against theories

- Is your principle supported by a behaviourist, cognitivist or humanist school of thought?

- Does it advocate a teacher-centred (objectivist) or learner-centred (constructivist) model of learning?

- Do you use a style of teaching based on pedagogy or andragogy?

- How do you **develop** the levels of learning – Bloom, Biggs or Gagné?

- Which motivation theory do you follow?

- Is the learning effective due to your methods of communication?

In completing this activity, you have created the opportunity to investigate a few of your principles and start to think about whether or not they are principles or whether they are hopes and wishes. Usually if your principle is not consistent practice or you can't justify it against theory then it may be a hope rather than a principle. Alternatively, when listening to others justify their principles you may realise that there are alternative ways of doing something. In these cases you may feel the need to develop your principles.

Identifying changes in your practice

As with many other teaching and learning activities, time and experience will mean that you re-think what you do in the learning environment and why you do things in a particular way. Reflection is the key to this development. Whether it is a deliberate act of reviewing your practice or an **ad hoc** decision based on experience (Schön 1983 and Kolb 1984), either will result in identifying things that you want to do differently. Being receptive to the need to develop is the key to successful reflective practice. A couple of good questions to ask at this point are:

- What principles would you *like* to be able to advocate?
- What principles do your lesson observers say you *should* develop?

What is the reason behind you not having these principles now – is it inexperience, inability or that you don't have the time or skills to develop them?

Identifying the change is sometimes the easy part. You will have your own ideas, and we all know somebody that tells us 'if I were you ...'. However, sometimes you may not know what to do to change, in which case you may benefit from seeking advice from managers, peers or mentors, listening to feedback from learners, or simply listening or asking questions in the staffroom.

Implementing change

Having analysed your current practice and considered the developments you wish to make you will finally be able to start thinking about how to make the changes.

The people who can help are:

- Your *tutor* on the diploma programme. They will have observed you and given you ideas. During the discussions in class you may have ideas of your own.
- Your *mentor* is an experienced practitioner in the same teaching area as yourself. They will be familiar with the curriculum and the learners so may have ideas they can share. Your organisation may also employ generic mentors who can help with wide-ranging teaching skills.
- Subject learning *coaches* are trained in supporting the staff teaching within curriculum areas and have access to an extensive range of material, so may be able to help in implementing your ideas.
- Other members of the *team* will have experience of delivering a similar subject and will certainly know the learners, although they may not have experience of sharing their knowledge or the time to spend lots of time with colleagues.

● Your *manager* will usually be quite experienced in terms of delivering learning and assuming you feel comfortable working with him or her, will be able to share with you the organisation's values which may help you understand your own principles.

The strategies that can help

Collectively known as continuing professional development (CPD) activities, the following will help you to learn of new ideas, suggest ways of implementing changes and provide the theory to support your ideas.

● researching using text books or the Internet
● professional discussions with colleagues
● attending in-service training events
● personal study
● problem-solving activities
● trial-and-error practice
● action research
● reflective journals or diary logs.

One of the most difficult yet important parts of implementing a change in practice is having the idea in the first place. So take the advice, be receptive to new ideas and become a reflective practitioner. Whether it works or not is sometimes immaterial. Many things that occur in your teaching seem like a good idea at the time, you should only feel pressured to change if things are not working or you are convinced that there is a better way of working. If your principles are resulting in your learners achieving in a timely manner and all of the necessary pieces of teacher administration are complete then chances are there's nothing much wrong, you may only wish to get more efficient.

You may find it helpful to document the changes you wish to make in an action plan. This will help you to prioritise your actions, keep focused on the developments and monitor success on the way. A suggested format for this might be:

What change or modification do I need to make?	Why?	Who can I ask to help me?	What cpd strategies will I need to engage in?	Done ✓ or ×	How will I know when the change is successful?
Example:					
One of the principles I wish to include in future sessions is to provide feedback to learners on how they are progressing in my lessons.	Theory suggests that it improves motivation. I want my learners to succeed.	My recent lesson observation stated that feedback was 'inconsistent' and that I should use 'constructive' feedback to learners following activities. Ask my mentor for ideas. Is there a corporate document that I should use?	Book appointment with mentor/tutor. Investigate the expression 'constructive'. www, text books. Ask if there is any guidance on intranet. Check cpd plan for any events or workshops (attend if and when).		ALL learners will be clear about what they have to do to improve their practical skills and coursework.

Glossary of terms

Ad hoc random, unplanned action

Critique detailed analysis

Develop advance or improve ability

Evaluation to form an idea about something, to measure its effectiveness

Identify to determine or recognise something

Learning preferences the individual's favoured way of learning

Reflection a considered opinion expressed in speech or writing; thoughts or considerations, developing ideas or thoughts

Self-assessment a method of confirming own ability

 SUMMARY

In this chapter we set out to achieve the following outcomes:

- Evaluate your own practice against theories and principles of learning and communication
- Identify ways of adapting and improving own practice
- Develop an action plan to meet development needs

Your Personal Development

In the first part of the chapter you identified and evaluated your current principles of learning and communication. In the activity you selected relevant or close principles in relation to planning, structure, differentiation and assessment. You then used these to fine tune your own principles and in the second activity, you justified them against previously learned theoretical models.

In the second part of the chapter you reviewed your principles and practice against perceptions of best practice, theory and advice offered. You then considered areas for improvement and change.

Finally, using a reflective model you have decided if change is necessary and how you would initiate any changes that were needed. You then considered how any resultant actions could be recorded in an action plan, together with an idea of how your action plan can be achieved.

Part Five
Continuing personal and professional development
(CPPD)

This is the fifth unit in your Diploma in Teaching in the Lifelong Learning Sector (DTLLS) qualification

Learning Outcomes	Assessment Criteria
Understand the role of the teacher in the lifelong learning sector	● Analyse and compare different teaching roles and contexts in the lifelong learning sector ● Evaluate own role and responsibilities with reference to area of specialism and as part of a team ● Analyse the impact of own beliefs, assumptions and behaviours on learners and others ● Analyse the impact of own professional, personal, interpersonal skills, including literacy, numeracy and ICT skills, on learners and others
Understand theories and principles of reflective practice, and models of continuing personal and professional development	● Analyse and compare relevant theories, principles and models of reflective practice ● Explain how theories, principles and models of reflective practice can be applied to own development as an autonomous learner
Understand own need for continuous personal and professional self-development	● Evaluate own approaches, strengths and development needs, including literacy, language and numeracy needs ● Use self-reflection and feedback to develop own knowledge, practice and skills, including literacy, language, numeracy and ICT skills ● Plan appropriate opportunities to address own identified learning needs
Understand and demonstrate ways in which engagement in CPPD activities has improved own practice	● Identify and engage in appropriate CPPD opportunities to keep up to date and develop in teaching and in own specialist area ● Evaluate the impact of CPPD activities on own professional practice, identifying any further learning and development needs

CHAPTER 21
(CPPD)

The role of the teacher in the Lifelong Learning Sector

LEARNING OBJECTIVES

The measurable outcomes that you will achieve by reading this chapter and completing the activities are:

- To describe the roles of the various providers of learning in the lifelong learning sector
- To identify the many roles of the teacher and the impact they have on learners
- To state how the main components of your job description and person specification meets the requirements of LLUK standards

This initial introduction seeks to help teachers to understand their role and therefore their professional requirements.

The Lifelong Learning Sector

The Lifelong Learning Sector covers a very diverse area of work. The sector covers community learning, further education, higher education institutions, work based learning, offender learning and the voluntary sector. Each meets the needs of its clients through education and learning funded either by government bodies – such as the Learning and Skills Council or Higher Education Funding Councils, or through direct government funding, for example offender learning, or through private or charitable funding from individuals and employers.

Community Learning

This responsive sector co-ordinates the work of adult learning, community education, family learning and youth work. It aims to address the demands of several key agendas: widening participation; social inclusion; customised provision; lifelong learning needs; community development; social needs; personal and social development. The Community Learning sector employs in excess of 170,000 people in England, 4,000 people in N Ireland, 11,000 in Scotland and 4,000 in Wales (source: LLUK: Staff Individualised Record 2005).

Further Education

This sector includes approximately 450 general FE colleges, tertiary colleges, sixth form colleges and independent and specialist colleges. Many of the colleges work in partnership with other members of the sector and are mainly associated with the delivery of education for 14–19 year old learners. Recent changes in funding have led to a shift from adult learning to the education of younger learners. Colleges are now tasked with supporting adult learning and training through direct realistic costing of provision. The sector covers a wide variety of subject disciplines and many specialist teaching groups, with many also working in HE, community and work based sectors as well as the more **vocational** and **academic** subjects. The Further Education sector employs in excess of 250,000 people in England, 6,000 people in N Ireland, 12,000 in Scotland and 9,000 in Wales (source: LLUK: Staff Individualised Record 2005).

Higher Education Institutions (HEI)

This sector covers universities, university colleges, and colleges of Higher Education (HE). Much of the work in universities is based around graduate and post graduate levels. There are trends to make the sector more diverse and accessible by including programmes which are more vocational and employment related. There are about 170 institutions employing in excess of 307,000 people in England, 6,700 people in N Ireland, 52,000 in Scotland and 24,000 in Wales (source: LLUK: Staff Individualised Record 2005).

Work Based Learning (WBL)

This sector includes the work around applied vocational training, national training programmes, specialist training programmes and private training. The work is closely linked to the needs of employers and in addressing subject shortages based on employment trends. Much of the work is funded by government funding councils but also by private sources. The sector employs in excess of 170,000 people in England, 4,000 people in N Ireland, 11,000 in Scotland and 4,000 in Wales (source: LLUK: Staff Individualised Record 2005).

Offender learning

This is a key priority and contributor to the Government's Skills for Life strategy and is a way of reducing offending behaviour.

Associated with the prison and probation services, offender learning is concerned with improving skills and employability. The sector is overseen by both The Department for Innovation, Universities and Skills (DIUS – for adult offenders) and The Department for Children, Schools and Families (DCSF – for school age and youth offenders). Learners aged between 10 and 18 are held in Young Offender Institutions (YOI), Secure Homes or Secure Training Centres. Those over 18 are held in adult prison establishments. Learning environments in over 140 establishments are overseen by the Learning and Skills Councils; there are 19 education providers as well as local authority provision. In addition to the education departments, training is also offered as part of normal work regimes. The sector is now funded and inspected under the auspices of the Learning and Skills Councils. It is the complexity of the provision that makes it difficult to accurately calculate the number of people employed as teachers in the sector because employers recruit locally and often sub-contract to other providers (Information provided with permission from Jandrell, Joint Youth Justice Unit, 2008).

Voluntary and Community Sector (VCS)

The third sector which is also sometimes known as 'the charity sector' or 'not-for-profit sector', includes organisations registered with the Charities Commission, housing associations, places of worship, NHS trusts and sport and recreational clubs, etc. The numbers working in the sector are huge, but are not recorded in such a way as to differentiate between those involved in teaching and those not. The sector works with groups such as those with disabilities or hard to reach groups and under-represented groups. Accredited learning is associated with basic skills and **ESOL**. Non-accredited learning is concerned with developing relationships and partnerships. This sector is overseen by the Office of the Third Sector, part of the Cabinet Office.

Areas of specialism

In the sector, teachers talk about subject disciplines and specialisms. There are many variables here for instance:

Disciplines – e.g. maths, public services, teacher training, child care, hairdressing. These are the subjects that teachers consider that they are proficient in teaching.

Specialisms – the contexts in which we deliver those disciplines – 14–16, 16–19, adult, offender learning, skills for life, community provision, WBL, etc. These cover the broad type of learner or area of delivery.

Roles – the term 'teacher' has been used as a generic term to cover the name given to one who teaches or initiates learning. It covers facilitator, tutor, instructor, lecturer, trainer, coach etc.

The skills required to teach within these specialisms are learned through experience, in-service training and development and research. The following is an overview of the main specialisms in which a teacher may find themselves.

Teaching 14–16 year olds

The teaching of younger learners within or in conjunction with the **post-compulsory** sector, has emerged from the recent changes in government policy resulting from Mike Tomlinson's report – 14–19 Curriculum and Qualification Reform (2004). It set out the following targets:

- Raise participation and achievement
- Improve functional skills
- Strengthen vocational routes
- Provide greater stretch and challenge
- Reduce the assessment burden
- Rationalise the curriculum.

The main outcome of the report was the implementation of the Diploma lines of vocational training. Many organisations were already working with schools to offer a vocational programme of study as an alternative option to academic study: 'The Increased Flexibility Programme'.

Teachers may teach younger learners within their institution or they may be required to teach in partnership with schools. The strategies of teaching are the same, but younger learners have different needs and the teacher should bear these in mind when preparing their sessions. There are a number of legislations and specialised codes of conduct for working with younger learners: The Children Act, Duty of Care, *In loco parentis*. See the section on Legislation and codes of conduct in Chapter 1.

The move from school to the lifelong learning sector (FE, WBL, etc.) can be daunting, some may see it as exciting, but there are differences that a younger learner will see when comparing their learning to their school experiences. These are:

- Classes are longer in FE timetables
- Post-compulsory learning is less teacher dominated
- Learners are treated as adults – although their immaturity sometimes restricts the development of independence
- Children are still developing emotionally and may act before thinking
- Instances of vocational programme being seen as second to academic routes
- Shift of teaching from teacher dependent models to learner centred independent strategies
- Older learners in classrooms
- Unsupervised periods (breaks, lunch etc.).

However well managed the change, young learners will experience a series of emotions arising from this new sense of freedom which may result in:

- Fear
- Lack of confidence

- Noisy outbursts
- Disruptive behaviour
- Transitional problems concerned with school to FE environments
- Apprehension and anxiety.

Many of these emotions could have a negative influence on teaching and learning, although teaching this age group is not always problematic; a teacher just needs to focus on specific skills. In order to ensure teaching and learning is effective the teacher should:

- Increase the importance of analysis of individual learning styles and creating Individual Learning Plans (ILPs) to chart progress
- Deliver an induction to introduce the differences between school and the LLUK organisation
- Create and maintain classroom rules
- Devise small chunks of activity to maintain interest, promote motivation and increase self-esteem
- Offer plenty of variety in classes
- Initiate relevant support mechanisms
- Follow recommendations to promote the care of younger learners, Protection of Children Act 1999, Every Child Matters and 'in loco parentis' – duty of care
- Prepare learners for the world of work
- Use rewards and sanctions to control behaviour
- Be patient; be in control (firm but fair)
- Praise and encourage at every opportunity
- Use strategies to develop rapport and mutual respect.

Teaching 16–19 year olds

Programmes for this age group are generally either vocationally based or academic subjects. Learners usually come into their programme of study from school and the main provider is the Further Education sector. Courses tend to be full-time and are funded by Learning and Skills Councils (LSC). Academic subjects, for example 'A' levels are usually, but not exclusively, delivered within Sixth Form Colleges or schools. Priority areas are based on national and local skills needs and funding is allocated accordingly. This leads to colleges having to plan their curriculum offer according to trends. Provision that is not a funding priority is offered on a **self-financing** basis. The needs of the age group are often very similar to those of the 14–16 groups. As they are usually entering directly from school, there has to be a period of personal development towards adulthood, and of course hormones play a big part in influencing behaviour at this age!

This influences the choice of teaching and learning methods. The teacher is responsible for developing autonomy and independence (of learning) in order to prepare the age group for further study or self-development. There is a notional development of pedagogy towards **andragogy**.

There is an assumption (remember that the first rule of teaching is 'Assume Nothing!') that learners entering at 16 are following their chosen career path and are eager to learn skills which will prepare them for employment. This group of learners should be seen as 'work in progress', a group in transition from childhood to adulthood. Whilst some have identified their preferred careers, others may need more guidance and direction and will benefit from 'taster' opportunities. Teachers involved with this age group, especially if on a vocational programme, are usually practitioners in the subject and have moved into teaching; this brings a wealth of technical knowledge into the classroom.

Some learners are in receipt of an Educational Maintenance Allowance (**EMA**). EMA is a means tested allowance paid to those over 16 who wish to remain in full-time education but are concerned about the financial implications of doing so. Those living in a home where the annual household income is less than £30,810 (2007–08 tax year) can qualify for a weekly EMA of up to £30.00 (2008) to support the cost of books, travel and equipment. Bonuses are paid for learners who meet progress and achievement targets. For more advice, learners can be directed to http://ema.direct.gov.uk/ to discover current information and application details.

The payments are not related to monies paid through Learner Support Fund or any other financial help paid to students.

ACTIVITY 1

Can you see what they see?

> Imagine you are a 14-year-old . . . or imagine you are a 16-year-old . . .
>
> How is your teaching different from school?
>
> Are the rules different? What about the sanctions?
>
> Is the classroom different?
>
> Is the relationship between teacher and learner different?
>
> How do you imagine a 14- or 16-year-old will feel?

You may wish to do this kind of activity at the start of a programme with younger learners and compare this with a repeated activity 6 or 12 months into the programme.

Teaching adults

The term given to teaching adults is andragogy (how adults learn) as distinct from how children learn. Adult teaching tends to be more learner-centred. Adults may come into the environment on work related training sessions or in recreational evening sessions. The teacher should remember that adults come into education with a range of life skills and previous educational experiences. They are generally independent and usually have clear goals for their learning – although there will be some variations (see the PTLLS section, Challenges and barriers to learning in Chapter 2 and Chapter 18, Principles and theories of learning and communication, in Part 4).

Adults expect:

- To be treated as adults
- Their teaching sessions to be relevant to their learning goals
- To be taught in a way that motivates and meets their needs.

There are different beliefs and expectations when it comes to the teacher's role; some adults expect the teacher to teach them, via loads of handouts and teacher led sessions – maybe similar to their own learning background. Others are independent and just need the teacher to facilitate their learning (learner-centred). Your role as the teacher is to identify this and reflect it in your choice of teaching strategies and promote a shared responsibility to learning. Teachers may need to coax adults from a '**chalk and talk**' style of learning to a more **autonomous learner**-centred style.

Teaching in the community

Recreational or social learning used to be within the funding responsibility of Local Education Authorities. Then in 1998 the Adult and Community Learning Fund was established with the aim of widening and increasing the participation in learning and improving the standards of basic skills. The fund set out to support those who would not normally participate in education or training and took learning out into the community rather than expecting the community to come to learning establishments. There were clear links between learning and social regeneration. The Fund ceased in 2004 when it was taken over by the Learning and Skills Council, with broadly the same mandate. However, in 2006 came a different funding methodology with priorities given to younger learners, with the result that less funding was available to adult community learning. Now, any provision offered is usually based on a self-financing strategy, which in some areas has resulted in a significant decrease in courses offered for recreational or personal interest outcomes.

Some key contributory factors in the changing view of ACL:

- FE for the New Millennium, DfEE (1998) in a response the Helena Kennedy's Learning Works says, 'The establishment of a learning society in which all people have opportunities to succeed'.
- Success for All (2002): Adult and community learning seeks to provide choice, raise standards and helps to meet skill needs.
- White Paper: 21st century skills: Realising our potential (2003), directed focus of learning to those required by employers to meet a skill need.
- Investing in Skills: taking forward the skills strategy (2003). LSC reconsidered the approaches to funding.

Teaching and supporting voluntary sector groups

The skills of teaching in this sector are broadly similar to teaching related to adults, children and community provision, because the features of the group are similar; venues and social environments may be different. There may be those with specialisms such as working with learners on the autistic spectrum, disabilities, non-English speakers, youth workers. There may be a high focus of working with multiple agencies to support the wider needs of learners.

Teaching and training in Work Based Learning (WBL)

This is the term used to identify those learners who are on Government sponsored training programmes, as opposed to Work Based Training (WBT), which refers to in-service training and development. There are initiatives to support young people to train for employment as well as schemes to support those who are unemployed or inactive and equip them with the skills they need to re-enter the world of work. There are/have been Youth Training Schemes (YTS), New Deal, Apprenticeships and Train to Gain as well as work related Foundation Degrees. Whilst work based learning schemes are usually associated with 16- to 24-year-olds, they are not limited solely to that age group.

Generally the programmes are a method of gaining employability skills through a combination of work based practice and training, which is usually day-release type at the premises of a training provider. Training Providers may be private training companies, small or large organisations or FE colleges; the link is the commitment to work with employers to ensure a skilled workforce. The skills are usually measured using qualifications such as National Vocational Qualifications (NVQs), Technical Certificates, and/or Key Skills, and are enhanced by Training Allowances. These used to be on a par with other government benefits paid to the trainees, but now employers are encouraged to recruit unqualified staff and pay them fair salaries, whilst receiving sponsored training. This has eliminated a lot of the 'cheap labour' arguments and by offering recognised qualifications has seen value and worth develop into the provision.

Teaching offenders

Offenders are often under-achievers (DFES, 2006: 7), particularly in respect of basic skills. These skills need to be improved if the challenge of reducing re-offending is to be achieved. The teaching of offenders is often challenging. Teachers have to balance the requirements of LSC and Ofsted with the additional demands of Home Office policy. Add to this the impact of working safely and securely and teaching and learning choices are often limited. Where possible, links to employers are seen as advantageous, but teaching therefore should advocate and recognise skills required to gain employment. Some take the opportunity to train or learn new skills either to while away the time or to create purposeful activity. The sector sees many **disaffected learners** and reluctance to learn is symptomatic of their previous experiences, fears, pressures and in some instances apathy. Teachers frequently have to deal with emotional and behavioural issues; the additional security aspects also constrain activities and movement. An offender's teacher, therefore, must work hard to improve self-esteem and advocate the value of learning in sometimes very difficult conditions. A teacher in this sector frequently works with very minimal resources; ILT teaching strategies such as Internet research are not available to offenders within many prison settings and many community offices do not have the training facilities of other training providers.

The roles of the teacher

As explained earlier, the term teacher is generic and includes many different functions in respect of teaching in the Lifelong Learning Sector. One definition of a teacher is 'one whose occupation is teaching'. Whilst not particularly helpful as a definition it leads us to thinking about what teaching is. This was originally reviewed in the PTLLS part of your award:

The role and functions of a teacher

- Designing programmes of study
- Planning and preparing classes
- Developing interesting ways of delivering learning
- Assessing the impact of learning
- Ensuring a safe learning environment
- Marking of work and giving feedback on outcomes
- Keeping records
- Contributing to the development of the programme
- Evaluating the effectiveness of the programme
- Keeping data about retention and achievement
- Having a duty of care
- Monitoring the progress of learners
- Acting within the professional codes
- Monitoring attendance and punctuality
- Contributing to the administration of the programme

- Entering learners for exams and tests
- Contributing to Quality Assurance requirements
- Acting as a role model
- Pastoral Care

Wilson (2008) Chapter 1

It is duties such as these that will appear on a **job description**. Therefore teaching is far more than just disseminating information to others. It requires many more skills and a lot of balancing of time to ensure everything gets done in a timely manner. The characteristics of a teacher will provide the basis of the '**person specification**' and will include:

Qualities of a teacher

- Patience
- Team player
- Organised
- Good communicator
- IT literate
- Innovative, creative
- Reflective
- Shows empathy and respect
- Fair
- Forgiving/compassionate
- Tactful
- Good sense of humour
- Enthusiastic
- Dedicated/committed
- Hard working

- Aspirational/inspirational
- Friendly
- Autonomous

This is a tough list to achieve, given that you have to do all of these tasks and be all of these characters to different people constantly during your working day, and probably some of them concurrently!

There are some distinct responsibilities that a teacher may be given. The major one to be considered here is the job of 'tutor'. This will probably be to a group of learners (maybe a specific cohort or qualification) and is the name given to an additional responsibility to support learners.

The class tutor

In this context I am referring to the role of the tutor as someone who provides academic and **pastoral** support rather than the generic term of tutor which is sometimes used as an alternative to teacher or assessor.

When operating within an inclusive environment, monitoring progress and providing continuity is paramount. The role of the class tutor and the provision of tutorial time are vital in creating a learning experience that is beneficial to everyone, although respecting boundaries is essential. There is a fine line between a tutor's role and those of a counsellor; both tutors and learners must be clear about those boundaries.

The role of the tutor and purpose of tutorials is one of supporting learning which will manifest itself in a variety of ways:

- Preparing for and monitoring learners whilst they learn and study
- Providing pastoral and emotional support – supporting the well-being of the learner

- Initiating introductory and diagnostic support – induction, study skills, ILP, initial assessment, preparing for inclusive learning
- Completing progress reviews and personal development reviews
- Addressing retention – looking for and pre-empting cause for concern, offering solutions to issues, and monitoring actions
- Providing opportunities for teacher and learner to communicate on a one-to-one basis
- Providing group development, e.g. citizenship, wider key skills
- Advising other teachers about characteristics of learners which are likely to impact on teaching and learning activities
- Completing target setting discussions towards achievement
- Developing communication skills of learners
- Developing learners' autonomy
- Addressing individual problems or concerns
- Showing that you care at individual level.

However, tutorials can be costly to operate, especially when delivering one-to-one tutorials. This is due to the time needed to ensure that every learner has a tutorial, thus making tutorials very time-consuming. Seeking accommodation that is appropriate to tutorials can also be problematic; small private rooms are not always available and if trying to do one-to-one interviews at the same time as being responsible for the whole group, it is very challenging – what does the rest of the group do whilst you are chatting to one individual? How do you maintain confidentiality under these circumstances? Another consideration when tutoring has to be concerned with learners' perceptions of the tutorial; some may consider it puts pressure on them (both staff and learners) or it appears threatening. However, if tutors demonstrate the value of tutorials and always express confidence in the process, it will result in a positive perception, rather than a negative one. This reinforces the need to teach learners about tutoring and its purposes. The benefits of operating a tutorial system significantly outweigh the disadvantages, and are usually a key part of a learning programme. Effective tutoring systems aid retention and achievement, which of course are the key processes measured in education and training.

In carrying out this role it is essential that tutors are selected and trained in the specific skills of being a tutor. It should not be assumed that everyone can tutor. As well as training in the documentation used by an organisation to record the process, a tutor needs many other skills. Walklin (2000: 254) lists functions that can be attributed to the role of the tutor as: catalyst and adviser; fact finder; auditor; technical expert; problem solver; advocate; reflector; solution provider; enabler; facilitator; influencer and implementer. Let us look at some of the skills needed to carry out these roles:

- Active listening – a tutor should *really* listen; don't interrupt other than to seek clarification or summarising. Look interested but not nosey. Value their opinion – even if it differs from yours and do not voice opinion or inflict your values on the learner, even when asked 'what shall I do?' or 'what would you do?' Respect pauses in the conversation; silence is usually thinking time, especially if your questioning is open and initiates reflection.

- Questioning and explaining – use open questions to encourage learners to reflect on their actions, consider cause and effect. Effective communication is essential, both parties need to be able to talk and understand, listen and hear. Non-verbal communication is also very important. In terms of questioning think about how those questions are asked:

  Open: What do you find difficult?

  Closed: Do you find assignments difficult?

  Leading: You are having difficulty with assignments.

  Hypothetical: What would happen if . . .?

  Reflective: How will you approach the assignment next time?

- Record keeping – usually called reviews, plans or similar. The purpose of the document should be to prompt the discussion, record what is said and what the agreed outcomes are.

- Planning – both the tutor and the learner should plan the tutorial. The tutor should have a fairly good idea of progress and pastoral issues relating to their learners and be able to recount them in tutorials; learners should know the types of discussion topics that will be mentioned so that they can begin to formulate their strategies to develop.

- Time management – ensure that everyone understands how much time is allowed. Manage that period well and if things look like being delayed or over-running take action to control it. A learner may also seek guidance on how to plan and use their time effectively.

- Praise, feedback, discipline – commenting about how well things are going, offering constructive feedback on progress and taking responsibility in dealing with problems are required to maintain rapport and the effectiveness of the process.

- Motivational interviewing or discussion – this is a strategy involving techniques to guide the learner into identifying and dealing with their own issues based on intrinsic learning values.

- Anti-discriminatory practice – tutoring without any bias or discrimination.

- Supporting the development of problem-solving skills by encouraging learners to solve their own problems in a supported way.

- Discretion and confidentiality – the tutor may be privy to information which is expressed within a private discussion. You may have to use your discretion about responding to what is said; if what you are told is best shared, then the owner of the information should be the one to share it; exceptions to this may occur if abuse is suspected or if an illegal practice is identified.

- Empathy (not sympathy), non-judgemental – the tutor should try to understand how things make the learners feel and keep opinions to themselves.

- Respect and socially correct – respect should be mutual and aids the development of a good relationship (rapport). There are social parameters to think about when conducting tutorials; respect of personal space, sitting to the side rather than opposite the learner.

- Flexibility – tutoring demands different styles and expectations to meet different learners, yet consistent in methodology and equality.

- Codes of practice and ethics – working within your Duty of Care (see PTLLS: Chapter 1, pp. 20–21).

The tutor may or may not teach the group, there are no particular guidelines on this; it may be beneficial to remain independent or be advantageous to get truly involved in both the learner's personal and academic development. You should follow your organisation's methods and remember that there are boundaries between the roles of the teacher, the tutor and the counsellor which should be clear in everyone's minds.

Tutoring, like any other part of teaching, is not without its problems. Tutors who do not prepare for tutorials are likely to end up with unfocused sessions without any meaningful outcomes; crossing the boundaries of tutoring and counselling can lead to ill-informed actions, imprudent use of time and is unprofessional. The tutor should know when to refer the issue to someone more qualified to deal with it. The tutor should balance their approach: not too authoritarian or too nonchalant. If it is found that the support provided is ineffective an evaluation should establish the cause: is it too supportive, meaning that your learner is not challenged to develop their own support mechanisms; you may need to question whether the support is (still) relevant.

Other responsibilities a teacher may undertake

Instructor One who is usually working in a practical session and would work to support and develop technical abilities. An example might be someone working as a Fitness Instructor (or coach) on a Sports programme. The role is usually different from teachers in that their role is more logically defined as a supporting role. This role is important as someone who is expert in the technical skill and works closely with learners to develop those skills. The instructor is perceived as less formal than the teaching role and so may engage well with learners who prefer an informal learning environment.

Trainer/Assessor One who may be working with individuals in training venues. It is a common role within NVQ based qualifications where learners are demonstrating competence rather than learning skills. The advantage of this role is the one-to-one strategy that is usually involved. This close working relationship quickly builds trust which creates confidence. If this type of learning is work based, then the learner is probably more relaxed as they are in familiar surroundings.

Facilitator This role is similar to an instructor but may differ in that the sessions are usually workshops in which learners are using discovery type of learning techniques, under the support of a subject specialist. This type of learning suits those learners who enjoy the freedom of a more experiential learning mode. Yet they have 'a back up plan' with the expert should they decide they need extra help or the learners need to be re-focused.

LLUK Professional Standards of Competence

Whatever the title of your role in the sector, your role is important in ensuring that learners have a valuable experience and achieve their planned targets.

Part 7, Wider Professional Practice, fully lists in Chapter 30 the New Overarching **Professional Standards** of Competence relating to teachers, tutors and trainers in the Lifelong Learning Sector. The standards, written by Lifelong Learning (UK), broadly categorise the areas of competence as:

- *Domain A – Professional values and practice.* This covers enabling learners' aspirations and goals to be achieved, working within the law and agreed codes of practice and within quality systems, whilst continually striving to improve own practice.
- *Domain B – Learning and teaching.* This covers implementing learning, inclusion, motivation, achieving goals, communication and liaising with stakeholders.
- *Domain C – Specialist learning and teaching.* This covers keeping up-to-date in subject, enthusing learners, statutory compliance in respect of subject and developing good practice.
- *Domain D – Planning for learning.* This covers promoting equality and diversity, meeting learners needs, negotiating learning, and evaluating the effectiveness of techniques.
- *Domain E – Assessment for learning.* This covers planning, designing and implementing assessment fairly, using feedback to promote learning and working within quality systems to monitor and evaluate assessment.
- *Domain F – Access and progression.* This covers initial assessment and career progression, supporting learners and maintaining own professional role.

The Standards describe the role and many of the responsibilities of the professional teacher. In this context 'professional' means qualified, paid as a teacher and engaged in the practice of teaching.

Your role and the Professional Standards

 **ACTIVITY 2**

1) Refer to a copy of your job description.

It may be generic for the role of 'teacher' rather than specific to a particular teaching role. If you do not already possess a copy your Human Resources department will advise you where it can be located.

2) Download a copy of the New Overarching Professional Standards from http://standardsverificationuk.org/documents/professional_standards_for_itts_020107.pdf.

3) Look at each of the duties described in your Job Description and identify which standard you are meeting by carrying out this action.

4) Create a table:

Duties in my job description	Links to Standards
Characteristics required in person specification	

5) Answer the questions:

Are there any duties that you are asked to do that you cannot link to the Standards?

Are there Standards that you do not/cannot cover in your current role?

6) Create a list of things (an action plan) to identify how you can meet the Standard fully. Use this to define your continuing professional development plan and discuss your findings at a meeting with your line manager or mentor.

Glossary of terms

Academic relating to education, school or scholarships

Andragogy how adults learn

Autonomous learner one who requires minimal guidance from the teacher

Chalk and talk teaching by traditional methods with focus on a blackboard

Disaffected learners no longer satisfied with the learning environment

Discipline a branch of knowledge

EMA Educational Maintenance Allowance

ESOL English for speakers of other languages

Job description a list of duties typical of the job role

Pastoral concerned with the well-being of learners

Person specification a list of characteristics required in the job role

Post-compulsory education after the age of 16, not mandatory

Professional Standards the minimum acceptable levels of performance of a competent teacher within the LLUK sector

Role a person's position within a function or organisation

▶

Self-financing generating sufficient income to cover costs and profit margins

Specialism a particular focus within the broader meaning of teaching

Vocational skills related to employment

 # SUMMARY

In this chapter we set out to achieve the following outcomes:

- Describe the roles of the various providers of learning in the Lifelong Learning Sector

- Identify the many roles of the teacher and the impact they have on learners

- State how the main components of your job description and person specification meets the requirements of LLUK standards

Your Personal Development

This chapter commenced by looking at the main areas of work within the Lifelong Learning Sector, those being: community and voluntary sectors, FE, HE, WBL and offender learning. Each was described in terms of the contribution it makes to the sector, although many areas overlap as they respond to their client market.

In the next section, we reviewed the various specialisms or learner types seen in the sector. Whilst avoiding stereotyping any particular type of learner, the section analysed some of the skills a teacher would need to teach the category of learner.

The role of the teacher was similarly reviewed, investigating the functions within a job role and exploring the many activities a teacher must demonstrate in their 'full' teaching role. Specific reference was made to the role of the tutor and their importance in providing pastoral support to learners. The tutor's role impacts on the learner's enjoyment of the programme and thus is a significant player in the retention and achievement strategies seen in the post-compulsory sector. The discussion then briefly considered other roles a teacher may undertake, or roles performed by others in the learning environment.

Finally, the link was made between professional standards and the teaching role. In the activity, you were provided with an opportunity to look at aspects of your job description and person specification and compare it with the Professional Standards issued by Lifelong Learning (UK). In carrying out this activity it may have identified ways in which you can improve your practice by modifying or developing your skills and knowledge, thus embarking on your continuing professional development.

CHAPTER 22
(CPPD)

Theories, principles and models of CPPD and reflective practice

LEARNING OBJECTIVES

The measurable outcomes that you will achieve by reading this chapter and completing the activities are:

- To explain the terms reflection and reflective practice
- To explain the general term continuing professional development (CPD)
- To describe the main theories and principles of reflective practice
- To identify key stages of the reflective process
- To describe the purpose of CPD

Continuing personal and professional development

In Part 2, Planning and Enabling Learning, Chapter 11, and Part 4, Theories and Principles for Planning and Enabling Learning, Chapters 18 and 20, we have looked briefly at reflection, reflective practice and theories of learning. We have considered models written by Dewey (1933), Kolb (1984), Schön (1983) and Brookfield (1985) and briefly described their relevance to learning. In this chapter, we will look at their importance to cpd and reflective practice. In PTLLS Chapter 4, we looked at post-lesson evaluation documents and reflective logs which remain useful in reflective practice.

Continuing Professional Development (**CPD**) and **reflective practice** are **intrinsically** linked. Quite simply, CPD is the act of gaining new skills and knowledge; **reflection** is making sure that the new skills and knowledge have an impact.

Different types of people teach; there is no particular type of person that will make a good teacher. In some trades and professions, experience leads to **mastery**; this is not true of the teaching profession, probably due to the main variable – the learner. Consequently, the teacher needs to constantly refine their skills. There are times when it feels like you need 'to run in order to keep up' with the sector.

Reflection
The way to ensure that
what worked yesterday will work today.

Whilst it is easy to blame learners for poor teaching, the blame should lie with the teacher's inability to adjust and modify their skills to meet their learner's needs. Unfortunately the plan used for the session last year cannot be wheeled out indefinitely without adjustment. The reflective practitioner has the confidence to take the good and bad outcomes on the chin and deal with them. Experience in teaching makes things easier; you'll build up a set of tried and tested ways of working and use peer and mentor support to share the highs and lows.

Defining the terms

First of all, let us list the terms that will be used in this section:

- Reflection
- Reflective Practice
- Continuing Professional Development – aka CPD
- Continuing Personal and Professional Development – aka **CPPD**

Reflection is an expression used to describe the act of thinking about occurrences, which for the teacher is their teaching role; it should be an essential part of their responsibility. It is more than analysis which is the expression used for collecting and understanding information; it is more than evaluation which is concerned with creating meaning from the information gathered. Reflection is the next stage – questioning the meanings. Reflective practice is the skill of being reflective. Continuing professional development is a collective term used to describe the many ways you can develop and improve your practice. Continuing professional development is not just going on courses, it is any activity which results in a change in practice. In summary, reflection is the process used to identify if and when development is required; CPD is the vehicle to provide that development, reflecting again, then ensures that the development is effectively used to raise performance.

Figure 22A explains the various stages of the reflective process, which starts with the teacher trying to analyse information about their performance and ends with them undertaking activities in order to improve their working practices.

Figure 22A The reflective process

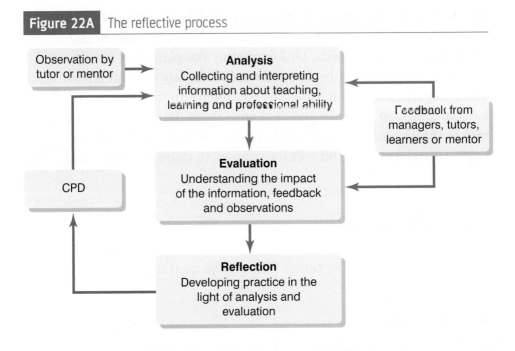

Reflection challenges the teacher to get out of their comfort zone and be receptive to change. It does, however, need skills which have to be learned or developed.

Skills required to reflect:

- Description
- Observation
- Critical analysis
- Evaluation
- Objectivity
- Open mindedness
- Rational thinking.

According to Bain (1999), in order to reflect effectively, the teacher needs to fully understand what has occurred and have the ability to make conclusions and recommendations based on experience, advice and hind-sight in a non-defensive manner. Atherton (2005: 1) suggests that 'real reflective practice needs another person as a mentor or professional supervisor, who can ask appropriate questions to ensure that the reflection goes somewhere and does not get bogged down in self-justification, self-indulgence or self-pity'. Finally, Moon (1999: 63), states the reflection is 'a set of abilities and skills to indicate the taking of a critical stance'.

Why do we need to engage in CPD?

The benefits of CPD are gained by all: the teacher, the teaching team and the organisation. The impact of the CPD benefits the learners because they are faced with professional, knowledgeable and committed staff.

The main benefits are:

- To increase credibility
- To build personal confidence
- To provide career development
- To enhance earnings
- To keep up to date with facts, technology and skills
- To maintain IfL membership
- To motivate and improve effectiveness
- To cope with change.

For the organisation you work for, CPD:

- Maximises staff potential
- Updates skills to reflect changing business needs
- Responds to change
- Improves morale
- Develops teams
- Raises efficiency.

The publication of the regulations for CPD (discussed in more detail in the next chapter) and the growth of the Institute for Learning as a professional body has formalised the need and purpose of professional development. Investing in staff in the form of CPD is expensive yet is a necessary business requirement. There is no specific formula for calculating the budget for CPD as it will be dependent on need and funding availability.

The theories of reflection as a learning tool

Learning and CPD are linked and this is particularly noticeable when looking at theories and **models**. The use of models to justify the practice of engaging with CPD is as important as the reverse; i.e., the development of models in the light of changing practices.

Most of the theories relating to reflection are derived from models associated with describing learning. It therefore has to be accepted that in the context of the theory, reflection is an experimental process to identify developments and CPD is the act of improvement or modification; both are therefore perceived as part of a learning process.

In the 1930s, Dewey (from the cognitivist school) first challenged traditional learning methods by talking about learning by experience. His notion of 'reflective action' was based on the idea that people constantly check their own performance and seek to develop but in order to learn they need to reflect (think about) their actions.

David Kolb's experiential learning cycle, shown in Figure 22B, is a model that explains how learning occurs. It is represented as a circle although there is not a particular starting point; dependent upon

Figure 22B　Kolb's experiential learning cycle

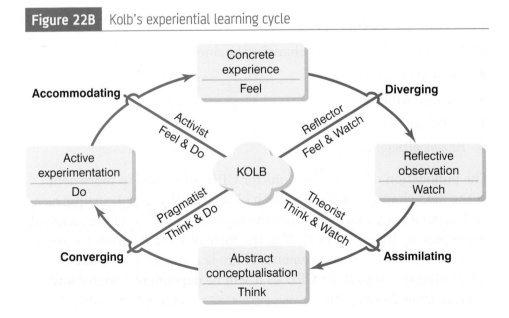

whether you are a 'thinker' or a 'doer' you will enter at different places in the cycle. The cycle is useful as an explanation of training, experiential learning and reflection. More recently, Peter Honey and Alan Mumford (1992) used this model as a means of explaining that people like to learn in different ways – as pragmatists, theorists, activists or reflectors.

In the illustration Figure 22B, you will see the three very similar models described below are super-imposed into one diagram. Whilst you will see, in this instance, three models, there could be an argument that they all say similar things, so the different models are not necessary.

In one model, Kolb's experiential learning cycle, he demonstrates the process of:

- *concrete experience* – undertaking an activity, feeling the emotion of the experience
- *reflective observation* – analysing it, watching oneself and considering what is going on around them
- *abstract conceptualisation* – thinking about why it happened, trying to understand why, and
- *active experimentation* – having another go at the activity, trial and error.

In another of his models, Kolb talks about the characteristics or preferences that people have during experiential activities:

- *Diverging* – those who avoid making assumptions
- *Assimilating* – those who absorb information
- *Converging* – those who follow patterns, and
- *Accommodating* – those who find ways to deal with issues, sometimes without a plan.

In the final model, Honey and Mumford devised a questionnaire to identify the preferred learning styles classifications and revised Kolb's four categories as:

- *Reflectors* – who like to consider why things happen in the way that they do; they like to feel (experience) and see (watching)

- *Theorists* – who must identify every possible eventuality to ensure they make the correct decisions; they think and watch what goes on around them
- *Pragmatists* – who will have a 'controlled' go, to test ideas and suggestions; they think and do
- *Activists* – the people who do; they enjoy the experience and aren't frightened to try out new ideas.

Putting all of these models together it is easy to see a link between Kolb's and Honey and Mumford's views. All believe that in order to develop you need to follow a process; different people will enter the cycle at different points but all will follow it around the circle back to their beginning. Although experiential learning is clearly linked to learning styles, Rogers (2002: 111) states that all of the learning styles are needed in order to develop practice, reminding us that the learning styles are preferences and not rules and that most people demonstrate multiple learning characteristics although they may be dominant in one particular style. The reference here to learning styles is to recognise that if people learn differently, then they will also use that learning in different ways and so a 'one size fits all' CPD strategy will not work. In reflective scenarios, teachers should also review the activity and the way they need to gain new skills and recognise and value differences.

It is also noteworthy, that Coffield (2004, 2008) is challenging current thinking and strategy and provides an alternative opinion on learning preferences. Although some say he is being mischievous in his publications, others feel that he is verbalising unsaid beliefs. He has listed 70 different learner preference theories and analysed 13 in detail. He argues against the widespread adoption of a particular style, particularly by managers and inspectorates. He does not dispute that people are different and like to learn in different ways, but he is against a generalised 'pigeon holing' to influence teaching styles.

Phil Race (2005) disagrees with the cyclical nature of Kolb's model. He finds the theories too wordy and perplexing. With a more modern view, he believes that learning starts with an issue and radiates out to encompass the change and development. He suggests, metaphorically, that it occurs in the same way that throwing a pebble into a pond starts the water rippling (p. 27). His theory therefore is known as

'Ripples'. In the shift from learning to reflection, he introduces the idea that there are five factors involved in successful learning and development:

- Wanting to learn
- Needing to learn
- Learning by doing
- Learning through feedback
- Making sense of things.

Commencing with the desire (need or want) to learn, a ripple effect is sent through the model with each stage having an effect on the next. The final stage of feedback may cause the ripples to return towards the middle again. The model is representative of a trial and error model when the teacher constantly reviews what is going on, modifying when necessary, and moving forward to achieve the desired result. The idea, presented by Race (2005) is shown in Figure 22C.

Figure 22C   Race's Ripples (2005, pp. 26–29)

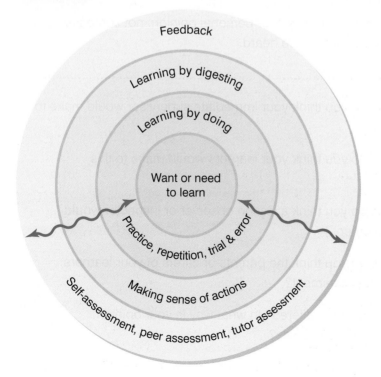

A model that you may find useful when thinking about development is that of Brookfield's Lenses. Brookfield (2007) suggests that sometimes we only see what we want to see and should look beyond our own beliefs and expectations. He suggests that reflective practitioners might want to look at problems through the eyes of others in order to get a bigger picture. He says: 'best teaching is critically reflective – constant scrutiny of assumptions about teaching' (2007: 2).

Let us consider the example in the following activity:

 **ACTIVITY 1**

Look at the following statement:

'A TEACHER SHOULD DESIGN DIFFERENTIATED ACTIVITIES IN EVERY CLASS'

What do *you* think? Try to give your personal opinion, not someone else's or something that you've heard.

Response ....

What comments do you think your immediate supervisor would make to this statement?

What comments do you think your learners would make to this statement?

What comments do you think a lesson observer or inspector would make to this statement?

What comments do you think the parents or carers of your learners would make to this statement?

Has your original opinion altered? In what way is your opinion influenced by other's responses?

Another study relates to the work of Donald Schön (1930–1997), who worked with Chris Argyris (1923–), concerning a model of 'theories of action'. Firstly, they expressed their opinions about learning and reflection. Very simply, they argued that people create their own theories in order to make sense of their actions, hence 'theory in action' (1974). In further work they describe learning as 'loops' (1978). In 'single-loop' learning if something goes wrong, a person thinks of another way and revises the action. In 'double-loop' learning, if something goes wrong the person asks themselves why and thinks of alternatives before having another go at the task. The double-loop idea is nearer the concepts of reflection in which the teacher would always question their performance in a bid to improve. However, whilst the idea challenges Kolb's opinion of learning being a cyclical process, this simplistic linear process does not recognise that sometimes in modifying the first situation you might also identify other necessary improvements, in which case a circular approach is more relevant.

Schön's (1983) second model is an effective suggestion for how reflection occurs. He suggests that there are two types of reflection. There are the reflections that occur which necessitate immediate response (reflection-in-action) and there are those reflections that occur after the event (reflection-on-action).

Reflection-in-action is the type of reflection that you and I might commonly describe as 'thinking on your feet'. It is an immediate response to something that happens in the classroom, for example, when touring the room following the launch of an activity you repeatedly hear from the groups that an important fact has either been misinterpreted or misunderstood, so you stop the activity and go over the fact again before re-commencing the activity. This is you reacting in favour of your learners by changing your lesson plan to meet their needs. This is why a lesson plan is a 'plan' and not a 'tablet of stone', so that you can be responsive.

Reflection-on-action is a more systematic, analytical approach to reflection. The reflection occurs after the event, rather than as it is happening. It is when you consciously evaluate your lessons with the aim of checking what went well and what needs to be modified next time you deliver a similar session. This is achieved through the writing of journals or post-lesson evaluation documents.

Bain (1999) *et al.* discuss levels of reflection, putting forward the notion that the ability to reflect improves with practice. They suggest that reflection is a spiral, broadly based on Kolb's Experiential Learning Cycle, but in which reflective ability increases with experience. This is also not unlike Bloom (1956) who also suggested that levels of learning move from low to high order skills.

At its lowest level, by an inexperienced teacher or student teacher, reflection is personal and generally descriptive. At the next level a (student) teacher will ask questions of themselves. In the next stage the teacher is able to relate the incident to previous experiences or current discussions. At the fourth level, the teacher is trying to understand why things happen. Finally, the teacher fully understands what has occurred and has the ability to make conclusions and recommendations to improve their practice.

Finally, a teacher may wish to look at a practice model.

'Teaching Squares' is a process of linking with colleagues to share experiences, observe practice and engage in dialogue about teaching and learning. The partnership approach is non-threatening.

Reciprocity and shared responsibility Assumes that partners in the process have different roles and therefore share risks	*Appreciation* Aids development in a positive way
Self-referential reflection Aids identification of own learning points and therefore becomes non-critical of others	*Mutual respect* Aids empathy and respect of others in the partnership

Wessely (2002) Teaching Squares

In teaching squares a group of four people, preferably from different disciplines, observe each other and engage in shared reflections. This is a good way of engaging in peer observations, which is undoubtedly an excellent method of improving performance and sharing best practice.

There have been many contributors to the field of reflection, less so for CPD, although the main contributors to CPD are the thousands of people who participate in it each year. Most of the work around reflection argues its worth as a means of improving individuals to cope with the demands of their profession. CPD is an outcome, but it can also be an initiator of further development. If CPD were to occur without any reflection, then it would be meaningless.

Recommended reading

Wessely, A. (2002) Teaching Squares: a handbook for participants.
    National Training Forum – www.ntlf.com/html/lib/suppmat/ts/
    tsparticipanthandbok/pdf
Pollard, A. (2005) *Reflective Teaching: Evidence Informed Professional
    Practice,* London: Continuum

Glossary of terms

CPD the abbreviation for continuing professional development

CPPD the abbreviation for continuing personal and professional development

Intrinsic motivation from within the person; natural desire

Mastery comprehensive ability

Models a description or example to represent an idea

Reflection a considered opinion expressed in speech or writing; thoughts or considerations, developing ideas and thoughts

Reflective practice thoughtful practice to develop skills

 # SUMMARY

In this chapter we set out to achieve the following outcomes:

- Explain the terms reflection and reflective practice
- Explain the general term continuing professional development (CPD)
- Describe the main theories and principles of reflective practice
- Identify key stages of the reflective process
- Describe the purpose of CPD

Your Personal Development

The chapter commences providing an opportunity to review things we know about reflection, reflective practice and CPD. The links between learning and reflection are noticeable when you look at the work done in theoretical research, providing many similarities in approach.

Initially we defined some key terms and explained what reflection and CPD means both to the teacher and the organisation. It describes a process of identifying current strengths and weaknesses and showing how improvement provides continuous opportunities for development. By providing some previously published opinions it offers the reader some suggestions for definitions.

The main theories discussed were those of Dewey, Kolb, Honey and Mumford, Race, Brookfield, Schön and Bain. Each theorist describes their opinion of reflection although they are broadly similar; they conclude that reflection is effective as a means of development.

The activity around Brookfield's theory provides the chance to think a little wider than personal viewpoints, aiming to change preconceived ideas and increase the significance that a teacher may attribute to CPD.

In the next chapter we will look at how we implement these ideas into everyday teaching life and how some other quality processes inform decisions made in respect of CPD.

CHAPTER 23 (CPPD)

CPPD and reflective practice in practice

LEARNING OBJECTIVES

The measurable outcomes that you will achieve by reading this chapter and completing the activities are:

- To identify and select your own approach to continuing personal and professional development (CPPD)
- To use reflection and feedback to plan your development and learning needs
- To describe the impact of the 2007 CPD regulations on teachers in the sector
- To identify appropriate CPPD activities
- To record the outcomes of CPPD activities and the impact they have on individuals, teams and organisations

Continuing personal and professional development (CPPD) is a process designed to improve performance. The most effective CPPD is that which is engaged in positively and thoughtfully. This chapter looks at the realistic ways that you can put CPPD into practice.

REVISION

Return to the following sections in Chapters 4, 11 and 17 to consolidate your previous learning.

PTLLS Chapter 4, Improving your own performance, pp. 104–107. This final section in Chapter 4 explains the stages of reflection from identification, through to analysis, evaluation and finally reflection and demonstrates the key components of a reflective log.

PEL Chapter 11, Reflection and reflective practice, pp. 246–261. This first section in Chapter 11 looks at the aspects of teaching that can be reflected upon and introduces some of the main theories. It describes the benefits of post lesson evaluation and gives an example of a post lesson evaluation document and a learning log.

ELA Chapter 17, Using assessment outcomes to develop yourself, pp. 338–345. The first section in this chapter gives a slightly different slant on reflection, when it considers how learners' results demonstrate the impact of your achievements in the classroom. It uses a reflective diary to describe reflection and a questionnaire to test assessment strategies.

Approaches to CPPD

Continuing personal and professional development is the outcome of a reflective process in which current levels of performance are analysed and evaluated to identify where you need to be. Again, it is worth noting what reflection really means.

> ### To practitioners, reflection means creating opportunities to pause and think about how effectively learning is taking place.

You can reflect on positive or negative experiences (both provide the opportunity to identify good and bad bits) and try and analyse why they are good or bad. You can learn from mistakes and successes. To learners, reflection means accepting pauses in classes in order to consolidate learning, so it is equally important to create reflective moments as well as participating in them.

Your ability to reflect and identify your development will depend upon:

- How you like to learn
- How urgent the change is required
- How much time you have available
- Your perception of your existing skills.

Most reflective practice occurs after what is described in many texts as a 'critical incident'. However, the use of the word 'critical' can be misconstrued. Although not intended, this appears to indicate something that has gone wrong, because one meaning of the word critical is 'a crisis point', somebody in a critical condition is considered to 'be seriously or gravely ill'. In the context of reflection, critical is meant more positively, meaning 'identifying the merits and faults of something'. A more expressive offering could be 'noteworthy event'. Whichever terminology you prefer, the key is to reflect on both the good and bad things that occur. It is equally as important to understand why something worked well as it is to understand why it didn't.

People perceive CPPD in different ways according to their opinion and the value they place on the situation. If the CPPD is compulsory, the teacher probably rebels against the purpose, however well meaning; those events that are voluntary offer more empowerment and therefore, are received in a more positive way. There are several approaches to CPPD in which you reflect on events and activities.

Action research – identifying areas of development and using the training cycle (identify, plan, implement, evaluate) to fine tune practice aiming for improved teaching. Action research may involve considering theory and comparing or developing your teaching according to reading and acquired knowledge.

Peer observation and review – pairs or small groups observe each other and investigate collective issues to identify and share good practice.

Action learning – problem-solving from real situations. Individuals and small groups reflect on elements of a session and set out to learn from their mistakes and successes. Action learning can also describe the 'tweaks' made during a session to respond to what is going on around you. This type of learning is 'thinking on your feet'.

Learning logs – critical incidents or noteworthy events are recorded, analysed and evaluated to establish the reasons behind effective and ineffective strategies. The teacher writes a descriptive piece about a teaching scenario and asks him- or herself why it worked or did not work. The reflection will also include strategies to address future modifications.

Dialogue – informal chats in the staffroom or over a coffee; in fact anytime the conversation turns to teaching and learning. The sharing of good ideas or strategies that work in a specific situation, a good resource found, the address of a useful Internet site or how they dealt with a particular learner.

Mentoring – using a critical friend or specialist teacher to discuss teaching, gain new ideas or fine tune practice. It is usually a confidential relationship, based on trust when two people can share challenges, successes and worries and together plan for better practice.

Case studies – written scenarios which lead individuals or groups to identify best practice or suggest ways of improving a given situation. This is a safe way of making suggestions prior to trying things out 'for real'.

Reading and research – topics are investigated using published materials. The individual reads many different strategies and analyses their preferred ways of working. By working in this way, some teachers feel more confident or safe to develop their practice knowing that they have investigated thoroughly.

Networking – attending meetings or conferences, working for related organisations, acting on committees or working parties brings a wealth of new ideas into a department, which can be shared with colleagues.

Teacher's TV – you can find teacher's TV either on the Internet (http://www.teacherstv/) or on the TV (Sky 880, Virgin 240 or Freeview 650). If using the Internet, when you are at the home page if you type FE into the search box, you will find some video clips, which can be used as information for you or as part of your teaching sessions. Don't forget to pass on good links to others in the staff room!

Regulations for teachers

Although a majority of teachers have engaged with professional development for many years, since September 2007, all teachers in England are now required to engage in CPD by statute. Continuing professional development, or more commonly CPD, is one of those terms that runs frequently from people's tongues, is very meaningful, but is rarely analysed to understand exactly what is meant by the expression. There are many definitions of CPD but first let us look at the phrase itself.

- Continuing means that it never ends; it is a continuous process.
- Professional means that it is focused on a specific role
- Development means that it is goal orientated.

Continuing professional development is not unique to the teaching profession. In 2002, a report to review performance measures in the construction industry in order to create an ethos of sustainability and professionalism, led to the publication of the 'Accelerating Change' report, in which it is advocated that CPD is a 'holistic commitment to structured skills enhancement and personal or professional competence' (Sir John Egan, 2002).

In September 2007, following much **research** and consultation, The Further Education Teachers' Continuing Professional Development and Registration (England) Regulations (Sl No 2007/2116) were launched. This statute requires that teachers register with the Institute for Learning (IfL) within a specified period and that all teachers must engage in continuing professional development (CPD) each year in order to maintain their registration and licence to practice.

From its publication, all existing teaching staff had until the 31st March 2008 to register with the IfL and beyond that date, all new staff had to register within six months of commencing their first teaching post. Teachers are required to renew their registration each April. In registering, teachers were committing to a professional code of conduct and agreeing to undertake and record their continuing professional development.

The amount of CPD a teacher should undertake is proportionate to the number of hours a teacher is employed. A full-time teacher should complete a minimum of 30 hours per year, and this is reduced pro-rata for part-time staff, to a minimum of six hours per year. A teacher is classified as anyone teaching on publicly funded courses or working within organisations in the wider lifelong learning sector. It does not currently apply to private training organisations although many are adopting the regulations as a 'best-practice' model.

In Scotland, teachers have been required to undertake CPD since the start of this millennium. Consequently, many of the lessons learned about implementing a CPD policy and the documentation to record CPD already exist. There is no need to 're-invent the wheel'. Strathclyde University define CPD as: '[a] continuous process of personal growth, to improve the capability and realise the full potential of professional people at work' (www.cll.strath.ac.uk/). Another definition from Scotland is 'anything undertaken to progress, assist or enhance a teacher's professionalism' (www.scotland.gov.uk/).

Recording CPD is the responsibility of the individual teacher; systems to do so are available in electronic and paper-based formats. There is not a specified recording device, although the IfL website provides a link to a software programme (**REfLECT**™) which not only records the activity, but provides a storage area for journals, planning documents and all linked paperwork. The teacher is required to account for their CPD during annual reviews or appraisals and can be set targets for CPD achievement by their line manager. The IfL will also audit members' records to ensure that what is being recorded as CPD is relevant and sufficient. Teachers have a professional responsibility to create CPPD goals, and to record and evaluate their development.

> 'CPD is most effective when practitioners reflect on their professional practice, develop a personal plan based on their identified needs and match this against their organisational context and development plan'

Institute for Learning 2008

Identifying your development needs

Continuing professional development (CPD) is any activity that is undertaken in order to help or develop a teacher's professionalism. The additional 'P' in CPPD stands for 'personal' recognising that a teacher may need to develop skills other than those deemed for professional development.

What constitutes CPD/CPPD:

- Development of functional skills – e.g. literacy, mathematics, ICT
- Development of personal skills – time management, problem-solving etc.
- Development of professional skills – e.g. subject specific updating
- Development of study skills – note taking, researching etc.
- Development of teaching skills – differentiating, planning, ILT etc.
- Development of legislative changes – copyright, health/safety, equality etc.

- Development of support skills – special educational needs, learner support
- Development of skills to embed functional skills into sessions
- Awareness of imminent changes in policy or practice
- Awareness of new management information systems
- Awareness of organisational processes and procedures
- Refreshing teaching skills.

Signposts to successful CPD include:

- Identify the starting point – what do you already know, what do you specifically want to find out
- Don't expect a quick fix – a one hour awareness or training session on a topic is unlikely to be the answer. You may need to go back to the classroom and practice the skills, fine-tuning them for you and your learners
- Different activities work for different people – some learn from books, some learn by watching, some listen to experienced practitioners; you'll need to find out what suits you – try a learning preferences questionnaire to help discover your preferred way
- Listen to the experts – they've probably had the same emotional development as you, they will have empathy with your situation and will be happy to guide, but they may only prompt the motivation to try things out, they may not have all the answers
- You are not alone – however foolish you feel, you are not the only person that is trying to tackle a problem – be it planning, behaviour, assessing, admin or whatever – always seek support
- Think wider than going on courses, sometimes the answer is closer to home than you think
- Take responsibility for your CPPD, empower yourself.

Using feedback and reflection to identify your development needs

Feedback comes to the teacher in many ways, and it is not always asked for! This feedback, however derived, should be the starting

Figure 23A

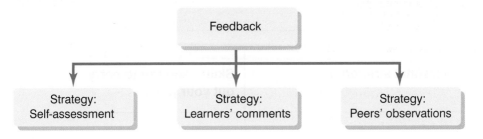

point for a reflection and any resultant action, through CPPD or direct action.

Strategy – self-assessment

Self-assessment starts with an initial assessment of current strengths and areas for development. The things that are identified will depend on some variables:

- Your experience
- Your environment
- Your organisation
- Your learners.

This is what makes your teaching unique. Others may have similar developments identified, but the context in which you make those developments is personal to you. The self-assessment will be your planning process. It may be useful to start your CPPD planning with a modified form of **SWOT** analysis. You should complete the next activity with the following documents to hand:

- Your job description and person specification
- Your department's most recent self-assessment report
- Your CV
- Your most recent appraisal and lesson observation report
- Your Individual Learning Plan – from ITT course.

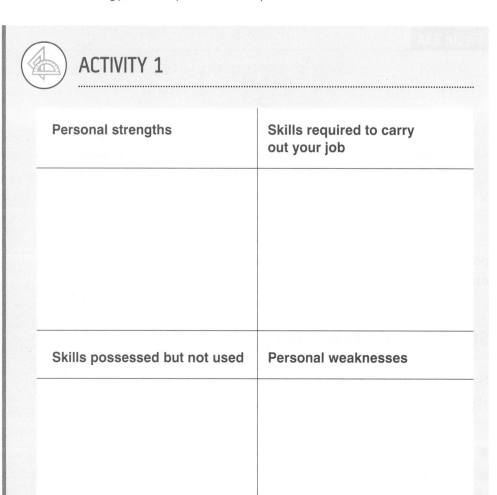

ACTIVITY 1

Personal strengths	Skills required to carry out your job
Skills possessed but not used	**Personal weaknesses**

Self-assessing is by far the most prolific and influential way of developing your practice. Only you honestly know what goes on in your sessions, the emotions you feel and the confidence and abilities you possess. Others may periodically enter your domain and make comment – which you may or may not eagerly grab – but you know the whole truth!

Post lesson evaluation is considered essential when teaching. More formally during your training you will be required to complete a post lesson evaluation checklist following many of the sessions used in your teaching practice evidence. As an experienced or qualified teacher this becomes less consistent and more informal. It is more likely that the post lesson evaluation will occur verbally or within the confines of your own mind. Obviously for future reference and evidence of development, these personal or verbal reflections are not as valuable as a CPPD **strategy**, but never discount the 'conversation' that you have with yourself when returning to the staffroom, or indeed the chat with the person sitting at the next desk.

Post lesson evaluation Here is a suggestion for a self-assessment checklist to use after a lesson, with some ideas on how to complete it.

Session:	
Date:	Time:
Group:	

Planning and preparation

Comment here about the quality and effectiveness of your documentation (SOW and LP), planned and actual outcomes, justification of (the planned variety of) teaching and learning strategies, proposed pace and timing of session.

Did the session go to plan?

What effect did your planning have on your preparation, confidence and focus?

Delivery

Comment here about the quality and effectiveness of the methods, including traditional and modern methods you used in the session, the differentiated strategies used, your resources, balance of teaching and learning

▶

activities, structure of session (beginning, middle and end), how your teaching strategies supported weaker learners and challenged more able learners.

You may also wish to reflect on how you made your lessons inclusive, advocating equality of opportunity and celebrating diversity.

Learning

Comment here about the quality and effectiveness of how learners engaged with you and the content, the level of learners' participation, how you raised motivation and enjoyment in the topic.

You might also wish to comment about how your session enhances and supports the Every Child/Learner Matters themes:

Being healthy; staying safe; enjoying and achieving; making a positive contribution; achieving economic well-being.

Learning is the most important factor of teaching. If learning does not happen then teaching is inadequate. How can I ensure learning occurs?

Environment

Comment here about the quality and effectiveness of the room layout, health and safety factors, impact that temperature had on learning, the facilities available and how you used them.

If an incident occurred, who do you need to report it to? (Sites or security, health and safety officer, line manager.)

Rapport

Comment here about the quality and effectiveness of your communication strategies (verbal, non-verbal and written), the learners' behaviour, how you dealt with any discipline issues, the effect of punctuality and attendance on learning.

Do you need to plan top-up activities for learners who missed this session?

Do you need to create a list of jargon used in sessions?

Do you need to follow up on any incidents in the session?

Assessment

Comment here about the quality and effectiveness of the different assessment methods used, the variety of methods chosen, whether or not learners achieved the planned outcomes, the style of Q&A used, and any homework set.

How do you KNOW that your learners have learned something in this session?

Can you identify exactly what each and every one of them achieved in the session?

Overall comments

What worked well? Why did it work well?

What was not successful? Why not?

How would you deliver this session again if you needed to?

What actions do you need to take – amending resources, addressing classroom management issues, etc.?

DOES THIS LESSON REFLECTION RAISE CPD ISSUES?

It is important also to mention at this stage, that you never stop learning and developing your teaching. Your teaching qualification is a bit like your driving test; the real learning starts afterwards. I have yet to meet the most experienced teacher who doesn't have a session they would rather forget and feel glad that they were not observed in. Equally, there is nothing like the feeling you have when you know that the session you've just delivered was fantastic!

The important thing to remember is to chat about both scenarios to try and find out why.

How to get a 'grade one'

Firstly, there is nothing wrong with a session that is graded three – that means that the learning experience for your learners was satisfactory. You have demonstrated many of the basics required of a teacher to initiate learning. It does mean that you can make both your teaching and your learners' experience better; reflection will help to achieve that – so will the help of an experienced teacher or mentor to initiate the ideas or motivate you into demonstrating them.

> ### 'There are few/no weaknesses identified in the lesson observation document, what else could I have done to get a grade one?'

This is one of the most frequent questions after an observation. Many teachers are good, which means that (in the observed session) the methods and activities they chose enabled learning to occur. It means that the learners responded well to activities and the lesson was well prepared, structured and executed. It is also pertinent at this time to note that the grade is attributed to the learning experience and not the individual teacher. The observer is measuring the amount of learning and the teacher's role in initiating that process. In this activity you might like to see how you are doing in **aspiring** to that grade of **excellence**: an outstanding lesson.

ACTIVITY 2

These are quotations from the Ofsted reports of various organisations, which *together* create the features of a Grade One lesson. In this activity you should read the statement and decide, using the self-analysis grid, how consistently you meet this standard. The key words highlighted express the grade one quality indicator.

Planning
'Teaching is **very** well planned and **all** courses have detailed and thorough schemes of work.'

I do this always	I do this sometimes	I rarely do this	I need to develop this

Classroom environment
'The displays of relevant technical information, charts, posters and students' work on the walls of the classrooms contributes to a **welcome** and **stimulating** learning environment.'

I do this always	I do this sometimes	I rarely do this	I need to develop this

Aims
'The aims of *every* lesson are displayed and **shared** with students at the start.'

I do this always	I do this sometimes	I rarely do this	I need to develop this

Recap
'Each lesson begins with an initial test, revision or review questions, which provides a **stimulating** start and a chance to **reinforce** students' understanding of earlier work.'

I do this always	I do this sometimes	I rarely do this	I need to develop this

▶

Presentation skills
'Teachers are knowledgeable and **enthusiastic**, and the best are **inspirational**, skilfully imparting their **passion** to students.'

I do this always	I do this sometimes	I rarely do this	I need to develop this

Variety of teaching strategies
'Teachers use a **wide** range of **imaginative** teaching strategies. These include revision games, group and pair work, debates and presentations.'

I do this always	I do this sometimes	I rarely do this	I need to develop this

Questioning
'Students are expected to **articulate** answers to questions in some **depth**, and are gently discouraged from monosyllabic responses.'

I do this always	I do this sometimes	I rarely do this	I need to develop this

Integration of key skills
'Key skills opportunities are **identified** by teachers, enabling students to **map and record** their key skills work appropriately.'

I do this always	I do this sometimes	I rarely do this	I need to develop this

Differentiation
'Activities have been devised that will **stretch and challenge** the more able students and also **enable** the weaker students to learn **effectively**.'

I do this always	I do this sometimes	I rarely do this	I need to develop this

Promotion of ILT

'Teachers offer useful and **interesting** website addresses to assist students with their research. Computer-based resources are used **effectively** for learning and **good use** is made of Internet research.'

I do this always	I do this sometimes	I rarely do this	I need to develop this

Assessment and targets

'Marking is **meticulous** and feedback gives students **clear** guidelines on ways to improve their work. Students are set **demanding** minimum performance standards at the start of their course.'

I do this always	I do this sometimes	I rarely do this	I need to develop this

Developing learner skills

'Students learn how to be **critical and analytical** as well as gaining good subject knowledge. They understand complex issues and theories, and demonstrate **high** levels of evaluative skills. Additional skills, such as group work and oral skills, are **well developed** through the teaching and learning methods used in the classroom.'

I do this always	I do this sometimes	I rarely do this	I need to develop this

Summation

'Learning is **constantly** checked and **summarised** well at the end of lessons.'

I do this always	I do this sometimes	I rarely do this	I need to develop this

Independent learning

'**Very high quality**, extra material is available for extension activities, some of which are on the college's intranet that students access at home.'

I do this always	I do this sometimes	I rarely do this	I need to develop this

▶

The grade one lesson has most, if not all of the left hand boxes ticked.

HOW DID *YOU* DO?

Identify three things that you are going to develop in order to aspire to that Grade One lesson.

1.

2.

3.

Modified from training activity devised and delivered by Bradley Lightbody, College Net (2008).

Strategy – feedback from learners

Another strategy to identify development in terms of teaching is that you seek feedback from your learners. You will probably find that your organisation undertakes surveys. These are generally quite specific and focused on the general learning experience. You may (or may not) see the full surveys, but the corridors are probably full of 'you said this . . . . and we did . . . .' types of posters. These are great to show learners and visitors that you listen to views and comments, but for this feedback to be effective for you, you need something a little more specific. This might be in the form of a 'Classroom Critical Incident Questionnaire' (Brookfield 2007).

Ask your learners:

- At what moment in the class did you feel most engaged with what was happening?
- At what moment in the class did you feel most distanced from what was happening?

- What action (by teacher or student) was most helpful?
- What action (by teacher or student) was most puzzling?

The answers to these questions should be able to tell you which of your teaching strategies are most effective. You should make sure, however, to question enough learners to get a sufficient response. You will find that learners have different preferences when learning and this will impact on their replies. This method can also be used when you want to try something new. Don't be frightened to say 'I'm giving this a go and at the end of the session I'll ask you about it'. **Learner Involvement** is becoming a high profile initiative and reflects the change towards a customer focused business model.

Strategy – feedback from peers

> ### There are two things that you can do with feedback from peers:
>
> ### use it
> ### or
> ### lose it

This section covers feedback from others. The word 'peer' covers:

- Colleagues informally making comments on your teaching in response to staffroom conversations
- Colleagues formally making comments on your teaching, through a peer mentoring system
- Subject learning coaches sharing good ideas and resources
- Teacher training tutors making assessments about your teaching
- Mentors offering advice on techniques seen in sessions and other teacher activities
- Managers making comments during annual performance and development reviews

- Lesson observation teams making judgements about your teaching and the impact it has on learning
- Internal verifiers validating decisions made during an assessment.

Good feedback will always start with sentences aimed at highlighting strengths seen. Constructive feedback continues with observations and suggestions regarding development areas. Effective feedback ends with the notion of an agreed plan for development. Contribute to the feedback by questioning or challenging statements to ensure you fully understand.

How the development ideas are expressed will vary according to the formality of the feedback activity. You may hear:

Consider this . . .

I wish I could . . .

Can I use . . .

Have you ever tried . . .?

Did you know . . .?

You need to . . .

If I were you . . .

Your receptiveness to feedback from peers will depend upon:

- Who those peers are
- Whether the feedback is positive or negative
- Whether or not you respect the peer
- If it is what you want to hear
- If there are further anticipated effects following the feedback.

The important thing here is to listen to the feedback, decide what you want or can do and reflect on how any identified improvements can be achieved or how the best practice can be shared.

Recommended reading

Appendix D, pp. 651–656 Teaching observations describes the process of being observed and what you can expect during and after the observation. It also describes the outcomes and judgements made following an observation.

Planning and recording CPPD

Planning your CPPD

Planning CPPD, like many other educational processes is becoming more business-like than in previous years. It used to be that if you 'fancied' going on a training event then generally it was allowed; rarely was it systematically planned and matched to a business strategy although most events were broadly relevant in educational terms. There is now a recognised process and hierarchy in planning CPPD:

Identified purpose of development
(teaching and learning)

↓

Specific strategic values and goals
(expressed in mission statements)

↓

Organisational targets
(set by government/funding bodies)

↓

Team targets
(identified through internal quality processes)

↓

Appraisal or performance review processes

↓

individual targets

Whilst identifying targets for an individual, the manager and teacher may agree on the development required in order to achieve those objectives, for example:

- To improve teaching and learning
- To improve success, retention and achievement of learners
- To meet curriculum change (new qualification types etc.)
- To address changes in policy, procedure or processes.

These would be written more specifically than stated here, but the list is offered as generic suggestions.

Recommended reading

For more advice on writing specific goals, see Planning, negotiating and recording learning goals in Chapter 6, pp. 143–146.

The next part of the process is the actual cycle of training. This follows a circular model of identifying training, designing or accessing training, implementing ideas and assessing and evaluating the impact. This will probably lead in turn to further identification of development needs.

There are a number of strategies that constitute CPPD, although the list is not exhaustive:

- Self or peer assessment opportunities
- In-service training events
- External events, conferences and seminars
- FE or HE courses
- Functional skill development
- Initial teacher training
- Updates on teaching and learning initiatives
- Committee membership
- Working party policy development groups
- Visits to other organisations
- Visits by other organisations
- Involvement with professional bodies
- Writing journal or magazine articles
- Professional reading or research
- Team or co-operative teaching
- Mentoring or supporting colleagues
- Evaluation resulting from lesson observations

- Participating in secondment or placement opportunities
- Curriculum analysis and review
- Curriculum planning and development
- Working with agencies – e.g. job clubs, careers service etc.
- Progression or succession development
- Working with stakeholders – e.g. parents, governors, awarding bodies
- Contributing to internal or external quality or audit teams.

When planning CPPD it must be realistic, otherwise it will not be achieved. You may need to prioritise ideas into lists:

Things I must do	Things I should do	Things I could do

These priorities will need to recognise the constraints listed earlier:

- The urgency demands imposed by self, peer or manager
- How significant the development is
- Time available to undertake the activity
- How enjoyable the activity is (learning preferences).

Just a word of caution here, analyse objectively, trying to avoid a 'cherry-picking' strategy which will ultimately result in inaccurate priorities being identified.

Recording your CPPD

Recording your CPPD is not just listing the types of activities you've undertaken. The value of CPPD is in how it has impacted on you, your learners, the rest of the teaching team or the organisation you work for. If it does not impact on any of the above, you should question the necessity in the first place. The economic and financial culture at the moment does not support CPPD activities that merely achieve comments such as:

> 'It was good to see that everyone was experiencing the same issue', or
> 'Lunch was good'.

There are two main records that you need to keep.

- The CPPD Plan
- The CPPD Record.

Both belong to the individual teacher and it is their responsibility to keep it up to date. However, the line manager should agree the Plan (if they haven't contributed to its preparation) and sign off the Record as being an accurate account of developments achieved in the stated period. The documents below are suggestions, you should use either RE*f*LECT™ or your organisation's paper or electronic recording systems.

CONTINUING PERSONAL AND PROFESSIONAL
DEVELOPMENT PLAN

COVERING THE PERIOD FROM: 2008–2009

Extract from entries:

Planned CPPD activity and date identified	Aims and desired outcomes of activity	Suggested methods to achieve the planned outcomes	Target date for completion	Actions
Performance Development Review: September 2008 Diversity Awareness	To identify key legislation and implications. To raise awareness of impact in lessons. To modify handouts to ensure all are inclusive	On-line diversity package on the Intranet	November 2008	Enrol for programme? how ? – check with Personnel? check date of next inset day
Lesson Observation Any identified actions	To improve the quality of teaching and learning	Mentor support	July 2009	Check with manager before embarking on activities requiring funding

TARGET CPPD HOURS: 30	IFL Membership No: AA123456 Organisation: A N Other Training

Name: Joe Bloggs

I agree to support the Continuing Personal and Professional Development plans identified above.

Manager's signature: Ima Boss   Date:

It is likely that a plan will include specific tasks to be achieved and some generic statements to ensure that you can respond to ongoing issues. The plan should not be entirely management driven. It should include personal aims. It is hoped that both the manager and the member of teaching staff will happily negotiate proposals which meet personal, team and organisational targets, which will allow for aspirational development and career progression, within any budgetary constraints.

CONTINUING PERSONAL AND PROFESSIONAL DEVELOPMENT RECORD				
COVERING THE PERIOD FROM: 2008–2009				
Extract from entries:				
Date of event/hrs	Nature of event	Why?	What did I learn from this?	How the organisation, teams and myself have benefited
27/10/08 7 hours cpd	Diversity Awareness Training Internal on-line programme of study	Identified in my PDR. This is becoming high profile and all staff are required to attend	What diversity means, what constitutes discrimination and how it impacts on teachers	I have been more conscious when creating handouts and workbooks to check for discriminating practices. I will now challenge unacceptable behaviours more confidently; my planning seeks to include a wider variety of experiences. In team meetings we discuss how to create more diversity into the curriculum

08/02/09	Managing workshops	My lesson observation suggested that this could be developed	Using the Internet I found a lot of information about workshops, mostly to do with setting clear learning goals	I ensure that at the start of each workshop I give 2-3 mins to each learner to check/identify what they wish or need to achieve in the session, I can then check that as I tour the workshop and/or study centre. At the end of the class I have something to measure their achievement against and set further goals for the next session or for their home study. X Ref workshop planner.doc
Three hrs	Research activity			

TOTAL No CPD HOURS	IFL Membership No: AA123456
10 hours	Organisation: A N Other Training

Name: *Joe Bloggs*

This document is agreed to be a true record of Continuing Personal and Professional Development undertaken.

Manager's signature: Date:

You should always record your CPPD, if only to act as a reminder of your development. It is not always easy to remember to do this systematically, but you should decide whether you are a paper person or an electronic person and stick to that system of recording. Each year you will be required to review your plan against achievements with your line manager.

Glossary of terms

Aspiring one's hopes and ambitions

Enthusiastic a grade one indicator meaning creating enjoyment and interest

Excellence a grade one indicator meaning to be exceptionally good at teaching

Imaginative a grade one indicator meaning creative or resourceful

Inspirational a grade one indicator meaning one who encourages learners

Learner Involvement customer service initiative about listening to learner's opinions

LP abbreviation for lesson or session plan

Passion a grade one indicator meaning a strong desire to teach

PDR abbreviation for performance development review; appraisal

Q&A abbreviation for question and answer

REfLECT™ Trade mark software recording system from IfL

Research an investigation

SOW abbreviation for scheme of work

Stimulating a grade one indicator meaning to excite or motivate

Strategy a systematic process

SWOT an analysis tool to identify strengths, weaknesses, opportunities and threats; used to assess current practice

SUMMARY

In this chapter we set out to achieve the following outcomes:

- Identify and select your own approach to CPPD
- Use reflection and feedback to plan your development and learning needs

- Describe the impact of the 2007 CPD regulations on teachers in the sector
- Identify appropriate CPPD activities
- Record the outcomes of CPPD activities and the impact they have on individuals, teams and organisations

Your Personal Development

In the first part of this chapter, following some quick links to earlier learning, you looked at some of the ways that you might engage in CPPD. Each approach was briefly described to give ideas about the different contexts in which they may be used.

In the next section, there was a review of the legislation that has formally introduced the notion of CPPD into every teacher's agenda.

The discussion around identifying development needs listed several ideas that may need to be addressed, together with some hints to ensuring CPPD is effective. This part also looked at receiving feedback as an initiator of development and how that feedback may be collected. The section on self-assessment used two activities to carry out this analysis. The first activity was a modified SWOT analysis in which you compared your current strengths and known development needs against the skills required to carry out your job. These ideas were progressed to consider how post lesson evaluation impacts on development. There is a detailed breakdown of how and what to write in an evaluation, with ideas, reflective questions, links to current initiatives and key prompts. The second activity is designed to raise teaching levels towards excellence. The activity, modified from a College Net training session, provides statements of merit and requires the individuals to assess their own performance at this high level and identify gaps. Using words such as inspirational and imaginative it raises the levels of performance. The section continues with information about feedback from learners and peers to improve performance, making suggestions about collecting and using feedback.

▶

In the latter part of the chapter, we focus on planning and recording CPPD. There is a review of the planning process which links hierarchy and dissemination of organisational needs to the training cycle. There follows a list of potential CPPD activities and a method of prioritising identified CPPD. The chapter concludes with a suggestion for a paper-based planning and recording system for your CPPD activities.

Part Six
Curriculum development for inclusive practice (CDIP)

This is the sixth unit in your Diploma in Teaching in the Lifelong Learning Sector (DTLLS) qualification

Learning Outcomes	Assessment Criteria
Understand the range of contexts in which education and training are offered in the lifelong learning sector	● Analyse ways in which the curriculum offer might differ according to the educational/training context ● Analyse ways in which delivery of curriculum might vary according to purpose and context, with reference to examples from own practice
Understand theories, principles and models of curriculum design and implementation and their impact on teaching and learning	● Analyse theories, models and approaches to curriculum design and their potential influence on outcomes for individual learners and groups ● Analyse the appropriateness of a particular curriculum in relation to individual learners or a cohort of learners
Understand the significance of equality and diversity for curriculum design, and take opportunities to promote equality within practice	● Analyse and explain ways in which equality of opportunity and respect for diversity can be built into curriculum design ● Analyse and explain the impact of social, economic and cultural differences on teaching, learning and achievement in own specialist area ● Explain ways to challenge discriminatory behaviours where they occur in the learning environment
Understand and demonstrate how to apply theories, principles and models to curriculum development and practice	● Apply theories, principles and models of inclusive curriculum to the design and implementation of programmes of study ● Justify proposals to improve the curriculum offer and evaluate their effectiveness where these have been implemented
Understand how to evaluate and improve own practice in inclusive curriculum design and development	● Analyse how theories, principles and models of inclusive curriculum design and development are used to inform own practice and the provision in own specialist area ● Evaluate own approaches, strengths and development needs, in relation to inclusive curriculum design and development ● Plan and take up opportunities to develop and improve own learning and practice in curriculum design and development

CHAPTER 24 (CDIP)

Curriculum in practice

LEARNING OBJECTIVES

The measurable outcomes that you will achieve by reading this chapter and completing the activities are:

- To describe the evolution of curriculum in the UK
- To identify strategies of delivering a curriculum model
- To analyse the effectiveness of curriculum
- To evaluate and improve curriculum and practice

The history of curriculum change

As you can imagine in this era of continuous change, the curriculum has also had its own developments, some as a result of legislation, others as a result of reports by respected individuals. Listed below are some of the highlights.

	Curriculum initiative
1870	First Education Act (Forster) set compulsory education for 5–13 year olds, which became free in 1891
1880	Attendance Officers enforce schooling for 5 to 10 year olds
1899	Leaving age raised to 12 years old
1902	Education Act (Balfour) established Local Education Authorities
1918	School leaving age was raised to 14 years old
1944	The Education Act (Butler), formalised primary, secondary and FE agendas. School leaving age was raised to 15 years old – implemented 1947
1951	GCEs introduced
1959	Crowther Report recommended FE for 15–18 year olds
1965	CSE introduced in Secondary Modern Schools, replacing School Leaving Certificate and a parallel qualification to the Grammar School GCE
1972	Leaving age raised to 16 years old
1973	Manpower Services Commission (MSC) set up
1978	Youth Opportunities Programmes (YOPs) introduced Warnock Report on Special Educational Needs
1980	White Paper 'A new training initiative: a programme for action' paved the way for YTS and TVEI initiatives

1983	Technical and Vocational Educational Initiative (TVEI)
	Youth Training Scheme – one year scheme (YTS) replaced YOPs
1985	FE Act – allowed colleges to self-fund some of its provision
	Green Paper 'Education and Training for Young People' expanded YTS to a two-year programme
	Certificate in Pre-Vocational Education (CPVE) introduced
1987	National Vocational Qualifications (NVQs) introduced, overseen by National Council for Vocational Qualifications (NCVQ)
1988	Education Reform Act (Baker), replaced GCEs and CSEs with GCSEs and introduced the National Curriculum to schools
	MSC became known as Training Commission
1989	Youth Training (YT) replaced YTS
1990	'Core skills' became collective name for literacy and numeracy
1991	White Paper 'Education and Training for the 21st century', saw FE colleges removed from Local Education Authority control resulting in 'Incorporation' in 1993
1992	FE and Training Bill – the FEFC was formed to fund all school/university academic education (about £11 billion), resulting in control being taken away from LEAs
	General National Vocational Qualifications (GNVQ) introduced as an academic equivalent to NVQs
	Ofsted established to inspect schools
1993	Adult Learning Inspectorate (ALI) formed to inspect publicly funded work-based learning for over 16s
1995	Modern Apprenticeships introduced
1996	J. Tomlinson Report – inquiry on behalf of the FEFC into FE provision for students with disabilities and/or learning difficulties – identified a need for a more inclusive curriculum
	Ron Dearing's Review of Qualifications (16–19 year olds) commissioned by School Curriculum and Assessment Authority (SCAA). It was largely ignored

▶

1997	Helena Kennedy reports on poor participation of minority groups in FE which resulted in Widening Participation themes
	NCVQ and SCAA amalgamated to become Qualifications and Curriculum Authority (QCA)
1999	Moser Report on literacy and numeracy resulted in targets for achievement of these basic skills
2000	Curriculum 2000 (Blunkett), saw the introduction of AS/A2 and AVCE qualifications in a bid to assimilate level 3 provision
	Learning and Skills Act
	Learning and Skills Council formed
2001	FE Teachers' Qualifications (England) Regulations rationalised teaching qualifications and introduced mandatory acquisition of a qualification
	New Deal introduced – qualifications for the long-term unemployed
	Offenders' Learning and Skills Unit (OLSU) formed
2002	Green Paper, '14–19, Extending Opportunities: Raising Standards' (DfES)
2003	Green Paper, 'Every Child Matters' resulted in the 2004 Children Act
2004	M. Tomlinson Report suggested reforms in 14–19 year curriculum, which was also largely ignored although did result in the 2005 White Paper, 'Education and Skills'
	OLSU's responsibility extended to policy and funding
2005	Merger of Ofsted and ALI announced
2006	White Paper, 'FE: Raising skills, improving life chances'
	Leitch Report, *Prosperity for all in the Global Economy: World Class Skills Personalising FE: Developing a vision for the future* (DfES)
	2020 Vision: Report of the Teaching and Learning in 2020 Review group

2007	World Class Skills: implementing the Leitch review of skills in England
	Announcement of School leaving age to be raised to 18
	ITT Reforms – IfL registrations – CPD requirement – QTLS/ATLS
	DfES split to become Dept. for Innovation, Universities and Skills and Dept. for Children, Schools and Families
2008	Education and Skills Bill
	New Diplomas introduced
	Joint letter from John Denham and Ed Balls outlining key challenges for the time
2013	School leaving age to be raised to 17 years old
2015	School leaving age to be raised to 18 years old

Based on Gillard (2007), Neary (2002)

Change in curriculum is necessary to respond to weaknesses in the current curricula. Policy change is usually as a result of political, economic, sociological, or technological changes. **Effective** curriculum must be responsive to the needs of learners and employers and by reflecting upon the needs of society, it provides teachers with the agenda for change and improvement. The policy changes in curriculum filter down to the 'chalk-face' as adaptations and amendments to the subjects taught, and so the teacher is required to change or modify what or how they teach.

The number of changes in curriculum direction recently has caused much frustration in the teaching and learning sector. It seems that initiatives alter strategy constantly; this means that teachers and trainers are always having to keep up with the changes in their working practices or updating skills and knowledge through their continuing personal and professional development. The professional teacher or trainer now has to accept the inevitable modifications and be pro-active in implementing changes. It is a natural **evolution**.

Why change?

- To develop to meet needs
- To correct previous errors
- To pre-empt future needs
- To reflect opinion
- For change's sake?

The curriculum choices in the Lifelong Learning Sector are now largely influenced by funding and that funding is now **demand led**. The funding bodies research the local labour market information to identify what the economy needs to fulfil employment and social need. They will only fund that which is essential, employers must fund their training needs and individuals must pay for their own development. Coffield (2008: 44) raises an argument in which he questions 'who is making the demand', and suggests that not

Figure 24A   Classifications of Curricula

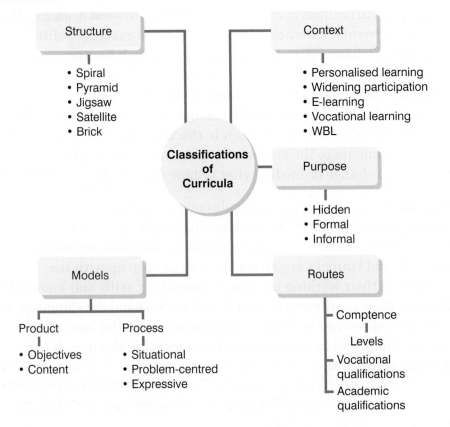

everything 'demanded' can be afforded. In essence, we are working at a time of rapid change; that change is our challenge. The 'curriculum choice' or options available are depicted in Figure 24A which consolidates all of the structures, models and routes in the contexts of the Lifelong Learning Sector.

Investigating the curriculum

PEST is a way of thinking about the external and internal factors that affect something. It is used extensively in the business sector, but it can also be applied to almost any aspect of teaching.

P	Political
E	Economic
S	Social
T	Technological

You may also see the analysis tool explained as 'STEP', it means exactly the same. PEST/STEP = political, economic, social, technological. Some more recent models have added additional letters:

PESTLE = adds legal and environmental.

Additional reading on PEST

....

http://www.businessballs.com/pestanalysisfreetemplate.htm
http://tutor2u.net/business/strategy/PEST_analysis.htm
http://marketingteacher.com/Lessons/lesson_PEST.htm

 ACTIVITY 1
....

PEST Analysis

Consider the current curriculum that you deliver. In recent years how has it changed, what is impacting on it at the moment and what does the future hold? Identify what is influencing those changes from the ideas given.

| **Figure 24B** | A curriculum PEST Analysis |

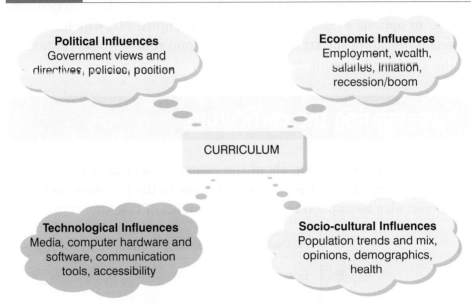

Implementing a curriculum

Having established the curriculum model that you are going to use, you then need to make it happen. Implementing the curriculum means making sure that all aspects of the teaching and learning match up with the chosen model.

Using a **mind map** to consider the relationship between curriculum and teaching and learning, you quickly realise that they are intrinsically linked, each affects the other. The curriculum model you choose will impact on the way the topic is taught and assessed. The availability of resources, physical and human, and the needs of the learners will impact on how the topic needs to be modelled.

If curriculum is defined as the planning and delivery of knowledge and experience in a transparent, effective manner (Chapter 2), then the teacher has a responsibility to create that effectiveness and **transparency** in the way they deliver the subject.

Figure 24C

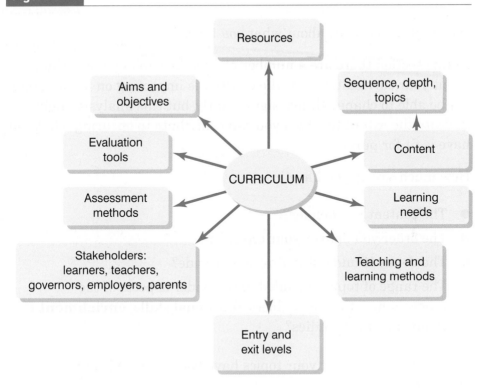

Resources

Aims and objectives

Sequence, depth, topics

Evaluation tools

Content

CURRICULUM

Assessment methods

Learning needs

Stakeholders: learners, teachers, governors, employers, parents

Teaching and learning methods

Entry and exit levels

Key Word – TRANSPARENCY

The curriculum must be clear: learners, teachers, employers and other stakeholders must be able to understand the purpose. The purpose will have an educational justification as well as meeting and responding to political, economic, social and technological requirements.

Key Word – EFFECTIVE

The curriculum must be easily understood and be able to be applied by teachers and learners in a measurable way. If it does not meet its purpose (defined above) then it is not effective. Educational institutions will also add value for money into this category.

Analysing the curriculum

Who makes decisions about what *you* teach?

In this section there are a number of questions to make you think about your curriculum and who or what is impacting on it. You might not be able to change things significantly, but this analysis might indicate the extent to which you can contribute to ensuring what you have is fit for purpose.

How much say do you have in:

- The content you deliver?
- The order you deliver your topics in?
- The depth of understanding you provide?
- The range of topics included in the wider aspects of the programme – the core subject, functional skills, **enrichment** or complementary studies?

How do you know that your topics have been 'received' and 'understood'?

Does your curriculum follow a product or process model?

Are there plans to modify the curriculum?

How does your curriculum address equality, diversity and inclusion?

What additional factors emerge from your curriculum, e.g. study skills, personal development, improvement in timekeeping, preparing learners for HE or work?

Evaluating curriculum

It is both good practice and a management requirement that the curriculum is evaluated. Rarely, however, do the likes of you and I get the opportunity to evaluate curriculum per se; we are more likely to evaluate our interpretation and implementation of the curriculum within our own organisation. It is important to review the provision against quality and performance standards. Generally these judgements are specified as:

Strengths

Areas for development

The term 'weakness' is used less often; it is more common to favour the expression 'development'. This in itself is an appropriate development in analysing the curriculum. The next change will be work on the difference between perceived 'strengths' and those aspects which are better described as 'positives'. The person undertaking the evaluation or judgement has to be mindful of the fact that quality initiatives are raising the norm; the strategies once considered as strengths are now, in certain circumstances, considered at best, satisfactory.

Satisfactory is no longer OK

Many of the strategies used to analyse strengths and areas for development are derived from the need to do two things:

- Reflect and improve individuals and organisations
- Comply with quality standards set by funding and inspection bodies.

Both of these outcomes are discussed in other chapters (reflection in CPPD and quality within WPP). At this point it is sufficient to comment that the teaching profession must always strive to improve towards excellence; to make the best learning experiences possible within the constraints of the organisation, and then some!

The tools or documents used to record the evaluations and judgements of performance are more commonly known as:

- Course review – a method of evaluating each course, qualification or programme of study. It will review previous achievement, methods of delivery and assessment, strengths and areas for development.

- Self-assessment report (**SAR**) – an official summary document to record the performance within a broader curriculum area and report its strengths and areas of development against key questions set by Ofsted.

Common Inspection Framework
Key Questions

- How well do learners achieve?
- How effective are teaching, training and learning?
- How well do programmes and activities meet the needs and interests of learners?
- How well are learners guided and supported?
- How effective are leadership and management in raising achievement and supporting all learners?

Ofsted (2008)

When evaluating the curriculum we are trying to establish the answers to those key questions; whether or not the key principles of teaching have been achieved and whether the political and organisational targets have been met. These two indicators very often cause a conflict; which is more important? Coffield (2008: 1) considers the imbalance between these two aspects and advocates a return to putting learners first. He suggests that the tide needs to turn:

'We are familiar with current practice: ritual genuflection is made to the central importance of learning, but the sermon swiftly becomes a litany of what the government considers to be the really key elements of transformation – priorities, targets, inspection grades and funding – and the topics of teaching and learning disappear from sight . . .'

He suggests that maybe we are losing focus on our priorities; is the way to improve the quality within the sector to concentrate on the teaching and learning, or is quality driven upwards by business processes and measuring performance against grades and targets? This may be, according to some, tongue-in-cheek research, but it is nevertheless thought provoking.

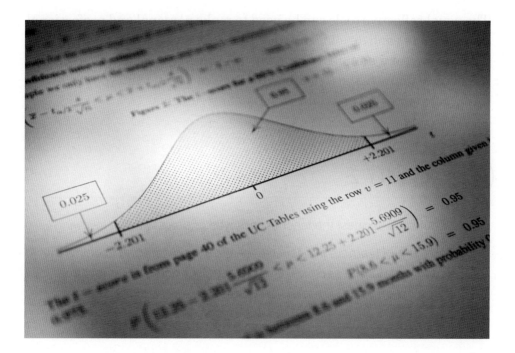

Conversely, the funding bodies believe that they also are considering learners by demanding that organisations who accept monies to fund provision ensure its quality and achievement effectively and efficiently, and the only way they can check this is by numbers – how many succeeded in achieving their target qualification? The only sanction they then have is to refuse to fund organisations that don't perform to their standards. Unfortunately, that means data, stats and more stats (and checks to make sure that the data and stats are correct!). This is why you are always being asked to report figures for attendance, achievement, quality audits and the like.

In order to balance these two opposing opinions it is important that we analyse the provision both by numbers (quantitatively) and by learner voice (qualitatively) and make decisions about improvement based both on opinion and performance. Therefore any document used to analyse the curriculum must include both facets. Whichever method of evaluation you use, the most important part of the process is 'closing the loop'. Having identified what is good and not so good about the provision, it is essential to devise a plan to build on the strengths and provide opportunities to develop where necessary.

The usual reflective tools can be used to make personal and professional improvements and develop practice. In the following activity you are asked to look at a number of familiar scenarios and decide what you might do to improve the situations. You will carry out this type of activity as part of your own personal development strategies.

 ACTIVITY 2

How would you suggest the teacher improves or deals with the following?

1. Retention of learners in a level 2 vocational qualification is below the benchmark for the sector. There are usually good enrolments but after a few months learners start to miss lessons and then some don't turn up at all. When the teacher rang one learner she said that she had got a job, so that was alright wasn't it?

2. Learners seem quite stressed around the end of the first semester. Each module, which is delivered by a different teacher, has an assessment which means several assignments are handed in together. When learners ask about this they are told that 'We [the teachers] have to check that all of the outcomes are met in each of the assignments, so they [the learners] should keep up to date with work to prevent it all needing to be done at the same time'.

3. The learners in a secure environment are told that they must do basic skills lessons. They are tested as they enter the establishment, some being transferred from other places. They do not see the point of the lessons. On occasions they refuse to work and can become aggressive. They rarely display these poor levels of motivation in their vocational subjects.

4. The exercise class in the village hall has been going for years. It is successful and learners return year after year. Newcomers join the class and follow the routines by watching the teacher or the more

experienced members of the group. The learners are always complimentary of the teacher, proven by their continued attendance. They are quite annoyed at the thought of the fees going up next term and have written to complain.

When answering the case studies above, try to analyse the curriculum module being used and the teaching and learning methods being used. Can the teaching team change their working methods to improve these situations?

Scenario 1

Teachers should consider how they manage attendance in classes and how they monitor progress; they may consider target setting to raise aspirations. In some situations learners may be able to be transferred into work based learning programmes so that they can continue to study whilst working.

Scenario 2

The teaching team should consider a more holistic approach to the setting of assignments, either by linking common criteria or by pacing the hand-in dates. The teaching staff might also consider how to support time-management skills by including workshops or catch-up activities into their schemes of work.

Scenario 3

Teaching teams should embed as many functional skills into the vocational curriculum as possible and make top-up activities interesting, contextualised and relevant. Where learners are being transferred into the establishment, a fuller history should be passed to the new teams.

Scenario 4

It seems here that the sessions are becoming more of a club so the teacher needs to turn it back to a learning environment. By tracking progress of skills learned and demonstrated in the routines and expressing these to learners it will revise their focus. A teacher should also stand back and watch the experienced learners, maybe setting advanced skills to challenge them or allowing them to peer mentor newer members. Unfortunately the funding changes mean higher fees, this should be sensitively explained to learners.

Curriculum is about what we teach, influenced by a number of factors and managed and controlled by a number of others, ourselves included. It is very often difficult to understand how a teacher can influence curriculum; they cannot at national level – even in this democratic society. They can, however, contribute to consultations at organisational level, and manipulate the implementation – i.e. at the classroom or training level. It is at this level that the teacher has the ultimate level of control and influence. Of course we must work within the constraints but flair, inspiration and passion are what the learners see, not the bureaucracy, and nor should they!

Glossary of terms

Demand led prioritised funding

Effective to produce the intended or desired result or outcome

Enrichment activities added to the curriculum or course to make a better learning experience

Evolution a gradual development

Mind map a visual representation of ideas

PEST an analysis tool to identify political, economic, social and technological influences

SAR Self-assessment report

Transparency overt, clear in meaning

 SUMMARY

In this chapter we set out to achieve the following outcomes:

● Describe the evolution of curriculum in the UK

● Identify strategies of delivering a curriculum model

● Analyse the effectiveness of curriculum

● Evaluate and improve curriculum and practice

Your Personal Development

In the first part of this chapter, we reviewed a brief history of education and curriculum. It is possible to see how the sector has evolved and responded to various reports and pieces of legislation that have been published. We also considered why the changes are necessary to ensure that 'UK plc' has the education system it needs and is proud of.

Using PEST as a tool to investigate change, we have looked at the external influences on education and the Lifelong Learning Sector. The first activity caused you to think about your own curriculum and attempt to map its own history and potential development.

Having established the macro-environment we looked closer to home to consider how pedagogy influences and is influenced by curriculum. We concluded that irrespective of the chosen curriculum, we need to be transparent and effective in our duties.

Whilst analysing the curriculum we sought to find out how much influence the teacher has in promoting the curriculum to learners, parents and employers. We also reviewed the parallel – how much the curriculum influences teaching.

Finally, we considered how curriculum is evaluated. In this instance we restricted the evaluation to that which we can control – namely, at organisational level looking at the quality systems locally available and deciding upon their effectiveness. We briefly reviewed Ofsted's key questions in respect of how they are used to evaluate curriculum.

In activity 2, in order to consolidate all aspects of the curriculum chapters you examined some typical problems. You were asked to identify the curriculum model used and how it could be developed to overcome the problems the teacher was having. This brought together everything you have learned so far about models and pedagogy and created a deeper learning by asking you to apply that knowledge in a different context.

CHAPTER 25
(CDIP)

Contexts of inclusive curriculum

LEARNING OBJECTIVES

The measurable outcomes that you will achieve by reading this chapter and completing the activities are:

- To define the meaning of curriculum in the Lifelong Learning Sector
- To describe the context of curriculum in current educational strategy
- To analyse the structure of the curriculum in the Lifelong Learning Sector
- To identify how equality, diversity and inclusion are met in curriculum design

The curriculum vision

In 2005, in a White Paper, the Department for Education and Skills (DfES), gave their vision for **curriculum** change. They were reviewing the current curriculum, based on GCSE and A levels and advocating the introduction of 'The New Diploma'. They announced curriculum reform to increase the number of learning routes available through qualifications which are:

> **'tailored to the talents and aspirations of individuals, better preparing young people for further study and/or skilled employment'.**

DfES (2005)

This has set the current agenda for teaching, tutoring and training in the Lifelong Learning Sector, namely **employability**.

Curriculum in the Lifelong Learning Sector is largely determined by the Qualifications and Curriculum Authority (a government agency set up to coordinate qualifications) and awarding bodies (organisations that write and accredit qualifications).

In 2007, the Department for Education and Skills was split. The two government departments now responsible for the sector are:

- Department for Innovations, Universities and Skills (DIUS)
- Department for Children, Schools and Families (DCSF).

This means that there are now two departments influencing the Lifelong Learning Sector.

Defining curriculum

To many, a curriculum is a course, something bigger than a single module or qualification. In reality, curriculum is more than a course;

it is the way the course is delivered, the content, the learning environment, the external and internal influences; it is the 'learning experience' (Smith 2002).

This publication defines curriculum as: a programme or model of study. The struggle to define the term is made all the more difficult due to different perceptions and beliefs. Albert Einstein wrote:

> **'I never teach my pupils; I only attempt to provide the conditions in which they can learn.'**

This adage reinforces the importance of the learners rather than the struggle to create an all encompassing definition.

In practice, when defining curriculum, you need to consider:

- The knowledge that teachers impart – the **syllabus**
- The process of teaching – the **pedagogy**
- The product of teaching – the assessment
- The style of delivery – the **praxis**.

Some definitions you may see include:

> 'All the learning which is planned and guided by the school, whether it is carried on in groups or individually, inside or outside the school.'
>
> John Kerr in Kelly (1983: 10)

> 'A programme of activities designed so that pupils will attain so far as possible certain educational and other schooling ends or objectives.'
>
> Grundy (1987: 11)

> 'On the one hand curriculum is seen as an intention, plan or prescription . . . on the other, it is seen as the existing state of affairs in schools.'
>
> Stenhouse (1975)

'The formulation and implementation of an educational proposal'.

> Jenkins and Shipman in Neary (2002: 40)

'The curriculum is all too simply whatever course we happen to be teaching at the time!'

> Dunnill in Armitage (2003: 192)

'A curriculum usually contains a statement of aims and of specific objectives; it indicates some selection and organization of content; it either implies or manifests certain patterns of learning and teaching, whether because the objectives demand them or because the content organization requires them. Finally, it includes a programme of evaluation of the outcomes.'

> Taba in Curzon (2004: 185)

ACTIVITY 1

Classroom activity

This activity is to consolidate your prior understanding.

Define the word 'curriculum'.

Each individual should write their definition on a Post-It™ note.

Use a pyramid activity – individual thoughts, shared and agreed with a partner, shared and agreed with another pair, and so on until one definition has been agreed by the whole group.

Some of the definitions seen before have included:

● A plan to specify the intended learning

● A group of modules to create a qualification

● What the teachers do with their students

● The government's instruction about what to teach

● The choices offered to create learning programmes

- A list of objectives to create an 'education'
- A philosophy of ideal learning.

How do your definitions compare?

Have you created the ultimate definition?

The curriculum context

Curriculum in its widest **context** isn't just about preparing or designing courses for your groups on a scheme of work. Of course you will consider the content, but you have to do that considering how your department or organisation works, and within policy or strategic constraints. There are several interpretations of curriculum; these are influenced by the context and are clearly linked to things in the political and funding agendas.

Firstly, the basics, let's look at the main contexts that you may be involved in.

Work-based learning (WBL)

In this curriculum the needs of employers are the major priority. The curriculum addresses the requirements of employers and aims to raise a learner's ability to gain employment.

Key words are: employability skills, employer engagement, apprenticeships, work experience.

Vocational learning

This is a curriculum type that addresses a number of stakeholders. It meets the learners' needs to have employment skills, the academic need to provide qualifications and the employers' needs to fill its vacancies with qualified staff.

Key words are: NVQ, Diploma, Foundation Degree.

Personal development

In this curriculum the needs of the individual are paramount. The curriculum is designed to address personal need, aspirational need, progression and transfer of skills and knowledge.

Key words are: personalised learning, enrichment, tutorials.

Widening participation

In this style of curriculum the needs of groups are considered. There will be socio-economic benefits. Including all people in the local community is the first priority. In some cases education is taken to the community so that venues are non-traditional locations, rather than the more traditional attendance at a local college of further education. Curriculum may be designed to suit a specific group of learners or specific issues relating to a group of learners.

Key words are: inclusion, adult and community learning.

E-learning

The curriculum is designed to be shared on-line to support self-study. This might complement other provision or be the sole strategy for learning.

Key words are: blended learning, virtual learning environment (VLE).

Figure 25A The contexts of curriculum

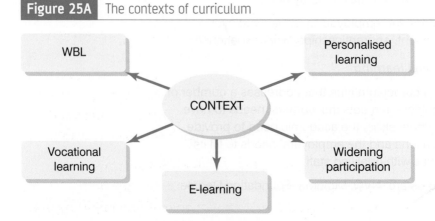

The structure of curriculum

There are many different ways of structuring a curriculum. According to Butcher (2006) and Neary (2002), there are five shapes:

Figure 25B The structures of curriculum

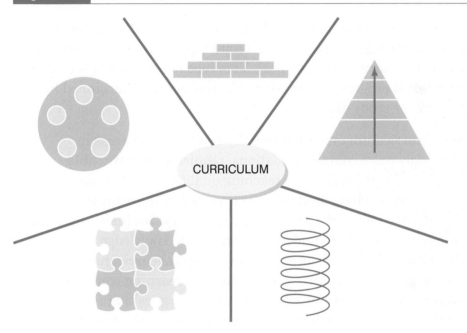

A brick design is where the subjects build upon each other and collectively create the final goal. It is a **linear** design of curriculum. A linear curriculum is based on the assumption that learning goes forward without being influenced on the way; one piece of learning leads to the next, etc. This model of curriculum could be described as 'a production line', in which learners enter education, follow their course and exit with quite a narrow development. In the current era of inclusivity, e-learning, skills for employment, this type of model seems inappropriate, because it does not consider that people are different, people come into education from a range of backgrounds and experiences; people want different things from their learning.

A satellite or subject based curriculum is where subjects are independent and not related to each other; however they do collectively make a very broad topic. An example of this might be in a programme called Art and Craft, which might include modules on still-life, printing, soft furnishings and calligraphy.

A jigsaw or co-ordinated curriculum is where each section is a topic in its own right and when collected together makes an overall goal. This might be seen in any **modular** course or maybe in an NVQ in which the units make the qualification, but can be accredited as stand alone qualifications. It is popular in vocational training.

A pyramid or integrated curriculum is where several different themes with a common goal link to make a final topic. They may increase in complexity before reaching a goal. This type of curriculum is common in vocational programmes in which the basics are underpinned by functional or study skills.

A spiral curriculum model continually re-visits topic areas in increasingly more complex situations, requiring **transferable** skills. An example might be a teaching qualification. The main concepts, say teaching methods, are revisited in the context of meeting learners' needs, developing **autonomy**, **inclusive** learning; and in each you have to understand and apply knowledge in a different way. Jerome Bruner advocated a spiral curriculum in which the topic themes constantly run through the learning which gets broader as knowledge and skills develop. He argues that this makes the transfer of learning into other contexts easier. His theory is based on a Piaget style of development in which 'practice makes perfect'.

Credit accumulation and transfer scheme

Commonly known as **CATS**, this is a way of creating values on qualifications. According to criteria implemented by awarding bodies, every module or subsection of learning is given a point score, based on its level, size, and learning outcomes. Qualifications, therefore, get a value which helps learners understand how they fit into single qualifications and how they compare with other maybe similar sounding qualifications, although caution is needed because the CATS system is not national and does have variants. The 'transfer' part of it allows a certain number of points gained in one qualification to be used towards another.

ITT qualifications and CATS points			
Qualification	**Module title**	**CATS**	**Level**
PTLLS	Award in Preparing to Teach in the Lifelong Learning Sector – PTLLS	6	3 or 4
Certificate in Teaching in the Lifelong Learning Sector (CTLLS)	Award in Preparing to Teach in the Lifelong Learning Sector – PTLLS	6	3 or 4
	Planning and Enabling Learning – PEL	9	3 or 4
24 credits	Principles and Practice of Assessment – PPA	3	3 or 4
	Option Unit	6	3 or 4
Diploma in Teaching in the Lifelong Learning Sector (DTLLS)	Award in Preparing to Teach in the Lifelong Learning Sector – PTLLS	6	4
	Planning and Enabling Learning – PEL	9	4
	Enabling Learning and Assessment – ELA	15	4
	Theories and Principles for Planning and Enabling Learning – TPPEL	15	4
	Option Unit	15	4
	Continuing Personal and Professional Development – CPPD	15	5
	Curriculum Development for Inclusive Practice – CDIP	15	5
120 credits	Wider Professional Practice – WPP	15	5
	Option Unit	15	5

In the Initial Teacher Training (ITT) framework, each module is given a value by LLUK. Qualifications are then written which must comply with the credit values and approved by LLUK. City and Guilds offer the qualifications above; other awarding bodies must follow the titles of the units provided by LLUK, but can re-name modules. Hence you may find 'Diploma' courses still called the Certificate in Education (Cert Ed).

In modular curriculum models, the units or modules with their values are clustered to make qualifications. Each module has its own learning outcomes and can be accredited individually or in the qualification cluster. Again, using ITT qualifications as an example, you see PTLLS and PEL are common to both the Certificate and the Diploma and form the basis of both qualifications. Similarly, in vocational programmes, units such as Health and Safety are common across broad curriculum areas.

Equality, diversity and inclusion in the curriculum

Firstly, inclusive practice is a requirement of discrimination laws. Amongst others, the Race Relations (Amendment) Act of 2002 requires every school (which can be extended to the Lifelong Learning Sector) to have a policy about diversity and challenging racism. Disability Discrimination laws also gave rise to statements about how an organisation addresses inclusion. It is not an optional way of teaching and designing learning. As a teacher you should think of it as an entitlement of learners rather than something that needs to be done when an instance occurs. It must be pro-active and not reactive and turn reactions into positive promotion of diversity. It is concerned with approaches to teaching and methods of assessing learning. In the curriculum it is a way of improving diversity by reflecting and mirroring the social picture. Diversity and curriculum synergy leads to enhanced learning and the raising of awareness.

By establishing and rectifying anomalies in equality a greater level of inclusion will be achieved. This might be by recognising under-representation or under-achievement in specific groups and creating strategies to address the imbalance.

An inclusive curriculum is one in which
all staff and students feel valued,
irrespective of age, gender, race and
disability, sexual orientation, religious
or personal beliefs, background or
personal circumstances. It is also one
to which all staff and students need
to be committed.

Talbot (2004)

Two documents, by the University and College Union (formerly NATFHE) make some useful suggestions to advise teachers, with some helpful and thought provoking case studies.

It suggests that 'the curriculum may provide space to promote Equal Opportunities' and offers ideas:

- Audit curriculum for instances of inequality and examples of celebrating diversity.
- Ensure language used is inclusive, non-discriminatory, being careful to make a good balance between political correctness and inclusion.
- Inclusive practices don't occur overnight; it takes time to make a systematic change, but don't devolve responsibility waiting for someone else to implement the change.
- Don't make assumptions about needs based on stereotype – always ask. For example: assuming the blind student needs their work in Braille, assuming the dyslexia student wants handouts on coloured paper. Anticipate but don't predict.
- Consider tasks carefully – when you set the homework to research this, download that – Can everyone access it? – It may be more than access to the equipment; there may be implications for the visually impaired.

- When using dictionaries, don't limit them to English dictionaries, provide translation from English into foreign language types.
- Allow time in your planning to modify materials.
- Reduce anxiety by providing detailed information about the course.
- Remember that not everyone will disclose their needs.

To ensure an inclusive curriculum, consider the following:

- Language
- Tone and voice
- Image
- Dress
- Ethics
- Connections
- Examples and role models
- Global perspectives
- Knowledge
- Teaching methods and resources
- Assessment and feedback
- Counselling and support
- Access.

Recommended reading

The University and College Union website at http://www.ucu.org.uk

Ensuring that the curriculum and all aspects of your teaching are inclusive is important; the learning environment that is created must be suitable and accessible to all.

SENDA

SENDA stands for the Special Education Needs and Disability Act (2001) and links strongly with the Disability Discrimination Act (1995) to such an extent that SENDA has become Part 4 of the DDA. This means that educational establishments must not treat a disabled person less favourably than anyone else. This applies not only to accommodation but equally to the services it provides. (See http://www.techdis.ac.uk/index.php?p=3_12_21.)

A useful website which notes cultural events, celebrations, holidays and even lunar phases is http://www.earthcalendar.net and can provide interesting facts to add to lessons.

Glossary of terms

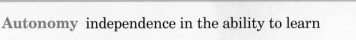

Autonomy independence in the ability to learn

CATS Credit Accumulation and Transfer Scheme

Context the setting in which learning occurs

Curriculum a programme or model of study

E-learning learning using electronic systems or equipment

Employability in a position or suitable to be employed

Inclusion finding opportunities to integrate all learners

Inclusive not excluding any individual or group of learners (adj.)

Linear in curriculum – single dimensional

Model a description or example to represent an idea

Modular a curriculum or programme made up from several modules or units

Pedagogy the skill or ability of teaching

Praxis practical skills as opposed to theoretical skills

Syllabus the structure of a qualification

Transferable something learned in one context used and applied to another

 ## SUMMARY

In this chapter we set out to achieve the following outcomes:

- Define the meaning of curriculum in the Lifelong Learning Sector
- Describe the context of curriculum in current educational strategy
- Analyse the structure of the curriculum in the Lifelong Learning Sector
- Identify how equality, diversity and inclusion are met in curriculum design

Your Personal Development

In the first part of this chapter, we reviewed the recent drivers moving curriculum strategy forward. This considered the national picture and the impact this has at regional and organisational level.

In defining the term 'curriculum' we sought to find an over-arching statement. This is made difficult due to interpretation, but in a classroom exercise, you engaged in an activity to consider and justify your interpretations.

The context of the Lifelong Learning Sector was explained in terms of learner types in order to further identify the link between national, regional and personal opinions. With a further classification, the curriculum was explained in terms of structure, which offers ideas on how the curriculum fits together.

Following on from the ideas around curriculum structure, we consider how the different components are given values (CATS) and interact to make the learning experiences seen in the sector.

Finally, the subjects of equality, diversity and inclusion are discussed and how curriculum must meet the demands of everyone: learners, employers, teachers, awarding bodies and other stakeholders. This section focused on the issues within the power of the teacher, namely: the impact of creating an inclusive curriculum.

CHAPTER 26 (CDIP)

Theories, principles and models of curriculum

LEARNING OBJECTIVES

The measurable outcomes that you will achieve by reading this chapter and completing the activities are:

- To state the main models and theories associated with curriculum design
- To establish the link between theories and principles of curriculum
- To describe the levels of competence
- To identify key factors in planning and designing curriculum

Models and theories of curriculum

Curriculum models are approaches or procedures for implementing a curriculum. Different **theorists** have opinions on the most effective way, which is dependent on the *context* of the learning. It is through curriculum models that concepts and theories move into practice, i.e. into teaching.

This section will focus on the main models of curriculum and note the main protagonists of each of them. Whilst many try to label curriculum in a particular style, it is more common that the teaching undertaken in the Lifelong Learning Sector will not wholly be in any one style. Several variants are noted; commonly, **curricula** are described as '**product**' or '**process**'. In its simplest of definitions, curriculum as a product depends on the setting of objectives which are the learning goals and the means by which learning is measured. A process model focuses on the relationship between learner and teacher and therefore looks at the delivery of learning, the methods by which the delivery is completed and the distance a learner travels; these are indicators of success.

Models of Curriculum		
PRODUCT MODELS **A prescriptive type**		
Objectives Model		*Content Model*
Tyler (1949) Bloom (1956) Davies (1976)		Hirst (1974)
PROCESS MODELS **Stenhouse (1975)**		
Situational Model	*Problem-Centred Model*	*Expressive Model*
Grundy (1987) Skilbeck (1976) Lawton (1983)	Boud (1991) Bruner (1966)	Eisner (1985)

The curriculum model chosen will determine the choices made in terms of teaching and assessment strategies; they will be influenced and in some cases predetermined by awarding bodies, organisational constraints, funding bodies and political initiatives.

Objectives model

Summary:

- Behaviourist in style
- Defines learning outcomes
- Establishes learning
- Organises learning
- Measures learning
- Prescriptive model.

In this model, the curriculum driver is what the learner needs to know. Outcomes are specified in terms of what the learner will be able to do at the end of a given period of learning. It is focused on the dissemination of facts, techniques and information to address those outcomes and may become a little **authoritative** in style. Assessment will always be against the specified outcomes, with teaching adapted to ensure that outcomes are met. Much vocational training is of this style and so the teacher will need to show how these learning chunks build to create the learners' goals; this will prevent any concerns a few learners may have about the purpose of the learning. The main criticism of the model is that it may have a tendency to provide shallow learning over a wide range of topics. Although many expect this organised style of delivery, some may feel as though they do not control their learning. In the worst (and very rare) reactions learners may become de-motivated and show a lack of commitment. The advantages of this style come from the way that it can be standardised, both internally and externally, so that teachers are confident, clearly guided and able to network with colleagues about issues as well as share resources and ideas. The model can be easily adapted to fully address the needs of learners by differentiating outcomes for different learners:

By the end of the session, *all* learners will be able to . . .

By the end of the session, *most* learners will be able to . . .

By the end of the session, *some* learners will be able to . . .

This strategy is useful:

- when linked to pass, merit and distinction levels of achievement
- when teaching different ability levels in sessions
- when delivering roll-on, roll-off modular sessions
- when working with learners with special educational needs
- when managing workshop sessions
- when coping with inconsistent attendance patterns.

Davies (1976) identifies verbs used in defining outcomes. He suggests that there are two types of verb used; those that are open to interpretation – for example: to know, to understand, to appreciate or to believe; and those that are clear in their meaning: to write, to identify, to solve, to construct, to list etc. (See also PTLLS, Chapter 3 and PEL, Chapter 7). His suggestion is widely advocated amongst teachers and inspectors who agree that the verbs in the first list are not easily measured and are very broad, thus making the second list preferable.

Bloom's Taxonomy of Learning, discussed in Part 4, Theories and Principles of Planning and Enabling Learning, Chapter 18, pp. 361–362, is used widely in an objectives model in order to define outcomes of learning.

Ralph Tyler is one of the main theorists of product or objectives based curriculum. In designing curriculum, he suggests (1949: 1) that teachers should question:

- The purpose of education
- The experiences likely to provide those purposes or outcomes

- The organisation required
- The measurement of the attainment of the purpose.

This is a very systematic approach; to be effective the curriculum must be measurable otherwise you will not know if the goals are reached. Those goals may be:

FORMAL – what a learner needs to know

INFORMAL – what is nice to know

HIDDEN – what you didn't mean a learner to know.

One of the criticisms of a product curriculum is that it leans towards behaviourist and cognitivist learning values, yet a rounder, wider curriculum would meet a more humanistic view. Current funding methods also encourage a product centred model. The product model can, therefore, be insular. In its favour, is the fact that an objective based curriculum is more reliable in that stakeholders are aware of the scope of the curriculum as it is easier to create a national standard, whereas process models can be more subjective.

Content model

Summary:

- Transmits existing knowledge
- Focus on intellectual development
- Defined by a syllabus
- Does not consider how.

The outcomes in this model are unspecified; it is an open rationale where learning follows ideas and concepts. It develops intellect based on scientific, philosophical, moral or artistic values. Assessment is around opinions and the use of theories rather than the recall of facts; the assessor marks around the exploration of the idea rather than a right or wrong statement. The teaching is aimed at initiating, searching and discovering ideas and cognitive values.

Process model

Summary:

- Content defined In cognitive terms
- Focus on learning how to learn
- Descriptive model.

As its name suggests this over-arching model of curriculum is concerned with content, i.e. the key components which make up the knowledge required of a specific topic.

A process model is concerned with all aspects of the topic – the content and its wider effects. It has its roots firmly grounded within humanist values. Curriculum planned in this way considers the individual learner and how they like to learn and how they need to apply their learning. Stenhouse (1975: 95) recognises that this model does not encourage a standardised approach to the delivery of learning or the outcomes of teaching and learning.

Situational model

Summary:

- Emphasis in context, culture, society
- Hidden curriculum
- Considers the learner's experience.

This model defines curriculum by the influences which impact upon it. This makes this a responsive model. In a situational model of curriculum, writers consider external and internal factors in order to create a curriculum that is 'fit for purpose'. Every stage of the design is analysed and must be appropriate to the purpose – from both the teachers' and learners' points of view.

Problem-centred model

Summary:

- Application of knowledge
- Discovery learning
- Reflective
- Active learning.

This curriculum model develops around the notion that learners need to be able to apply their knowledge to solve problems and create opportunities in order to move forward in their learning. Bruner's spiral model (1966) is one theory associated with problem-centred curriculum saying that new ideas are a result of previous learning. In problem-centred activities, the facts and theories explored are generally restricted to those that have an impact on the issue at hand; the problem helps to consolidate and apply the learning. The problem may be devised by the teacher in which case the learning outcomes can be pre-empted or they can be devised by the learner in which case the learning is more ad hoc. At any one time learners can be working on different areas of the topic or field of learning. The teaching is a discovery model and follows the development of reflection (Kolb, Schön) in order to bring about the learning. This type of curriculum develops higher or deeper levels of learning. Assessment tends to be a mixture of checking understanding of key facts and underpinning them by concurring with opinions and reflections.

One downside to this style is that curriculum may not be fully covered and 'additional' problems will have to be set in order to complete the learning; this is more of a problem when combining an outcome-based assessment curriculum, with a delivery model following a problem-solving learning curriculum.

Weyers (2006) made some suggestions for active learning strategies to enhance learner engagement when following these more open activities:

1   Organise information

2   Highlight important information

3   Make information meaningful

4   Check and refine learners' understanding of topic

5   Promote transfer of information and 'generalisability'.

Quite simply, this means that the learning must not be so random that it is difficult to assimilate into the context of the learning, and it should always be checked to ensure that learners understand what they are finding out and are able to put it into their own words or situations.

Expressive model

Summary:

● Personal goals

● Experiential learning.

This curriculum is concerned with personalised and/or experiential types of learning. Learners explore issues of their own desire or interest; they are intrinsically motivated. This model suits those who are well prepared or experienced in learning. Skills for learning how to learn will have already been acquired, or will be being delivered alongside, probably through an instructional or objective based method of curriculum. Teaching this type of curriculum will be facilitative. Assessment is more about the journey than the specific learning outcomes. Art curricula frequently exploit the expressive abilities of its learners to develop their attitudes to the subject.

Primary and secondary curriculum

In some contexts one curriculum model is used wholly when delivering learning. This is the primary route – which in my experience tends to be outcome related, if only because success can easily be measured and standardised and so becomes the main way of writing qualifications. However, as teachers we are individuals, we are encouraged to meet learners' needs as individuals and we like doing things our own way and sometimes that means amending our curriculum, through modifying our teaching methods. The amendments should not compromise the way we (need to) deliver our topic, thus we may use more than one curriculum model – hence secondary curriculum.

 **ACTIVITY 1**

Consider a recent reflective activity – something related to your teaching that you have thought about recently. Examples might be:

● Why a particular resource worked well.

● Why a lesson for one group worked well, but when repeated with a different group was unsuccessful

● Why *are* Monday mornings so difficult?

● Why the chat to X worked to improve commitment.

Now think about the basic teaching skills (planning, methods, assessment, resources) you have learned so far and establish a link between those basics and how you have modified the skills to make them work for you.

Idea/recent reflection:

_____

Skills/knowledge applied:

_____   _____

_____   _____

_____   _____

_____   _____

How did you modify your practice to overcome a problem?

_____

_____

_____

_____

This activity works to stimulate ideas about the links between objective and problem-centred models of curriculum. It can also serve as a reflective activity to develop own practice.

You have just completed an activity in which you have related information learned from an outcome based curriculum model – planning techniques, teaching and learning methods, assessment strategies, managing your classroom; and used those basic skills in a different context to solve a problem. This is an example of how the ideals of two models can be integrated successfully, or how the curriculum content spirals to develop deeper understanding. It is quite normal to see a different approach to learning being used to create deeper learning required in higher level programmes. A word of warning though, changing models half way through a programme can be confusing, and you will probably still be constrained by parameters of the primary curriculum.

ACTIVITY 2

Consider your own curriculum:

Is it purely one curriculum style or a bit of a mixture? Identify the primary and (if applicable) the secondary curricula you apply in your teaching.

Primary:

Secondary:

Your interpretation of these curricula will show in your scheme of work and lesson plans.

Annotate your scheme of work to show curriculum styles.

The hidden curriculum

The hidden curriculum is defined as:

> ## That which a learner learns that is not planned as part of their main syllabus.

A teacher should always consider the positive aspects of a hidden curriculum. Some of the things which may be described as hidden are very beneficial. The wider social and personal development aspects of learning can be covered easily under this heading. For example: encouraging learners to turn up on time will help them keep a job when they complete their study, yet is a common example of one of the things a teacher does to develop learners which does not get recorded on the scheme of work.

Is the hidden curriculum a valid method of developing autonomy and responsibility?

Very often the 'hidden curriculum' is not hidden to the teacher; it is a valuable component of the academic or vocational specifications. It may be that some developments are hidden to make them more palatable to reluctant learners. The whole notion of the 'readiness agenda' means that many of the skills required to develop to the next stage and often taught are not included in the scheme of work. They should be included to give them their true acknowledgement within the learning experience.

ACTIVITY 3

List aspects of your curriculum which occur but are not planned.

Describe the positive and negative effects of each aspect.

Positive aspects	Negative aspects

The Readiness Agenda

Learners are always ready for the next stage of their development

Classroom	Learning	Higher Education
Role	Work	Job
Success	Return	Independence

(Lewisham College 2002, www.lewisham.ac.uk)

Curriculum routes

The competence model

Competence models are derived from an outcomes model of curriculum. The competences are a set of performance standards that a learner is able to know, understand or demonstrate by the time they complete their learning. NVQs and many vocational qualifications are written as competence models. NVQs focus on job specific training.

Figure 26A Competence model

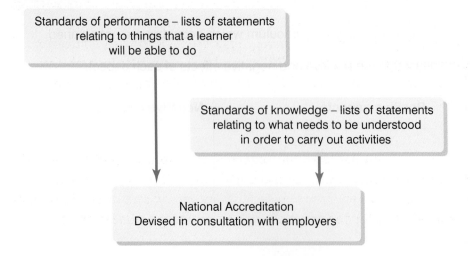

Standards of performance – lists of statements relating to things that a learner will be able to do

Standards of knowledge – lists of statements relating to what needs to be understood in order to carry out activities

National Accreditation
Devised in consultation with employers

Levels of competence

The levels below are used to determine the stage someone is at in terms of their ability, or the level a qualification is awarded at, or to provide an aspirational goal for learning.

Level one Competence which involves the application of knowledge in the performance of a range of varied work activities, most of which are routine and predictable.

Level two Competence which involves the application of knowledge in a significant range of work activities, performed in a variety of contexts. Some of these activities are complex or non-routine and there is some individual responsibility or autonomy. Collaboration with others, perhaps through membership of work group or team, is often a requirement.

Level three Competence which involves the application of knowledge in a broad range of varied work activities performed in a wide variety of contexts, most of which are complex and non-routine. There is considerable responsibility and autonomy and control or guidance of others is often required.

Level four Competence that involves the application of knowledge in a broad range of complex, technical or professional work activities performed in a variety of contexts and with a substantial degree of personal responsibility and autonomy. Responsibility for the work of others and the allocation of resources is often present.

Level five Competence that involves the application of a range of fundamental principles, across a wide and often unpredictable variety of contexts. Very substantial autonomy and often significant responsibility for the work of others and for the allocation of substantial resources feature strongly as do personal accountabilities for analysis, diagnosis, design, planning, execution and evaluation.

QCA (2004)

The vocational model

Sometimes called Vocationally Relevant Qualifications (VRQs), they do not have the same status as NVQs, although they are still designed to be relevant to the subject. First Diplomas, National Certificates and Diplomas and Foundation Degrees fall into this category. This means that they can be delivered in a learning environment, whereas the NVQs are a training tool. Very often there is a link to the world of work through work experience, visiting speakers or work activities.

The academic model

These are routes based on theoretical knowledge of the subject, although many will contextualise the learning. Commonly, some subjects within the National Curriculum (GCSE/A levels) and Higher Education provision fall into this category. Recent curriculum initiatives have sought to offer alternatives to academic study, especially within the 14-year-old choices.

The links between principles and curriculum design

Now let's put all this together in a way that demonstrates the connections between the theory and what is done in the classroom.

Principle

I structure my teaching to meet my learners' needs.

Practice

- Ensure that there is a balance between curriculum and learning reflected in teaching methods and assessment strategies used.
- Avoid 'teaching' – focus on 'learning'. This is where the sessions always consider what the learner needs to get out of the session, i.e. seeing learning from the learners' perspective. Brilliant teaching does not always equate to effective learning.
- Explain to learners what is going to happen. This might be through course handbooks, stating aims and outcomes, or negotiating individual targets.
- Integrate easy and hard facts evenly and mindfully through group work, discussion groups, role plays to create opportunities for everyone to develop ideas and concepts.

Theory

- Objectives model (if outcomes defined).
- Process or expressive models (if negotiated outcomes).
- Jigsaw or pyramid structure of curriculum.

Principle

I always move from the known to the unknown when delivering topics.

Practice

When delivering the curriculum, use a variety of strategies to identify what learners already know. This may be on many different levels:

- Checking qualifications required pre-entry – for example, a National Diploma applicant needs between three and five GCSEs to enter the programme.

▶

- Tests to determine suitability – for example, competence checks to ascertain levels or diagnostic tests to check literacy levels, etc.

- Discussions to find out about background – for example, advice, guidance or interviews prior to enrolment sessions or before a learner progresses to the next level.

- Recap activities at beginning of sessions – for example, to refresh the mind of last week's lesson, or, check understanding before moving on within the topic.

- Task analysis or formative assessment during topic – for example, checking learner knows the basics before extending or developing a topic. Learning to drive is a good example of how a topic develops in complexity.

- Integrated tasks – for example, assignments that consolidate learning from a variety of subject areas taught.

Theory

- Objectives model.

- Problem-solving model – in latter part of programme.

- Brick or pyramid structure of curriculum.

Principle

I deliver my lessons in order to develop deeper learning.

Practice

This involves developing learning so that a fuller understanding is retained; a more holistic strategy. This is particularly important in order to be able to apply a basic skill in different contexts. This development of *'critical thinking'* is based on a learner's ability to apply or analyse information and use it in different ways. This will be commensurate with the levels of learning; you wouldn't expect the same analytical abilities in level one and level three learners, but it can still be present. This *'constructive alignment'* means the balance between your teaching and assessment strategies matching the levels of learning and curriculum outcomes.

One of the main things we do in the classroom to develop deeper learning is to teach basic skills or study skills to learners. With these basic *building blocks* they are able to 'hang' additional information and achieve in their studies. Another strategy commonly seen is the *'must know, should know and could know'* style of deciding on topics to be taught. In this style, the specified topics are taught as a priority and according to time constraints or how quick learners grasp the ideas, additional information is added which might be slightly outside of the syllabus. There is a danger associated with this strategy; and that is the tendency to teach to exams or assignments without even covering all of the required outcomes which is demonstrating neither deep nor shallow learning. Although there are not many teachers who in the last few weeks of a module are not concentrating on getting those last few pass criteria out of learners!

Theory

● Bloom's Taxonomy, Biggs.

● Problem-centred model.

● Spiral structure of curriculum.

Principle

I endeavour to deliver the curriculum in an efficient way.

Practice

Whilst not a primary consideration for the teacher, working within the constraints of the funding methodology will impact on the delivery. Those managing the curriculum will make demands of the teacher which seem to be of lesser importance than the teacher's primary role of imparting knowledge, but nevertheless the teacher must take into consideration:

● Statistics – current performance measured against required performance.

▶

◀

- Rules – number of learners required in the room, utilisation of staffing hours, number of guided learning hours (GLH) required to deliver topic.
- Environment – accommodation, equipment.
- Market – research, intelligence, competitors.
- Costs – funding source, learners' contributions, remitted fees, full cost provision.
- Staffing – skills, availability.

Theory

- Coffield (2008).
- Objectives model – related to funding.
- Jigsaw structure of curriculum.

Designing curriculum

Curriculum design is the planning and delivery of knowledge and experiences in a transparent, effective manner. The key words used here are:

- *Transparent* – the purpose both in educational and sociological terms must be clear to all.
- *Effective* – easily understood with the ability to be applied by teachers and learners in a measurable way.

Many teachers will not need to know how to plan and design their own curriculum, given that most of the work is already within established frameworks. However, if you are given the opportunity to influence the shape of a curriculum it is worth knowing where to start.

One strategy which encourages thought on the subject is to note external influences – the macro-environment. By jotting down ideas you will be able to be pro-active in creating ideas, solutions or answers to the issues that impact on how the curriculum is planned and designed.

Once the major external influences have led you to plan and design your curriculum framework – it will probably lead you to a particular model – then the next series of influences need to be addressed. These are more associated with internal influences.

Finally you will consider the advantages and disadvantages of the current and proposed models, trying to ensure that it complies with everything everyone is asking you to meet. A tough challenge!

With any type of curriculum model there are basic ideas which steer the process of learning:

> Learning is PLANNED – ideas introduced, links to previous and future teaching.
>
> Learning is DELIVERED – teaching techniques, management of the classroom and assessment for learning.
>
> Learning is EXPERIENCED – by the learners, recommended by learners and employers.

All three parts must be right for any curriculum to be effective. We will revisit the strategies governing effectiveness in the next chapter.

One idea for putting all of these ideas together in order to analyse them, is to do a **SWOT** analysis:

Strengths	Weaknesses
What is good about the current model?	Why is the current curriculum model not working?
Does it meet the needs of learners and employers?	Which areas of the teaching and learning are not providing what you want?
What are the good parts of the programme – staffing, resources?	Do you need a different skill-set to deliver the change?
What is the potential?	
Opportunities	*Threats*
Are new employers moving into the area?	What might prevent a successful implantation of a new model – staff, resources?
What policies and practices would benefit from the development?	Is it affordable?
Is it going to lead to more efficient processes?	Is it achievable?
Is there a market?	Are your competitors ahead of you?

Once you have done all of the research you will have an idea of the 'how', 'when', 'why', 'what' and 'where' possibilities. This will shape your curriculum.

Glossary of terms

Authoritative a self-confident or assertive method of teaching

Curricula plural of curriculum

Curriculum a programme or model of study

Process curriculum focuses on the delivery of learning

Product curriculum focuses on the outcome of learning

SWOT an analysis tool to identify strengths, weaknesses, opportunities and threats; used to assess current practice

Theorist someone who creates an idea or explanation of something

 SUMMARY

In this chapter we set out to achieve the following outcomes:

- State the main models and theories associated with curriculum design
- Establish the link between theories and principles of curriculum
- Describe the levels of competence
- Identify key factors in planning and designing curriculum

Your Personal Development

In the first part of this chapter, we have looked at the two main types of curriculum and the sub-divisions resulting from the work and ideas of a number of theorists. We also have considered issues around primary, secondary and hidden curricula. Finally, in the first part of this section, we have reviewed the various routes available to learners and the competence framework designated by QCA for current use in determining the level a qualification is awarded at.

Next we looked at linking the ideas learned. That is, the principles by which we set our standards, how practice is directed to achieve those standards and how the models of curriculum influence or position us. This section is linking the intrinsic values of the teacher to the extrinsic values impacting upon the teacher.

In the last part, we looked at the basics of planning and designing a curriculum and the principles, practice and theory that need to be considered.

Part Seven
Wider professional practice
(WPP)

This is the seventh unit in your Diploma in Teaching in the Lifelong Learning Sector (DTLLS) qualification

Learning Outcomes	Assessment Criteria
Understand the concept of professionalism and core professional values for teachers in the Lifelong Learning Sector	● Discuss key aspects of professionalism in the context of the Lifelong Learning Sector ● Explain ways in which equality of opportunity and respect for diversity can be built into teaching and learning practice ● Discuss the contribution of learning to personal development, economic growth and community regeneration ● Analyse the impact of own professional values and judgements on teaching and learning
Understand key issues in relation to professional conduct and accountability in the Lifelong Learning Sector	● Discuss the implications and impact of government policies on teaching and learning in the Lifelong Learning Sector ● Discuss the roles of regulatory bodies and systems and inspection regimes in the operation of the Lifelong Learning Sector ● Interpret ways to apply relevant statutory requirements and underpinning principles in relation to teaching own area of specialism ● Analyse own responsibilities in relation to the above
Understand and apply principles of evaluation, quality assurance and quality improvement	● Review and compare a range of principles and approaches to evaluation ● Explain differences and the relationship between evaluation and assessment ● Analyse the role of evaluation within quality assurance to inform and promote quality improvement
Understand and demonstrate how to contribute to QA and QI systems and procedures	● Work with others to develop and improve the effectiveness of evaluation processes ● Evaluate the validity and reliability of data collected and the effectiveness of the methods/instruments used, with reference to own learner(s)
Understand how to evaluate and improve own wider professional practice	● Evaluate own approaches, strengths and development needs, in relation to professional practice ● Plan and take up opportunities to develop and improve own wider professional practice

CHAPTER 27
(WPP)

Professionalism in teaching

LEARNING OBJECTIVES

The measurable outcomes that you will achieve by reading this chapter and completing the activities are:

- Describe the term professionalism
- Explain the professional values that underpin teaching
- Identify benefits of independent learning on personal development

Defining professionalism

> A set of collectively held norms that regulate teaching according to values and practices.

Craig and Fieschi (2007: 2)

Professionalism refers to a style of behaviour; it is something that is deemed appropriate to the job role. There is not a list of professional behaviours, but LLUK describe professional values (LLUK 2006), and organisations will create their own codes of conduct. There is also common sense. Teachers are in control of their own professionalism and it is the ability to self-regulate that will prevent difficult situations arising. It is, therefore, a good idea to link new teachers with more experienced staff to help them through these sometimes unwritten rules.

Professionalism is also determined by the systems in which we work. The ever changing way in which teaching is planned, delivered, assessed and monitored, calls for another level of professionalism. Either through desire or necessity, teachers cope well with the changes they face; in fact so well that the change itself has become the norm, and we constantly look for new curriculum ideas, new ways of creating income, developing provision to meet the requests from employers and learners. This is what we do; it is the professional within us that leads us to keep up to date and in tune with what's going on around us.

The move from a **vocational** occupation into the teaching profession is usually under-estimated. The Lifelong Learning Sector relies significantly on the skills and experience of its workforce and their ability or desire to want to make a difference by passing on those skills to a new group of learners. The expectations of those entering the profession is great; however highly qualified in their subject, new teachers are required to undertake teaching qualifications. The role of a teacher is broader than that of teaching. A teacher is also an administrator, tutor, assessor, quality assurer, and analyst. Teaching is a profession, not a job.

The professional approach to work does come at a cost: the commitment to teaching. Teachers have to balance their home and workplace activities. The teacher does a significant amount of planning, preparation, and marking at home. This makes for a more 'professional' approach to teaching, but it conflicts with family life. There do not seem to be enough hours in the day to do everything that needs to be done; hence the need to 'take work home'. Even our learners expect this commitment. Students seem quite shocked to see their teacher at the local supermarket and handing in a piece of work on one day and expecting it marked for the following day's class is not unusual (although frustrating when they have left it until the last minute anyway!). It is important to get the work/life balance correct whilst maintaining a professional approach. Alarmingly, according to the University and College Union (UCU 2007), teachers, on average, do 11 hours of unpaid overtime each week. Be careful and sensible with regard to this issue and be realistic in what you can and will do.

Davies (2006) in talking about professionalism in the sector says that teachers come into teaching from many backgrounds; some are **graduates**, some are experienced practitioners in their vocational subject. It is this diverse background of the teaching staff that helps to make the Lifelong Learning Sector what it is today. People come into teaching because they want to share their experiences and knowledge to others, they complement their backgrounds with a teaching qualification, register with a government agency (the Institute for Learning) and become known as professionals. This is then conferred as 'Qualified Teacher Learning and Skills' (QTLS); the Further Education equivalent to QTS (Qualified Teacher Status) in schools, and thus they embark on their career. In order to maintain QTLS a professional teacher has to keep up-to-date through engagement with a CPD process. A full-time lecturer is expected to participate in 30 hours of continuing professional practice each year. This amount is reduced for fractional or sessional staff to a minimum of six hours.

Professionalism also includes the ability to teach well. Therefore, many of the standards expected of teachers refer not only to a behaviour and a code of conduct but also to an ability. It is these abilities that are explained in the Professional Standards (LLUK 2006) and demonstrated whilst undertaking teacher training qualifications. When qualified our professionalism is also maintained through continuous development and monitored through processes such as observing teaching and learning activities.

IfL's Code of Professional Practice

This is a series of statements, badged under the title 'PROMOTE' that relate to teachers and will apply to all of those people registered with the Institute for Learning.

> Behaviour 1 – Professional Integrity
>
> Behaviour 2 – Respect
>
> Behaviour 3 – Reasonable Care
>
> Behaviour 4 – Professional Practice
>
> Behaviour 5 – Criminal Offence Disclosure
>
> Behaviour 6 – Responsibility during Institute Investigations
>
> Behaviour 7 – Responsibility

https://ifl.ac.uk/services/docs/1269/CodeofProfessionalPractice.pdf

Professional values, knowledge and practice

The Standards for Teachers, Tutors and Trainers (LLUK 2006) set out three types of professionalism. The *values* that underpin everything we do, the *knowledge* necessary to complete tasks well and the application of *teaching* skills. These are set out in their Standards – see Chapter 30.

The *values* cover topics such as:

- learner's progress and achievement
- equality and inclusion

- teacher's reflection and development
- communication and collaboration
- working within codes of conduct
- quality of teaching and learning
- motivating learners
- integrity of assessment.

These have also been described as our principles in earlier chapters. The values set out the standards we hope to achieve every time we meet our learners. By working in this way we are deemed to be professional and our managers can measure our performance to confirm competence and therefore confirm our professionalism.

As professionals we are also required to know and understand how to make the values listed above happen. By engaging with your Teacher Training programme and participating in training events within your organisation, your knowledge increases to cope with the changes in the sector. Similarly, there are standards of performance that are required in the classroom and staffrooms. What constitutes professionalism will vary according to the circumstances in which the teaching takes place; the standards of professionalism will always be high.

Baume (2006) identified five elements required in teaching:

- Context – in what setting the teaching is undertaken
- Goals – what the teaching is intended to achieve
- Knowledge – what the teacher should know about effective teaching
- Virtues – what values, principles or codes of practice inform the teaching
- Competences – what the teacher needs to be able to do in order to teach effectively.

Baume describes these elements in the context of European Higher Education; we are lucky in that the Lifelong Learning Sector Standards are clearly defined and agreed on a national level.

Some of the professional practice standards advocated by LLUK include:

- Encouraging progression and development (AP1.1, FP2.1)
- Promoting equality and inclusivity (AP3.1, BP2.1, DP1.1, FP3 2)
- Improving through feedback and evaluation (AP4.2, BP2.6)
- Sharing good practice (AP4.3)
- Communicate and collaborate (AP5.1, BP3.1, BP3.4, FP4.2)
- Conform to statutory and organisational codes (AP6.1, EP5.1)
- Establish safe and purposeful learning environments (BP1.1)
- Motivate and encourage learners (BP1.3, CP2.1)
- Promote and develop autonomy (BP2.3)
- Plan and prepare sessions (DP1.2, DP1.3)
- Use a variety of methods and resources in sessions (BP2.2, BP2.4, BP5.1, CP3.1)
- Assess learners (EP1.2, EP1.3, EP2.1, EP3.1)
- Keep up to date in specialism (CP1.1)
- Be literate, numerate and technologically up to date (CP3.4, CP3.5).

You can download a copy of the standards from www.lifelonglearninguk.org.

But what about the assumptions; the things that experience teach us: our common sense. Where do we find out about those? Silly things like not knowing the code to the staff toilet can seriously influence how we perform; our confidence may be reduced and it may appear as a poor level of professionalism. Our professionalism is affected by the professionalism of those around us. On your first day in a new organisation, you will be told many things, sometimes to a point of overload; people are trying to be helpful but it is sometimes difficult to take everything in. A piece of advice here: at the end of the first day, make sure you know the name and phone number for your line manager, a mentor (or similarly experienced colleague) and a member of the admin team. With these points of reference there will not be many pieces of information you won't be able to find out – if they don't know the answer to your question, they'll know who to ask!

How do you know what you don't know?

	Detail	Help through . . .
The basics	Toilets, rest areas, work rooms Timetable – diary commitments Breaks, tea kitty arrangements Security codes Log-on passwords Stationery requisition Emergency procedures Pay procedures Staff room etiquette – noise, space, ring tone on personal mobile, etc.	Induction Line manager Administrative staff Health and Safety Manager Personnel
The protocols	Use of IT equipment Use of reprographic equipment Policies and procedures Staff and student Charters Specialist rooms and equipment	Mentor Line Manager **Intranet** or **VLE** Advanced Practitioner
The inter-actions	Learner/teacher relationships Dress codes Behaviour code Use of phones/computers for personal use Classroom etiquette and rules	Experienced staff Mentor
Using information	Pro-formas for lesson plans, schemes of work etc. Forms to record learners' progress and achievement Use of computer based management information systems (**MIS**) Applying for funding for development	Intranet or VLE Mentor Experienced staff MIS administrative staff CPD Manager

Ways to improve professionalism

Whilst the organisation in which you work will provide opportunities for personal development, the only person empowered to develop your professionalism is yourself. There are a number of activities and tactics that will help:

- Strive to develop your experience from initial teacher training through to advanced practice
- Professionals in the classroom strive to be inspirational, are enthusiastic and teach with a passion
- Participate in CPD activities to keep up to date with initiatives
- Continually look for new or better ways of working
- Know what is expected of you
- Engage positively in feedback sessions from lesson observations and peer observations
- Set standards for learners to help you manage your time and workload
- Be realistic when asked to do things; better to do a few things well than loads of things badly
- Don't be afraid of saying 'no'
- Undertake a variety of activities to multi-skill and position yourself for future change
- Influence and promote change and development
- Set yourself challenges
- Read publications and journals for teachers
- Look at Teachers TV (http:www.teachers.tv/)
- Highlight useful websites in your 'favourites' box
- Encourage others to progress
- Celebrate when things are successful
- Promote good practice.

The impact of learning on personal development

It sounds obvious, but to initiate your development you will need to learn new skills and reinforce existing ones. Professional development is not something that is done to you, it is yours for the taking, and therefore you will need to take a pro-active stance. The key word in describing independent or autonomous learning is 'responsibility'. The individual knows what they want, how they want it and when they want it. Teachers improve their professionalism by developing their own autonomy and, equally, improve their learner's ability to develop by increasing theirs too. The more independence and autonomy you have, the more confident and professional you appear; the more autonomy your learners have, the easier your teaching role is, in that you become less of a teacher and more of a facilitator of learning.

The independent learner has a number of characteristics:

- They like to control the pace of their learning
- They are able to manage and control the direction of their learning
- They work happily without teacher support or require only minimum help
- They have the ability to self-assess objectively
- They have good time management skills

- They are intrinsically motivated
- They are self-directed
- They are aware of their own learning preferences
- They are fully aware of their own needs and how those needs will be met
- They are confident
- They like to learn through experience (Kolb, Schön).

Independence in learning will ensure that the teacher remains aware of, and responsive to, their surroundings and thus maintains their professionalism. However, you can also maintain your professionalism without being independent. Look at the activity below and find out how you like to develop.

 ## ACTIVITY 1

Are you an independent learner?

Rate yourself:

1	=	I strongly agree with the statement
2	=	I agree with the statement
3	=	I neither agree nor disagree with the statement
4	=	I disagree with the statement
5	=	I strongly disagree with the statement

Statement	1	2	3	4	5
I can set aside dedicated time to study					
I am able to organise my time well					
I prioritise my workload well					

I know what my goals are					
I know where to get information about a range of topics					
I am confident in reading and referencing material I find in books					
I can use search engines to find information					
I am a good communicator					
I have good levels of study skills					
I am focused when researching and reading					
I am objective when I analyse my strengths and areas for development					
I am highly motivated					
I enjoy learning					
I only require occasional support from tutors					
I am a reflective person					

If you have ticked statements mainly in columns 1 and 2, then you are someone who likes to learn independently. If you have mainly ticked statements in columns 4 and 5, I would suggest you are someone who benefits from attending courses to learn new skills. If you have ticked mainly in box 3 or ticked unevenly across the table, then you have the potential to become an independent learner; you are able to initiate your own learning yet like group learning and value your progress being monitored by a tutor.

Everyone controls their own learning to a certain extent, as we become more confident, experienced and self-aware the autonomy develops so that full independence occurs and the teacher develops and learns with minimal interventions from others.

Glossary of terms

Graduates people who have a degree

Intranet internal computer based communications network

MIS Management Information Systems, computer based data storage software

VLE Virtual Learning Environment

Vocational relating to learning the skills of an occupation

 SUMMARY

In this chapter we set out to achieve the following outcomes:

- Describe the term professionalism
- Explain the professional values that underpin teaching
- Identify benefits of independent learning on personal development

Your Personal Development

In the opening paragraphs of this chapter we looked at a definition of professionalism, especially in the context of the teacher. We explored aspects of the teaching role and explained various descriptors of professionalism. The section also considered the importance of Lifelong UK's professional standards for teachers, tutors and trainers in the sector and how they are used to indicate a professional approach to teaching.

The chapter progressed with a list of some of the things 'you need to know but, maybe, are too frightened to ask'. It also suggested who might be able to answer those questions for you. The text listed a number of ways that you could demonstrate professionalism.

Finally, it considered the importance of developing autonomy as a means of demonstrating a professional approach to work. Whilst in this context it looked at the independence and autonomy of the teacher, it also suggested that developing autonomy in your learners is advantageous. The last activity showed a self-assessment questionnaire, which was designed to discover how independent you are and what that means to your own learning preferences and development strategies.

CHAPTER 28 (WPP)

Quality management

LEARNING OBJECTIVES

The measurable outcomes that you will achieve by reading this chapter and completing the activities are:

- To define and state the difference between quality assurance and quality improvement
- To compare and contrast the main quality agencies and systems
- To list and describe ways of assuring and improving quality
- To evaluate the effectiveness of quality management in improving performance

Defining the terms

There are a number of expressions that you will come across when talking about quality. Although they have different meanings, you will sometimes come across them being interchanged; they all come under the generic term of Quality Management (QM). QM is initiated at organisational level and monitored in the sector by external agencies.

- **Quality Control** – checks the integrity of the process
- **Quality Assurance** – systematic checks to provide confidence
- **Quality Improvement** – a process to improve the reliability of quality systems.

> ## Quality means doing it right when no-one is looking.

Henry Ford

Much of the discussion in this section is concerned with the quality management relating to the sector in general and provides a basis for understanding why things happen and thus develops an empathy with the broader aspects of quality. The specific aspects of quality that most teachers will come across are those surrounding:

- Verification and moderation on behalf of awarding bodies to validate the certification of achievement
- Assessment and evaluation processes surrounding inspection by agencies such as Ofsted and IiP
- Analysis of performance at course level to collect information about learners' achievements
- Judgements about the learner's experience collected through lesson observation.

Before you embark further in this chapter, consider where you are now in terms of controlling quality within your teaching.

ACTIVITY 1

List five ways you know or can check on how good your teaching is.

1

2

3

4

5

Need a clue?

- Who checks your teaching?

- How do you know if your learners enjoy their sessions?

- What happens after you've marked work?

- How do you know how well you are doing?

Quality control

Quality control (QC) is checking the quality of the goods produced or services provided to ensure that bad workmanship is minimised and faulty goods or poor service provision is not passed onto the customer. In the Lifelong Learning Sector the customers are our learners, their employers, parents or carers; the 'goods' are the learning experience and the 'services' are the support and business functions.

The quality control systems that you will find in educational establishments include:

- Course review
- Self-assessment reports

- Observations of teaching and learning
- Learner satisfaction surveys
- Complaints cards
- Internal verification/moderation.

Verification and moderation are discussed in PTLLS, Chapter 5 and Enabling Learning and Assessment, Chapter 16.

Quality assurance

Quality assurance (QA) derives from a business model. QA is a process that manages quality control systems to reassure managers and other **stakeholders** that systems are in place to undertake those checks.

Quality assurance ensures that goods and services (i.e. the learning experience) are fit for purpose, value for money, performed to a high standard and meet legal requirements. QA also provides a mechanism to intercept and identify error which can then be corrected. Accurate and effective identification of strengths (and how to build upon them) and areas for development are crucial to the success of an organisation.

The quality assurance systems that you will find in educational establishments include:

- Teaching and learning strategies
- Internal review/inspections
- SAR validation boards
- **Learner voice** processes
- Standardised documentation
- Programme, course or tutoring files and **audits**.

External quality assurance strategies used to confirm and validate quality include:

- Ofsted inspection
- IiP/Matrix/ISO assessments

- Framework for Excellence assessment
- External verification.

Quality improvement

Quality improvement (QI) is a strategy to list improvements and record how and when they will be achieved. By then recording the successful completion of the action, the 'loop is closed' and the revisions become the new QC process. Quality improvement is less effective when top-down; it needs to originate from within the organisation, with contributions from everyone.

The quality improvement systems that you will find in educational establishments include:

- Quality Improvement Plans
- Quality Improvement Boards
- Annual Assessment Visit
- **Standardisation** of assessment committees.

Quality management

Quality management (QM) is the driver that plans, implements and monitors the use of systems and procedures to control and assure the quality of goods and services. In the Lifelong Learning Sector our 'goods' are teaching and learning activities; services are things like student services, personnel, finance, administration, MIS, etc. The notion of quality practices has been evolving for a number of years. Some names associated with quality are:

Joseph Juran (1904–2008) – acclaimed writer and consultant who investigated a problem and cause system and advocated training and accountability as a major contributory factor to ensuring quality.

Walter A. Shewhart (1891–1967) – who is associated with quality control methods for production systems in order to improve reliability. He initiated the Cycle of Learning and Improvement – Plan–Do–Study–Act.

W. Edwards Deming (1900–1993) – who was inspired by the work of Shewhart and is widely acknowledged for developing processes to control quality, especially in America during WW2 and Japan in the 1950s. He modified Shewhart's Cycle to read Plan–Do–Check–Act which still forms the basis of many quality processes.

Henry Ford (1863–1947) and Karl Friedrich Benz (1844–1929) – associated with developing quality processes in the automotive industries.

Total quality management (TQM)

The motto for **TQM** principles is an attitude of 'right first time'; it is a 'zero tolerance' to poor quality. Quality is at the heart of the TQM organisation with everyone doing their part to ensure everything hits the highest of standards.

Figure 28A	A TQM Model for Education

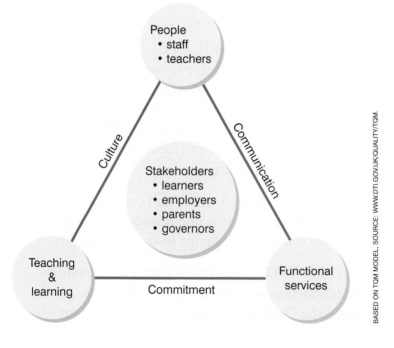

BASED ON TQM MODEL, SOURCE: WWW.DTI.GOV.UK/QUALITY/TQM.

In the diagram, the stakeholders (the learners, employers, parents and governors) are central to the organisation. Surrounding them are the various things they will experience – the people, the support or functional services and of course, the teaching and learning. To maintain quality, the systems and procedures need to be communicated and understood by all, there needs to be a commitment to quality and quality improvement, and ideally, the organisation should be known as one in which quality and improvement are embedded into the culture of the organisation.

 ACTIVITY 2

A Case Study

Joe is an experienced teacher on the ND in Health and Social Care and Society Health and Development Diploma. He also delivers Functional Skills, English and provides support and assessment to learners on the Level 2 NVQ in Care.

He works predominantly in the Care department; functional skills delivery are part of a wider support team, facilitating apprentices on a number of qualifications. Joe is quite confident with the ND programme; he has been teaching on the programme for a number of years. The Diploma is brand new. The functional skills aspect of the work is OK; the difficulties arise from lack of motivation from learners, but Joe is quite used to being creative to raise learners' interest. The work on the Care NVQ is also brand new for Joe, and he is finding the transition to these different styles of working challenging.

His manager for the Care department has asked him to comment about the ND course he works on. Although the learners Joe teaches do well on his unit, this is not the same for the qualification overall. His manager is trying to find out what might be the reasons for this.

Joe is being asked to comment upon achievement, teaching and learning, learners' enthusiasm and interest, support for learners and leadership of the programme. This is broadly in line with the Common Inspection Framework.

● How will the answers to these questions help Joe's manager to develop the National Diploma?

● What other quality initiatives might provide additional information?

● What recommendations might arise from the scenario?

Joe is also about to complete the first part of his course review for the new Diploma line. He feels this is difficult because he has little to compare with what he is doing. What support would you give to Joe?

Joe has just found out that the External Verifier is visiting the training company next month. As Joe is a new member of the team, the verifier is asking to speak to him. He is not looking forward to this, yet doesn't want to let the team down.

● What advice would you give to Joe to help him prepare for the visit?

● What information do you think he will need?

● How does this activity aid quality improvement?

This case study will have caused you to reflect on some of the things that Joe (and you) do in your normal daily routines to ensure that your learners have the best possible experience your organisation can provide.

In the next activity, you are asked to think a little more systematically and list some quality initiatives and their purposes.

ACTIVITY 3

In your normal teaching life, list the quality processes that you participate in.

List others that you know occur, but do not directly involve you.

Quality Activity	Main aim or purpose of the activity	Frequency

From your list, which quality activity has the biggest influence on you, and why?

_____

_____

_____

_____

Agencies directing quality management

Quality Assurance Agency (QAA)

Established in 1997, the organisation seeks to safeguard and help to improve the academic standards and quality of higher education in the United Kingdom. It is funded through subscriptions from Universities and project work undertaken for funding bodies.

(Source: www.qaa.ac.uk)

Lifelong Learning UK (LLUK)

An independent employer-led sector skills council responsible for the professional development of staff working in the sector. It supports the work of:

- community learning and development
- further education
- higher education
- libraries, archives and information services, and
- work based learning.

(Source: www.lluk.org)

Standards Verification UK (SVUK)

A subsidiary of LLUK for the verification of Initial Teacher Training and Workforce Development. It works closely with organisations who offer Initial Teacher Training qualifications in order to standardise and quality assure the delivery.

(Source: www.standardsverificationuk.org)

Institute for Learning (IfL)

Formed in 2002, the IfL is the professional body for teachers, trainers, tutors, student teachers and assessors in the Further Education and Skills sector. It covers:

- Adult and community learning
- Emergency and Public Services
- FE Colleges
- Ministry of Defence
- Armed Services
- The Voluntary Sector
- Work Based Learning.

The organisation seeks to raise the professional status of teaching professionals. The IfL was elected as the body to confer ATLS/QTLS when the revised regulations for teachers were published in September 2007, resulting from 'Equipping our Teachers for the Future' 2004.

Sector Skills Councils (SSC)

One of a number of organisations who represent occupational sectors. They represent employers, write occupational standards and offer professional services. They used to be called National Training Organisations (NTOs) and help underpin the standards for NVQs.

Learning and Skills Improvement Service (LSIS)

Formerly the Quality Improvement Agency (QIA), it strives to ensure that the sector is known for its excellence and offers itself as a critical friend to organisations in order for them to achieve and perform to their fullest potential. The QIA was initially formed as a governmental response to the White Paper – *Further Education: raising skills, improving life chances* (March 2006). During 2008 the QIA, together with the Centre for Excellence in Leadership (CEL), became known as the Learning and Skills Improvement Service.

(Sources. www.qia.org.uk and www.centreforexcellence.org.uk)

Ofsted

The Office for Standards in Education is the government department tasked with the role of inspecting quality and standards in education and training organisations. It publishes its findings on its website and thus it creates the opportunity for stakeholders to review quality of provision prior to deciding which educational establishment to attend. It uses a 'Common Inspection Framework' (CIF) to set the performance standards. The questions in the CIF are answered in the organisation's self-assessment report (SAR), which demonstrates how high quality is achieved, sustained and improvements are ensured.

(www.ofsted.gov.uk)

Equivalent organisations:

Wales – Estyn (www.estyn.gov.uk)

Scotland – HM Inspectorate of Education (www.hmie.gov.uk)

Northern Ireland – Department for Education (www.deni.gov.uk)

IQER – Integrated Quality and Enhancement Review – inspection tool for checking Higher Education provision in FE colleges

Audit companies

Building upon the best practices seen in the accountancy sector, auditors are a familiar contributor to quality management. They are used by organisations as consultants and by government agencies as inspectorates. Their role is to validate the accuracy of information.

The subsequent reports enable organisations to implement improvement and government agencies can use the outcomes to risk assess the integrity of their providers. Audits regulate the business processes and provide third party assurance of (usually) financial stability.

The 'big four' companies are:

Pricewaterhouse Coopers

Ernst and Young

KPMG

Deloitte

A rising leader providing audit services to the UK public sector is Tribal.

Awarding bodies

The quality assurance system used by awarding bodies is called either External Verification or External Moderation. Vocational qualifications such as NVQs tend to be verified, while academic and vocationally related qualifications (VRQs) tend to be moderated. The process is similar; it is a way of ensuring that organisations who deliver qualifications on behalf of an awarding body do so with rigour and integrity. The process starts with a planned visit (or desk-based activity) during which the nominated representative of the awarding body looks at work which has been delivered, assessed and internally quality assured within the centre. The 'centre' is the name given to the college or training provider offering the qualifications. If everything is satisfactory the awarding body will authorise the issue of certificates. It also has the ability to restrict activity in centres that do not perform to the required standard. A visit concludes with a report detailing good practice and areas for development. These can then be transferred to the organisations Quality Improvement Plan.

Systems to manage quality

Common inspection framework

An organisation is inspected and graded on its ability to self-regulate. It seeks answers to the following questions when deciding upon how good an organisation is:

1. How well do learners achieve?
2. How effective are teaching, training and learning?
3. How well do programmes and activities meet the needs and interests of learners?
4. How well are learners guided and supported?
5. How effective are leadership and management in raising achievement and supporting all learners?

Depending upon the answers to the questions and the evidence supplied to prove the responses, organisations are graded according to their performance and excellence. The grades applied are:

1. Outstanding
2. Good
3. Satisfactory
4. Inadequate

(Source: http://www.ofsted.gov.uk/publications/2434)

Self-assessment

As well as having a sound theoretical purpose (analysis, evaluation and reflection), self-assessment is also a requirement of funding bodies. Each year, the Learning and Skills Council requires organisations to present their self-assessment report. A self-assessment report makes two judgements: it measures the performance of the organisation and makes a judgement on the organisation's capability to improve. Ofsted check the accuracy of this self-regulation during the four-yearly visits. Usually the process starts with a course team co-ordinator preparing their annual course review, which is collated into programme area Self-Assessment Reports (SAR), broadly in line with Subject Sector Categories. These are then further collated into an overall SAR which provides the answers to the questions posed in the Common Inspection Framework.

SUBJECT SECTOR CATEGORIES	
1 Health, Public Services and Care	2 Science and Mathematics
1.1 Medicine and Dentistry	2.1 Science
1.2 Nursing and Subjects and Vocations Allied to Medicine	2.2 Mathematics and Statistics
1.3 Health and Social Care	
1.4 Public Services	
1.5 Child Development and Well Being	
3 Agriculture, Horticulture and Animal Care	4 Engineering and Manufacturing Technologies
3.1 Agriculture	4.1 Engineering
3.2 Horticulture and Forestry	4.2 Manufacturing Technologies
3.3 Animal Care and Veterinary Science	4.3 Transportation Operations and Maintenance
3.4 Environmental Conservation	
5 Construction, Planning and the Built Environment	6 Information and Communication Technology
5.1 Architecture	6.1 ICT Practitioners
5.2 Building and Construction	6.2 ICT for Users
5.3 Urban, Rural and Regional Planning	
7 Retail and Commercial Enterprise	8 Leisure, Travel and Tourism
7.1 Retailing and Wholesaling	8.1 Sport, Leisure and Recreation
7.2 Warehousing and Distribution	8.2 Travel and Tourism
7.3 Service Enterprises	
7.4 Hospitality and Catering	

▶

◄

9 Arts, Media and Publishing	10 History, Philosophy and Theology
9.1 Performing Arts	10.1 History
9.2 Crafts, Creative Arts and Design	10.2 Archaeology and Archaeological Sciences
9.3 Media and Communication	10.3 Philosophy
9.4 Publishing and Information Services	10.4 Theology and Religious Studies
11 Social Sciences	12 Languages, Literature and Culture
11.1 Geography	12.1 Languages, Literature and Culture of the British Isles
11.2 Sociology and Social Policy	
11.3 Politics	12.2 Other Languages, Literature and Culture
11.4 Economics	
11.5 Anthropology	12.3 Linguistics
13 Education and Training	14 Preparation for Life and Work
13.1 Teaching and Lecturing	14.1 Foundations for Learning and Life
13.2 Direct Learning Support	
	14.2 Preparation for Work
15 Business Administration and Law	
15.1 Accounting and Finance	
15.2 Administration	
15.3 Business Management	
15.4 Marketing and Sales	
15.5 Law and Legal Services	

(Source: www.lsc.gov.uk) accessed Aug. 2008

The LSC recommends a six stage process to quality improvement, which fits into the business cycle:

1. New SAR and QIP written
2. SAR and QIP submitted to LSC
3. HMI Annual Assessment Visit evaluates SAR
4. LSC Annual Planning Review
5. Inspection (current period between 2005–2009)
6. Annual Review and Inspection outcomes feed into the new SAR.

(Source: Quality Improvement and Self-Assessment. May 2005. LSC.)

Framework for Excellence

This is a recent quality assessment tool, devised by the Learning and Skills Council (LSC), which aims to improve performance by setting 'clear, unambiguous standards of excellence that all providers will want to achieve, so that they can demonstrate the quality of their provision'.

The Framework comprises three 'dimensions', each with two or three key performance areas (KPAs) and each having Performance Indicators (PIs). Wherever possible it uses information and results from other audit and inspection strategies.

Dimension 1	Dimension 2	Dimension 3
Responsiveness	*Effectiveness*	*Finance*
KPA 1a: Learners	**KPA 2a: Quality of Outcomes**	**KPA 3a: Use of Resources**
Performance indicators	Performance indicator	Performance indicators
Learner views	Success rates	Funding economy
Learners' destinations		Resource efficiency
		Use of capital
KPA 1b: Employers	**KPA 2b: Quality of Provision**	**KPA 3b: Financial Management and Control**
Performance indicators	Performance indicator	Performance indicators
Employer satisfaction survey	Ofsted inspection grade	Accountability
Amount of bespoke training		Financial planning
		Internal control
		Financial monitoring
		KPA 3c: Financial Health
		Performance indicators
		Solvency
		Sustainability
		Status

(Source: http://ffe.lsc.gov.uk/)

Programme self-assessment and action document (PSAAD)

This is higher education's equivalent to self-assessment reports for the Learning and Skills Sector. The document collates information regarding enrolments and achievements, feedback from external examiners and future actions required to improve. It provides an annual commentary on the performance of HE programmes. This document is also relevant to those who teach HE in the FE context.

Investors in People (IiP)

A set of standards designed to recognise and value the importance of people and their contributions to business improvement. It mirrors the teaching/training cycle in that the standards reflect the planning, implementation and evaluative stages development. The Standards seek to address the answers to the following questions and assessors gather evidence from both managers and employees.

Developing strategies to improve the performance of the organisation

1. A strategy for improving performance of the organisations is clearly defined and understood
2. Learning and development is planned to achieve the organisation's objectives
3. Strategies for managing people are designed to promote equality of opportunity in the development of the organisation's people
4. The capabilities managers need to lead, manage and develop people effectively are clearly defined and understood.

Taking action to improve the performance of the organisation

5. Managers are effective in leading, managing and developing people
6. People's contribution to the organisation is recognised and valued
7. People are encouraged to take ownership and responsibility by being involved in decision-making
8. People learn and develop effectively.

Evaluating the impact on the performance of the organisation

9. Investment in people improves the performance of the organisation
10. Improvements are continually made to the way people are managed and developed.

(Source: http://www.investorsinpeople.co.uk)

International Organisation for Standardisation (ISO)

ISO is recognised throughout the world, and due to language differences have adopted ISO as their acronym. Based on the training cycle, it enables organisations to work more efficiently and effectively by checking that the systems and procedures are implemented consistently throughout the organisation. There are over 17,000 different standards covering a wide variety of sectors, disciplines and initiatives. The two most commonly seen in the Lifelong Learning Sector are those associated with quality management and environmental management. The current series for quality is the ISO 9001 standard and the ISO 14001 is the standard for environmental management. These international standards certify the process rather than the product.

(Source: http://www.iso.org)

Matrix assessment

Matrix standards are service standards relating to information, advice and guidance. Assessment looks at the work of those involved in giving assistance to learners as they embark on their post-compulsory learning. There are eight standards:

Delivering the service:	Awareness
	Defining the service
	Access to information
	Support in exploring options.
Managing the service:	Planning and maintaining the service
	Staff competence and support
	Feedback from customers
	QI through evaluation.

(Source: http://www.matrixstandard.com)

PQASSO

This stands for Practical Quality Assurance System for Small Organisations. Primarily for the voluntary sector and small businesses, it has wide ranging criteria covering planning, services, monitoring and evaluating. It is an off-the-shelf QA system, written as a book to describe the system and offering a step-by-step approach for businesses. It covers the following aspects of business:

- Planning
- Governance
- Leadership and management
- User-centred service
- Managing people
- Learning and development
- Managing money
- Managing resources
- Communications and promotion
- Working with others
- Monitoring and evaluation
- Results.

The PQASSO Quality mark also provides users with an accreditation to recognise their quality systems.

(Source: www.ces-vol.org.uk)

Charter Mark

The Charter Mark focuses on customer service and makes standards for communications and consultation. It ensures people's opinions are heard.

In 2008 the Charter Mark was replaced by Customer Service Excellence. It is a quality assurance system to encourage and enable organisations that deliver an understanding of the needs and preferences of their customers and local communities.

(Source: www.cabinetoffice.gov.uk)

Learning PROBE

This is an analysis tool specifically designed for the learning and skills sector, which focuses on processes. It was designed in 2001 by the Learning and Skills Development Agency (LSDA) and the Confederation of British Industry (CBI). It allows comparisons to be made against peers and other benchmarks. It aids the identification of strengths and weaknesses and helps to develop a programme of continuous improvement. It is not a standard, rather a method of self-regulation.

(Source: www.cbi.org.uk)

Peer review

This is an effective strategy which looks at initiating collaborative arrangements for similar organisations to review each other. For example, participating in self-assessment panels, shadowing lesson observers to standardise grading. It builds upon the notion of transparency in quality assurance systems, sharing good practice and seeking advice from objective observers.

Quality improvement plan (QIP)

This document, which is written following a review and evaluation of performance, records what needs to be developed and how it will be achieved.

Suggested format for a QIP

QUALITY IMPROVEMENT PLAN

Area for development	Actions required	Success indicator	By whom	By when	Review	Met Y/N
In this section you should write the development point, for example:	In this section you should identify the various activities you need to carry out in order to achieve an improvement	How will you know that your actions have achieved the desired result?	In this section you should identify someone whose responsibility it is to ensure success	In this section you should identify a realistic date by which you can confirm whether or not improvements have been achieved	In this section you can identify a point at which you will check how you are progressing with the actions and therefore check that you are on target to achieve success	
Achievement on Level 2 programme is below national benchmark	Design a course handbook Include study skills to the programme Monitor tutorial documentation to confirm effective advice is being given	Achievement rate increased to match National benchmark	Course tutor Course Team	July 2010	December 2009 - check handbook issued to learners October 2009 - check scheme of work includes study skills December 2009 and March 2010 - audit tutorial records, observe a tutorial	

If there are a number of areas for development it may be necessary to prioritise the order you address them in. Developments on your plans can be:

- *Essential* – Failure to develop in this area will have significant effects on provision.
- *Desirable* – Systematic developments arise from routine quality processes or in response to initiatives.
- *Aspirational* – Developments which would enhance provision, but which only need to be carried out if time and skills allow.

Risk assessment

Assessing risk is both an internal process and one that is undertaken through audit and inspection. In the context of quality management, it checks that an organisation is able to objectively evaluate its ability to improve. The assessment indicates how much risk is associated either with the organisation per se, or with individual procedures.

Organisational risk assessment provides the LSC and Ofsted with an indication of the frequency and intensity of inspection required. Procedural risk assessment provides the organisation with an indication of how effective a department or area is. Risk assessment can also be applied when prioritising improvements which are necessary.

Risk assessment is a final measure in terms of quality which identifies the amount of risk that failure to implement an action incurs. Organisations should carry out their own business risk assessment.

For example:

A significant risk to providers of education and training is 'failure to recruit learners'. Every organisation should have a plan to ensure that this doesn't happen, or what it has to do if recruitment is lower than anticipated.

Other risks include:

- Failure to secure funding

- Failure to pay suppliers

- Failure to meet targets for success

- Failure to meet needs of learners/local businesses, etc.

External bodies will also make risk assessment on organisations regarding their ability to provide services to learners. For example: awarding bodies use their external verification processes to assess the risk of centres in being able to provide rigorous assessment of their qualifications. If the risk is high then centres will be subjected to more careful scrutiny.

The LSC assesses the risks associated with funding training organisations and colleges; if targets for success and financial security are not met then they will not continue to engage with the organisation for learning contracts.

ACTIVITY 4

In this activity you should discover which quality initiatives are implemented in your organisation. A few are listed to give you a start . . .

Initiative	Last done	Key staff involved	Key purpose	Key outcome
Ofsted Inspection				
Self-Assessment Report				
Quality Improvement Panel				
Annual Assessment Visit				
Awarding Body Verification or moderation				
Investor in People				
Framework for Excellence assessment				
Observation of Teaching and Learning				

Use the information contained in this chapter, but also talk to other members of staff, especially the management team and more experienced teachers. Don't be frightened to ask questions such as:

- Why do we do this?
- What benefits result from these activities?
- How do they improve performance of individuals, teams and the organisation as a whole?

Finally, there is no single QA system which is suitable for all providers in the sector and covers all aspects of the business of learning. Some systems are undertaken voluntarily, others are an accepted requirement. The important thing is to ensure that the outcome of quality initiatives leads to a development and that an organisation can prove it has done so; thus every development identified whether successfully actioned or not, needs to be completed, thus the loop is closed. The purpose of quality management is to ensure organisations are consistently effective and efficient in their work.

 ## ACTIVITY 5

Following on from the previous activities, list two things that you are going to do differently or improve upon now that you are more aware of quality standards in your organisation.

Activity	Who can help?	How will you know that you've made an improvement?	When do you hope to have achieved this by?

Recommended reading

Ewans, D. and K. Watters (2002) *Using quality schemes in adult and community learning: a guide for managers*, Learning and Skills Development Agency.

Ravenhall, M. and M. Kenway (2003) *Making a difference: leading and managing for quality improvement in adult and community learning*, Learning and Skills Development Agency.

Sallis, E. (2002) *Total Quality Management in Education*, Routledge.

Glossary of terms

Audit an official inspection by an independent person

Learner voice term given to processes which gather feedback from learners

Quality Control checks the integrity of the process

Quality Assurance systematic checks to provide confidence

Quality Improvement a process to improve the reliability of quality systems

Self-regulation the ability to check own performance without asking others

Stakeholder people with an interest in the organisation

Standardisation a process to confirm decisions and create norms

TQM Total Quality Management

 # SUMMARY

In this chapter we set out to achieve the following outcomes:

- State the difference between quality assurance and quality improvement
- Compare and contrast the main quality agencies and systems
- List ways of assuring and improving quality
- Evaluate the effectiveness of quality management in improving performance.

Your Personal Development

The first part of this chapter is concerned with explaining the meaning of quality control, quality assurance, quality improvement and quality management. It looks briefly at the historical evolution and influences and sets out to justify the importance of such systems and processes. In the first activity you analyse where you are starting from in terms of awareness of quality initiatives.

You engage in three further activities; one which sets a scenario in the form of a case study and asks you to consider teaching and learning processes and requires you to suggest improvements or advice to the tutor; the second requires you to review current quality initiatives at your organisation; in the third you are required to think more widely about quality events in your organisation, their benefits and the outcomes they achieve. You have also analysed the impact of these initiatives on the organisation, stakeholders as well as yourself.

The middle part of the chapter lists and briefly describes the more common agencies and models used to implement quality management. Some of these are obligatory to the organisation; some are taken up in a more voluntary manner.

The closing part looks at the overall outcome of quality management, namely the improvements necessary to drive the business forward. It also looks briefly at risk assessment and the importance of understanding the implications of failing to have or comply with a quality management strategy.

In the final activity you were asked to consolidate what you have learned so far and link it to your practice. You have identified at least two things that you will do differently and given yourself a CPD plan for improvement.

CHAPTER 29 (WPP)

Writing and presenting your research project

LEARNING OBJECTIVES

The measurable outcomes that you will achieve by reading this chapter and completing the activities are:

- To explain the key terms associated with research
- To devise a research title and plan your research project
- To prepare and justify the research methods
- To structure an academic essay
- To identify key components of the project
- To demonstrate sound ethical values in your research project
- To recognise your development against minimum core standards

Research presentation skills

Many of the pieces of assessed work you have undertaken during your Diploma course have taken the form of essays and small projects, supported by evidence from your teaching. In the assessment for this unit you will be asked to investigate a topic of your own choosing, related to the Lifelong Learning Sector, and present it as a piece of research or critical analysis. (Refer to your Course Handbook for detailed information about the assessment criteria.) It may also be called an academic essay, a study, an enquiry or critique; it may even be described as a mini thesis or dissertation project. Don't be too concerned, they all mean broadly the same thing although they may be presented slightly differently. In essence, an academic research project is a formal piece of writing and follows a set pattern of presentation. The university or college at which you are studying will have the definitive guide on how it is to be presented; this section aims to guide you through that process.

> ### Research is fundamentally a problem solving activity which addresses a problem or tests a hypothesis.

Anderson (1990: 4)

Anderson (1990: 3–4) believes that there are five sorts of researchers:

- *Tenacious* – those who believe that something is true
- *Authority based* – those who rely on experts to establish what something is
- *Rationalist* – those who predict and generalise based on logic
- *Axiological* – those who participate in 'insightful observation', unsystematically making conclusions
- *Scientific* – those who systematically analyse data.

There is another type; the *Researcher* who needs to achieve their Diploma in Teaching and hasn't got the faintest idea of where to start!

Getting started

If you have been given the topic title you can disregard this first section, although it may be useful if your topic title is very general. First of all, list things that are relevant, interesting or useful to you. For each idea you need to think about what is involved, where information is available from. Talk to colleagues, friends and tutors. Try a spider diagram to collect your thoughts. Choose something with plenty of information in books or on the Internet. Obscure titles may be interesting but will give you hours of reading – assuming there have been some publications.

The topic should be something related to the Lifelong Learning Sector. It is difficult to write a list of topics, because it will be outdated too quickly, but, so as to get you started here are some of the more generic themes:

Educational initiatives Government policy	Investigate the impact of recent reports published by government bodies or contribute to issues currently being consulted upon. Ideas for these will be found in the press, TV and professional or vocational journals/magazines.
	A review of policy is contained within the College Net site www.collegenet.co.uk and provides a useful resource for educational investigation.
Equality and diversity	A popular topic at the moment, but planning inclusive teaching to meet individual needs has been around for a while, and can always be developed. ▶

◀

Social issues/ demographics	Widening participation in which education and training is available to everyone is not new, but social trends and community regeneration impact on the topic greatly. It may be worth investigating whether your curriculum is addressing priorities, needs and future developments.
National strategy/ curriculum	Government targets and initiatives will continue to impact on the Lifelong Learning Sector. Age of learners, funding, skills needs, school leaving age, new qualifications will always be worth a look at.
Responsive-ness	We must meet needs of learners, employers, parents and external agencies. Within the sector there are learners with special educational needs, gifted and talented learners, disadvantaged and disaffected groups. How we continue to meet the needs of the diversity in the LLS is worth a look.
Personal or professional development	Strategies at the forefront are mentoring, CPD, reflective practice. How do you see the best way to improve teachers' performance? Similarly, learners are required to complement their studies with functional skills, personalised learning and employability skills – these are the current ideas. How is it impacting on and supporting vocational learning?
Legislation	There seems to be an ever changing and developing need to meet legal requirements, either due to the fact that a new law appears or the changes to the learner profile in the training rooms: caring for younger learners, anti-discrimination, teacher professionalism, health and safety, Why not investigate the latest piece of legislation and how it affects teaching and learning?

Hopefully, you are no longer staring at a blank sheet of paper, but if you are and you have exhausted all of your ideas then consult your tutor, who will provide some inspiration. If your paper is overflowing, then consider which aspect you want to focus on to reduce your research.

Keep these early notes; they will be useful in the future when you have a 'dry' moment.

Bell (2005)

Planning your essay

It is useful to plan your ideas and talk them through with your tutor. You might find the following planner useful.

RESEARCH PLANNER
Main question
What are you hoping to find out about?
Sub questions
Do some parts of the question above need further clarification or explanation?
Topics to be covered
List topics
Main literature sources
List books, web addresses, journals
Research methodology
Questionnaires, interviews, action research etc. Why?
Hypothesis
What you are hoping to achieve, prove, argue against etc.

The opening line in any essay is the most difficult. A good way to start is:

'The purpose of this project/study is to . . .', then use verbs such as 'describe', 'analyse', 'define', 'determine', 'examine', 'consider'. Then continue with a descriptive phrase like 'the extent to which', 'how', 'factors which', 'the implications of', 'the reasons underpinning', 'the preferences or effects of' or 'the characteristics of' and then follow with your topic. You should ensure your question is contextualised.

For example:

> 'The purpose of this study is to analyse the extent to which changes in funding methodologies will impact on enrolments.' A case study of one curriculum area in an Inner City College.
>
> 'The purpose of this study is to establish the underlying factors which influence the delivery of catering [or any other subject] to learners whose first language is not English [or any other specific need].'
>
> 'The purpose of this study is to investigate the impact of the introduction of the New Diploma [or any other new initiative] on the delivery of Health and Social Care to younger learners [or any curriculum area].'
>
> City and Guilds titles include:
>
> 'The extent to which learning can contribute to the personal development, economic growth and community regeneration of your learners.'
>
> 'How government policies and initiatives impact on own role and teaching and learning in the Lifelong Learning Sector.'
>
> 'Examine the impact of own professional values and judgements on teaching and learning.'

By defining your question or title in this way you should be able to keep a tight focus on your research (or ramblings!). It also enables the reader to fully understand what you are trying to achieve and in what **context**. Keep going back to your title question to check that you are still on the point and are in fact answering it!

The structure of a research project

The correct order to present your research project is:

1   Title

2   Abstract – a summary of the question, research and conclusions*

3   Introduction – context, parameters, acknowledgements, etc.

4   Literature review – findings, observations and summary of published (**secondary**) research

5   Research methodologies – how you approached your own (primary) research**

6   Data results and discussion – what the primary research told you**

7   Conclusions and recommendations

8   **Reference** list

9   Appendices

Presenting your research paper

Look at your University or College's Student Handbook for more detail, but in summary:

- Word process or type the essay.
- Use double line spacing in a font such as Arial; size 11 or 12 are typical.
- Long quotes should be in single line spacing with double indents; no quotation marks are needed.
- Quotes in main body of text should be in 'quotation marks'.
- Left hand margin should be about 1.5 inches (4 cms) wide, the right about 1 inch (2.5 cms). This allows for hole-punching and binding.

*The 'abstract' (section 2), is presented at the beginning of the presented work, however it is the last thing you will complete. The purpose of an abstract is to give the reader an overview of the content and findings of your project. It is useful to readers (especially if your work is published) to know what your essay is about to save them reading the whole lot). Again, check whether or not you are expected to present an abstract.

**Check whether or not you are expected to include primary research (sections 5 and 6) in your study. It may be that you only need to present the secondary research, i.e. a summary of that which is already published.

- Number your pages.
- Do not use abbreviations, e.g. 'don't'. If using a title like NVQ, ensure you write it in full the first time it is used in the text with the abbreviation in brackets afterwards. For example 'National Vocational Qualification (NVQ)'.
- Use the correct referencing system, Harvard is widely used and most colleges and universities provide detailed examples – if not: Google – Harvard.

It is not the tutor's job to proofread, check grammar or spelling or interpret meaning. Your essay must use standard English language conventions, be fluent and coherent. If the reader is distracted by errors, your work cannot be easily read and they will return it to you for amendment. However, the occasional spelling or grammar error may be ignored or alerted in the margins without any major impact on the final mark.

You should write your essay knowing that the reader is an intelligent person, but they may not be wholly conversant with your topic.

Writing a literature review

This part of your essay is a summary of all published material on your topic. It should be restricted to what is already written and not include your opinion, hearsay or talk about your practice. It is one of those things that you will either find easy to complete or struggle with; practice makes perfect!

One of the first things you need to come to terms with is that it represents others' opinions. You can find different authors' opinions and use them to argue for and against topics, but what you think at this point is not relevant. You will use your primary research to argue your points later in the essay. In other words, comments are only **valid** if published or proven. (This is where I struggled, because being a pragmatist, I do things because they feel right and they work, I do not necessarily do things because somebody else says it works. I, therefore, found literature reviews quite difficult in the beginning and had to learn to write in this way.)

If using Harvard referencing, the way you will write is like this:

When paraphrasing an author's opinion:

> Author (year) argues that . . . . You do not need quotation (speech) marks as you are changing words, but be careful not to change the original author's interpretation.

When making a short direct quotation from a book or article:

> Author (year, page) states ' ... .' In this case you are citing exactly, so you should put the quote in quotation marks. If you need to add a word in order to link the quote to your text, use square parenthesis [ ] to indicate this. Some people prefer to put the page number at the end of the quote. That is fine, whichever method you choose, be consistent throughout your work.

When making a long quotation from an article:

> Follow the same strategy as for short quotes but put the quotation onto separate lines, use indents both sides to identify the quote; you do not need quotation marks, the presentation alerts the reader to the fact that it is a quotation.

Remember that, whilst this section is a series of quotes and opinions, it does need to have a beginning, middle and end and the text should flow, rather than just being a collection of quotes. This is the part that takes practice, so ask you tutor to look at draft reviews until you are confident in this style of writing. (See also Appendix C, Study Skills.)

Research methodology

This simply means the way you are going to organise your research. It is a significant part of graduate and post graduate programmes. The terminology sounds quite complicated, but fortunately most Diploma students will only have to read about a topic and then evaluate the impact it has on your teaching or planning.

Bell (2005: 8) describes five types of research classifications:

> '**qualitative, quantitative**, ethnographic, survey and action research'.

This is a very basic classification in order to familiarise you with some of the terms used. Below are several other styles (**paradigms** or frameworks) that a researcher can use. The research method will affect the choice of research tool selected.

> *Historical study* – is based on that which exists. No new ideas are developed. You would use qualitative tools to prove your points.

> *Descriptive study* – is an analysis of current practice and views. Tools used to collect data are qualitative or quantitative in style to explain facts or practices.

> *Narrative enquiry* – is the use of stories/experience to identify good models of practice. It needs to be **triangulated** by other research to justify its worth. Research tool will be qualitative in style.

> *Experimental or quasi-experimental* – the researcher's observations are monitored and compared to that which is known. The experiment or sample is randomly selected, except in quasi method when it is manipulated by the researcher.

> *Correlation study* – where predictions are related to other facts or theories. The **variables** are analysed.

> *Ethnographic study* – is used to establish cultural or sociological values and interventions to find out what things mean. It is usually an observation of human nature/learners' behaviour. It will be supported by qualitative method of collecting research data.

> *Programme evaluation* – a practical analysis to question what we are doing. It can be a formative or summative evaluation. It is not strictly academic research but may encompass research methodologies.

> *Case study* – an **eclectic** (diverse) mix of other methods, usually using **empirical** (observational or experiential) research. It is used to test a hypothesis. A word of caution – you may be biased and therefore the research could be unreliable.

Empirical research – an activity that uses direct or indirect observation as its test of reality, which is then balanced against known objects/theories/documents.

Policy research – an exploration of social issues within a real-life context, attempting to rationalise meaning and make recommendations.

Grounded theory – an enquiry based on theories or concepts which are established. Usually qualitative analysis. Theories evolve during the study.

Action research – the analysis of an activity (e.g. teaching in a particular style) carried out by the researcher and an evaluation and self-reflection of its effect and impact. Sometimes known as critical theory.

Research tools

This is a list of ways to collect primary source data. It is useful to collect this type of information to strengthen your arguments which may have been collected through secondary sources.

Census – a complete collection of data from the whole organisation, cohort, population.

Surveys – a representative sample of above. Data is collected by questionnaires, telephone or face-to-face interviews. The rationale behind the sample should be explicit. Sometimes a pilot study is required to establish the **reliability** of the sample chosen. In probability **sampling** the sample is truly representative of the population; in non-probability sampling it is skewed. With either it can be randomly decided who will participate in the survey or stratified/sub-divided into groups before deciding who is selected. In clustering, particular sections are selected.

For example, in an academic institution:

Random – every 10th name is selected.

Stratified – grouped into teachers, managers, students then selected by, for example, every 10th name.

Clustering – grouped into departments irrespective of position and then every 1 in 10 departments is selected.

One of the biggest problems to justify is the sample size. It should be large enough to be representative yet small enough to manage.

Questionnaire – they are the most used and abused method of data collection. You should always test your questionnaire before distributing it, maybe do your own thought-shower to try and anticipate responses. The questions should be clear and unambiguous; open rather than closed. Multiple-choice is easier to collate than short answer which may have as many answers as you sent out questionnaires. You could always add an 'any other comment' box. In the 'Likert' questionnaire (Rensis Likert, 1932 in Anderson 1990: 211–213), you face the respondent with a statement to which they can agree or disagree, usually using a three to seven point scale. However, if you rate a response using odd numbers you will encourage respondents to sit on the fence without committing to one side or the other. It is preferable to give an even number of choices to prevent this.

Not all of the questionnaires that you send out will be returned. This will probably be due to one of three main reasons: no contact (the person has moved, changed phone number, or email address), a refusal to respond (on average 25 per cent of people refuse to participate in questionnaires) or a large proportion are unable to respond (the most common reasons being – 'I don't understand the questions' or 'I haven't the time').

You can enhance the number of responses by:

- Piloting questionnaire to check questions
- Preparing selected people for responding, e.g. phone call
- Stamped addressed envelope with letter
- Use stamps not franked mail – makes it more personal
- Follow up request, if filling the form is a problem they may answer your questions over the phone
- Offer benefits/treats to respondents.

Interviews – these can be structured, semi-structured or unstructured in style. In all cases they should be planned. The responses will be different in each interview style. The style varies from prescriptive to anything goes; and remember you have to consolidate the responses.

An interview may follow a questionnaire to elicit underlying issues; it may be sent to a smaller sample or those who indicated they would be available for further discussion. You may wish to tape the interview – remember to get permission first. Interviews can be by phone or in person or maybe in an e-chat forum; you should always pre-arrange a time and indicate how long it will take. Focus groups are an assembled group of respondents rather than one to one and usually include a discussion type of response rather than specific answers. When conducting an interview you will need skills in explaining, paraphrasing and listening.

Analysing the data

Quantitative data When presenting data it is not sufficient to say '32 per cent of respondents entered the course with x and 6 per cent with y.' The analysis is 'So what?' Did the x group need more/less tutorials than y? What were the final achievements in relation to entry requirements?

Do not use just 'per cent' in your analysis. 100 per cent could be 1 person or 500 people, the emphasis, importance and meaning will alter according to the numbers involved.

Numeric skills – Averages You will use numeracy skills when analysing your data and when you present the findings, especially if you use percentages, averages and graphical presentations.

Mean – add all the numbers and divide by the number of numbers

Median – The mid value. Write numbers in order and find the mid point

Mode – Most frequently occurring value

Range – difference between highest and lowest value

Interquartile range – mid range data is used; upper and lower quartiles are disregarded

Standard deviation – the degree to which the upper/lower values vary from the mean. Usually presented as a percentage.

Graphs present a visual image and as such are easier to read; far more so than tables.

Ethics in research

Ethics are the standards by which the essay is validated. It ensures that contributor's views are respected and the opinions made are well thought out and presented without bias, i.e., the conclusions made can be trusted. It also protects confidential aspects of the primary research.

> Ethical research involves getting the informed consent of those you are going to interview, question, observe or take materials from. It involves reaching agreements about uses of this data, and how its analysis will be reported and disseminated. And it is about keeping to such agreements when they have been reached.
>
> Blaxter *et al.* (2001) in Bell (2005: 46)

The following are things to consider and protect during research:

Authority – seek explicit permission to review personal documentation and do not copy without such permissions.

Encroachment on privacy – beware that you respect others' values and beliefs, especially those of vulnerable groups.

Integrity – your research should be bona fide and not damaging, slanderous, libellous or offensive.

Protocol – you will need to explain the purpose of using the information to the authorising institution as part of the process of seeking permissions.

Security – you will need to comply with the Data Protection Act (1998) and subsequent amendments.

You have a responsibility to minimise:

Risk – informants should have the right to discontinue or abstain from answering particular questions.

You are accountable for:

Anonymity – nobody should be able to identify comments made in a questionnaire/essay, not even the researcher. The disadvantage to this is that without coding on questionnaires, it means that you can't follow up survey replies.

Confidentiality – as a researcher you commit to protect and respect the privacy of anything/anybody mentioned in data collection.

Copyright – this protects the original author of the work. It is forbidden to replicate some items. You can make personal copies for research purposes without breaking copyright rules, so long as you cite accurately. Under copyright 'personal' means only you; you must not reproduce it for anyone else.

Honesty – you will always be truthful and accurate.

Intellectual ownership – the person who created the original idea, thought or concept owns the idea; however, your employing organisation may include a statement about this. You should establish the organisation's protocol regarding who owns the work.

Plagiarism – do not paraphrase or use words or concepts that are not your own without accurately referencing them.

Respectfulness – of culture, opinion, values.

Transparency – no hidden agenda.

You should always make assurances about confidentiality – and keep them. You can invite contributors to read drafts or the finished item to check this. Remember: litigation is rife and you (the researcher) are responsible for what you write.

Academic misconduct Plagiarism is when a writer knowingly uses the language or beliefs of someone else and represents them as their own. In many essays, your marker will write 'source' in the margin which indicates that you have failed to acknowledge the originator of the material. This is a minor offence. More serious, however, is the growing use of 'cut and paste' on significant or entire pieces of work.

This is a serious breach and may result in a failed piece of coursework or other disciplinary sanction.

Plagiarism is also when a student misquotes or changes words or paraphrases without reference.

Your marker will recognise your style of writing and be alerted if it changes. Also, when marking a number of essays on a given topic, experienced tutors are familiar with typical quotations used. They will also note if different or obscure references are cited. I have been known to type a sentence into Google if I am suspicious and usually find the article as quickly as the original search. It is then easy to prove the plagiarism as you possess the source document to compare with the student's work.

Collusion (or copying) is regarded equally as serious as plagiarism in academic misconduct. Usually the same guides and sanctions apply. There is however, a difference between collusion and group work. In group work you will work together to research a topic and then use similar information as the basis of an individual essay. The key expression here is 'individual essay'. In group work it is not one essay written by a group member and copied for the group to submit in their portfolio. If in doubt, always state the extent of the research that is done as a group and that which is independent.

Concluding your research

Start by re-reading the essay and note the key points. Answer in rough the following:

> Are there further issues/developments/recommendations?
>
> What are the key outcomes of the literature?
>
> How does the literature confirm or disprove your **primary data**?
>
> How does the research link to your hypothesis/practice/ understanding?

This should give you a format to conclude your essay.

The abstract

Now you can go back to that summary activity at the beginning of your project. In your abstract you should state the purpose of the research, what you found out and summarise the findings and conclusions. It should never introduce new material but give future readers a flavour of what is contained in the main body of the text. It is extremely useful to fellow researchers to save time in future research.

Word counts

Most assignment guides or briefs will specify the number of words recommended for the essay. As a rule, this must be adhered to, although a tolerance of plus or minus 10 per cent is usually acceptable. As a (rough) guide, there will be an average of about 450 words to a page, based on a font such as Arial in a 12 point font-size. The reader of your assignment won't actually count the words, much is done on trust, but they are quite experienced and will be able to approximate the words. You should always note the word count in your essay.

When you plan your essay, it is advisable to break the word count down to plot how many words you will use in the introduction, main body and the conclusion. You should also watch for words that indicate the balance expected if you have to cover a number of aspects.

Appendices are usually presented in addition to the specified word count but **bibliographies** are usually included, as are introductions and **contextual** statements. You should always double check this with your tutor.

Some examples:

Type	Abstract	Introduction	Literature review	Methodology	Data analysis	Conclusion	Total
Basic essay		250 (25%)			600 (60%)	150 (15%)	1000
Project or study	50	200			600	150	1000
Mini research	100	500			1900	500	3000
Research or investigation	100	500	800	600	500	500	3000
Academic research	100	800	1400	1000	900	800	5000

Last thoughts

- The preferred reference style in most universities and colleges is HARVARD citation – but please check this out before you start.
- Keep focused on your research question by identifying sub-questions or key words; don't get side-tracked into other areas – however interesting.
- Keep in dialogue with your tutor.
- Keep a note of all books, journals read and Internet sites visited. Include everything you'll need to produce in the reference list. If you note a quote, write down the page numbers – better still photocopy it.
- Internet sites are not necessarily valid or reliable research. Be cautious.
- Save your work regularly as you write and don't forget to make back-up copies on a memory stick, floppy disk or CD-Rom. Email it to a friend (not fellow course member) for safe keeping.

- Ensure that any conclusions are those ascertained from the research and not your own feelings.
- Remember that small pieces of research may not give fully representative outcomes.

Recommended reading

Lawrence Stenhouse (1975) on Action Research

Donald Schön (1983) on reflective practice

Glaser and Strauss (1967) on grounded theory

Brewer (2000) on ethnography

Denscombe (2002) on social research

Opie (2004) on educational research (highly recommended)

Wragg (2002) on interviewing

http://www.scholar.google.com; type key word 'research methods' or 'educational research' for lots of links

UK Official Statistical Publications – http://www.statistics.gov.uk

Department for education and Science – http://www.dfes.gov.uk/index.htm

University or College Intranet or VLE

Times Educational Supplement – http://www.tes.co.uk

Guardian Educational – http://educationGuardian.co.uk

Higher Standards, Better Education for All – http://www.dfes.gov.uk/publications/schoolswhitepaper/pdfs/DfES-Schools%20White%Paper.pdf

Study Skills Tip Sheet – http://www.wlv.ac.uk/lib/systems/tipsweb.htm

Harvard Guide – http://www.staffs.ac.uk/uniservices/infoservices/library/learn/cite.php

General advice – http://www.mdx.ac.uk/www/study/research.htm

Minimum Core Skills

Literacy
In gathering your research and writing your essay, you will:

- Find, and select from, a range of reference material and sources of information, including the Internet

- Use and reflect on a range of reading strategies to interpret texts and locate information or meaning ▶

- Write fluently, accurately and legibly on a range of topics
- Select appropriate format and style of writing for different purposes and different readers
- Use spelling and punctuation accurately in order to make meaning clear
- Understand and use the conventions of grammar consistently when producing written text.

During interviews with colleagues and during research tutorials, you will:

- Express yourself clearly, using communication techniques to help convey meaning and enhance the delivery and accessibility of the message
- Show the ability to use language, style and tone in a way that suits the intended audience
- Use appropriate techniques to reinforce oral communication, check how well the information is received and support the understanding of those listening.

Numeracy
In collecting, interpreting and analysing your questionnaires, you will:

- Process and analyse data
- Make sense of data
- Select appropriate format and style for communicating findings.

Information and communication technology
In presenting your essay, you will:

- Express yourself clearly
- Communicate with ICT in a variety of ways that suit and support the intended audience
- Use ICT systems
- Find, select and exchange information
- Develop and present information.

Glossary of terms

The words used in research are sometimes quite daunting. From my own bitter experience I can relate to the fact that some words seem over-complex and may be designed to make the process seem far more intellectual than necessary. Here I aim to de-mystify some of those words:

Bibliography a complete list of everything investigated during the research, in alphabetical order

Context/Contextual describing the setting to aid understanding

Demographic the structure of the population

Eclectic a mixture or diversity

Empirical based on observation or experience rather than theories

Enquiry an investigation

Ethics the acceptable rules or behaviours of research

Hypothesis a supposition or belief

Paradigm a model or framework

Primary data is when the source (respondent) is present. For example – questionnaires, interviews, case studies

Qualitative data based on the analysis of opinion

Quantitative data based on the analysis of numbers

References a list of material cited in the research essay, in alphabetical order

Reliability (in research) the consistency of the measurement. Qualitative data is less reliable than quantitative data

Sampling the probability or non-probability of the data

Secondary data is when the originator is absent. For example books, journals etc.

Triangulated the validation of one set of data against other sets

Valid (in research) measured accurately to elicit reliable outcomes

Variables the analysis or acceptance that not everything will fit in the box

SUMMARY

In this chapter we set out to achieve the following outcomes:

- Explain the key terms associated with research
- Devise a research title and plan your research project
- Prepare and justify the research methods
- Structure an academic essay
- Identify key components of the project
- Demonstrate sound ethical values in your research project
- Recognise your development against minimum core standards.

Your Personal Development

This chapter looked at how you will present essays in response to questions about wider professional practice. Some ideas of things impacting on the profession are explored in the opening section and include topics relating to policy, curriculum, demographics, legislation and professional development.

The information in the chapter sets out to look at what is meant by a research project or academic essay and considers how it is structured. It specifically tries to help with deciding on your topic and how you would make a proposal prior to commencing the essay. It also summarises the basic dos and don'ts in terms of presentation techniques.

The chapter continues looking at the academic features of literature review, methodology and data analysis and how they help the researcher to make judgements and strengthen opinions. This part also looks at how numeracy skills are used and developed.

Finally, the chapter concludes with comments about how to ensure the essay is valid and ethically sound. There are a number of further reading suggestions, based on both how to research and what to research. As the terminology is particularly academic, key words are explained both in the text and in the glossary of key words.

CHAPTER 30 (WPP)

Professional standards for teachers, tutors and trainers

Chapter reproduced with the kind permission of 'New overarching professional standards for teachers, tutors and trainers in the lifelong learning sector', Lifelong Learning UK, December 2006.

Domain A: Professional values and practice

The practice of teaching is underpinned by a set of professional values that should be observed by teachers, tutors and trainers in all settings. This domain sets the standards for these values and their associated commitments.

PROFESSIONAL VALUES

Teachers in the lifelong learning sector value:

AS1   All learners, their progress and development, their learning goals and aspirations and the experience they bring to their learning

AS2   Learning, its potential to benefit people emotionally, intellectually, socially, and economically, and its contribution to community sustainability

AS3   Equality, diversity and inclusion in relation to learners, the workforce, and the community

AS4   Reflection and evaluation of their own practice and their continuing professional development as teachers

AS5   Collaboration with other individuals, groups and/or organisations with a legitimate interest in the progress and development of learners

They are committed to:

AS6   The application of agreed codes of practice and the maintenance of a safe environment

AS7   improving the quality of their practice

PROFESSIONAL KNOWLEDGE AND UNDERSTANDING	PROFESSIONAL PRACTICE
Teachers in the lifelong learning sector know and understand:	*Teachers in the lifelong learning sector:*
AK1.1 What motivates learners to learn and the importance of learners' experience and aspirations	AP1.1 Encourage the development and progression of all learners through recognising, valuing and responding to individual motivation, experience and aspirations

AK2.1 Ways in which learning has the potential to change lives	AP2.1 Use opportunities to highlight the potential for learning to positively transform lives and contribute to effective citizenship
AK2.2 Ways in which learning promotes the emotional, intellectual, social and economic well-being of individuals and the population as a whole	AP2.2 Encourage learners to recognise and reflect on ways in which learning can empower them as individuals and make a difference in their communities
AK3.1 Issues of equality, diversity and inclusion	AP3.1 Apply principles to evaluate and develop own practice in promoting equality and inclusive learning and engaging with diversity
AK4.1 Principles, frameworks and theories which underpin good practice in learning and teaching	AP4.1 Use relevant theories of learning to support the development of practice in learning and teaching
AK4.2 The impact of own practice on individuals and their learning	AP4.2 Reflect on and demonstrate commitment to improvement of own personal and teaching skills through regular evaluation and use of feedback
AK4.3 Ways to reflect, evaluate and use research to develop own practice, and to share good practice with others	AP4.3 Share good practice with others and engage in continuing professional development through reflection, evaluation and the appropriate use of research
AK5.1 Ways to communicate and collaborate with colleagues and/or others to enhance learners' experience	AP5.1 Communicate and collaborate with colleagues and/or others, within and outside the organisation, to enhance learners' experience
AK5.2 The need for confidentiality, respect and trust in communicating with others about learners	AP5.2 Communicate information and feedback about learners to others with a legitimate interest appropriately and in a manner which encourages trust between those communicating and respects confidentiality where necessary

AK6.1 Relevant statutory requirements and codes of practice	AP6.1 Conform to statutory requirements and apply codes of practice
AK6.2 Ways to apply relevant statutory requirements and the underpinning principles	AP6.2 Demonstrate good practice through maintaining a learning environment which conforms to statutory requirements and promotes equality, including appropriate consideration of the needs of children, young people and vulnerable adults
AK7.1 Organisational systems and processes for recording learner information	AP7.1 Keep accurate records which contribute to organisational procedures
AK7.2 Own role in the quality cycle	AP7.2 Evaluate own contribution to the organisation's quality cycle
AK7.3 Ways to implement improvements based on feedback received	AP7.3 Use feedback to develop own practice within the organisation's systems

Domain B: Learning and teaching

The values set out in Domain A support and inform all the commitments, knowledge and practice set out in the other domains.

PROFESSIONAL VALUES

Teachers in the lifelong learning sector value:

AS1	All learners, their progress and development, their learning goals and aspirations and the experience they bring to their learning
AS2	Learning, its potential to benefit people emotionally, intellectually, socially, and economically, and its contribution to community sustainability
AS3	Equality, diversity and inclusion in relation to learners, the workforce, and the community
AS4	Reflection and evaluation of their own practice and their continuing professional development as teachers

AS5   Collaboration with other individuals, groups and/or organisations with a legitimate interest in the progress and development of learners

They are committed to:

BS1   Maintaining an inclusive, equitable and motivating learning environment

BS2   Applying and developing own professional skills to enable learners to achieve their goals

BS3   Communicating effectively and appropriately with learners to enhance learning

BS4   Collaboration with colleagues to support the needs of learners

BS5   Using a range of learning resources to support learning

PROFESSIONAL KNOWLEDGE AND UNDERSTANDING	PROFESSIONAL PRACTICE
Teachers in the lifelong learning sector know and understand:	*Teachers in the lifelong learning sector:*
BK1.1 Ways to maintain a learning environment in which learners feel safe and supported	BP1.1 Establish a purposeful learning environment where learners feel safe, secure, confident and valued
BK1.2 Ways to develop and manage behaviours which promote respect for and between others and create an equitable and inclusive learning environment	BP1.2 Establish and maintain procedures with learners which promote and maintain appropriate behaviour, communication and respect for others, while challenging discriminatory behaviour and attitudes
BK1.3 Ways of creating a motivating learning environment	BP1.3 Create a motivating environment which encourages learners to reflect on, evaluate and make decisions about their learning
BK2.1 Principles of learning and ways to provide learning activities to meet curriculum requirements and the needs of all learners	BP2.1 Provide learning activities which meet curriculum requirements and the needs of all learners

▶

BK2.2 Ways to engage, motivate and encourage active participation of learners and learner independence

BP2.2 Use a range of effective and appropriate teaching and learning techniques to engage and motivate learners and encourage independence

BK2.3 The relevance of learning approaches, preferences and skills to learner progress

DP2.3 Implement learning activities which develop the skills and approaches of all learners and promote learner autonomy

BK2.4 Flexible delivery of learning, including open and distance learning and on-line learning

BP2.4 Apply flexible and varied delivery methods as appropriate to teaching and learning practice

BK2.5 Ways of using learners' own experiences as a foundation for learning

BP2.5 Encourage learners to use their own life experiences as a foundation for their development

BK2.6 Ways to evaluate own practice in terms of efficiency and effectiveness

BP2.6 Evaluate the efficiency and effectiveness of own teaching, including consideration of learner feedback and learning theories

BK2.7 Ways in which mentoring and/or coaching can support the development of professional skills and knowledge

BP2.7 Use mentoring and/or coaching to support own and others' professional development as appropriate

---

BK3.1 Effective and appropriate use of different forms of communication informed by relevant theories and principles

BP3.1 Communicate effectively and appropriately using different forms of language and media, including written, oral and non-verbal communication and new and emerging technologies to enhance learning

BK3.2 A range of listening and questioning techniques to support learning

BP3.2 Use listening and questioning techniques appropriately and effectively in a range of learning contexts

BK3.3 Ways to structure and present information and ideas clearly and effectively to learners

BP3.3 Structure and present information clearly and effectively

BK3.4 Barriers and aids to effective communication

BP3.4 Evaluate and improve own communication skills to maximise effective communication and overcome identifiable barriers to communication

BK3.5 Systems for communication within own organisation	BP3.5 Identify and use appropriate organisational systems for communicating with learners and colleagues
BK4.1 Good practice in meeting the needs of learners in collaboration with colleagues	BP4.1 Collaborate with colleagues to encourage learner progress
BK5.1 The impact of resources on effective learning	BP5.1 Select and develop a range of effective resources, include appropriate use of new and emerging technologies
BK5.2 Ways to ensure that resources used are inclusive, promote equality and support diversity	BP5.2 Select, develop and evaluate resources to ensure they are inclusive, promote equality and engage with diversity

Domain C: Specialist learning and teaching

The values set out in Domain A support and inform all the commitments, knowledge and practice set out in the other domains.

PROFESSIONAL VALUES

Teachers in the lifelong learning sector value:

AS1   All learners, their progress and development, their learning goals and aspirations and the experience they bring to their learning

AS2   Learning, its potential to benefit people emotionally, intellectually, socially, and economically, and its contribution to community sustainability

AS3   Equality, diversity and inclusion in relation to learners, the workforce, and the community

AS4   Reflection and evaluation of their own practice and their continuing professional development as teachers

▶

AS5   Collaboration with other individuals, groups and/or organisations with a legitimate interest in the progress and development of learners

They are committed to:

CS1   Understanding and keeping up to date with current knowledge in respect of own specialist area

CS2   Enthusing and motivating learners in own specialist area

CS3   Fulfilling the statutory responsibilities associated with own specialist area of teaching

CS4   Developing good practice in teaching own specialist area

PROFESSIONAL KNOWLEDGE AND UNDERSTANDING	PROFESSIONAL PRACTICE
Teachers in the lifelong learning sector know and understand:	*Teachers in the lifelong learning sector:*
CK1.1 Own specialist area including current developments	CP1.1 Ensure that knowledge of own specialist area is current and appropriate to the teaching context
CK1.2 Ways in which own specialism relates to the wider social, economic and environmental context	CP1.2 Provide opportunities for learners to understand how the specialist area relates to the wider social, economic and environmental context
CK2.1 Ways to convey enthusiasm for own specialist area to learners	CP2.1 Implement appropriate and innovative ways to enthuse and motivate learners about own specialist area
CK3.1 Teaching and learning theories and strategies relevant to own specialist area	CP3.1 Apply appropriate strategies and theories of teaching and learning to own specialist area
CK3.2 Ways to identify individual learning needs and potential barriers to learning in own specialist area	CP3.2 Work with learners to address particular individual learning needs and overcome identified barriers to learning
CK3.3 The different ways in which language, literacy and numeracy skills are integral to learners' achievement in own specialist area	CP3.3 Work with colleagues with relevant learner expertise to identify and address literacy, language and numeracy development in own specialist area

CK3.4 The language, literacy and numeracy skills required to support own specialist teaching	CP3.4 Ensure own personal skills in literacy, language and numeracy are appropriate for the effective support of learners
CK3.5 Ways to support learners in the use of new and emerging technologies in own specialist area	CP3.5 Make appropriate use of, and promote the benefits of new and emerging technologies
CK4.1 Ways to keep up-to-date with developments in teaching in own specialist area	CP4.1 Access sources for professional development in own specialist area
CK4.2 Potential transferable skills and employment opportunities relating to own specialist area	CP4.2 Work with learners to identify the transferable skills they are developing, and how these might relate to employment opportunities

Domain D: Planning for learning

The values set out in Domain A support and inform all the commitments, knowledge and practice set out in the other domains.

PROFESSIONAL VALUES

Teachers in the lifelong learning sector value:

AS1   All learners, their progress and development, their learning goals and aspirations and the experience they bring to their learning

AS2   Learning, its potential to benefit people emotionally, intellectually, socially, and economically, and its contribution to community sustainability

AS3   Equality, diversity and inclusion in relation to learners, the workforce, and the community

AS4   Reflection and evaluation of their own practice and their continuing professional development as teachers

AS5   Collaboration with other individuals, groups and/or organisations with a legitimate interest in the progress and development of learners

▶

◀

They are committed to:

DS1 Planning to promote equality, support diversity and meet the aims and learning needs of learners

DS2 Learner participation in the planning of learning

DS3 Evaluation of own effectiveness in planning learning

PROFESSIONAL KNOWLEDGE AND UNDERSTANDING	PROFESSIONAL PRACTICE
Teachers in the lifelong learning sector know and understand:	*Teachers in the lifelong learning sector:*
DK1.1 How to plan appropriate, effective, coherent and inclusive learning programmes that promote equality and engage with diversity	DP1.1 Plan coherent and inclusive learning programmes that meet learners' needs and curriculum requirements, promote equality and engage with diversity effectively
DK1.2 How to plan a teaching session	DP1.2 Plan teaching sessions which meet the aims and needs of individual learners and groups, using a variety of resources, including new and emerging technologies
DK1.3 Strategies for flexibility in planning and delivery	DP1.3 Prepare flexible session plans to adjust to the individual needs of learners
DK2.1 The importance of including learners in the planning process	DP2.1 Plan for opportunities for learner feedback to inform planning and practice
DK2.2 Ways to negotiate appropriate individual goals with learners	DP2.2 Negotiate and record appropriate learning goals and strategies with learners
DK3.1 Ways to evaluate own role and performance in planning learning	DP3.1 Evaluate the success of planned learning activities
DK3.2 Ways to evaluate own role and performance as a member of a team in planning learning	DP3.2 Evaluate the effectiveness of own contributions to planning as a member of a team

Domain E: Assessment for learning

The values set out in Domain A support and inform all the commitments, knowledge and practice set out in the other domains.

PROFESSIONAL VALUES

Teachers in the lifelong learning sector value:

AS1	All learners, their progress and development, their learning goals and aspirations and the experience they bring to their learning
AS2	Learning, its potential to benefit people emotionally, intellectually, socially, and economically, and its contribution to community sustainability
AS3	Equality, diversity and inclusion in relation to learners, the workforce, and the community
AS4	Reflection and evaluation of their own practice and their continuing professional development as teachers
AS5	Collaboration with other individuals, groups and/or organisations with a legitimate interest in the progress and development of learners

▶

◀

They are committed to:

ES1   Designing and using assessment as a tool for learning and progression

ES2   Assessing the work of learners in a fair and equitable manner

ES3   Learner involvement and shared responsibility in the assessment process

ES4   Using feedback as a tool for learning and progression

ES5   Working within the systems and quality requirements of the organisation in relation to assessment and monitoring of learner progress

PROFESSIONAL KNOWLEDGE AND UNDERSTANDING	PROFESSIONAL PRACTICE
Teachers in the lifelong learning sector know and understand:	*Teachers in the lifelong learning sector:*
EK1.1 Theories and principles of assessment and the application of different forms of assessment, including initial, formative and summative assessment in teaching and learning	EP1.1 Use appropriate forms of assessment and evaluate their effectiveness in producing information useful to the teacher and the learner
EK1.2 Ways to devise, select, use and appraise assessment tools, including, where appropriate, those which exploit new and emerging technologies	EP1.2 Devise, select, use and appraise assessment tools, including where appropriate, those which exploit new and emerging technologies
EK1.3 Ways to develop, establish and promote peer- and self-assessment	EP1.3 Develop, establish and promote peer- and self-assessment as a tool for learning and progression
EK2.1 Issues of equality and diversity in assessment	EP2.1 Apply appropriate methods of assessment fairly and effectively
EK2.2 Concepts of validity, reliability and sufficiency in assessment	EP2.2 Apply appropriate assessment methods to produce valid, reliable and sufficient evidence

EK2.3 The principles of assessment design in relation to own specialist area	EP2.3 Design appropriate assessment activities for own specialist area
EK2.4 How to work as part of a team to establish equitable assessment processes	EP2.4 Collaborate with others, as appropriate, to promote equity and consistency in assessment processes
EK3.1 Ways to establish learner involvement in and personal responsibility for assessment of their learning	EP3.1 Ensure that learners understand, are involved and share in responsibility for assessment of their learning
EK3.2 Ways to ensure access to assessment within a learning programme	EP3.2 Ensure that access to assessment is appropriate to learner need
EK4.1 The role of feedback and questioning in assessment for learning	EP4.1 Use assessment information to promote learning through questioning and constructive feedback, and involve learners in feedback activities
EK4.2 The role of feedback in effective evaluation and improvement of own assessment skills	EP4.2 Use feedback to evaluate and improve own skills in assessment
EK5.1 The role of assessment and associated organisational procedures in relation to the quality cycle	EP5.1 Contribute to the organisation's quality cycle by producing accurate and standardised assessment information, and keeping appropriate records of assessment decisions and learners' progress
EK5.2 The assessment requirements of individual learning programmes and procedures for conducting and recording internal and/or external assessment	EP5.2 Conduct and record assessments which adhere to the particular requirements of individual learning programmes and, where appropriate, external bodies
EK5.3 The necessary/appropriate assessment information to communicate to others who have a legitimate interest in learner achievement	EP5.3 Communicate relevant assessment information to those with a legitimate interest in learner achievement, as necessary/appropriate

Domain F: Access and progression

The values set out in Domain A support and inform all the commitments, knowledge and practice set out in the other domains.

PROFESSIONAL VALUES

Teachers in the lifelong learning sector value:

AS1   All learners, their progress and development, their learning goals and aspirations and the experience they bring to their learning

AS2   Learning, its potential to benefit people emotionally, intellectually, socially, and economically, and its contribution to community sustainability

AS3   Equality, diversity and inclusion in relation to learners, the workforce, and the community

AS4   Reflection and evaluation of their own practice and their continuing professional development as teachers

AS5   Collaboration with other individuals, groups and/or organisations with a legitimate interest in the progress and development of learners

They are committed to:

FS1   Encouraging learners to seek initial and further learning opportunities and use services within the organisation

FS2   Providing support for learners within the boundaries of the teacher role

FS3   Maintaining own professional knowledge in order to provide information on opportunities for progression in own specialist area

FS4   A multi-agency approach to supporting development and progression opportunities for learners

PROFESSIONAL KNOWLEDGE AND UNDERSTANDING	PROFESSIONAL PRACTICE
Teachers in the lifelong learning sector know and understand:	*Teachers in the lifelong learning sector:*
FK1.1 Sources of information, advice, guidance and support to which learners might be referred	FP1.1 Refer learners to information on potential current and future learning opportunities and appropriate specialist support services
FK1.2 Internal services which learners might access	FP1.2 Provide learners with appropriate information about the organisation and its facilities and encourage learners to use the organisation's services, as appropriate
FK2.1 Boundaries of own role in supporting learners	FP2.1 Provide effective learning support, within the boundaries of the teaching role
FK3.1 Progression and career opportunities within own specialist area	FP3.1 Provide general and current information about potential education, training and/or career opportunities in relation own specialist area
FK4.1 Professional specialist services available to learners and how to access them	FP4.1 Provide general and current information about a range of relevant external services
FK4.2 Processes for liaison with colleagues and other professionals to provide effective guidance and support for learners	FP4.2 Work with colleagues to provide guidance and support for learners

Appendices

A   Optional units

B   Abbreviations

C   Study skills

D   Teaching observations

E   Teaching qualifications

Minimum core

Throughout your qualification you are required to show evidence of how your are meeting the minimum core of literacy, language, numeracy and information communication technologies (ICT). Some teaching-related activities, mapped to the minimum core are included within Chapter 10.

Appendix A Optional units

Your Diploma in Teaching in the Lifelong Learning Sector (DTLLS) includes two further units which should be selected from a range of options. One option unit will be delivered during the first year of your award and will be accredited at level four; it will have a value of 15 credits. A second option unit will be delivered in year two and accredited at level five, also worth 15 credits.

Full lists of the options and the learning outcomes, which are being added to regularly, are available on the Lifelong Learning UK website – www.lluk.org.

There are restrictions on how the units can be combined. The 'Rules of Combination' should be discussed fully with your tutor before embarking on collecting evidence for your chosen options.

Level 4

Title	Credit level	Credit value
Evaluating learning programmes	4	3
Preparing for the coaching role	4	3
Preparing for the mentoring role	4	3
Delivering employability skills	4	6
Equality and diversity	4	6
Managing behaviours in the learning environment	4	6
Principles and practice of instructional techniques	4	6
Specialist delivery techniques and activities	4	6
The coaching and mentoring roles	4	6

▶

Title	Credit level	Credit value
Preparing to use e-learning and e-assessment in the lifelong learning sector	4	9
Planning and assessing for inclusive practice (ESOL)	4	9
Planning and assessing for inclusive practice (Literacy)	4	9
Planning and assessing for inclusive practice (Numeracy)	4	9
Working with individuals and groups in the learning environment	4	9
Working with the 14–16 age range in the learning environment	4	9
Learning in the community	4	10
Developing and managing resources within the lifelong learning sector	4	15
Effective partnership working in the learning and teaching context	4	15
Inclusive learning and communication for specialist teachers of learners with cognitive learning difficulties (excluding specialist provision for dyslexia)	4	15
Inclusive practice	4	15
Managing and responding to behaviours in a learning environment	4	15
Managing programmes in the lifelong learning sector	4	15
New and emerging technologies and the creative/performance arts	4	15
Professional development planning	4	15
Professional practice skills	4	15
Teaching a specialist subject	4	15

http://www.lluk.org/3080.htm and http://www.lluk.org/3081.htm (accessed 30.10.08)

Level 5

Title	Credit level	Credit value
Embedded approaches to literacy, language and numeracy within vocational and other subjects for integration within diploma programmes	5	6 + 9
Application of new and emerging technologies within the curriculum	5	10
Counselling skills awareness for the teacher	5	10
Developing management skills	5	10
Action learning to support development of subject specialist pedagogy	5	15
Action research	5	15
Developing and managing resources within the lifelong learning sector	5	15
Effective partnership working in the learning and teaching context	5	15
Enabling learner independence and self determination for specialist teachers of learners with cognitive learning difficulties (excluding specialist dyslexia provision)	5	15
Inclusive practice	5	15
Planning and enabling learning for specialist teachers of learners with cognitive learning difficulties (excluding specialist dyslexia provision)	5	15
Professional development planning	5	15
Reflective practice skills	5	15
The lifelong learning sector	5	15
Tutoring and course leadership in the lifelong learning sector	5	15
Working with the 14–19 age range in the learning environment	5	15

http://www.lluk.org/3082.htm and http://www.lluk.org/3083.htm (accessed 30.10.08)

Your provider may not offer every option on the list as a traditionally taught provision; you may need to engage in private study to complete assessment activities. Alternatively, a provider might be receptive to either accrediting previous learning or achievement or offer alternative learning methods, for example on-line or distance learning packages. Any work presented for assessment should clearly meet the learning outcomes specified by LLUK. For example, an in-service programme for equality and diversity must be mapped to the LLUK standards for it to be validated and accredited by a provider.

Optional units currently available from City and Guilds

Diploma options (part one) – level 4

- Inclusive practice
- Managing and responding to behaviours in a learning environment
- Developing and managing resources in the lifelong learning sector
- Planning and assessing for inclusive practice (ESOL)
- Planning and assessing for inclusive practice (literacy)
- Planning and assessing for inclusive practice (numeracy)
- Working with the 14–16 age range in the learning environment
- Professional development planning
- Teaching a specialist subject
- Equality and diversity
- Preparing for the coaching role
- Preparing for the mentoring role
- Evaluating learning programmes
- Developing employability skills
- Principles and practice of instructional techniques
- Specialist delivery of techniques and activities
- The coaching and mentoring role

Diploma options (part two) – level 5

- Developing and managing resources within the lifelong learning sector
- The lifelong learning sector
- Integrating literacy, language and numeracy into the learning of vocational and other subjects
- Planning and practising embedded approaches to raise learner achievement
- Working with the 14–19 age range in the learning environment
- Inclusive practice
- Professional development planning
- Developing management skills

http://www.cityandguilds.com/cps/rde/xchg/SID-A0312A53-C16929EA/
cgonline/hs.xsl/35590.html?search_term=Diploma%20options
(accessed 30.10.08)

Appendix B Abbreviations

AAIA	Association for Achievement and Improvement through Assessment
ACL	adult and community learning
ADHD	attention deficit hyperactivity disorder
AI	awarding institution
ALI	Adult Learning Inspectorate
APEL	Accreditation of Prior Experience Learning
APL	Accreditation of Prior Learning
ARG	Assessment Reform Group
ATLS	Associate Teacher Learning and Skills
AVCE	Advanced Vocational Certificate in Education
BSA	Basic Skills Agency
BSL	British Sign Language
BTEC	Business and Technology Education Council
CADET	consistent, accessible, detailed, earned, transparent
CATS	Credit Accumulation and Transfer Scheme
CPD	continuous professional development
CPPD	continuing personal and professional development
CTAD	Cambridge Training and Development
CTLLS	Certificate in Teaching in the Lifelong Learning Sector
CV	curriculum vitae
DCSF	Department for Children, Schools and Families
DfES	Department for Education and Skills
DIUS	Department for Innovation, Universities and Skills
DTLLS	Diploma in Teaching in the Lifelong Learning Sector
EFL	English as a foreign language
EM	external moderator
EMA	Educational Maintenance Allowance
ESOL	English for speakers of other languages
EV	external verifier

F4E/FFE	Framework for Excellence
FE	further education
FEHQ	Framework for Higher Education Qualifications
FEnto	Further Education National Training Organisation
GCSE	General Certificate in Secondary Education
GLH	guided learning hours
GNVQ	General National Vocational Qualifications
HE	higher education
HND	Higher National Diploma
IA	initial assessment
ICT	information and communications technology
IfL	Institute for Learning
ILP	individual learning plan
ILT	information learning technology
ITT	initial teacher training
IV	internal verification
LCD	liquid crystal display
LLUK	Lifelong Learning UK (Sector Skills Council)
LP	lesson plan
LSC	Learning and Skills Council
MCQ	multiple choice question
MIS	management information system
NCFE	Northern Council for Further Education
NQF	National Qualifications Framework
NQT	newly qualified teacher
NVQ	National Vocational Qualifications
OCN	Open Colleges Network
OHP	overhead projector
OHT	overhead transparency
OTL	observations of teaching and learning
PAT	portable appliance testing
PDR	Performance Development Review

PEST	political, economic, social, technological
PTLLS	Award in Preparing to Teach in the Lifelong Learning Sector
Q&A	question and answer
QCA	Qualifications and Curriculum Authority
QTLS	Qualified Teacher Learning and Skills
SAR	self-assessment report
SEN	special educational needs
SENDA	Special Educational Needs and Disabilities Act (2001)
SOW	scheme of work
SSC	Sector Skills Council
SWOT	strengths, weaknesses, opportunities, threats
TQM	total quality management
URL	universal resource locator
VLE	virtual learning environment
WBL	work-based learning
WBT	work-based training
YTS	Youth Training Scheme

Appendix C Study skills

This section has nothing to do with your qualification; it is about *how* you learn.

The same philosophy can be adapted for your learners: there is more to teaching than teaching the subject matter. We assume that by the time our learners reach us in the post-compulsory sector, they have learned how to learn. *This is an assumption.*

Learners enter colleges and training providers with their various previous experiences of learning. We aim to develop autonomous learners who are able to achieve their qualifications and reach their full potential. They will, if you help them by teaching them how to do this. You are no different. To your tutor you are a learner!

Therefore, by the end of this section you will be able to:

- List the skills required in order to develop study skills
- Describe the safety issues relating to studying
- State the ethical values which underpin study
- Identify the most appropriate locations for personal study
- Explain the skills of note-taking
- Explain the skills of efficient reading
- Summarise the most effective strategies for time management
- List the key components of writing essays
- State the most common sources of information
- Use the Internet effectively
- Use a search engine
- Describe how to reference your sources using Harvard referencing system
- State the meaning of some common Latin words

- Describe a way to declare authenticity
- Specify the meaning of plagiarism
- Explain the meaning of the main command words in assessment
- List some alternative words for 'said'.

What are study skills?

These are the skills which help you to learn your subject. It is not a passive activity; you need to help your tutor to develop the skills by talking to them, attending tutorials and reflecting on feedback. Study skills include note-taking, efficient reading and research and accurate citation in well-structured essays. *How do you learn?*

Everyone is different. Some learners like to learn by seeing things; they are called *visual* learners. Some learners will learn by listening to things; they are called *auditory* learners. The last category is those learners that like to do things; they are called *kinaesthetic* learners. All of these relate to our senses: hearing, seeing, touching. How you learn and study will depend on your senses.

Safety issues

Ensure that the area in which you work has got a desk and chair that is comfortable and adjustable. If using a computer, be careful not to look at the screen for too long without taking a break.

Ethics and values

There are really two considerations here. One is the fact that should you decide to use a tape recorder in the class you should notify and seek permission from your peers and the tutor. The teacher training learning environment is one in which people need to be comfortable to speak openly about a range of issues and students may be a little self-conscious if the discussion is recorded.

The second is to do with citation. It is not acceptable to pass off other people's views, opinions and writings as your own. You can cite them, but must always acknowledge the original source. Every organisation will advise on the relevant method of doing this. Similarly, if you are using primary research, for example questionnaires in your essay, you should always ensure that there can be no link back to the originator and protect their anonymity.

Where to study

- Somewhere with few distractions and interruptions.
- Somewhere quiet. If background noise (music) is necessary, then keep the volume low. Avoid the temptation to sing along with your favourite artist.
- Somewhere with suitable furnishings: a desk big enough to have a computer, a place to write, and a place to keep your reference books or notes.
- An area to keep your study things separate from other uses of the space.
- Suitably ventilated, comfortable and light.

Note-taking skills

Thinking is quicker than speaking, so use this time to think about what your teacher is saying. This time allows you to understand what is being said.

Speaking is quicker than writing, so be selective when listening to your teacher and only write key things.

You may make your notes in a linear format (subheadings and written text), plain text (loads of writing in a prose style), or diagrams (for example spider diagrams or pictures).

Some examples of different types are:

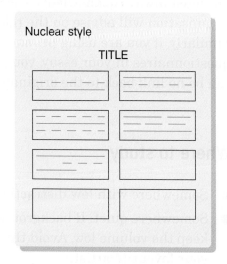

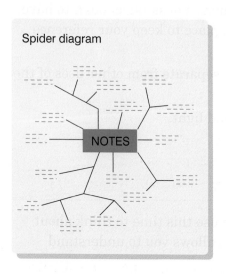

- Listen for key words. Develop your ability to use key words by asking the teacher to stress them or write them on the board.
- Don't try and write everything down, it is not supposed to be dictation!
- Are you sitting where you can hear and see everything?
- If you are continuing a topic from a previous session, then re-read your notes before attending the next session. This acts as a

reminder, helps the transition from the known to the unknown and reminds you to ask about things you didn't grasp first time or have not retained.

- Always have sufficient resources. Be prepared. Pencils need sharpening and pens run out of ink!

- Perhaps a tape recorder would help if you have difficulty in listening and writing at the same time, but check permissions before switching on.

- Use a highlighter pen or coloured pencils/crayons to identify important facts.

- Use abbreviations to help you write quickly in class, but be consistent or you'll forget which abbreviations you've used. Some examples:

   (a) assmt = assessment;

   (b) fdbk = feedback;

   (c) t&l = teaching and learning;

   (d) sow = scheme of work;

   (e) LP = lesson/session plan;

   (f) diff'n = differentiation.

- Number handouts and put the corresponding number in your notes to remind you about additional information.

- Check a citation source if you plan to use printed material in lessons or study.

- Organise your notes. For example, use either different pages for different topics, or arrange notes in chronological order, or arrange them according to your assignment topics, or separate class and research notes.

- Leave white space around your notes so that you have room to add things later.

- Write legibly. Notes are for your use only, so don't bother too much about 'best writing' or spelling, as long as you can read them later. New vocabulary should be spelled correctly – with a definition.

- Rewrite notes to help deepen the knowledge.

Reading skills

Reading is the method of finding out information; you will do this when researching topics or trying to develop understanding. Depending upon why you are reading, you will read in one of three ways:

Skim This is a brief look at something, possibly looking at the introduction, the chapter outline and summaries before deciding whether or not the subject matter is relevant to you.

Scan This is a more detailed look at a particular topic or relevant section. You can use indexes to find appropriate readings. It will enable you to broadly describe the content, without any specific detail.

Digest This is when you read thoroughly. Every word will be considered until you fully understand the meaning. You will be able to describe in detail the author's points and may know some by heart. It is a very slow way of reading so needs to be both focused and necessary.

You should follow reading with writing. Make notes on key points and remember to fully reference the book title etc., for future use. There is nothing worse (and this is learned from bitter experience) than trying to use a brilliant quote but not being able to remember which book it was in, or remembering the book but having to re-read it to find the page reference.

Time management skills

I haven't got the time!

I know. It is difficult balancing all of the things that have to be done, so here are some ideas to help:

1   Identify what has to be done and by when. There are only 24 hours in a day, so decide when you will do your study. Writing an assignment at two in the morning the day before it is due is not

evidence of well-planned study time. Especially when you email it to your tutor and expect feedback and amendments before tonight's class!

2   Fit study time into your life: realistically

- Work
- School run
- Watching TV
- Me time
- Prep for lessons
- Domestic responsibilities.

Try keeping a diary for seven days, just to check what you actually do in a week. If you like a practical or technological way of doing this then you will find many questionnaires on the Internet which help you to plan your time: however, never underestimate how long things take to do.

- Plan your study needs. Start from when work has to be handed in and work backwards. Set yourself 'by now I should have done . . .' targets.
- Be in control.
- Persuade the family to respect your study time.
- Try to get quality time. Half an hour of good time is better than two hours of faffing about!
- Always meet the deadline – better a referral than a fail. If you hand something in your tutor will give you focused feedback which may give you a clearer direction. If you don't hand in anything, you may struggle and enter the spiral of more work, less time etc.
- Be strict with yourself. Are you researching something on the net or surfing? Do you *really* need to look at your emails now?

Essay writing

The hardest part of an essay is the start. There is nothing more daunting than staring at a blank sheet of paper, so always be clear about what you are going to write about. Plan the essay, and run it past your tutor or mentor for advice. Make notes about what you feel it is important to include. Keep going back to it to check that you are still on track and not waffling.

You may find writing an essay plan easier than just starting to write. You may also like to show it to your tutor in tutorial to check that you are on the right lines. This is a typical example:

ESSAY PLAN
Essay title:
Introduction *For example:* The essay will review/analyse [topic] and summarise key issues relating to . . .
Main themes to be included are: ✳   ✳   ✳ ✳   ✳   ✳ ✳   ✳   ✳
Information sources will be: ✳ ✳ ✳
Expected summary or outcomes of essay:

Every essay needs structure, that is, a *beginning*, a *middle* and an *end*.

1   At the start of your essay, tell the reader what they can expect to read about; this is usually directly linked to the assessment criteria. If you have to put the essay into context, now is the time to do it. By the end of your introduction, the reader should have a clear understanding of what to expect and what you aim to discuss.

2   The middle is about the content. It is about what you said you were going to write about in the introduction. Make sure your points follow a logical order and if you are using quotations ensure that they are relevant and don't disjoint the essay. Your tutor may advise you to write this in the third person, or they may prefer you to talk about your own experiences and link this to the theory. Check this out.

3   Finally your essay needs an ending. If you wish to evaluate and reflect on your future development, write this before you summarise your essay; do not introduce anything new in the section. In this part you need to tell the reader what they have just read, so it may be helpful to go back to the start and check what you said you were going to do, and ask yourself if this is what you did.

Make a draft of the essay:

● Does it flow?

● Spell-check your work – most computers have a program to do this, but please check that the language is set as UK English and not US English.

● Proofread your work – remember that 'fro'/'for' and 'from/form' are bona fide words. They are a common typing error, but their misuse will not be picked up using a software spell-check.

● Check presentation at this point. Watch for headings at the bottom of pages or tables that go over two pages. I know that this type of thing isn't in the criteria, but you are working as academic professionals so your work should be at that standard.

● Save frequently and make back-up copies.

● Do not use abbreviations in a formal essay.

● Use double line spacing as this gives you and your tutor plenty of space for comments.

Make a note of references as you find them and write the reference list or bibliography as you use the quotes. That way you won't forget any.

If you get stuck, leave a space and carry on writing about something that you are not stuck on. Then ask you tutor for guidance on the difficult bit. When you are in a writing mood, keep going . . .

To get brownie points for your essay:

- Check that it is logical and coherent
- Ensure it is well structured
- Relate theory to practice
- Proofread and spell-check
- Check that it makes sense.

Information sources

You will find helpful information for your study in:

- textbooks
- journals
- magazines
- study centre intranet/VLEs
- the Internet
- newspapers
- dictionaries
- encyclopaedias
- thesaurus.

Remember that your class notes are also there to be used, as is your tutor.

Using the Internet

The World Wide Web is a mass of information. Some of it is useful, some of it is not. Because anybody can write stuff and put it on the

Web, it might not always be accurate, so if you are using the Internet for a project or assignment, stick to the more reliable sources.

When you find something good, download it to your computer and save it, rather than wasting paper printing everything off. You can then read it and get the really good bits to include in your work. *Do not* just cut and paste it. This does not demonstrate your understanding. To comply with copyright, you may take a personal copy of information from a website, but must not make multiple copies for your class. You can give learners lists of useful URL (universal resource locator) addresses. If you do want to quote from the Internet, you can, but you must write the source in your bibliography in the same way as you would reference a book. For example:

www.igotitfromtheweb.co.uk (accessed on 09/09/2009)

Using search engines

This is a huge database of things on the Internet. The more commonly used search engines are Google, Ask and Yahoo. You should use a search engine to help you locate information. Write in key words; forget the small words or common words as they will give you too many 'hits'. Unless you want info from abroad, click the tab for 'UK only' search, as this will also help in finding information and research relevant to this country.

Avoid words that are very common, such as 'research about learning', because that will give you too many listings (hits).

Usually the best information is found in the first 10 listings, anything after that tends towards obscurity.

If you've got thousands of hits, go back and refine your search. Try using Boolean Logic (http://www.internettutorials.net/boolean.html) to filter your search.

Be careful choosing the words you input to the search engine, both in terms of how common the word is and also in terms of alternative meanings.

You can use a search engine to do a quick plagiarism check by typing in a sentence from a piece of work, or an obscure reference. The link is usually in the first few websites.

Harvard referencing

Harvard referencing is a style of citation. Its purpose is to acknowledge the original ownership of the thought. Failure to use a citation style and passing off other people's work as your own is plagiarism. Plagiarised work is likely to be failed and may result in exclusion from the programme.

In an essay you are likely to use either direct quotes or paraphrasing.

Direct quotes are when you write the author's words exactly as they were presented in the document, and they will be in quotation marks ('. . .'). You should type exactly, so if it is an American work you may well see 'z' instead of 's' in words, or color not colour. *Do not alter it;* if you cite correctly the reader will know it is an American work and you will not be penalised for such errors. Long quotes, say of more than four lines, should be in their own space on the page and indented on both sides. You do not need quotation marks in this instance because it is obviously a quote. If the rest of your work is in double line spacing, then these long quotes would be in single line spacing. The purpose of quotation marks, indenting and different line spacing is to make them stand out. What you are saying is 'hey! here is a quote, and I'm not trying to hide it.' Any quotation should be introduced with the author's surname and the year of publication and page in brackets.

Paraphrasing is when you are expressing the idea, but putting it into your own words, maybe condensing the idea. This must still be cited using Harvard referencing; just because you've put it into your own words does not make it your thought.

For example:

Wilson (2008: 47) said: '. . .'

Wilson (2008: 46–9) states: '. . .' This is used when a quote goes over two or more pages or if you are paraphrasing a section.

The reference list at the end of the work is a list of all of your sources used in the text. A bibliography is a list of everything you have read, some of which you haven't used. It is more common to present a reference list. There should be a clear link between the names and dates in the text and the names and dates in the reference list. Books are listed in alphabetical order by author and presented:

Author surname and Initial/s (year) Title of the book. Location of Publisher: Publisher's name.

The title of the book is written as presented on the book cover So It May Have Capital Letters In Funny Places. You would either underline, **embolden** or *italicise* the title to make it stand out.

It will look like this:
Wilson, L. (2008) *Practical Teaching: A guide to PTLLS and CTLLS.* London: Cengage Learning.

For a magazine or newspaper, you should write the journalist's name, article title, paper title, date and page of article. It will look like this:

Smith, B. 'How to write an essay', *Popular Magazine.* 12/03/2009, pp. 23–5.

For class notes or handouts, it is similar to magazine articles, so the information you need is: the teacher's or group's name, class notes and lesson title, date. It will look like this:
Brown, P. Class notes: Module 4. 30/09/09, or
Group A. Class notes: Module 4. 30/09/09

Citing from the Internet

You should follow the same rules. If you can identify the author from the site then use it as you would a book. Alternatively you can use anon (anonymous) or the organisation's name. In the reference list at the end you should make the link to author or organisation. The URL becomes the 'book title' and you should add (accessed on [date]) instead of publisher details.

Jones, M. www.igotitfromtheweb.co.uk (accessed on 09/09/2009)

For fuller details of how to reference, ask your tutor for their guidance document, or type the key word 'Harvard' into a search engine on the Internet.

Latin words

et al. – and others, usually a number of contributors to a text

ibid. – in the same source

loc. cit. – in the passage or place cited

op cit. – in the work already cited

de facto – in reality, according to practice – in actual fact

in loco parentis – in the place of a parent

ipso facto – by that very fact or act

q.v. – referring to text in a work – which see

sic – literally used as spelled or given.

Authenticity

You will probably be asked by your tutor to make a statement at the end of your work to confirm that it is your own work. This statement may look like:

> I confirm that the work submitted is my own work, and that no part of this work has been submitted to another organisation or towards assessment for another qualification.
>
> *Linda Wilson*
>
> October 2007
> Word Count: 3,500

Plagiarism

Plagiarism is when a writer uses somebody else's work without saying so, or expresses someone else's opinions as their own. Even if you reference work, you are only allowed to use a small amount of that text (copyright and licensing laws govern this). This is a problem given the amount of information on the Internet, which is easily pasted into your own essays. Educational organisations do not tolerate plagiarism. You can prevent being accused of plagiarism if you *reference* your sources. Referencing is used to acknowledge the rightful owner (the author, the learner or the teacher).

Command words

These are the words that you will see in assignments; they instruct you to carry out a particular action. You will also use similar words in your lesson plans in order to identify outcomes. See also Chapter 3 – Lesson plans and outcomes.

Analyse	To examine in detail; to discover meaning
Complete	To make whole or perfect to ending
Demonstrate	To show or prove by reasoning or practical skill
Deliver	To carry out; to produce or perform
Describe	To give an account of
Evaluate	To assess the value or worth of something
Explain	To make something clear by giving a detailed account of relevant facts, circumstances
Identify	To determine or list availability or identity of something
Investigate	To examine thoroughly and systematically in order to discover the truth

▶

Justify	To prove validity
Obtain	To get or acquire something
Outline	To state the main features or general idea of something
Plan	To devise a purpose
Prepare	To make ready for an event, to construct or equip
Present	To show or exhibit something
Produce	To bring into existence, to make something
Reflect	To look back upon something and effect changes
Research	To carry out investigations into a subject or problem
Review	To look at or examine (again), to look back on
State	To express something clearly in speech or writing
Summarise	To express concisely the main outcomes
Use	To put into action

Different ways to say 'said'

When you are writing and referencing in your essays, you will often open the sentence with 'author said', you may vary this with 'stated' but may wish to include other variants:

Advocate, agree, allege, argue, articulate, assert, believe, certify, claim, comment, confirm, contend, contest, debate, declare, defend, define, dictate, disagree, enunciate, explain, express, imply, indicate, insist, maintain, make a case, mention, observe, profess, recommend, refer, reflect, remark, report, stipulate, subscribe, suggest, tell us, think, voice.

Summary

I hope that you will find this section useful as you complete the many tasks required of you in order to gain your qualification. Please remember that the most valuable study aids available to you are your tutor and your mentor.

Appendix D Teaching observations

This section is to reassure you about the purpose, process and possible outcomes of your teaching observation. They may be called:

- Teaching Observations
- Lesson Observations
- Teaching Practice Observations
- Session Observations
- Observations of Teaching and Learning (OTL)

Observations are your opportunity to showcase your expertise. They are very daunting, and it doesn't matter how long you have been in teaching, it remains traumatic to be observed. Observers know this and take this into consideration.

Teaching, traditionally, is a 'behind closed doors' activity, so it is not surprising that in order to find out how effective teaching and learning is, it must involve opening those doors.

Part of your teacher training programme will include observations of your teaching. Most probably these observations will be carried out by your tutor/assessor, i.e. the person responsible for making assessment decisions to prove your competence and so gain your award. However, you should also prepare for observations by others. Your mentor will provide particular guidance because he or she is likely to be from the same subject area that you teach in and therefore can advise on content, handling a particular group and level. You may also be observed as part of the organisation's self-assessment process: this will be by a trained observer who is looking to make judgements about the quality of the learners' experiences.

	CTLLS	DTLLS
Total number of teaching hours to be undertaken during the programme	30	150
Total number of observations during the programme	3	8

Who may watch you teach and why?

- The teacher training team – to assess your abilities against teaching competences
- The teaching (or lesson) observation team – to make judgements about the organisation's performance
- A mentor – to advise and guide your development
- A peer – to share ideas
- Ofsted inspector – to make judgements about the quality of the education or training provider
- Internal verifier/moderator – to validate the accuracy of your assessment decisions
- A manager – to monitor your performance and gather information from yourself and your students about programme delivery.

How to prepare for a lesson observation

Prepare your lesson as usual, although it will probably be a little more thoroughly done for an observed session.

An observer will spend between 40 minutes and an hour-and-a-half in your class. The average time spent observing is an hour. If your teaching session is timetabled for an hour, then your observer will see the entire lesson, but if it is longer, then they will use your lesson plan to make decisions about the part of the lesson that isn't observed. They may see any part of the lesson, although different people may want to focus on different aspects or alternatively, if there are a large number of observations to do, it will be when your session can be fitted in to the observer's workload.

Your mentor will probably come in by invitation and focus on an aspect of the session that you have already spoken about. The teacher training team will probably like to see the beginning or the end of the session, because these are the most difficult parts and they will be able to advise you more developmentally. Their visit will be expected. The lesson observation team or Ofsted inspection team will come in unannounced, although you will know that there is a significant likelihood of a visit.

Your observer will not participate in the lesson. They may, if the structure of your lesson permits, interview some learners. Questions they may ask learners include:

- 'Can you explain to me what you are doing today?' The observer is trying to find out if your learners know what they are trying to achieve, and may compare their answers with your stated learning outcomes.

- 'Do you usually do (specify an activity)?' The observer is trying to find out if what they are seeing in the lesson is typical and if you vary the methods in your lessons. They will compare this to the scheme of work.

- 'Are you working on any assessments/assignments at the moment?' The observer is trying to find out how learners are progressing, if they are getting timely feedback, or if there is any kind of assessment plan. They may compare this with paper evidence you have supplied.

They are trying to make judgements about the learners' experiences on the course and the impact your teaching has on the learners' experiences and will need to validate their judgements by cross-referencing evidence.

What documents to have available for the observer

When you are being observed, it makes sense to prepare a pack of documents for your observer. They need to make decisions about your teaching and some of their questions can be answered quite easily by providing certain things. For example: they need to find out if you are prepared for your class, so a copy of your lesson plan provides sufficient evidence to prove that you are.

Lesson (session) plan to demonstrate you are prepared and that your lesson has a clear beginning, middle and an end, using a range of teaching and learning methods, differentiated strategies and assessment plans.

A scheme of work to put this lesson into context with what has happened previously and what is planned for the future.

A class profile to explain about the group, its characteristics, and unique circumstances. This is particularly important if you are aware of particular issues that impact on the session. For example: x is unlikely to participate in this session because . . . or there are x authorised absences this week. You may provide the tutor file if you are the group's personal tutor. You are trying to provide the observer with information about what has led you to deliver the session in the way that you have. You may also wish to provide additional information to support current trends – for example, how you meet the Every Child Matters strategy or how you ensure your lessons meet equality and diversity agendas.

Assessment file with details of assessment plans, tracking and progress sheets, examples of marked work, or feedback given to learners.

Register to show attendance and punctuality over a period of time.

Handouts and teacher's notes copies of everything used in the session and notes about links to websites or books used. You may include a teaching or teacher's file to show consistency and variety.

What happens after the observation?

The observer may not stay until the end of the session. Usually they will try to leave at an appropriate time; for example, during some group work or at a break time so as to cause the least disruption to the flow, but it is not always possible. Don't worry if the observer gets up and leaves the room. They will try and say goodbye, but they will not deliberately interrupt the lesson, so may just get up and go, with a brief nod.

What happens next depends on who observed you. Observations that are carried out for development purposes will have a detailed feedback session immediately afterwards. These will usually be pre-arranged, especially if your lesson is planned to continue after the observation. The observer may give you cursory feedback, with an opportunity to arrange a more detailed session later.

The lesson observation team, and particularly the Ofsted inspectors, may give brief strengths and weaknesses as feedback, but it will be minimal. This is because the purpose of their observations is judgemental, not developmental. It will seem uncomfortable not to receive detailed feedback but it is quite common, so don't feel threatened.

Ten key points to survive your observation

1 Be prepared and keep your lesson plan to hand.
2 Lay out your desk with the resources you will use in the class, it saves time fumbling around for that board pen later!
3 Sit the observer out of your eye line, but where they can see what is going on.
4 Slow down, take deep breaths and try to overcome your nerves.
5 Give your observer plenty to read; whilst they are reading they are not watching!
6 If you are nervous, don't hold a piece of paper in front of you, it wobbles as you tremble.
7 Don't hide behind the desk, move around the room to check what's going on or just to remove a barrier.
8 Have lots of activities that engage your learners, group work, gapped handouts, discussion groups and practical activities. The observer is looking for active learners.
9 Start the lesson promptly. Have an opener activity whilst you take the register and settle the group.
10 End the lesson with a means of assessing learning – quiz or nominated questions.

Observation outcomes

Depending on the nature of the observation, you may or may not have a judgement offered to you.

Your mentor may not give you any kind of grade; they are using the observation to initiate reflective practice.

The teacher training observer has to decide whether your teaching meets the criteria (laid down by LLUK) or not. The decision will therefore be 'pass' or 'refer'.

The lesson observation team and Ofsted inspectors will grade you as either:

Grade one – outstanding

Grade two – good

Grade three – satisfactory

Grade four – inadequate.

Ofsted inspectors will not reveal the grade, nor will some lesson observation teams; it depends on the policy of the organisation. In either instance, you should be able to ascertain your grade by the judgements offered in the strengths and weaknesses feedback. Listen for the cue words: good, very good, exemplary, satisfactory, poor, etc.

Appeals against judgements

Hopefully you will not need to read this part, but if you do think that your observer has been unprofessional or has made an inaccurate judgement, read on.

The first course of action should be to discuss this with the observer; it will probably be that you want to justify your actions. Would a class profile have negated the need for this? Hopefully, your observer will meet you to discuss the outcome and the reasons why they made the decision.

If you cannot reach an amicable outcome, then you should report the matter to your line manager. Be prepared that one of the ways to mediate might be another observation.

Appendix E Teaching qualifications

In summary, from September 2007.

New staff

All new employees will work towards Qualified Teacher – Learning and Skills (QTLS) within five years of appointment, using the new qualification structure. This period gives them plenty of time to acquire a qualification, develop personal functional skills and widen, through CPD, academic and pedagogic skills. Private trainers or visiting speakers are exempt. (*The Further Education Teachers' Qualifications (England) Regulations 2007*)

Existing staff

Existing staff – employed since 2001 – will have a Level 4 qualification (e.g. C&G 7407 stage 1, stage 2, Cert Ed/PGCE). Staff employed before 2001 may have other qualifications, such as C&G 7306/7 or TCOS, which are Level 3 qualifications, but are encouraged to update them to Level 4. (*The Further Education Teachers' Qualifications (England) Regulations 2001 – Statute 1209*)

All staff

All staff must register with the Institute for Learning and undertake regular continuing professional development. (*The Further Education Teachers' Continuing Professional Development and Registration (England) Regulations 2007*)

The qualification structure for new entrants and unqualified teaching staff

The level of qualification for Associate Teacher Learning and Skills (ATLS) or Qualified Teacher Learning and Skills (QTLS) is determined by the role the teacher undertakes. Every teacher will be expected to complete the Award in Preparing to Teach in the Lifelong Learning Sector (PTLLS – C&G 7303). The Certificate in Teaching in the Lifelong Learning Sector (CTLLS – C&G 7304) is for those who are working as Associate Teachers. The Diploma in Teaching in the Lifelong Learning Sector (DTLLS – C&G 7305 – In university awards this is equivalent to Certificate in Education) is for those working in a full teacher role.

Table to compare new qualifications

Qualification	Number of guided learning hours of contact	Credit value	Number of teaching practice hours	Number of observed teaching hours
PTLLS Intro Award Level 3 or 4	30 glh	6 credits	30 mins micro-teach	30 mins
CTLLS Assoc Role Level 3 or 4	120 glh	24 credits (of which 6 from PTLLS)	30 hours	3 hours
DTLLS Cert Ed Full Role Level 4 Year 1 and Level 5 in Year 2	360 glh	120 credits (of which 15 from CTLLS)	150 hours	8 hours

PTLLS 6 CATS	CTLLS APL = 9 CATS	DIPLOMA (YR 1) 45 CATS	DIPLOMA (YR 2) 60 CATS	120 Credits
PTLLS 6 CATS	CTLLS 18 CATS			24 Credits
PTLLS 6 CATS				6 Credits

Descriptors for teaching roles

Associate teacher role (irrespective of hours worked)

Will teach predominantly in one of the following ways:

- From pack/pre-prepared materials and therefore has fewer responsibilities in design of curriculum and materials
- On a one-to-one basis
- A programme confined to a particular level/subject/type of learner (i.e. does not develop or deliver a full range across a curriculum area)
- Short courses.

Assessor/trainers, instructors, adult and community learning (ACL), work-based learning (WBL) and uniformed services will fall into this category

Full teacher role (irrespective of hours worked)

Will take on the full professional responsibility by:

- Using materials they have designed and evaluated
- Working across a range of levels, subjects and learner types
- Working across or contributing to a range of programmes of varying lengths
- Engaging in the wider role of teaching, e.g. tutoring, advice and guidance etc.

Unit titles and content

PTLLS   Award in Preparing to Teach in the Lifelong Learning Sector

6 credits, offered at Level 3 and Level 4

5 learning outcomes

Threshold qualification required by all teachers

CTLLS
 Preparing to Teach in the Lifelong Learning Sector (as above)

 Planning and Enabling Learning (Level 3 or Level 4 – 9 credits – 6 outcomes)

 Principles and Practice of Assessment (Level 3/4 – 3 credits – 6 outcomes)

 Option Unit * (6 credits)

DTLLS
 Preparing to Teach in the Lifelong Learning Sector (as above but Level 4)

 Planning and Enabling Learning (Level 4 – 9 credits – 6 outcomes)

 Enabling Learning and Assessment (Level 4 – 15 credits – 6 outcomes)

 Theories and Principles for Planning and Enabling Learning (Level 4 – 15 credits – 4 outcomes)

 Option Unit * (15 credits)

 YEAR TWO

 Continuing Personal and Professional Development (Level 5 – 15 credits – 4 outcomes)

 Curriculum Development for Inclusive Practice (Level 5 – 15 credits – 5 outcomes)

 Wider Professional Practice (Level 5 – 15 credits – 5 outcomes)

 Option Unit * (15 credits)

Note:

Option Units (*) are varied and subject to development. For up-to-date information please refer to Lifelong Learning (UK).

Glossary

Academic relating to education, school or scholarships

Achievement meeting learning goals

Achievement data the number of students who achieved their qualification, usually expressed as a percentage of those who completed

Acronym an abbreviation or series of initial letters which together make another word

Ad hoc random, unplanned action

ADHD attention deficit/hyperactivity disorder

Affective domain concerned with emotions and values

Affective concerned with emotions and values

Aim a broad statement of intent

Analysis a detailed examination

Andragogy how adults learn

APL accreditation of prior learning

APEL/APL accreditation of previous experience and/or learning

Approval permission to deliver qualifications on behalf of an awarding body

Aspiring one's hopes and ambitions

Assessment to make a judgement about something, a measurement of achievement

Attainment reaching the goal or qualification aim

Audit an official inspection by an independent person

Authenticity to establish who wrote/owns the subject

Authoritative a self-confident or assertive method of teaching

Autocratic a domineering approach to teaching

Autonomous learner one who requires minimal guidance from the teacher

Autonomy independence in the ability to learn

Awarding bodies the people who devise the qualifications and award the certificates

Behaviourist a school of thought associated with responses to stimuli

Benchmark a standard or point of reference to compare performance

Bibliography a complete list of everything investigated during the research, in alphabetical order

Blended learning a mixture of traditional and modern/computer learning technologies

Body language using conscious or unconscious gesture to express feelings

BTEC Business and Technology Education Council; a qualification title part of Edexcel; an awarding body

Buzz group activities small groups interact with the teacher to gather answers

C&G City and Guilds; an awarding body

CADET© consistent, accessible, detailed, earned, transparent

CATS Credit Accumulation and Transfer Scheme

Certificate a recognised outcome of a programme of study

Chalk and talk teaching by traditional methods with focus on a chalkboard

Chronological in date order

Code of conduct a set of standards governing professional values

Cognitive domain concerned with thinking skills

Cognitive concerned with thinking skills

Cognitivist a school of thought associated with thinking processes

Communication a means of sending and receiving information to share or exchange ideas

Competence the knowledge of or ability to do something

Concept an idea

Confidentiality secrecy of information

Constructive a term used to imply helpful feedback

Constructivism a learner-centred model of learning

Context the setting in which learning occurs

Context/Contextual describing the setting to aid understanding

CPD continuous professional development

cppd the abbreviation for continuing personal and professional development

Criteria the standard of competence

Critical analysis a detailed examination resulting in an opinion or argument

Critical incidents events that have a significant effect

Critique detailed analysis

Curricula plural of curriculum

Curriculum a programme or model of study

Deep learning learning which is memorised and fully understood

Demand led prioritised funding

Democratic a style of teaching based on negotiation and shared values

Demographic the structure of the population

Demography a study of population trends

Develop advance or improve ability

Diagnostic assessment assessment used to identify capability or skill level

Differentiation catering for the needs of all learners to reduce barriers to learning

Direct assessment evidence of the learner's work

Direct feedback/communication clear and unambiguous link

Disaffected learners no longer satisfied with the learning environment

Discipline a branch of knowledge

Discovery learning finding things out through research, investigation and discussion

Disengaged uninvolved with learning

Distractor incorrect answer choices in MCQs

Diversity valuing and celebrating the differences in people

Domain an area or section of learning; a classification

Due diligence pro-active investigation to help prevent future incidents occurring

Dyscalculia associated with difficulties in making sense of numbers and calculations

Dyslexia associated with a difficulty in reading and interpreting words and symbols

E-assessment electronic versions of assessment

Eclectic a mixture or diversity

Effective to produce the intended or desired result or outcome

Efficient productive working without waste

Ego self-importance or personal identity

E-learning learning using electronic systems or equipment

EMA Educational Maintenance Allowance – a grant paid to learners to support their further education

Embedded fixed firmly in the vocational context

Empirical based on observation or experience rather than theories

Employability in a position or suitable to be employed

Empowered given responsibility for something

Enquiry an investigation

Enrichment activities added to the curriculum or course to make a better learning experience

Enthusiastic a grade one indicator meaning creating enjoyment and interest

Equality the state of being equal or the same

Equality of opportunity legislation and focus on gender, age, culture etc.

ESOL English for speakers of other languages

Ethics the acceptable rules or behaviours of research

Evaluation to form an idea about something by measuring its effectiveness

Evolution a gradual development

Excellence a grade one indicator meaning to be exceptionally good at teaching

Experiential learning learning by trial and error

Extended question a question that involves a long answer

Extrinsic motivation motivation derived from the outside of the person

Facilitator one who supports or stimulates learning

Fail an assessment decision; not at pass standard

Feedback verbal or written comments about the assessment intended to bring about improvement

FEnto Further Education National Training Organisation

Font a type or style of lettering in a printed document

Formative continuous assessment

Formula a mathematical rule

Functional skills basic skills of literacy and numeracy

Gestaltist a school of thought associated with the whole learning process

Gifted and talented learners highly skilled or adept

Goal an aim or desired result

Grade a level or degree of competence

Grading the degree of competence, pass, merit, distinction

Graduates people who have a degree

Group learning collaborative learning techniques

High order most thorough level of learning

HND Higher National Diploma

Holistic the big picture; the whole curriculum

Hub the centre

Humanist a school of thought associated with the meeting all human needs

Hypothesis a supposition or belief

Ice-breaker an activity used to introduce learners to each other

ICT information communication technology

Identify to determine or recognise something

Idiosyncrasies a particular way of behaving

ILP individual learning plan

ILT information learning technology

Imaginative a grade one indicator meaning creative or resourceful

Impact an effect; an influence

Inclusion finding opportunities to integrate all learners

Inclusive not excluding any individual or group of learners (adj.)

Indirect assessment evidence or opinion from others

Indirect feedback/communication a link via a secondary method

Induction a formal introduction to a programme/role

Initial assessment an assessment tool to identify and establish potential or aspirations and discover facts

Inspectorate e.g. Adult Learning Inspectorate, Ofsted

Inspirational a grade one indicator meaning one who encourages learners

Instructor direct or commanding delivery of information

Integrity having values and principles

Interact to have an effect on

Intervention an interruption

Intranet internal computer-based communications network

Intrinsic motivation motivation from within the person; natural desire

Intuitive instinctive; apparently natural behaviour

Invigilation supervision of examination candidates

Ipsative self-assessment against standards of competence

IT information technology

IV internal verification

Jargon language, words or expressions of a specialist occupation

Jigsaw group activities small groups discuss different themes within a topic, which are collated by the teacher at the end of the activity

Job description a list of duties typical of the job role

Journal a diary

Judgement a decision about an assessment

Justified text even distribution of words across the page within fixed margins

Justify explain and prove something

Key the correct answer in a MCQ

Laissez-faire a non-interference model of teaching; learner-devised; a laid-back approach

Language written or spoken communication

Learner-centred the learner dominates the learning environment

Learner involvement customer service initiative about listening to learner's opinions

Learner voice term given to processes which gather feedback from learners

Learning to gain knowledge or a skill; what the learners do during a session

Learning environment general term for where learning occurs

Learning goals what a learner sets out to do

Learning needs things which will help a learner to achieve their goal

Learning outcome the result of a learning session

Learning preferences the individual's favoured way of learning

Learning styles analysis of how learners learn

Lesson plan a written structure for a session

Level 3 a position within the NQF indicating the value of a qualification

Linear (in communication) a message following a direct line

Linear (in curriculum) single dimensional

Literacy the ability to read and write

LLUK Lifelong Learning (UK) Sector Skills Council

Low order a superficial level of learning

LP abbreviation for lesson or session plan

Mastery comprehensive ability

MCQ multiple choice question

Mind map a visual representation of ideas

Minimum core standards of competence in language, literacy, numeracy and ICT

MIS management information systems, computer based data storage software

Models a description or example to represent an idea

Modular a curriculum or programme made up from several modules or units

Motivation enthusiasm or interest

NCFE Northern Council for Further Education; an awarding body

Negative reinforcement feedback that inhibits practice and lessens motivation

Negotiation agreement and compromise towards outcome

Neo-behaviourist a school of thought which believes learners are driven by goals

NQF National Qualifications Framework

NQT newly qualified teacher

Numeracy the ability to use numbers

Nurture development of characteristics, beliefs or attitudes

NVQ National Vocational Qualification

Objective a specific statement of intended outcome

Objectivism a teacher-centred model of learning

OHP overhead projector

OHT overhead transparency

On-programme a term to describe a period of learning

Opener activity a short activity at the start of session to set scene, create learning ethos and engage learners quickly

Opener an activity at the beginning of a session

Outcome result or consequence of assessment

Paradigm a model or framework

Participation to take part in

Pass assessment decision relating to satisfactory performance

Passion a grade one indicator meaning a strong desire to teach

Passive learning in which the learners accept teaching with little or no active response

Pastoral concerned with the well-being of learners

PDR abbreviation for performance development review; appraisal

Pedagogy the skill or ability of teaching

Performance criteria standards of required competence

Person specification a list of characteristics required in the job role

PEST an analysis tool to identify political, economic, social and technological influences

Philosopher someone who studies theories, attitudes or beliefs

Plagiarism to pass off somebody else's work as your own

Policy course of action by an organisation

Positive reinforcement feedback that enhances practice and improves motivation

Post-compulsory education after the age of 16, not mandatory

Praxis practical skills as opposed to theoretical skills

Primary data is when the source (respondent) is present. For example: questionnaires, interviews, case studies

Principle a set of values or beliefs promoted by the teacher; a rule or moral code

Product curriculum focuses on the outcome of learning

Professional Standards the minimum acceptable levels of performance of a competent teacher within the LLUK sector

Profile an outline of the characteristic traits of a particular person

Programme of study a structured list of sessions

Psyche the human mind or spirit

Psychology the study of the human mind or behaviour

Psychomotor concerned with physical, practical and co-ordination skills

QA (quality assurance) an official system to establish the quality of something such as an assessment

Q&A abbreviation for question and answer

QCA Qualifications and Curriculum Authority

Qualification a skill that makes someone suitable for a job

Qualitative data relating to opinions or thoughts

Quality Assurance systematic checks to provide confidence

Quality Control checks the integrity of the process

Quality Improvement a process to improve the reliability of quality systems.

Quantitative data relating to statistics and number

Questioning querying inviting responses

Rapport a common understanding

Rationale the reasons for an action

Recreational learning a skill for pleasure

Reference a list of material cited in the research essay, in alphabetical order

Referencing a source of information

Reflection a considered opinion expressed in speech or writing; thoughts or considerations, developing ideas or thoughts

Reflective practice thoughtful practice to develop skills

REfLECT™ Trade mark software recording system from IfL

Registration an official list of entrants on a qualification

Reliability (in assessment) a strategy to ensure that assessment decisions are consistent

Reliability (in research) the consistency of the measurement. Qualitative data is less reliable than quantitative data

Research an investigation

Restricted response limited choices in answers

Retention the number of students who complete their programme

Role a person's position within a function or organisation

Rote teaching by repetition, e.g. learning multiplication tables

Sampling the probability or non-probability of the data

Sanction a penalty for disobeying rules

SAR self-assessment report

Scheme of work a document listing sessions within a programme

Screen shot a visual image from a software program reproduced into a document to support understanding

Secondary data is when the originator is absent. For example books, journals etc.

Self-assessment (an individual) a method of confirming own ability

Self-assessment (an organisation) an organisation's ability to monitor and quality assure its provision

Self-financing generating sufficient income to cover costs and profit margins

Self-regulation the ability to check own performance without asking others

Sensory learning learning which relies on the five senses

Session a period of learning

Shallow learning learning which is retained for a short period

Snowball (pyramid) group activities pairs discuss then form gradually larger groups to gain a consensus of opinion on a topic or subject

SOW abbreviation for scheme of work

Specialism a particular focus within the broader meaning of teaching

Spider diagram a visual form of note-taking to collect thoughts

Spiky profile mixed levels of learning within topic

Stakeholder people with an interest in the organisation

Standard an agreed level of competence

Standardisation a process to confirm decisions and create norms

Stem the term given to a question in a MCQ

Stimulating a grade one indicator meaning to excite or motivate

Strategy a systematic process

Success recognition of achievement

Success rate the number of students who complete and achieve their qualification, usually expressed as a percentage of those who commenced

Sufficiency to check that there is enough evidence to cover the criteria

Summative final or summary assessment

Surface learning shallow understanding of topic

SWOT an analysis tool to identify strengths, weaknesses, opportunities and threats; used to assess current practice

Syllabus the structure of a qualification

Target an objective or focused path towards a specified outcome

Taxonomy a classification

Teacher-centred the teacher dominates the learning environment

Teaching to impart knowledge or a skill; what the teacher does during a session

Theorist someone who creates an idea or explanation of something

Theory an explanation or proof of an idea

TQM Total Quality Management

Tracking a method of recording progress

Transferable something learned in one context used and applied to another

Transmission type in communication, a message passing from one to another

Transparency overt, clear in meaning

Triangulate measuring by different perspectives

Triangulation/Triangulated the validation of one set of data against other sets.

VAK visual, auditory and kinaesthetic learners – different ways learners like to learn

Valid (in research) measured accurately to elicit reliable outcomes

Validity a strategy to ensure that judgements are made against criteria

Value something which is important

Variables the analysis or acceptance that not everything will fit in the box

Verbal exposition teacher-talk

VLE (virtual learning environment) – a modern teaching and learning style using computer technologies

Vocational relating to learning the skills of an occupation

Vocational learning skills related to employment

VRQ vocationally related qualifications

WBL (work-based learning) learning that takes place predominantly in the workplace

Reference and bibliography

Books and publications:

Anderson, G. (1990) *Fundamentals of educational research*, Basingstoke: Falmer Press.

Argyris, C. and D. Schön (1974) *Theory in Practice: increasing professional effectiveness*, San Francisco: Jossey Bass.

Argyris, C. and D. Schön (1978) *Organizational learning: A theory of action perspective*, Reading, Mass: Addison Wesley.

Armitage, A. *et al.* (2003) *Teaching and Training in Post-Compulsory Education*, 2nd ed. Maidenhead: Open University Press, McGraw Hill.

Assessment Reform Group (1999) *Assessment For Learning: Beyond the Black Box*, University of Cambridge, School of Education.

Bain, D., R. Ballantyne, J. Packer and W. Mills (1999) 'Understanding journal writing to enhance student teachers' reflectivity during field experience placements', *Teachers and Teaching; theory and practice*, Vol 5, No 1, pp. 23–32.

Bandura, A. (1994) *Self-efficacy* in V.S. Ramachaudran (ed) (1998) *Encyclopedia of human behaviour* (Vol 4, pp. 71–81) New York: Academic Press.

Basic Skills Agency (2006) *Identifying and meeting needs*, London: DfES.

Belbin, M. (1993) 'Team Roles at Work' in Meredith, M. and R. Belbin (1993) *Management Teams: why they succeed or fail*, Oxford: Butterworth: Heinemann.

Bell, J. (2005) *Doing your Research Project: A guide for first-time researchers in education, health and social science*, 4th ed. Maidenhead: Open University Press.

Berne, E. (1964) *Games people play*, New York: Grove Press.

Biggs, J. (1987) *Student approaches to learning and studying*, Melbourne: Australian Council for Education Research.

Biggs, J. (1999) *Teaching for quality learning at University*, Buckingham: Society for Research into Higher Education and Open University Press.

Biggs, J.B. (2003) *Teaching for quality learning*, 3rd ed. Buckingham: Society for Research into Higher Education and Open University Press.

Black, P. and D. Wiliam (1998) *Inside the Black Box*, London: Kings College.

Bloom, B.S. (ed.) (1956) *Taxonomy of Educational Objectives: Handbook 1, Cognitive Domain*, London: Longman.

Bloom, B.S. (ed.) (1964) *Taxonomy of Educational Objectives: Handbook 2, Affective Domain*, London: Longman.

Boud, D. (1995) *Enhancing Learning Through Self-Assessment*, London: Kogan Page.

Boud, D. and Feletti, G. (eds.) (1991) *The Challenge of Problem-Based Learning*, London: Kogan Page.

Brewer, J. D. (2000) *Ethnography*, Buckingham: Open University Press.

Brookfield, S. (ed.) (1985) *Self-Directed Learning. From theory to practice*, San Francisco: Jossey-Bass. http://www.infed.org/biblio/b-selfdr.htm.

Bruner, J. (1996) *The Culture of Education*, Cambridge, MA: Harvard University Press. http://tip.psychology.org/bruner.html.

Budge, D. 'Tasting the Assessment Soup', *Times Educational Supplement*, 18 February 2005.

Butcher, C., C. Davies and M. Highton (2006) *Designing Learning: from module outline to effective teaching*, Abingdon: Routledge.

Child, D. (2004) *Psychology and the teacher*, 7th ed. London: Continuum.

Coffield, F. (2008) *Just suppose teaching and learning became the first priority*, London: LSN.

Coffield, F., D. Moseley, E. Hall and K. Ecclestone (2004) *Learning styles and pedagogy in post-16 learning: a systematic and critical review*, London: LSRC.

Cohen, L., L. Manion and K. Morrison (2000) *Research Methods in Education*, 5th ed. Abingdon: Routledge Falmer.

Cohen, L., L. Manion and K. Morrison (2004) *A guide to Teaching Practice*, Abingdon: Routledge.

Clutterbuck, D. and S. Hirst (2003) *Talking business: making communication work*, Oxford: Butterworth Heinemann.

Cohen, L., L. Manion and K. Morrison (2004) *A guide to Teaching Practice*, 5th ed. Abingdon: Routledge Falmer.

Cooper, R. (1996) 'Identifying real differences in thinking and learning styles', *National Journal of Vocational Assessment: Assessment Matters*, Issue 2, Spring: pp 3–5.

Cowley, S. (2003) *Getting the Buggers to Behave*, 2nd ed. London: Continuum.

Curzon, L.B. (2004) *Teaching in Further Education*, 6th ed. London: Continuum.

Dave R.H. (1970) in Armstrong R. J. et al (1975) *Developing and Writing Behavioural Objectives*, Tuscon, Arizona: Educational Innovators Press. First reference at a Berlin conference in 1967.

Davies, I. K. (1976) *Objectives in Curriculum Design*, New York: McGraw Hill.

Davies, L. (2006) *Towards a new professionalism in the further education sector*, CPD Update, London: IfL.

Deming, W. (1996) *Out of the Crisis: Quality, productivity and competitive position*, Cambridge: Cambridge University Press.

Denscombe, M. (2002) *Ground Rules for Good Research*, Buckingham: Open University Press.

Department for Education and Employment (1999) *A Fresh Start – Improving Literacy and Numeracy (The Report of the working group chaired by Sir Claus Moser)* London: DfEE.

Department for Education and Skills (2001) *Adult Literacy: Core Curriculum including spoken communication*, London: DfES.

Department for Education and Skills (2001) *Adult Numeracy: Core Curriculum*, London: DfES.

Department for Education and Skills (2005) *14–19 Education and Skills, (A response to the Tomlinson Report, 2004)*, London: DfES.

Devany, A. (2007) *Equality and Diversity*, (unpublished) St George's Centre, Birmingham.

Dewey, J. (1916) *Democracy and Education*, New York: Macmillan.

Dewey, J. (1933) *How We Think. A restatement of the relation of reflective thinking to the educative process* (Revised edn.), Boston: D. C. Heath. http://www.infed.org/thinkers/et-dewey.htm.

Dewey, J. (1938) *Experience and Education*, London: Collier Macmillan Publishers.

Ecclestone, K. (1996) *How to assess the Vocational Curriculum*, London: Kogan Page in Gray, D., C. Griffin and T. Nasta (2005) *Training to Teach in Further and Adult Education*, 2nd ed. Cheltenham: Stanley Thornes.

Egan, J. (2002) *Accelerating Change*, Department for Trade and Industry.

Eisner, Elliot W. (1985) *The art of educational evaluation: a personal view*, London: Falmer Press. http://www.infed.org/thinkers/eisner.htm.

Fawbert, F. (2003) *Teaching in Post-Compulsory Education: Learning, Skills and Standards*, London: Continuum.

FEnto (2004) *Including Language, literacy and Numeracy Learning in all Post-16 Education. Guidance on curriculum and methodology for generic initial teacher education programmes.* March 2004, Further Education National Training Organisation/National Research and Development Centre for adult literacy and numeracy.

Further Education Funding Council (1996) *Learning Works: The Kennedy Report*, Helena Kennedy QC.

Gagné, R.M. (1985) *The conditions of learning*, 4th ed. New York: Holt, Reinhart and Winston.

Gardner, H. (1983) *Frames of Mind, the theory of multiple intelligences,* New York: Basic Books.

Glaser, B. and Strauss, A. (1967) *The discovery of grounded theory*, Chicago: Aldine.

Gray, D., C. Griffin and T. Nasta (2005) *Training to Teach in Further and Adult Education*, 2nd ed. Cheltenham: Stanley Thornes.

Grundy, S. (1987) *Curriculum: product or praxis?*, Lewes: Falmer Press.

Hillier, Y. (2005) *Reflective teaching in Further and Adult Education*, 2nd ed. London: Continuum.

Hirst, Paul H. (1974) *Knowledge and the Curriculum*, London: Routledge.

Honey, P. and A. Mumford (1982/1992) *The Manual of Learning Styles*, Maidenhead: Peter Honey Publications.

Hopkins, D. (2002) *A teacher's guide to Classroom research*, 3rd ed. Maidenhead: Open University Press.

Huddleston, P. and L. Unwin (2002) *Teaching and learning in Further Education*, 2nd ed. Abingdon: RoutledgeFalmer.

Kandola, R.S. and J. Fullerton (1994) *Managing the Mosaic: Diversity in Action (Developing Strategies)*, Chartered Institute of Personnel and Development.

Kelly, A. (1983) *The Curriculum, Theory and Practice*, 4th ed. London: Paul Chapman.

Knowles, M. (1984) *The Adult Learner: a neglected species*, 3rd ed. Houston, Texas: Gulf Publishing.

Kolb, D. (1984) *Experiential Learning: experience as a source of learning and development*, Englewood Cliffs, NJ: Prentice-Hall.

Kyriacou, C. (2007) *Essential Teaching Skills*, 3rd ed. Cheltenham: Nelson Thornes.

Laird, D., E. Holton and S. Naquin (2003) *Approaches to Training and Development*, 3rd ed. US: Perseus Books.

Lawton, D. (1983) *Curriculum Studies and Educational Planning*, London: Hodder and Stoughton.

Lightbody, B. (2008) *Ofsted Grade One Reports*, Training Handout modified from *Outstanding Teaching and Learning* (with permission). Update, Issue 2, April 2005, Batley: College Net.

LLUK (2004) *Addressing literacy, language, numeracy and ICT needs in education and training: defining the minimum core of teachers' knowledge, understanding and personal skills. A guide for teacher education programmes*, July 2004, Lifelong Learning UK/FEnto.

LLUK (2006) *New overarching professional standards for teachers, tutors and trainers in the Lifelong Learning Sector*, November 2006, Lifelong Learning UK.

LLUK (2007) *Addressing literacy, language, numeracy and ICT needs in education and training: defining the minimum core of teachers' knowledge, understanding and personal skills. A guide for teacher education programmes*, June 2007, The Sector Skills Council for Lifelong Learning.

Maslow, A.H. (1970) *Motivation and Personality*, 2nd ed. New York: Harper and Row.

McClelland, D. (1988) *Human Motivation*, Cambridge: Cambridge University Press.

McGregor, D. (1960) *The Human Side of Enterprise*, Columbus, Ohio: McGraw Hill.

McQuail, D. and S. Windahl (1993) *Communication models: for the study of mass communications*, 2nd ed. NJ: Prentice Hall.

Moon, J. (1999) *Learning Journals: a handbook for academics, students and professional development*, London. Kogan Page.

Neary, M. (2002) *Curriculum Studies in Post Compulsory and Adult Education: A teacher's and student teacher's study guide*, Cheltenham: Nelson Thornes.

Opie, C. (2004) *Doing Educational Research*. London: Sage.

Pearsall, J. (ed.) (2001) *Oxford English Dictionary*, 10th ed. Oxford: Oxford University Press.

Peter, L.J. (1969) *Why things go wrong*, London: Bantam Books.

Petty, G. (2004) *Teaching Today: A practical guide*, 3rd ed. Cheltenham: Nelson Thornes.

Race, P. (2005) *Making learning happen*, London: Sage.

Reece, I. and S. Walker (2006) *Teaching, training and learning: A practical guide*, 6th ed. Sunderland: Business Education Publishers.

Riding, R. and S. Raynor (1998) *Cognitive styles and Learning strategies: Understanding style differences in learning and behaviour*, London: David Fulton Publishers.

Rogers, A. (2002) *Teaching Adults*, 3rd ed. Maidenhead: Open University Press, McGraw-Hill Education.

Rogers, C. (1969) *Freedom to Learn*, Columbus, Ohio: Merrill.

Schön, D. (1983) *The Reflective Practitioner*, San Francisco: Jossey-Bass.

Shannon, C. and W. Weaver (1949) *A mathematical theory of communication*, Urbana: University of Illinois Press.

Skilbeck, M. and Reynolds, J. (1976) *Culture in the Classroom*, London: Open Books Publishing.

Skinner, B. (1984) *The Shame of American education*, American Psychologist, Issue 1984:11.

Stenhouse, L. (1975) *An introduction to Curriculum Research and Development*, London: Heinemann.

Talbot, C. (2004) *Equality, Diversity and Inclusivity: Curriculum Matters*, Birmingham: Staff and Educational Development Association.

The Further Education Teachers' Continuing Professional Development and Registration (England) Regulations 2007, SI No 2007/2116.

Tummons, J. (2007) *Becoming a professional Tutor in the Lifelong Learning Sector*, Exeter: Learning Matters (1).

Tummons, J. (2007) *Assessing in the Lifelong Learning Sector*, 2nd ed. Exeter: Learning Matters (2).

Turner, C.H. (1990) *Corporate Culture: From vicious to virtuous circles*, London: Random House Business Books.

Tyler, R.W. (1949) *Basic Principles of Curriculum and Instruction*, Chicago: University of Chicago Press.

Walklin, L. (2000) *Teaching and Learning in Further and Adult Education*, Cheltenham: Nelson Thornes.

Wallace, S. (2007) *Teaching, tutoring and training in the Lifelong Learning Sector*, 3rd ed. Exeter: Learning Matters Ltd.

West-Burnham, J. and M. Coates, (2005) *Personalized Learning*, Stafford: Network Educational Press.

Weyers, M. (2006) *Teaching the FE curriculum*, London: Continuum.

Wilson, L. (2008) *Practical Teaching: A guide to PTLLS and CTLLS*, London: Cengage Learning.

Wragg, E. C. (2002) 'Interviewing', in M. Coleman and A. R. J. Briggs (eds.), *Research Methods in Educational Leadership and Management*, Paul Chapman Publishing, pp. 143–148.

Web sourced references:

Assessment Reform Group. http://arg. educ.cam.uk/publications.html (accessed 29 09 07).

Atherton, J.S. (2005) *Learning and teaching: reflection and reflective*

practice, On-line UK: http://www.
learningandteaching.info/learning/
reflecti.htm (accessed 01 04 08).

Barriers to Learning, http://www.open.
ac.uk/inclusiveteaching/pages/inclusive-
teaching/barriers-to-learning.php
(accessed 30 12 06).

Baume, D. (2006) *Towards a meta-
framework for European standards
for teaching in higher education*, www
.nettle.soton.ac.uk:8082/framweworks
(accessed 01 08 08).

Behaviourism, http://simplypsychology.
pwp.blueyonder.co.uk/behaviourism.
html (accessed 01 03 08).

Berne, E. *Transactional Analysis*, http://
www.businessballs.com/transact.htm
(accessed 12 05 07).

Bloom's Taxonomy, www.businessball.com/
bloomstaxonomyoflearningdomains.
htm (accessed 22 03 08).

Brookfield, S. (2007) *Becoming a critically
reflective teacher*, stephenbrookfield.
com (accessed 26 03 08).

Conner, M. (2007) *Learning from
Experience: Ageless Learner*, http://
agelesslearner.com (accessed 19 02 08).

CPD: Teaching in Scotland, *An overview
of the cpd framework and requirements for teachers in Scotland* (2003)
www.scotland.gov.uk/Resources/Doc/
47021/0023973.pdf (accessed 26 03 08).

Craig, J. and C. Fieschi (2007) *DIY
Professionalism: futures for teaching*,
www.nationalschool.gov.uk/policyhub/.
General Teaching Council (accessed
01 08 08).

Curriculum Design, http://www.ssdd.bcu.
ac.uk/crumpton/curriculum-design/
curriculum-design.htm (accessed
14 06 08).

Department for Education and Skills
(2006) *Reducing Re-Offending
through skills and employment – next
steps*, London: DFES, Home Office,
Department for Works and Pensions,
http://www.dfes.gov.uk/publications/
offenderlearning/ (accessed 14 06 08).

Gillard, D. (2007) *Education in England:
a brief history*, www.dg.dial.pipex.
com/history/ (accessed 04 07 08).

Guidelines on the procedure of
Professional Review and Development for Teachers in Scotland

(2004), www.scotland.gov.uk/
Resource/Doc/ 26487/0023803.pdf
(accessed 26 03 08).

Hattie, John (1999, 2003) http://www.
education.auckland.ac.nz/uoa/fms/
default/education/staff/
Prof.%20John%20Hattie/Documents/
Presentations/influences/
Influences_on_student_learning.pdf.

Inclusive Learning, http://www.open.ac.
uk/inclusiveteaching/pages/inclusive-
teaching/learning-environment.php
(accessed 12 05 07).

Lasswell, H. (1976) *Power and Personality*,
www.cultsock.ndirect.co.uk (accessed
08 03 08).

Lawrence, E., H. Heasman and P. Smith
(circa 1995) *Equal Opportunities and
the Curriculum*, Natfhe http://
www.ucu.org.uk/media/pdf/s/4/
EqualOppCurriculum_1.pdf (accessed
20 07 08).

Learning Theories, http://tip.psychology.
org/ (accessed 01 03 08).

McGregor D., www.businessballs.com/
mcgregor.htm, information about
McGregor's Theory X and Theory Y
motivation (accessed 08 03 08).

NATFHE, A guide to Language, http://
www.ucu.org.uk/media/docs/3/0/
eqlang_1.doc (accessed 20 07 08).

QCA (2004) Levels of Competence,
http://www.qca.org.uk/14-19/
qualifications/index_nvqs.htm
(accessed 20 07 08).

Qualifications and Initial Teacher
Training, www.lifelonglearninguk.org
(accessed 12 09 07).

Resources for FE from Lightbody, B.,
College Net Training. www.collegenet.
co.uk (accessed 25 04 08, with
permission).

Scottish Funding Council (2006)
*Overcoming barriers; enabling
learning. Planning, designing and
delivering the full time FE curriculum
in Scotland's Colleges,* HM Inspectors
for Education and Scottish Funding
Council (October 2006) http://www.sfc.
ac.uk (accessed on 12 05 07).

Smith, M.K. (1996, 2000) *Curriculum
theory and practice,* The encyclopedia
of informal education, www.infed.org/
biblio/b-curric.htm.

Smith, M.K. (2002) *Jerome S Bruner and the process of education,* The encyclopaedia of informal education, http://www.infed.org/thinkers/bruner.htm (accessed 12 06 08).

Staff Individualised Record (2005) www.lluk.ac.uk (accessed 14 04 08).

UCU and Equal Opportunities, http://www.ucu.org.uk/media/pdf/s/4/EqualOppCurriculum_1.pdf (accessed 10 06 08).

Quality agencies and systems:

www.dti.gov.uk/quality/tqm

www.qaa.ac.uk

www.qia.org.uk

www.centreforexcellence.org.uk

www.ofsted.gov.uk

www.estyn.gov.uk

www.hmie.gov.uk

www.dcni.gov.uk

http://www.iso.org

http://www.ofsted.gov.uk/publications/2434

www.lsc.org.uk

http://ffe.lsc.gov.uk

http://www.investorsinpeople.co.uk

http://www.matrixstandard.com

www.ces-vol.org.uk

www.cabinetoffice.gov.uk

www.cbi.org.uk.

Index